ABBAS AMANAT is Profess
author of *Pivot of the Uni*
*Iranian Monarchy, 1831–1896* and of *Imagining the End: Visions of Apocalypse from the Ancient Middle East to Modern America*, both published by I.B.Tauris.



"Abbas Amanat is among the brightest stars in the firmament of historians who have treated Shi'i millenarian movements in depth. He always avoids the easy temptation to dismiss them as outbursts of irrational fanaticism, instead patiently tracing their roots in social discontent and teasing out the significance of their often recondite writings. Any historian can mine the British archives for imperial reactions to such popular manifestations; but Amanat is among the few with the linguistic and historiographic skills to be able to offer us the inside story, full of drama, texture and immense local significance. Those who wish to understand the Iranian Shi'i tradition must come to terms with this essential aspect of it. No better guide than the magisterial Amanat could be found."

– *Juan R. I. Cole, Richard P. Mitchell Collegiate Professor of History, University of Michigan*

"In these important essays, written in the two decades since the publication of his definitive study of the Babi movement, *Resurrection and Renewal* (1989), Abbas Amanat firmly places the apocalyptic aspects of Shi'ism on the map of modern scholarship, ending the book with a fascinating chapter on their current manifestations in post-revolutionary Iran."

– *Saïd Amir Arjomand, Distinguished Service Professor, State University of New York, Stony Brook; Director of the Stony Brook Institute for Global Studies; and President of the Association for the Study of Persianate Societies*

"Abbas Amanat's penetrating and insightful studies of the inter-relationship of Shi'ism and messianism in modern Iran will set the agenda for future scholarship in this area. His conclusions are thoughtful, measured and compelling in equal measure. This is a book of mature scholarship, free of histrionics, and establishes a new benchmark for the study of apocalyptic theologies in modern Islam generally, and in Iranian Shi'ism in particular. It should be required reading for all who wish to understand the place of religion in Iranian politics and society and move beyond current facile and hackneyed media analyses."

– *Robert Gleave, Professor of Arabic Studies, University of Exeter*

LIBRARY OF MODERN RELIGION

1. *Returning to Religion: Why a Secular Age is Haunted by Faith*
Jonathan Benthall
978 1 84511 718 4

2. *Knowing the Unknowable: Science and Religions on God and the Universe*
John Bowker [Ed]
978 1 84511 757 3

3. *Sufism Today: Heritage and Tradition in the Global Community*
Catharina Raudvere & Leif Stenberg [Eds.]
978 1 84511 762 7

4. *Apocalyptic Islam and Iranian Shi'ism*
Abbas Amanat
978 1 84511 124 3

5. *Global Pentecostalism: Encounters with Other Religious Traditions*
David Westerlund
978 1 84511 877 8

6. *Dying for Faith: Religiously Motivated Violence in the Contemporary World*
Madawi Al-Rasheed & Marat Shterin [Eds.]
978 1 84511 686 6

7. *The Hindu Erotic: Exploring Hinduism and Sexuality*
David Smith
978 1 84511 361 2

8. *The Power of Tantra: Religion, Sexuality and the Politics of South Asian Studies*
Hugh B. Urban
978 1 84511 873 0

9. *Jewish Identities in Iran:*
*Resistance and Conversion to Islam and the Baha'i Faith*
Mehrdad Amanat
978 1 84511 891 4

10. *Islamic Reform and Conservatism:*
*Al-Azhar and the Evolution of Modern Sunni Islam*
Indira Falk Gesink
978 1 84511 936 2

11. *Muslim Women's Rituals: Authority and Gender in the Islamic World*
Catharina Raudvere and Margaret Rausch
978 1 84511 643 9

12. *Lonesome: The Spiritual Meanings of American Solitude*
Kevin Lewis
978 1 84885 075 0

# *Apocalyptic Islam and Iranian Shi'ism*

ABBAS AMANAT

I.B. TAURIS
LONDON · NEW YORK

Published in 2009 by I.B.Tauris & Co Ltd
6 Salem Road, London W2 4BU
175 Fifth Avenue, New York NY 10010
www.ibtauris.com

Distributed in the United States and Canada Exclusively by Palgrave Macmillan
175 Fifth Avenue, New York NY 10010



Library of Modern Religion, Vol. 4

ISBN: 978 1 84511 124 3 (HB)
ISBN: 978 1 84511 981 2 (PB)

A full CIP record for this book is available from the British Library
A full CIP record is available from the Library of Congress

Library of Congress Catalog Card Number: available

Typeset in Sabon by Ellipsis Books Limited, Glasgow

Printed and bound in Great Britain by CPI Antony Rowe, Chippenham

## CONTENTS

## PART 3
### *Clerical Encounters with Modernity*



## PART 4
### *Satan and Salvation in the Islamic Revolution*

# *Preface*

In the summer of 2005 I visited the ancient city of Kashan, my ancestral homeland. An old center of Shi'ism on the edge of the Iranian central desert, Kashan was known in the geographical nomenclature of the pre-twentieth century as the "abode of the faith" *(Dar al-Iman)*, and it is not an exaggeration to suggest that the city has remained loyal to its old epithet up to this day. This is evident, at least in appearance, if we judge the religiosity of the inhabitants by the numerous signs of Muharram, "mourning associations" *(hay'at-i 'azadaran)* in every quarter of the city, vast numbers of black banners with sentimental messages hanging across the city's thoroughfares commemorating previously obscure events of the Shi'i calendar – and by their sheer signs of piety. The face of the city betrayed a mix of old Shi'i loyalties and, perhaps, forced conformity.

Seeking relief from the offensive heat of mid-afternoon in the back alleys of a half-ruined old neighborhood, I came across a religious structure in a state of surprisingly good repair. The tilework at the top of the portal read "Sadra Husayniya; Center for the Husayni Mourning Society" *(Husayniya-Sadra, Markaz-i Hay'at-i Husayni)*. The date of the repair underneath was 1356 in the Persian solar calendar (1977); a year before the Islamic Revolution. As a forum for performing the Muharram ceremonies, this Husayniya, presumably a Qajar structure, was still undergoing new repairs. The interior archway leading to the central platform was adorned with typical blue tilework – for which Kashan is known – quoting a hadith in praise of the House of the Prophet *(Ahl al-Bayt)*. Their names were followed on the edge of the archway by the name of seventy-two martyrs of the battle of Karbala. In the center of the domed platform there was a huge *nakhl* (literally: palm tree); a massive wooden heart-shaped structure covered with black cloth and with verses embroidered around a central medallion in praise of Imam Husayn ibn 'Ali, the Third Shi'i Imam and the Lord of the Martyrs *(Sayyid al-Shuhada)*. The verse in the center of the medallion read: "Salute to Husayn the Martyr." Each year on the

10th of Muharram during the Ashura procession the *nakhl*, symbolizing the coffin of Imam Husayn, is brought out of the Husayniya on the shoulders of the mourners and carried in the heart of the procession.

Everything in the Husayniya seemed familiar in a typical Shi'i Muharram surrounding. But when I walked closer to the *nakhl,* a small graffiti caught my attention on the base of the large structure, written with a felt pen and in a coarse hand. It read: "Yearning is our faith" *(entezar mazhab-i mast)*. The message took me by surprise. As a student of messianic Shi'ism who for more than thirty years was engaged with its diverse expressions, this was an unexpected revelation. Some quarter of a century after the victory of the Islamic Revolution, and sixteen years after the death of its leader, Ayatollah Khomeini, the messianic *imam* of that revolution, here I was encountering an almost subversive messianic message of eternal yearning for the return of a savior, and of all places on the base of a symbolic edifice commemorating the "Lord of the Martyrs," whose tragic fall in the battle of Karbala virtually defined Shi'ism. According to Shi'i traditions, the Mahdi's revenge of Husayn's blood will initiate an apocalyptic battle of cosmic proportion that precedes the Day of Resurrection and the End of Time.

The message made me think about the person who must have written the subversive message, possibly in haste; a message that resonated deeply and recurred repeatedly in this ancient land. Thinking of Kashan's messianic past, I later recalled the wonderful inscription that was glazed inside a fourteenth-century hoof-shaped ceramic bowl describing a holy dream by a faithful Shi'i Kashani who saw the First Imam, 'Ali ibn Abi-Talib, leading him into a tent where he was received by a young man with a glowing countenance. He was none other than the Mahdi himself. The dream narrative that led to the construction of yet another "stepping site" *(qadamgah)*, highlights the undercurrent of messianic aspirations in Iran's popular piety, something virtually parallel to the cult of Jamkaran in today's Iran, celebrated regularly near Qom and not far away from Kashan.[1]

The recitation of the sufferings of Karbala and the House of Husayn, a staple of the mourning sessions known as *rawza-khani* in all Shi'i centers, also reminded me of the origins of the tradition.

Significantly, works such as Mulla Husayn Kashifi's *Rawdat al-shuhada* (Meadow of the Martyrs) has a sentimental undertone parallel to the tone of today's messianic narrative.[2]

Thinking of subversive messianism outside the narrative of Karbala and martyrdom but still in the Shi'i context, one can think of the support for the remarkable Nuqtavi movement in Kashan and its vicinity. It was in Nasrabad, northwest of Kashan and one of the centers of Nuqtavis, for instance, that in 1592 the Safavid ruler Shah 'Abbas I struck the first blow against the movement by slaying a number of Nuqtavis supporters of Isma'ili background. They were accused of sedition and heresy. The Nuqtavis were expecting that the turn of the Islamic millennium would end the old order and initiate a new Persian prophetic cycle.[3] Two hundred and fifty years later, near the 'Attarha city gate in Kashan, Hajji Mirza Jani, a merchant and later the first historian of the Babi movement, welcomed Sayyid 'Ali Muhammad Shirazi the Bab, the founder of the Babi movement. Captivated with the impending advent of the Imam of the Age, Jani's encounter with the Bab came in the wake of a holy dream that made him believe he would soon encounter the Mahdi. He was one of the first Babis of Kashan.[4] In the following decades, and for more than a century, Kashan and its surrounding hinterland became a thriving center for the Babi and then the Baha'i community which survived in a semi-clandestine state despite many difficulties. Their "cause" *(amr)*, like the Nuqtavis', centered on the idea that the Islamic revelation cycle had come to its natural end and a new prophetic cycle, complementary to the revelations of the past but suitable to the advancing needs of humanity, had arrived.

The Muslims and the Babis (later Baha'is), the extinct Nuqtavis, the commemoration associations of today's Kashan, and the Husayniyas and the *ta'ziya*s, are to me facades of a religious tradition that resonates with modern Iranians today. Kashan indeed is a microcosm of the Iranian religious complexity and a window into how it has evolved over time, and especially over the past two centuries. As Iran became more Shi'i than ever in its history, very few Baha'is, or indeed any other religious minority, survived in Kashan and in the surrounding villages.[5] The greater Shi'itization of Kashan is a microcosm of Iranian demographics and Iran's collective psyche. A homogenized majority devoid of diversity could become more obsessed with ideological or religious convictions; and in the Iranian case, more captivated with a new reading of the Occultation of the Imam and his Return. In today's Islamic Republic such domestic and international "enemies," mostly imagined, are necessary to make the ideology of waiting viable and the persecuting mentality of its sponsors potent.

The idea for this book – a collection of articles written over twenty years – came to me while I was unaware of the impressions mentioned above. Yet I can now see a connection and I hope the reader does too. The chapters are mostly on apocalyptic and messianic Islam and its offshoots as well as the judicial, clerical, and ritualistic dimensions of Shi'ism in Iran and the neighboring lands. In book form I am hoping they render a coherent narrative and demonstrate the diversity of religious experiences in the Shi'i world and, more specifically, reveal the importance of messianic religion as its defining character.

The need for giving more serious attention to such messianic and utopian impulses is self-evident given their revival in contemporary Iran. Thirty years after the Islamic Revolution of 1978–9 and a century after the Constitutional Revolution of 1906–9, today's Iran more than at any time in its recent history is caught in a messianic euphoria, with speculations about the advent of the Mahdi and whatever such appearance is meant to accomplish. A generation ago such aspirations were dormant, if not dead. They were no longer a mainstay of religious debate, and certainly not part of the secular discourse of the Pahlavi era. Their revival hence deserves an explanation. It is questionable to what degree the current enthusiasm about the Hidden Imam is a genuine reflection of the Iranian people's ideals and aspirations or, arguably, their indoctrination, or their frustrations. Whatever is the case, it also appears that the excitement felt for the Mahdi is exploited, if not manufactured, by some influential circles and their subordinates to serve their purpose. It may reflect clerical anxieties of irrelevance and a desire to recapture lost ground. It may also serve to invent enemies and feed paranoiac fears and ultimately nurture dangerous ideological ambitions.

Allowing for some latitude, it may also be said that Mahdistic speculations are the outcome of unresolved theological debates within Shi'ism that, strange as it may appear, have resurfaced at this crucial juncture. One may attribute it to old conservative suspicions in the face of rational modernity, whether secular or religious. There is an unwillingness on behalf of clerical circles and their associates – what I would call the conservative Qom clique (though they are not all located in Qom) – to entertain a historical approach to the development of religion and the demands of time, and hence reconsider ancient doctrines of Occultation and Return. In effect messianism ties to re-examining the very fundamental assumption of Islam's timeless perfection. After three decades of experimentation under the Islamic Republic, the messianic resurgence may also be seen as a desire by those other than the conservative clique, such as religious dissenters, to depart from arcane modalities of Shi'i theology and ultimately to adopt a form of modernity that can reconfigure the promised utopia of Shi'ism.

The chapters in this volume are intended to offer a progression from the general to the specific while following a chronology. The Introduction offers an overview of Shi'ism and its messianic dynamics. Part 1 depicts general features of apocalypticism. Chapter 1 looks at apocalyptic paradigms in Middle Eastern salvation religions and their diffusion worldwide. It attempts an alternative reading of millenarian movements which at times parts with conventional interpretations. Chapter 2 reviews a resurgence of apocalypticism in modern Islam, both Sunni and Shi'i. Part 2 looks at apocalyptic trends and martyrdom narratives at the outset of the modern period. Chapter 3 is about the Nuqtavi movement in the Timurid and Safavid periods (fifteenth to seventeenth centuries), its doctrinal innovations, memories of the pre-Islamic past, and the movement's reception in Iran. Nuqtavism, as demonstrated here, is almost a post-Islamic counter-religion – and in some respects a precursor to the Babi movement of the nineteenth century. Its mystico-materialist worldview, with a shade of humanism and proto-nationalist awareness, is particularly striking. Chapter 4 examines the canonization of the Karbala narrative in the *Rawdat al-Shuhada*. First emerging in the late Timurid period, Kashifi's compilation was destined to play a crucial part in the Persian awareness of Shi'ism and its tragedies. Moreover, this chapter explores the correlation between commemorating Husayn and the expansion of the Safavid empire to eastern Iran in the early sixteenth century. It also explores the content analysis and biographical traits behind the text. Chapter 5 looks at aspects of Babi thought, an alternative reading of Iran's rich messianic tradition. As an afterthought to my 1989 *Resurrection and Renewal,* this chapter offers a content analysis of the Bab's major work, the *Bayan*, trying to make sense of the linguistic neology of the text and the dissident message of the context. I tried to detect traits of an indigenous modernity in his movement, novel to history of Shi'i Islam, while touching on weaknesses embedded in the Babi millennial message.

Part 3 examines aspects of clerical Shi'i encounters with modernity, be they polemical debates, evolving clerical authority, or inventing an Islamic political ideology. Chapter 6 is a study of the mujtahids' reactions to Christian evangelicalism in the early nineteenth century. The polemics of the missionary preacher Henry Martyn, the co-translator of the New Testament into Persian, generated a vast polemical literature known as "refuting the padre." The genre illustrates a willingness on the part of the Iranian scholars to respond with confidence to the theological challenges of Christian Europe. Chapter 7, on the other hand, scrutinizes the nature of clerical hierarchy and the emergence of the "source of emulations" *(marja'-i taqlid)* in the nineteenth century as a higher source of clerical authority. It may be said that the idea of Supreme Exemplar, as it evolved in the latter part of the nineteenth century and early twentieth century, offered a virtuous figure in the absence of the Hidden Imam, one that was deemed imperative in countering the forces of modernity. Though never institutionalized as an office (nor probably could it ever be), the Supreme Exemplar, it is argued, was primarily determined by the organizational and political acumen of its holder (or holders). Chapter 8 seeks to answer why the doctrine of "Guardianship of the Jurist" proposed by Ayatollah Khomeini evolved, or more accurately deviated, from the notion of *marja'iyat* and why in the process it transformed a primary judicial concern of the clerical establishment into a political ideology. It was argued that by politicizing the function of the jurist, the revolutionary doctrine of guardianship strived to compensate for the practically obsolete shari'a as a legal system and for the jurists' reluctance for more than a century seriously to engage with legal and theological modernity.

Part 4 looks at two aspects of post-revolutionary Iranian religion. Chapter 9 explores the notion of the Great Satan as a strategy of demonizing the American Other in order to discipline the revolutionary Self. It argues that the origin of such Othering is to be traced not so much in the Islamic, and especially Qur'anic, sources. Rather, it may be located in a secular context, and more specifically in the demonology of Cold War propaganda. Chapter 10 concludes the volume by returning to messianic aspirations in contemporary Iran and surveys diverse but interrelated expressions in popular piety, in the press and on the Internet, in the pronouncement of the Iranian President, and in the appearance of proto-messianic preachers. The chapter ends with general observations about the nature of messianic revival and its implications for today's Iran.

Scholarship on modern Iran as a whole is thriving, yet studies of the messianic dimension of Iranian religions, especially in early modern and modern times, are still lagging. There are no doubt a number of brilliant historical analyses, but much more remains to be done. This book would like to locate itself at the juncture of these two paths and I hope it has succeeded in further illuminating the complexity of this fascinating world without compromising historical objectivity.

Abbas Amanat
New Haven, Connecticut

# *List of Illustrations*

# *Acknowledgment and Citations*

I would like to thank many friends and colleagues who over the years and at various stages shared with me their thoughts, their bibliographical knowledge, or rendered other assistance in the production of these chapters. Among them are Saïd Amir Arjomand, Magnus Bernhardsson, J.J. Collins, Farhad Daftary, R.M. Gleave, Frank Griffel, Mahnaz Moazami, Hossein Modarressi, C.V. Pedersen, the late Franz Rosenthal, Erfan Sabeti, Foad Sanei, Fereydun Vahman and Heidi Walcher. The writing of this book was made possible in part by a grant from Yale MacMillan Center for International and Area Studies. My thanks are due to the Director, Ian Shapiro, for facilitating this grant.

The following is the list of chapters as they originally appeared in various volumes of collected essays. My gratitude is due to the publishers concerned for permission to reproduce them in this volume. There are negligible corrections throughout. The Introduction and Chapter 10 are published here for the first time.

"Apocalyptic Anxieties and Millennial Hopes in the Salvation Religions of the Middle East," in *Imagining the End: Visions of Apocalypse from Ancient Middle East to Contemporary America*, edited with M. Bernhardsson (London and New York: I.B.Tauris, 2001), 1–19.

"The Resurgence of the Apocalyptic in Modern Islam," in *Encyclopedia of Apocalypticism*, ed. J.J. Collins, B. McGinn, and S. Stein, 3 vols. (New York: Continuum, 1998), vol. 3, ed. S. Stein, 230–64.

"The Nuqtawi Movement of Mahmud Pashikhani and his Persian Cycle of Mystical-Materialism," in *Essays in Mediaeval Isma'ili History and Thought*, ed. F. Daftary (Cambridge: Cambridge University Press, 1996), 281–98.

"*Meadow of the Martyrs:* Kashifi's Persianization of the Shi'i Martyrdom Narrative in the Late Timurid Herat," in *Culture and Memory in Medieval Islam: Essays in Honor of Wilfred*

*Madelung* (London and New York: I.B.Tauris for the Institute of Isma'ili Studies, 2003), 250–75.

"The Persian *Bayan* and the Shaping of the Babi Renewal in Iran," in *Religious Texts in Iranian Languages: Symposium Held in Copenhagen, May 2002*, ed. F. Vahman and C. V. Pedersen, Historiske-filosofiske Meddelelser 98 (The Royal Danish Academy of Sciences and Letters, Copenhagen, 2007), 337–50.

"Mujtahids and Missionaries: Shi'i Responses to Christian Polemics in the Early Qajar Period," in *Religion and Society in Qajar Iran*, ed. R. M. Gleave (London: RoutledgeCurzon, 2004), 247–69.

"In Between the Madrasa and the Marketplace: The Designation of Clerical Leadership in Modern Shi'ism,'" in *Authority and Political Culture in Shi'ism*, ed. S. Arjomand (Albany, NY: SUNY Press, 1988), 98–132.

"From *ijtihad* to *wilayat-i faqih:* The Evolving of the Shi'i Legal Authority to Political Power," *Shari'a: Islamic Law in the Contemporary Context,* ed. A. Amanat and F. Griffel (Stanford: Stanford University Press, 2007), 120–36.

"Khomeini's *Great Satan:* Demonizing the American Other in Iran's Islamic Revolution," *U.S.-Middle East Historical Encounters: A Critical Survey*, ed. A. Amanat and M. Bernhardsson (Gainesville: Florida University Press, 2007), 142–61.

# *Note on Transliteration and Style*

The transliteration system adopted for Persian and Arabic is that of the *International Journal of Middle East Studies* but without diacritical marks (and despite its phonetic shortcomings such as the sound *e* represented as *i* and *o* as *u*, arising from the field's pro-Arabic bias). Both letters *hamza* and *'ayn* are represented by a "straight" apostrophe, silent *h* in Persian and Arabic by *a,* and silent *waw* in Persian by *w.* The Persian *izafa* in proper names and titles is not represented. The Arabic definite article *al-* is not assimilated to the noun. Persian works with Arabic titles are transliterated in Arabic.

Well-known place names are written in their common form (as in the *Oxford Atlas*), and less familiar place names are transliterated. *Iran* instead of *Persia* is used throughout but *Persian* is preferred over *Iranian* for culture and society in the pre-twentieth century contexts and occasionally to identify individuals. Dates are as in the Islamic lunar calendar and indicated with Q. (for *Qamari*) wherever necessary. In all instances Christian (Gregorian) calendar equivalents are given.

# *Introduction*

Shi'ism in Iran has always embraced diverse, even contesting, religious experiences. It has given birth to messianic aspirations and numerous apocalyptic movements, of which the most significant is the Safavid movement, the genesis of today's Shi'i Iran. It has also produced a conservative body of scrupulous jurists with an enduring legal legacy that is at the core of today's clerical establishment. It has generated a folk religion with gripping rituals and mourning ceremonies, and it has spawned speculative, mystical and philosophical schools of great sophistication unique in the Muslim world. Most notably, it has generated a radical Islamic ideology, and subsequently an Islamic Revolution, that for the first time in Shi'i history brought to power the Shi'i clerical establishment. Iran has been a fertile ground for the growth and survival of Shi'ism almost from its beginning and has given it state support, at least since the sixteenth century in the face of Sunni hostility. It was, and still is, an essential core of Iranian identity and a dominant feature in the shaping of Iranian history even before the Safavid period (1501–1732), when it was declared the state's official creed.

## *Chronology and Modalities*

To provide a rudimentary framework for the historical development of Shi'ism in Iran, we may identify at least seven overlapping historical episodes. First, from proto-Shi'i trends of the time of the Shi'i imams in the eighth and ninth centuries to the Shi'i legal and hadith scholarship of the ninth to eleventh centuries as represented by the Persian Nawbakhti family and later by theologians such as Shaykh Ja'far Tusi and Ibn Babuya. Second, the movements of dissent inspired by Zaydi and Isma'ili (and Qarmati) brands of Shi'ism against the caliphate and Sunni establishment active during the ninth to thirteenth centuries. Among these the most well known is the community of the Alamut and other Isma'ili fortresses in the twelfth and thirteenth centuries. Third, the Sufi-Shi'i trends of the post-Mongol period between the fourteenth and sixteenth centuries, with implicit or explicit messianic expressions of which the Safavid movement was the most powerful synthesis. Fourth, the speculative endeavors of the philosophical schools of Isfahan and Shiraz in the seventeenth century, represented by the likes of Sadr al-Din Shirazi and its resonances throughout the eighteenth and nineteenth centuries. Fifth, the hadith and legal scholastic studies of the sixteenth to nineteenth centuries represented by such influential theologians and jurists as 'Abd al-'Ali Karaki (d. 1533), Mulla Muhammad Baqir Majlisi (d. 1699) and Sayyid Muhammad Baqir Bihbahani, the founder of the Usuli school (d. *c.*1792) that endured in Najaf, Isfahan, and Qom circles. Sixth, the messianic aspirations in the nineteenth century that began with the Shaykhi school, culminating in the Babi movement (and leading to the emergence of the Baha'i Faith as an alternative religion that consciously differentiated itself from Islam). Seventh, modern developments in clerical and communal Shi'ism in the late twentieth century and the politicization of Iranian Islam that culminated in the Islamic Revolution of 1979 and its aftermath, the establishment of the Islamic Republic.

This schematic periodization roughly covers the course of Iran's political history during most of the Islamic era. At times Shi'ism acted as an institutional force buttressing political power – as in the Buyid period (the ninth century, often known as the "Shi'i century"), and more emphatically during the Safavid period, when the majority of the population converted to Shi'ism, and the Qajar period (1785–1925), when the state incorporated symbols of Shi'i identity. At other times it contested political power, for instance when it resisted the Ash'arite Sunni orthodoxy in the Saljuqid era (eleventh and twelfth centuries) or when the powerful Shi'i clerical establishment resisted, though did not subvert, the Qajar state, and during most of the Pahlavi period (1925–79). The correlation is not accidental. Shi'ism proved itself capable of operating in more than one mode accommodating power when necessary, and even legitimizing it, or adversely rebelling against it by resorting to a vast reservoir of memories of suffering and resistance.

It is of course arguable how far beyond the blanket label of Shi'ism one can draw a common doctrinal thread among many disparate currents in over a millennium of Iranian Shi'i experience. This is a formidable challenge, though not entirely impossible, as this book aims to demonstrate. Doubtless, there is a sea of difference between the legalistic Shi'ism of the madrasas of Najaf, Isfahan, and Qom, and the radical Shi'ism of the Alamut, and the Babi millennialism of the nineteenth century. Like any other religious experience Shi'ism evolved over time and adjusted to different climates and circumstances. Yet the ninth-century Shi'i theologian Ja'far Tusi and the thirteenth-century great Shi'i scientist, philosopher and statesman Nasir al-Din Tusi had more in common than just their birthplace. One can also draw a comparison between two Shi'i revolutionaries: the twelfth-century Hasan Sabbah, the Old Man of the Mountain, who founded the Alamut counter-state and the twentieth-century Ayatollah Khomeini, the founder of the Islamic Republic – a comparison that goes beyond the fact that the former was born in Qom (and initially was a Twelver Shi'i) and the latter spent many years of his life in Qom teaching a kind of philosophy that Nasir al-Din Tusi first contemplated while studying in the library of Alamut castle.

It is also noteworthy that the first Babi believer, Mulla Husain Bushru'i, came from a small village of Zirak in central Khurasan with a predominantly Isma'ili population composed of the remnants of the Isma'ilis of Qohistan (Kuhestan), an important stronghold of Nazari Isma'ilis centuries before. He went to study Shi'i legal and theological texts – the kind of texts produced by Ja'far Tusi and Nasir al-Din Tusi – in the madrasas of Najaf and Karbala, but rebelled against the scholastic training of the Usulis and opted for the Shaykhi proto-messianic mystical theology. Shaykh Ahmad Ahsa'i, a multidisciplinary scholar from the Shi'i region in north-east Arabia who was the founder of the Shaykhi school, detracted from Mulla Sadra's philosophy while being greatly shaped by it, an example of the "anxiety of influence" perhaps. Sayyid 'Ali Muhammad Shirazi, the young Bab to whom Bushru'i was attracted, himself was fascinated by the "cabalistic" tradition of letters and numbers that was for centuries studied in crypto-Isma'ili circles in the Ahsa' province in eastern Arabia and later by the Isma'ilis, the Hurufis and the Nuqtavis in the Iranian environment. The city of Shiraz, where the Bab was born and bred, was an old center of Sufism which Shi'i peripatetic dervishes frequented while criss-crossing remote lands from India to Arabia, Iraq and Anatolia.

Ayatollah Khomeini's ancestors, though not dervishes, immigrated as Shi'i clerics to Kashmir and Lucknow (the capital of the Shi'i Awdh kingdom) but later returned to Iran – an example of the fluidity of the Shi'i communities. In Qom Ayatollah Khomeini taught the Islamic mysticism of Ibn al-'Arabi, himself a practitioner of numerology, and the philosophy of Avicenna and Mulla Sadra before being rebuked by the strict anti-philosophy Shi'i jurists in the city. Not unlike Khomeini, three centuries earlier Mulla Sadra himself, fearing denunciation of the Shi'i 'ulama of Isfahan, first took refuge in a small village around Qom and later resided in Shiraz.

Yet despite bonds of geography and continuity in textual tradition and in scholastic training, Shi'ism accommodated a wide range of ideas and practices across dispersed communities. To some observers, Hamilton Gibb for example, diversity meant that Shi'ism often served as an ideological blanket to cover heterogeneous trends of dissent in Islam. It is more realistic to think of it, however, as variations on a theme: a core idea and many diverse expressions. The core idea, as Shi'is denoted, was devotion to the House of the Prophet and more specifically "love for the House of 'Ali" *(hubb-i Al-i 'Ali)*. The story of the Imams, their sacred leadership of the community and their usurped right as successor to the Prophet of Islam are part of this legacy. Devotion to the House of the Prophet is evident in all doctrinal modalities of Shi'ism. We may identify at least four modes of expression – as the chapters in this volume aim to demonstrate – at times distinct from one another but more often enmeshed and intermingled. The most prevalent, and widespread, is what may be called commemorative Shi'ism, revolving mainly around the image of Imam Husayn, the Third Shi'i Imam, and the mourning rite associated with his martyrdom in 680. The Husayn cult – as we may loosely call it – was celebrated in the ceremonies of Muharram and the recitations of tragedies of Karbala and had a wide appeal to Iranian believers who commemorated it since at least the ninth century. Commemorating the martyrdom of a fallen hero is not without precedent in pre-Islamic Iran. The mourning for the murder of Iraj – the primordial representation of Iran – is seminal to the *Shahnama*. More distinct is the martyrdom of the prince Siyavush in the *Shahnama*, who falls victim to a sinister plot. The collective memory of his martyrdom, the rite of *Suvashan*, was celebrated as late as the early Islamic centuries. The Husayn cult was urban as well as rural, intense and emotional and invariably tied up with the grassroots Muharram mourning.

Somewhat independent of Husayn's martyrdom narrative, but complementing it, is the veneration of 'Ali, the First Shi'i Imam, as champion of justice, affection and self-sacrifice. As a role model intended for the rulers to emulate, this devotion should be seen as more of an establishment cult that crosses social boundaries to tie the rulers to the ruled. Naming 'Ali as the ultimate patron saint, and "attaching to him bonds of clientship" was often invoked by the rulers of the Safavid era and later to stress not only duty and virtue but also legitimacy. For centuries, the notion of "governance" and "guardianship" (Ar. *wilaya;* Per. *wilayat*) of 'Ali as the just successor to the prophet of Islam entailed political legitimacy. Even in the twentieth century, the doctrine of the "Guardianship of the Jurist" *(wilayat-i faqih)*, the founding doctrine of the Islamic Republic of Iran, is a legalistic interpretation that is ultimately grounded in the old principle of Ali's legitimacy.

Along with the notion of governance was also the idea of the "friendship" of 'Ali as a patron saint, a belief long treasured by the Shi'i-Sufi orders such as the Ni'matullahis and their sub-branches and by the grassroots Khaksar (or Jalali) mendicant dervishes. Veneration for 'Ali also tied mainstream Shi'ism with powerful, but often rustic, communities of Ahl-i Haqq in the western Iranian periphery. Often labeled as "extremist" (*ghulat;* better translated as exaggerationist) by their opponents, the Ahl-i Haqq, Nusayris and the Alawites are but three variations on the theme of 'Ali veneration holding him as the "silent one" *(samet)* complementing the Prophet of Islam as the "speaker" *(natiq)* who articulates the apparent truth of the religion.

Memories of Husayn and 'Ali were crucial for messianic manifestations in Shi'ism. The Mahdi (the guided one; the savior) in Shi'ism is not only from the House of the Prophet and a progeny of 'Ali, but, more importantly, is the "riser" (*qa'im*) who avenges all that went wrong in Shi'i sacred history and all the sufferings that 'Ali, Fatima, Husayn, their family and supporters sustained. He restores their rightful place in history, for the apocalyptic scenario in Shi'ism is essentially reconstructed on the narrative of Karbala. The Shi'i self-image is not limited to victimization. Hope for restoration in the narrative of apocalyptic Shi'ism – as will be argued in the following chapters – is remarkable because it generates hopes beyond vengeance, especially in the Iranian environment, hopes that potentially, and at times actually, lead to conceiving a new order beyond Islam. In effect both the legitimacy claim and the martyrdom paradigm associated with 'Ali and Husayn respectively serve as powerful motives to make the Shi'ite Mahdi the initiator of a new supra-prophetic cycle. The revival of elements of the Zoroastrian apocalyptic tradition is evident in trends ranging from early Isma'ilism to Nuqtavism of the late Middle Ages, and the Babi movement in the middle of the nineteenth century.

Even in today's Iran the cult of the Mahdi is not absent, having been resuscitated and co-opted by some circles in the Islamic Republic and blessed by the president and the state propaganda machine. Nearly thirty years into an Islamic Revolution, which itself was rich with apocalyptic motifs, this revived enthusiasm may reflect frustration with the current direction and leadership of the Islamic regime.

## *Legalistic Shi'ism and the Jurist Establishment*

Beyond developing reverence for Husayn, affiliation with 'Ali and the messianic yearning for the Mahdi, the Twelver *(Ithna 'Ashari)* brand of Shi'ism also produced an enduring scholastic interpretation. It promoted the collection of the "traditions" (hadith) of the Prophets and eleven of the Shi'i Imams along with the text of the Qur'an and limited use of logic in order to build up an elaborate legal system that since at least the seventeenth century tended to discipline Shi'i individual and communal lives in Iran (and far more than was ever possible among the Shi'i communities in the Sunni-dominated Iraq and Lebanon). With varying degrees of success the jurist class *(fuqaha)* came to dominate not only madrasa education, the production of legal texts, the religious courts and most charitable endowments (*awqaf*) but also the control of mosques, at least through indirect means. Their control over these institutions was never complete, because their authority was continually undermined not only by their own lower ranks, but also by popular and mystical forms of Shi'ism, and occasionally by messianic trends.

The overall advantage of the mujtahids (jurisconsults or legal experts qualified to form legal opinions) as custodians of Islamic law gave them enormous social prestige and even political edge. Yet as some chapters in this book argue, the legalistic interpretation of Shi'ism, despite its complexity and pre-eminence and despite the jurists often enjoying the overt support of the state authorities, never fully resolved the structural issues of leadership and hierarchy. Nor in more recent times were the issues of legal modernity ever addressed even at a rudimentary level. The 'ulama (plural of *'alim*: learned, scholar; defining the legal establishment) as an interest group, to use the sociological term, by and large remained profoundly conservative in their attitude towards law and legal reforms, the acceptance of any major doctrinal innovation, and in recent times towards cultural toleration, social pluralism, gender equality and a secular polity.

In some respects Shi'i law paralleled the archaism in most ritualistic religions including both Jewish Talmudic law and the Zoroastrian law of the *Vedivdad* and their preoccupations with ritualistic acts, complicated laws of cleanliness and dietary prohibitions. Such legal conservatism, needless to say, is typical of religious communities that are historically disempowered, persecuted and held in minority status. Clinging to given laws, traditions and rituals was thus considered – and vigorously advocated by the legal authorities, the rabbis, the *mubads* and the Shi'i jurists – as the steadfast display of communal loyalty and means of survival against incentives for conversion to majority religions and abandoning the ways of the forefathers. Yet in the Iranian case, such an argument is clearly problematic, given that Shi'ism enjoyed state sponsorship since the early sixteenth century (not to mention the patronage the Shi'i jurist enjoyed under Ilkhanid rule [1256–1335]) and the fact that Shi'ism was internalized by the majority, at least in the Iranian center (as against the Sunni peripheries), since the seventeenth century.

Yet throughout the Safavid and the Qajar periods, Shi'i jurisprudence, and to some extent Shi'i theology, became increasingly petrified and, in terms of applicability, largely irrelevant. Especially in the course of the late nineteenth and the early part of the twentieth century, mainstream jurisprudence refused to allow room for any form of modernity, whether adaptive or indigenous. As late as the 1930s modernizers such as Shari'at Sangelagi were soundly repudiated, and even the incorporation of aspects of Shi'i jurisprudence into Iranian civil and penal codes in the early Pahlavi era was frowned upon or ignored by the high-ranking jurists of Qom and Najaf. In the 1960s and 1970s such modernist critics as 'Ali Shari'ati (1933–77) were shunned by the jurist establishment as blasphemous, if not heretical. His critique of the Shi'i jurists' preoccupations with intricate but useless details of rituals and outmoded legal methods hardly amounted to a shift in legal paradigm or rethinking arcane practices. Yet his message of revolutionary Shi'ism was soon adopted by the younger generation of clergy who preferred to abandon the arduous task of rethinking Shi'i law and theology in favor of political Islam and the irresistible lure of an Islamic revolution.

Thus the answer to the question as to why conservatism was integral to the Shi'i establishment remains an elusive one. It can of course be argued that Sunni law, generally speaking, was no more accommodating to the contingencies of modernity than was Shi'ite law, and, a few exceptions aside, it remained just as hostile to innovativeness. Sunni law also enjoyed state sponsorship in the Ottoman times, as in Khedivate Egypt, and a somewhat elevated status in British India. Yet even the few exceptions – Muhammad Abduh in Egypt and Sayyid Ahmad Khan in India are the most prominent examples – failed to carry the day, for they too were soundly defeated by the discourse of legal conservatism.

One important motive for this defensive attitude towards social change no doubt was the jurists' inherent isolation in the madrasa environment and their reluctance to be engaged with the public beyond the sheer necessities arrogated to the *qadis* and *muftis* in the Sunni world and less formally assigned to the mujtahids in Shi'i Iran. In turn, the highly elaborate and speculative aspects of devotional rituals and contractual laws and regulations of the shari'a were sharply truncated and remained unenforceable beyond the limited jurisdiction of the religious courts. The rise of the Usuli school in the nineteenth century, as argued in this book, was an attempt to break through the juristic isolation. Yet in reality Usulism failed to nurture legal innovation and explore new avenues of dealing with the needs of Iranian society. The Usuli *ijtihad* (a legal exercise; making opinions based on sources of Shi'i law) accepted limited rationalization and hence a broader application of law than did the rival Akhbari school, but the bookish quality of the Islamic law, Shi'i and Sunni alike, despite its impressive theoretical foundation

– as for instance in the extensive study of the "roots of jurisprudence" *('ilm al-usul)* – hardly ever facilitated a serious rethinking of the old legal framework and principles.

The bookish nature of the study of law is evident in a huge number of glosses, commentaries and marginalia produced since the late Safavid period and in the whole scholastic production of the madrasa. Madrasa culture was well versed in traditional skills, especially rhetoric and disputation, but defiant of the realities of a changing society around it. Indeed the very political radicalization of the clerical establishment in the latter part of the twentieth century may be attributed to its reluctance to engage in legal modernity. Moreover, the clerical establishment's intellectual isolation, and political marginalization during the Pahlavi era made radical voices such as Khomeini's more audible. Political radicalization in effect was a convenient means of obfuscating clerical reluctance to face the profound problems that riddled the Shi'i scholastic interpretation of the shari'a. Broadly speaking, the failure to come up with effective answers to the modern legal, moral and rational dilemmas of Iranian society persuaded twentieth-century radical clerics to seek the high road of opposition to the state and blame the Pahlavi regime, and more especially Reza Shah, not only as a totalitarian instrument of modernity but primarily as an enemy of the faith.

## *Revolutionary Shi'ism and Post-Revolutionary Prospects*

Clerical opposition to the legitimacy of the Pahlavi state, which is part of the imagined history of the contemporary Shi'i establishment (partly based on the undue emphasis in Western scholarship on the 'ulama's opposition to the Qajar state) has little ground in historical reality. In purely theoretical terms Shi'ism rejected the legitimacy of any form of state, Shi'i or otherwise, before the advent of the Mahdi; the belief that all temporal powers, as has often been observed, are considered unjust was carried almost to the point of anarchistic idealism. Yet throughout the history of clerical Twelver Shi'ism we can hardly detect serious evidence of the active rejection of the upholders of temporal power and even less evidence of the theoretical substitution of temporal authority. Before Ayatollah Khomeini's doctrine of the Governence of the Jurist in the 1970s, no Shi'i jurist of any importance (save for one dubious case reported from the late Safavid era) ever proposed the creation of the jurists' political governance *(wilayat al-hukm)*. If the clerical leadership ever claimed authority outside the madrasa – and that only in the Qajar period – it was purely a judicial one, that is, the "judicial authority" *(wilayat al-qada)*. In practice this meant resistance to the state's creation of a centralized judiciary that would be regulated by a codified body of laws and legislations. The intense hatred that radicalized clerics like Ayatollah Khomeini reserved for Reza Shah was primarily because the latter eventually established such a system – itself a major objective of the Constitutional Revolution – at the expense of the mujtahids and their monopoly over the religious courts.

Equally important was a kind of "turf war" that was waged throughout the nineteenth century between the increasingly affluent high-ranking 'ulama in the cities and the agents of the state over social prestige, material privileges, and popularity. As the prestige and credibility of the Qajar state diminished for lack of military, administrative, and political effectiveness, the Shi'i 'ulama came to represent a class of urban notables willing and able to establish a sphere of influence through the collection of religious taxes and dues, control of endowments and mosques, and private economic and commercial enterprises. In turn, the preservation of these material and political interests rather than any ideological and doctrinal differences generated rivalries and, occasionally, open conflict with government agents, as with other mujtahids and with other urban notables.

Among the effective weapons in the hands of both the high-ranking mujtahids and the lower ranks of preachers, who were often in competition with their senior colleagues, were the exploitation of the easily excitable masses of followers and students of the madrasa; the provocation of sectarian and urban divisions between the Ni'matis and Haydaris, the Shaykhis and the Mutisharri'a; repeated anti-Sufi, anti-minority and anti-heresy campaigns; crusades against European infidels of all sorts, Russian armies and English missionaries; at times boycott of modern innovations and in the Pahlavi era a ban on the public presence of women.

In due course what became a hallmark of the Shi'i clerical establishment in Iran, and its extension in Iraq, and part of its communal culture was fetishistic avoidance and frowning defiance of anything new, novel, and unfamiliar, anything that appeared to threaten the inner core of the community of followers upon which was built their power and influence. In that regard, the Shi'i establishment did not differ in conservative spirit, although it did in means and methods, from any other clerical establishment at a certain stage of its passage to modernity: the Catholic Church, Calvinist Puritanism, Rabbinical Judaism, and Hindu Brahmanism.

What, however, differentiates the Shi'i clerical establishment in the twentieth century from these counterparts is a modern claim to political power, and the radical means of achieving power through an ideological revolution. This is the latest modality that characterizes Shi'ism in Iran (and now increasingly Sunni Islam as well). The Islamic Revolution was in effect the redefining of clerical aspirations no longer congruent with the temporal power of the state but in competition with the state and eventually taking control of the state. To achieve this, the Islamic Revolution modernized the clerical establishment not only by exploiting modern means – most effectively through mass media – but by modernizing its message. It also borrowed from populist and socialist ideologies of the twentieth century. Legal modernity by and large was resisted, however, except in matters of sheer contingency. Though there emerged in the aftermath of the revolution an Islamic constitution and an Islamic parliament – replacing the mostly secular constitution and the National Consultative Assembly of the previous era – the Islamic Revolution also installed a "Guardian Jurist" to control, supervise and monitor all affairs of the state and a Guardian Council to oversee the parliament and to veto legislations deemed contradictory to the shari'a.

The relics of the Shi'i clerical past further persisted in an old communal culture and what may be called the Qom *esprit de corps*, a binary worldview of good versus evil, and the incorporation of elements of dissident messianic Shi'ism, to which in the past clerical Shi'ism had always remained hostile. Most significant was the sharpening of gender boundaries by monitoring the chaste covering of the female body and hence Islamic society's "honor" *(namus)* and effectively trying to push women out of the public space – though evidently with little success – and denying them full professional privileges and equal legal status.

Iranian Shi'ism thus is likely to remain distinct from other Shi'i communities in Iraq, Lebanon, Bahrain and elsewhere. The complex history of Shi'ism's intermingling with Iran's culture and society, its diverse modalities and the way they interplay, the decisive majority status of Shi'is in Iran and the Islamic Republic's political and ideological claims generated dynamics that differentiates today's Iranian Shi'ism from other expressions of Islamic fundamentalism in the Sunni world. Today's post-revolutionary Iranian society displays diverse, even conflicting, characteristics: on the one hand disillusionment with the ideologies and rhetoric of the Islamic Revolution, combined with a cynicism typical of societies under oppressive rule and an even more typical thirst for receiving, absorbing and enjoying non-Islamic mores and fads forbidden by the regime, especially on the part of the new urban middle class. On the other hand, Iran during the past three decades has witnessed an undeniable revival of what may be called a "folk" religiosity especially visible at the grassroots level; deeply Shi'i in its ethos though not necessarily committed to the project of political Islam. The prospects for intermingling these seemingly contesting trends may determine the future of Shi'ism in Iran and define the evolving Iranian identity.

Beyond popular religiosity, since the Islamic Revolution some Iranian laity and clergy have engaged in a discourse of modernity that aims to build on the revolutionary legacy of the past to redefine the pertinence of Islam and Shi'ism and their place in context of Iranian society and culture as well as in the Muslim world and even globally. Informed by philosophy and theory more than history or social realities, this post-revolutionary discourse displays exciting signs of vitality that in many respects are rooted in the Shi'i dynamics of the past.

A current of Islamic neo-modernism spearheaded by the Abdolkarim Soroush is but one example. An articulate student of philosophy, who since the outset of the Revolution gradually moved to what may be called an Islamic dissident camp, has been advocating a certain elasticity in Islam as a religious construct which, though possessing a sacred core – a set of a prioris – also evolves over time as a force that shaped Muslim societies and cultures but that also is shaped by them. His epistemological distinction between religious truth and the evolving human understanding of this truth, what he calls the theory of "contraction and expansion" *(qabz va bast)* though essentialist and arguably ahistorical in essence, is nevertheless a significant and refreshing development. Informed by the Popperian "critical rationalism," over the past three decades Soroush's quest for flexibility in Islamic thought and practice has led him to a greater recognition of the need for toleration, acceptance of change, and the inevitability of religious progression in time. Albeit through the mystical prism of the thirteenth-century Persian mystic and poet Rumi, he came to recognize that conservative interpretation of the shari'a has reached an existential dead end from which it can not escape unless the realities of modernity are acknowledged. In his recent pronouncements one may even sense an ambivalent call for rethinking the sacred religious core in such fundamental beliefs as Prophethood and the Imamate. Soroush thus appears to have come closer than any contemporary thinker to the theme of cyclical renewal in Shi'i Islam even though we have yet to see in his approach to Islamic thought a clear break from conventional notions of Islam as an eternal divine message and in turn greater acknowledgment of religion as a historical construct. He seems to have stopped at the threshold of such a paradigmatic shift.

Dissenting reformists among the clergy such as Mohsen Kadivar, Mohammad Mojtahed Shabestari, Hasan Yousefi Eshkevari, and Muhammad Khatami also offered alternative readings to doctrinal positions of the Islamic Republic, readings which led to their harassment, arrest, and imprisonment. Mohsen Kadivar, who has critiqued the Islamic Republic's absolutist interpretation of the doctrine of Governance of the Jurist and its fundamental contrast to the precedence in Shi'i past, seems to advocate a conditional return to the Shi'i historical preference for diffused leadership, striving for the emergence of a civil society, and even clerical dissociation from political power. He also highlighted the Islamic judicial impasse in coping with modern issues of gender, human rights, toleration, clerical monopoly of power, and advocacy of religious militancy. Dealing with these sensitive yet inescapable choices, Kadivar and like-minded reformers aim at a new interpretation of Islam without denying the legitimacy of the Islamic Republic.

Mujtahid Shabestari, another clerical thinker, on the other hand resorts to an epistemological discourse somewhat similar to the Sufi and Sufi-Shi'i mystical readings of Islam. He calls for recognizing the limitations of religious knowledge and scriptural instruction and their inapplicability to the material, and more specifically scientific and technological, sphere of human existence. He moreover views as essential the hermeneutical understanding of Islamic scripture and traditions as a key to Muslim societies' adaptability to the contingencies of modern times and in effect the implicit recognition of human agency.

Naturally all these thinkers (and the reformist movement often associated with President Mohammad Khatami since the mid-1990s) in various degrees recognize "Islam" not merely as a religious belief system or a historical construct but as an organizing principle upon which an Islamic republic can be viably built. Such a proactive stand may well be understood not merely in terms of personal conviction or utopian aspiration but also because the Islamic Republic over the past thirty years has offered a forum for these religious intellectuals despite their opposition to the mainstream, or perhaps because of it. In cautiously distancing themselves from the reality of the Islamic state and its actors and their advocacy of a freer and more open society, these thinkers have made a courageous move. If sustained, this is no doubt a new phenomenon in the history of clerical Shi'ism with potential ramifications for the very viability of the Islamic Republic and the Guardianship of the Jurist.

The reformist trends stand in contrast to the doctrinaire outlook of the ideological commissars of the Islamic Republic. Mostly influenced by German idealist philosophy and a reinterpretation of the Shi'i theosophy of the Mulla Sadra school, these facilitators of the Islamic regime – among them Reza Davari, a teacher of philosophy and an influential ideologue, and Hadad Adel, a former speaker of the Islamic Parliament and a translator of Kantian philosophy – have their intellectual roots in the debates of the 1960s and 1970s, inspired by proponents of neo-traditionalism. They included Henry Corbin, the celebrated French scholar of Islamic theosophy and mysticism, who in those decades unearthed a trait of Shi'i theosophy and esoteric thought particular to Iran. Ahmad Fardid, the "oral philosopher" with the dubious credential of coining the problematic notion of *gharbzadagi* (Westoxication) espoused a post-metaphysical synthesis of Heideggerian philosophy, Persian mystical poetry, and the Islamic philosophy of the School of Isfahan. Hussein Nasr, an influential scholar of Islamic philosophy and an uneasy liaison between Shi'i madrasa learning and Pahlavi secularism, was the first to offer an accessible (though arguably nostalgic) reading of Iran's rich tradition of Islamic philosophy. In the early years of the Islamic Revolution the legacy of this complex anti-modernist discourse, through a handful of its students (and many enthusiasts), set the theoretic grounding for the ascent of theocratic absolutism. Driven by a search for Islamic "authenticity" impervious to Western Enlightenment and its sins, the strange blend of madrasa conservatism, conspiracy theory and xenophobia, and customized Heideggerian philosophy, they offered the rhetorical ground for the consolidation of conservative forces in today's Iran.

The ongoing debates between reformists and conservatives are nonetheless cerebral and thus elitist in nature, often confined to religious intellectuals and their cliques. It thus may prove to be less relevant to the future direction of the Islamic Republic, and even less important to the future of Iranian Shi'ism. What may prove to be more pertinent are generational changes and undercurrents within Iranian society beyond the richness of Islamic ideology. Released by the Revolution, and three decades later, younger Iranians seem to have taken a direction of their own largely independent of the preached ideologies. This is evident in a desire for global interconnectedness through the Internet and the popular culture associated with it, artistic and cinematic expression, and engaging in issues of women's rights, environment, freedom of the press, pluralism and human rights that are at odds with ideological Islam and outside the traditional strictures of normative Shi'ism. One may discern in this new discourse – which is still informed by the dynamics of Shi'ism – a deliverance from the yokes of dogmatism and repression.

# PART I

# *Apocalypticism in the Islamic Middle East*

## CHAPTER I

# *Apocalyptic Anxieties and Millennial Hopes in the Salvation Religions of the Middle East*

> A thousand years I can await your boon,
> Whenever you come is a moment too soon.
>
> Sana'i

At the turn of the third Christian millennium, the secularized Gregorian Christian calendar of our time has reached an almost global recognition beyond its religious origins. Millennialism in the context of non-Western societies thus may make sense even though Iran observes a solar Islamic calendar of its own. Six years into the third Christian millennium much of the public euphoria surrounding the millennial turn seems to be at a low ebb, even though in many minds the events of September 11, 2001 and subsequent developments seem to signal the prelude to a real apocalyptic calamity. After all, the al-Qaeda leader, Osama Bin Laden, may very well be seen as an apocalyptic figure, a savior in the eye of the beholder and an ultimate villain in the eye of multitudes of his enemies.

The rise of neoconservatism in the United States and the rhetoric of the "War on Terror" at times also resonate with familiar apocalyptic motifs; first with the fall of the Taliban regime in Afghanistan in 2002, which seemed to many the triumph of good over evil, and then with the invasion of Iraq in 2003, which landed the United States in what appears to be one of the gravest errors ever committed in the history of U.S. foreign policy. With the U.S. setbacks, no clear line seems any longer to differentiate the forces of good from the forces of evil. The religious climate of post-September 11, however, remained intensely polarized, with growing terrorist attacks, evangelical calls for eliminating the evil of Islamic radicalism, and fear of nuclear confrontation.

What may come out of this religious and political fermentation is difficult to predict. Yet one thing is clear. Beyond the "War on Terror" and fear of nuclear proliferation there are deeper and more lasting catastrophes in the offing, global warming being one example; genocide and widespread human suffering is another – as if the whole world is now facing an unprecedented fear of a catastrophic turn, albeit expressed through motifs different from those in the Book of Daniel, the Book of Revelation or the Shi'i messianic prophecies. Yet apocalyptic anxieties abound and patterns of response are not far different.

This is all the more reason to reflect on the scholarship dedicated to the origins and evolution of apocalypticism as a historical phenomenon, its multifaceted manifestations and its lasting grip on the human imagination. Appropriate to the postmodern information society, the primary concern at the recent millennial turn was a trivial anxiety about computers' dating malfunction, the so called Y2K problem or the Millennium Bug (now almost completely forgotten); an apt reminder of similar fears of chaos and hopes for ultimate redemption in different calendaric junctures and in diverse cultures. The complex recurrence of millennial paradigms is intrinsically tied to humanity's striving to imagine, anticipate, and help bring about a tormenting End, and through that agony a fresh beginning.

Whether historical or exegetical in approach, the comparative scholarship of apocalypticism as a phenomenon confirms the presence of common themes in all religious traditions that originated in the Middle East. Despite the peculiarities of each tradition, all of them demonstrate the interplay between archetypal motifs and indigenous cultures both in medieval and in modern times. It is primarily this shared apocalyptic legacy of salvation in Judaism, Zoroastrianism, Christianity and Islam that helped shape not only the theological perspective and eschatology of these religious communities, but also served as a driving force behind major currents in human history from the rise of new institutional religions to political revolutions and intellectual movements. In addressing these themes, beyond conventional understandings of millennialism, there are political, cultural and social manifestations. These almost invariably originated in the ancient Middle East, where the earliest paradigms of the apocalyptic narrative were shaped.

## *The End Paradigm*

Perhaps the most recognizable feature in the Middle Eastern narrative of the final events, the End paradigm in the Zoroastrian and Jewish traditions, is that it operates as a reverse process to the myth of the beginning, what is often identified as the binary of the *zeitgeist* and the *endgeist*. As in other nature-orientated cosmologies, the eschatological narrative of the final events commemorates a seasonal cycle. Despite much variation, this powerful motif relies on celestial and agricultural imagery to convey a sense of continuity in the cycle of life and death, an essential feature of any enduring socio-religious cosmology. In the salvation religions of the Middle East the binary of the Beginning and the End paradigms is particularly powerful since it generally functions as a strategy to resolve the tension engendered by the problem of theodicy. The struggle between good and evil, in existence since the dawn of creation, will culminate in a destructive final battle in which the victory of the forces of good over evil will be followed by divine judgment and the reward of timeless bliss.[1]

Unraveling mysteries of the End paradigm has long been the preoccupation of believers, whether as commentators of the encoded messages of the scriptures or, more often, as human agents called upon to realize the scenario of the End. In any given situation, the millennialists tend to engage in some form of temporalizing past prophecies and demonstrate the imminence, or near imminence, of the End in their own time and place. Applying prophecies to contemporary settings, needless to say, is as distinct from the modern historical or critical reading of the scriptures as it is from the ahistorical timelessness usually attached to the prophecies by "authoritative" exegeses, be they Augustinian church dogma, the Talmudic halakha, or the consensus of the Muslim 'ulama. By denying altogether the apocalyptic meaning of the prophecies (or what is considered by millenarians as prophecies), the authoritative readings often relegate these prophecies to an unspecified distant future far from this-worldly access and safely curtailed by implausible preconditions. This is indeed the rationale behind the prohibition shared by all "orthodox" traditions to "set the time" of the End, an obvious precaution against millenarian textual subversion and the urge for temporality.

To temporalize the prophecies and other scriptural evidence, whether literally or allegorically, millennialists have employed various strategies to make their evidence speak out the anticipated End and the events preceding it. The act of prognosticating the End necessitates a preoccupation with time reckoning and calendaric. Equally common was the wide usage of the occult sciences, especially numerology and esoteric knowledge of letters. To the chiliastic adept, sacred dates and deadlines encoded in the verses of any given scripture, and in the sayings of prophets and saints (as well as in non-textual evidence), were mysteries urgently awaiting decipherment. Indeed the whole material world, with its seasonal changes and natural and human calamities, was seen as a text to be read with esoteric methods mastered by millennialists through rigorous study, mortification, intuition, dreams and mystical experiences.

The alternative reality that emerged out of temporalizing endeavors, beneath the apparent reality accepted and enshrined by authoritative exegeses, was particularly apt for cyclical reckoning. Both centennial and millennial, these cyclical courses were based on conventional calendaric and its variants. More often they were calculated from primal dates in a sacred text. Sacred chronology, especially in creation narratives, was favored, or even more specific dates such as those present in the Book of Daniel, the assumed date for the birth of Jesus, the *Hijra* of the Islamic Prophet, or the assumed Occultation of the Twelfth Imam in Shi'ism. In particular, the notion of millennium, and its correlation to the events of the End, held a firm grip over the apocalyptic calendaric in all Western religions. As a unit of time reckoning, millennium is a Babylonian invention. But it was probably in the Zoroastrian tradition of Iran that the millennium *(hazarag)* first earned an apocalyptic significance. It connoted the duration of a thousand-year cycle in the finite battle between the forces of good and evil, a cyclical struggle that shapes the whole of human history and will eventually end in the triumph of the Lord of Wisdom and his associates over Ahriman.[2] The events of the End therefore came to be linked in Zoroastrianism, as in the Hebrew tradition, and later in other apocalyptic literature of the Middle East, with thousand-year periods, which were either explicitly or implicitly cyclical or, as in the conventional Christian apocalyptics, a one-time occurrence leading to an irrevocable End. Respectively, the centennial turns, as decimal denominations of the millennium, were often associated with temporary lapses of order. The spirit of decadence that has fallen upon humanity was to be rejuvenated with the turn of a new century. The Islamic notion of the "renovator of the beginning of the century" (i.e. of the *Hijra* calendar) and perhaps even the idea of *fin de siècle* in modern Western cultures, acknowledge such a centennial renewal. On a smaller scale, celebrating the beginning of a new year in most cultures also conveys a sense of cyclical renewal. The Persian celebration of the Nowruz at the vernal equinox, for instance, commemorates seasonal renewal as a token of the millennial turn.

Millennialism and other forms of apocalyptic calendaric hence appear to be inherent to all Middle Eastern religions. It may be argued that they are far more essential for continuity of the sacred and its perpetual renewal than our modern utilitarian notion of linear time and the concept of progress. Time cycles thus may be seen as regulatory means of placing utopian and eschatological aspirations, and whatever is associated with the Beginning and the End, within a humanly conceivable time frame. Those who sifted through the sacred text for evidence of the End, labored over the esoteric methods of discovering the encoded message, and subjected themselves and their followers to a rigorous course of abstinence, penitence, and social exclusion, viewed the certainty of such calendaric calculations as indispensable and indisputable. For them the millennial turn (and other forms of calendaric cycles) had a momentary urgency and the potential to actualize apocalyptic aspirations. These individuals and communities, by taking upon themselves the divine charge of bringing closer the hour of the End, attempt to fulfill the conditions scripted in the text. In a millennial momentum, common to all apocalyptic trends, a crucial shift occurs from dormant aspiration to keen ambition. This turning point invariably pertains to crossing a psychological barrier, one which divides adherence to the established belief system from an experience of rebirth and in turn discovering a communal identity with like-minded individuals.

Playing an active part in temporalizing the apocalyptic scenario, the participants view their role, and that of their opponents, as divinely ordained though not entirely devoid of human initiatives and strategies. This curious mix of the scripted and the improvised, the providential design and its human deciphering, is germane to most apocalyptic currents. It stands to determine the nature of their unraveling, whether peaceful and "optimistic," radical and destructive, or more often a combination of the two. Yet in all instances urgency for arriving at the divine judgment, salvation, and millennial bliss remain the ultimate goal. In the visions of the End we observe the ideals of generations, utopian dreams and nightmares, fanatical obsessions with providential plan, and prospects for a regressive or a progressive future; a mirror to societies' innate fears and aspirations.

Predictably, millennial visions frequently contrast prevailing legal, theological, and even pietistic norms of their time. Furthermore, they were in conflict with the authorities, religious and temporal, who represented these norms or served as their guardians. The history of millenarianism in all Western religions is suffused with clashes (to use a Weberian concept) between priests and prophets. Yet precisely this antinomian quality of the apocalyptic experience, even in its speculative and tangential manifestation, brings to bear an imaginative alternative to the sanctified dogma. Whether crude and naive at their inception or fully developed and articulated, these trends sought creative directions untenable in prevailing theology, if not altogether prohibited by it. Yet not all millennial trends were forward-looking in their doctrinal disposition or inclusive in their social message.

Moreover, some mystics and theologians, even philosophers, who were not overtly millenarian in their recognized thinking, at times subscribed to millennial paradigms to put across their most speculative, controversial, and utopian thoughts. Covert millennialism, for the greater part, still remains unexplored. Engagements of these speculative millennialists, overt or covert, did not, however, exclude a vast array of those individuals labeled as crackpots, eccentrics, and fanatics – those who crowded the history of popular apocalypticism. Nor can one stop noticing at times, in the same millennial environment, contrasts and compromises of glaring magnitude. A not so subtle coexistence of the mundane and the sublime defined many apocalyptic quests. An uneasy marriage of anger, violence, and intolerance with peace and acumen, of naiveté and demagogy with sophistication and creativity, and of folk beliefs with venerable erudition, characterizes the inspirational ramshackle upon which millennial edifices were often built.

Contradictions aside, in their morally sharpened worldview, millenarians reject the legalistic and ritualistic strategies for salvation as offered by religious authorities (though they often do incorporate the mystical and the ascetic). In their effort to save the world from evil, millennialists often demand total justice, material plenty, and, at times, liberation from the yoke of religious or secular law by seeking an end to the prevailing order. In their estimation such an order equates with absolute evil on account of its presumed corruption, injustice, and the decadence that it had brought upon God's community.

## *Cycles and the Advent of the Messiah*

A unifying motif in speculative millennialism, and a converging point of the absolute and the relative in this mode of thinking, is the concept of cyclical renovation. Imagining the End, whether a literal or allegorical annihilation of the physical world, necessitates a chaotic jolt to facilitate a new beginning. Millennial currents, except perhaps for the most "pessimistic" and doctrinally inarticulate, subscribe to one form or another of cyclical rebirth so as to place the convulsions of the End in a broader, and humanly more tolerable, scheme. Such apocalyptic deconstruction is not an entirely aimless or nihilistic process. While it often reflects the violent aspirations of the persecuted and the deprived, it also guarantees the continuity of the human race in celestial or terrestrial forms; be it the timeless bliss of an otherworldly paradise or in the post-apocalyptic reality. Such reality adheres to postponed prophecies and anticipations but also may attempt to build an earthly community on the perceived celestial model. Isma'ili messianism offers at least two examples of post-millennial community: the tenth-century Qarmati state of Bahrain and the Nazari Isma'ilism of the Alamut after the declaration of the Resurrection *(Qiyamat)* in 1164. The Babi movement in Iran after the conference of Badasht in 1848, which declared the end of the Islamic dispensation, may also be viewed as post-millennial; a spirit that in many ways continued to shape the *zeitgeist* of the Baha'i Faith during Baha'ullah's time. Of post-millennial trends in Judaism one example is the Sabbatean Donmeh, the crypto-Jewish followers of Sabbatai Zevi of the seventeenth century. Among several Christian examples in recent times we may note the emergence of the Seventh Day Adventists after the collapse of the Millerite movement in 1844.

Inevitably, all apocalyptic currents subscribe to some form of symbolism, for it is difficult, even for strict literalists, not to read some level of allegory into admonishing prophecies of the Hebrew Bible, the terrifying imagery of the Book of Revelation, or the warnings of the Qur'an and the hadith. At least in early Christianity, even St. Augustine's post-millennial doctrine, which denied the possible occurrence of an earthly apocalypse, could not be argued without resorting to some metaphorical devise. Yet literal interpretations of the End are more likely to adhere narrowly to a sequence of prophesized events and to identify all heroes and villains in an apocalyptic scenario.

Symbolic interpretations of the End, in contrast, are more likely to acquire a historical perspective, reading a hidden moral drama behind the textual description and seeking an imaginative, and even progressive, view of the future. Here the End paradigm is consciously employed to justify a doctrinal break with the existing "orthodoxy." The divinely consecrated orthodoxies, whether the church, the shari'a, or the Talmudic law, are considered timeless and eternal and can not be perceived as terminable except with the occurrence of an apocalyptic End.

The theme of progression (or regression), associated with symbolic interpretations of apocalyptic texts, views cyclical phases of human history as purposeful movements in time in either forward or backward directions. The metaphor commonly employed in apocalyptic literature, such as in Zoroastrianism, is that of a tree, reflecting both a seasonal cycle and a gradual growth at the turn of each cycle; hence spiral turns. The effectiveness of the tree metaphor, which also is manifest in the Book of Daniel, is in the fact that movement in time could be seen either as a process of maturation and strength or, alternatively, regression toward eventual, though distant, demise. In either case, this spiral movement in time was distinct from the notion of immutable cycles often upheld by ancient Mesopotamian, or Egyptian, cosmologies whereby the eternal renewal of the time cycle does not result in any progression or regression.

The myth of the four kingdoms in the Book of Daniel (chapters 4 and 7), and its Zoroastrian and Greek versions, mourns the eclipse of a golden age, symbolized by the golden branch, to be followed at later cycles by depreciated ages of silver, bronze (or iron), and clay.[3] Such a conception of time, presumably representing the metallurgical revolutions of ancient times, denotes nostalgia for a golden past, contempt for the degenerate present, and a gloomy future. This regressive view of history, however, is not entirely devoid of potentials for a dynamic, and even forward-looking, future. The end to the age of clay eventually comes with conflagration of the entire material world and reconstruction in the golden age. As late as in the Bab's *Bayan* in nineteenth-century Iran, we encounter the "tree of the truth" conceptualizing a progressive revelation within the context of the past and future prophetic cycles.

The act of cosmic reconstruction revolves around the figure of a human savior. The rebirth *(farashkart)*, an essential notion of Zoroastrian eschatology, is firmly tied with the advent of a charismatic figure, who is probably the prototype for saviors in other religions of Middle East. The divine mandate and miraculous powers of the Saoshyant, who is of sacred origin, epitomizes the forces of good and leads the armies of his human and angelic supporters in a cosmic battle that ends with the destruction of evil and the reconstitution of the original and lasting order. In Judaism, the Day of the Lord *(yum adunay)* similarly commences with the advent of a messianic savior, the Mashiah, and culminates in the salvation of the People of Israel from the yoke of slavery. The Christ's Second Coming, which initiates the *parusia*, brings about the millennial era (or ends it, according to the post-millennialists doctrine), and in Islam, especially in Shi'ism, the appearance of the Mahdi initiates the process of the great revolt *(khuruj)* culminating in the Resurrection *(qiyama)* and the Day of Judgment *(yaum al-din)*.

In all these apocalyptic scenarios the power and charisma of the savior is countered with those of his arch opponent and mirror image. The Zoroastrian Ahriman (who is not humanly personified) is mightier than the Hebrew Bible's Belial, the Christian Antichrist, and the Islamic Dajjal, yet they all in various degrees serve as the personification of evil, an agent whose enormous deceptive capacity and whose tyranny and terror run supreme at the outset of the apocalyptic chaos before being eventually vanquished in the hands of the savior and his army.

Not surprisingly, apocalyptic messianism through the ages has been the genesis of new religious currents and a predominant mode of prophetic expression. Jesus' own call for salvation and the birth of Christianity could not be fully explained without the apocalyptic spirit that consumed the Judeo-Hellenistic world of the first century. Nor can the essence of Muhammad's early mission be fully understood without the apocalyptic admonitions, the foreseen calamities, and the terror of the Day of Judgment, apparent in the early suras of the Qur'an. In more recent times, Luther's call for reforming the Catholic Church, Sabbatai Zevi's claim to be the Jewish messiah, Sayyid 'Ali Muhammad the Bab's claim to be the Shi'i Mahdi and the evolution of his movement into the Baha'i Faith, Joseph Smith's Church of Jesus Christ of the Latter-Day Saints, and other American indigenous religions should be seen as a conscious fulfillment of the messianic role conceived on ancient biblical and Zoroastrian models.

Messianic prophets emerge not only in a milieu of apocalyptic expectations, but their doctrinal unfolding and course of action tend to re-enact the apocalypse. In time, the movements they initiate tend to evolve in conjunction with the dynamics of their surroundings and in response to the whims and wishes of their supporters. There is a gradual shift from being precursors and agents to being the savior who fulfills the scriptural prophecies. As a millennial manifestation, a savior may preside over a new dispensation and consciously engender a new religious system that even crosses the ancient biblical divide between prophethood and divinity.

In their post-apocalyptic phase messianic movements seldom succeed in entirely transforming the pervasive apocalyptic notions in a given religious culture. Regardless of their success or failure to fulfill their perceived prophecies and regardless of becoming a conspicuous socio-religious force, messianic movements retain the intense expectation for an imminent paradisiacal bliss. In due course, therefore, the paradigm of the impending End is to be relegated into a supra-temporal space. Such a post-apocalyptic shift seems necessary, inadvertently perhaps, to allow a gradual routinization of the prophetic charisma and the emergence of an institutionalized creed. The alternative is to be reduced to sectarian marginality or altogether to be thrown into the repository of dormant memories only to be retrieved as the raw material for re-emerging apocalyptic trends of later times. It goes without saying that beyond the initial phase, once a messianic movement comes of age, to sustain the momentum in any organized religion often proves impossible. Without resorting to some form of future recurrence, possibly another millennial return, such anticipations are inherently viewed as subversive.

## *Millenarian Movements and Social Change*

With few exceptions, millennial movements in Western religious traditions acquired a distinct socio-cultural dimension discernable in their social composition as well as in their explicit, or dormant, social message. Almost invariably they are socially inclusive movements which tend to break across class and other social barriers and create a momentary spirit of unity and equity within the community of believers. Anticipation of some form of divine judgment, though based on individual, rather than collective, deeds and misdeeds, is often translatable into a message of social justice. Moreover, the ultimate test of salvation in the anticipated Last Judgment is adherence and loyalty to the messianic upholder of the truth, an act of individual choice, rather than to the deeds of one's ancestors, tribe, or community.

Individual choice, however, is curtailed by an intense sense of group identity which enacts and fulfills the scripted prophecies. This uneasy mix of voluntary choice and collective destiny has often been a source of attraction to the deprived – whether perceived or real – the underprivileged, the marginalized, and the socially exiled. Promises of plenty and justice, or more likely vengeance, abound in apocalyptic literature, combined with ideals of love and sexual liberty, the breaking of gender barriers, prosperity and immortality, offering a collective consciousness that is grounded in shared memories. Predictably, any millenarian melting pot rendered an ethnic, occupational, and class amalgam with the implicit leitmotifs of modern nationhood and even conscious nationalism.

By the same token the apocalyptic rationale not only offers a frame of analysis for understanding human social behavior across social divides but also a source of solace and hope in moments of crisis. The apocalyptic outlook rationalizes real or perceived human suffering by treating it as providential design to expedite the millennial relief. Devastating wars, pandemics, genocide, earthquakes and floods, were hence perceived as God's destruction of sinful, tyrannical rule, his punishment of the arrogant and the corrupt and vindication of the victims.

Moreover, though most "positive" apocalyptic images and values are masculine and decidedly patriarchal, millenarian movements in pre-modern times were among the very few to offer social channels through which women could excel and even occupy positions of leadership. Ann Lee, the principal founder of the Shakers, shared her founding role with the twelfth-century German apocalyptic nun, painter and composer Hildegard of Bingen and with Fatima Qurrat al-'Ayan (also known as Tahira), a leading Babi leader and chief advocate of the break with Islam. Such prominence contrasts with the misogynic imagery of Judeo-Christian and Islamic apocalyptics, which usually associate femininity with evil and women as deceptive agents of sin. The Whore of the Babylon of the Book of Revelation had other counterparts.[4]

The presence of women may in part be attributed, at least in the Islamic context, to the antinomian self-perception that placed millenarians on a different plane from society at large as paragons of a value-free paradise. Millenarian communities often, though not as a rule, found in the very notion of the End a liberation from restrictive socio-religious norms such as marital sanctions, which were grounded in women's subordination and controlled sexuality. The End meant a deliberate transgression of these norms, whether the removal of the facial veil and other infringements of the prevailing dress code, appearance in the company of men in public, even the annulment of marriage and redefining the accepted notions of family.

Promise of paradisiacal bliss also meant in reality equal access to the limited material resources available to the community of believers. At times this gave rise to communistic practices of shared land and property, be it the believers' own or the spoils of wars waged against unbelievers. A spirit of remorseful austerity and egalitarian discipline were additional leitmotifs, but the momentum created by these practices seldom engendered democratic values. Millennial visions, in theory as well as in practice, remained largely akin to absolute power, a manifestation, so millenarians tended to believe, of God's absolute might and glory transfused through the savior, to His community. At their height, few millenarian movements were hotbeds of democratic ideals, though in their post-apocalyptic phase some nurtured a greater pluralistic outlook, perhaps because of a diffused leadership. Others remained firmly committed to the original absolutist culture and even reinforced it.

For the same basic reason most millenarian movements, at least at their climax, were not favorable toward liberal ideals of religious tolerance and diversity. Nor were they all committed to a peaceful spread of their message of salvation. The quest for expansion at various regional, national, and international scales often propelled millennial programs for action into instances of vengeance and the eradication of doctrinal enemies. Desperately imprisoned in the confines of their own convictions, millennial dreams could easily turn into nightmares prescribed in the apocalyptic literature.

Alternatively, they could themselves become victims of society's undue suspicion and fury. Labeled as dangerous heretics, they were targets of torture, massacre, enslavement, and mob frenzy, often even more violent than their own apocalyptic visions. Frequently the fragile social structure of these movements could not withstand the joint forces of religious authorities and the allied state. Too often millenarian communities were wiped out of existence outside history books or the memory of their sectarian progeny. Those communities that possessed enough coherence and stamina to sustain a semblance of group identity often developed pacifist strategies of survival. Belief in an ascended, hidden, lost, or unidentifiable savior, who at some point in time will return to relieve the community from the oppression and torment to which it has been subjected, is a common feature of so many failed, or delayed, millenarian movements.

## *Millennialism as a Field of Study*

Millennialism (or apocalypticism) emerged as a field of social and intellectual studies (in the humanities and social sciences) beyond Christian biblical studies first with the publication in 1957 of Norman Cohn's seminal study *In Pursuit of the Millennium*, and in 1960 with Vittorio Lanternari's comparative study, *The Religions of the Oppressed: A Study of Modern Messianic Cults*, and the 1962 collection of essays *Millennial Dreams in Action: Studies in Revolutionary Religious Movements* edited by Sylvia Thrupp. Nearly half a century later, millennialism still is the subject of a wide and lively academic debate including and beyond the Judeo-Christian tradition and with numerous studies on millenarian currents in cultures as far and wide as Chinese, Buddhist, Hindu, Islamic, Pre-Columbian American, indigenous African, Latin American, and Pacific Islands. The ancient cultures of Egypt, Mesopotamia, Zoroastrian Iran, and Greece have been scrutinized for comparable notions of the End and the highly diverse manifestations of millennialism in the Judeo-Christian world from ancient Hebrew to the Judeo-Hellenistic, to the Byzantine, medieval and early modern European, Russian and modern American also have been subjects of major studies.

Moreover, the study of apocalyptic themes in pictorial art, literature, music, and cinema has generated a substantial body of scholarship. Today, the study of millennialism no longer stands out, as it once probably did, as an extraordinary, even embarrassing, fascination with the implausible and insignificant few on the fringes of the religious mainstream or anarchists seeking to destroy the consecrated social order. Those who subscribed to these modes of thinking and participated in these movements are also not invariably seen as revolutionary expressions of the weak and the underprivileged. Rather, millennialism is now appreciated, as an influential current, or undercurrent, comprehensible on its own terms; modes of thought and action which, though too often skewed, suppressed, or obliterated from the master narrative of any given culture, often leave recoverable traces in the subtext for today's students to reconstruct an alternative narrative.[5]

The comparative study of millennialism offers an intriguing prospect. Yet it also poses insurmountable problems of epistemology and method. Questions of definition (e.g. how does millennialism differ from apocalypticism?), the meaning of prophecy, and methods of textual analysis, even within an indigenous religio-cultural tradition, pose prohibiting complexities. And so does the comparative study of movements that gave historical substance to these millenarian aspirations. Any plan for establishing a comparative framework for millennialism should thus be substantially modified in the hope of arriving at a unifying theme of reasonable originality and plausibility; a theme that has not yet been fully addressed in the current literature.[6] The Middle Eastern origins of apocalyptic and millennial motifs, as well as their intricate interplay with their indigenous settings, add to the complexity. These complementary themes –

namely the paradigmatic origins of millennialism and their realizations in a specific time and place (in Islamic Iran, for instance) – are further complicated by the rich heterogeneous interactions among four religious traditions: Zoroastrianism, Judaism, Christianity, and Islam.[7]

The question of inadequate sources and problems of interpretation also looms large. These and similar exegetical and historiographical issues thus lead us to two essential points: first, that study of millennialism has developed certain tools and techniques to recover from the text, and "between the lines" so to speak, the suspect evidence usually not discernable by conventional methods of source criticism. Yet unearthing what is buried in the text, especially what is generally considered as embarrassing or dangerous by the religious authorities, no matter how skillfully done, leaves much room for divergence. Inevitably, the textual ambiguities persuaded students of millennialism to offer a multiplicity of contesting interpretations. The debate about the significance of the year 1000 in medieval Europe for instance raises important questions concerning its very significance in stimulating the popular imagination.[8]

The Hurufiyya movement in the fourteenth and fifteenth centuries in the Iranian world, on the other hand, sought alternative means to understand the secrets of the text, particularly through cabalistic preoccupation with letters of the Qur'an. This was an attempt to go beyond the established norms of interpretation by adopting a hermeneutical approach.[9] Similarly, certain recurring features in the rich Iranian messianic tradition since the Safavid period should be comprehended within its own apocalyptic hermeneutics.[10]

Textual ambiguities nonetheless have persuaded many philologists, biblical, Zoroastrian, and Islamic scholars to try to reconcile, or gloss over, inherent paradoxes in apocalyptic literature in favor of an authoritative exegesis that would "make sense." Through this unavoidable, though often uninspiring, exercise, the exclusive exegetical approach generally circumvents not only hermeneutical subtleties but also the historical context. The circumstances leading to the emergence of a given apocalyptic trend and its evolving development, if ever explored, were because they meant to provide additional clues, to buttress the authoritative version rather than problematize it. The case in point is modern Islamic scholarship, which relies solely on the "authoritative" narrative at the expense of the apocalyptic message of the early Meccan suras in the Qur'an.[11]

Second, when the socio-historical context of apocalypticism is addressed – increasingly in recent decades by social historians or by anthropologists and sociologists of religion – the focus is shifted from doctrinal expressions, namely what millenarians have said, to socio-economic factors conducive to the shaping of the movements and their evolution. In contrast to philological and textual preoccupations, the objective here is to sift selectively through ideas and aspirations of the claimants and their community of believers as a source for unraveling social hierarchies, political and anti-colonial grievances, and economic disadvantages. Revolutionary movements with millenarian coloring, however, were often treated as typical of all millenarian movements, as a mode of social protest anticipating modern ideological and anti-imperialist currents of later times.

Both the textual scrutiny and socio-historical approach, however, seldom tried to study these currents in their totality or dealt with them in their own terms, though often they paid homage to the idea. Most notably, the social-psychological interpretation of apocalypticism relied on the theories of relative deprivation and trauma of sudden transition in order to address the complexity of the apocalyptic phenomenon. The theory of relative deprivation, for instance, offers the very perception of social, political, and cultural depravity, whether real or perceived, as the prime motive for the apocalyptic syndrome.[12] A corollary of this theory of apocalypticism is that of disaster and swift socio-economic displacements: collapse of the empires, as in the Zoroastrian apocalypticism of Iran; rupture of a closely knit social fabric, as in the experience of the Babylonian Diaspora; the disrupting effects of rapid industrial and technological revolutions, as in Europe of the nineteenth century; the intrusion of an alien culture or imposition of colonial socio-economic regimes, as in Latin America, Africa, and the Islamic world.[13]

Without denying the triggering effect of such factors, and their implications for the social composition and doctrinal formulation of these movements, still neither of the two theories takes sufficient account of the hermeneutical legacy, or legacies, on which millennial discourses were articulated. The experience of sharing the mysteries of the text and the signs of the End, expounding a certain rhetorical discourse, and taking part in a scripted course of action, are dimensions of a millennial rationale, which is at the heart of the notion of "community of interpretation."[14] Through memory or text, an apocalyptic experience retrieves an esoteric temporality, articulates its own rationale, and engenders a sense of adherence more compelling for believers than any ulterior motive. Frequent recurrence of apocalyptic expressions within certain cultural settings – Judeo-Hellenistic, Perso-Shi'i, American Protestant, and Latin American Catholic, to name a few – may best be understood if the pivotal role of apocalyptic hermeneutics is seriously taken into account.[15]

## *Apocalyptic Dynamics in the Contemporary Context*

It is not an exaggeration to suggest that millenarianism in its varied manifestations, whether progressive or regressive, allegorical or fundamentalist, has been an important vehicle for social protest and revolutionary fervor. In modern times, it has been observed, secularized millennialism also fueled revolutionary aspirants and rendered subtle undertones to ideologies as diverse as the Philosophy of Progress, the American and the French Revolutions, the scientific positivism of the nineteenth century, Marxism and its various manifestations, and even Fascism and Nazism in the Third Reich. More recently, a variety of popular science fiction and pseudo-scientific theories, and more substantially, the environmental debates and critiques of technomania, may be seen as examples of the latent millennialism of our times. In most cases, it is true, the millennial paradigm remains a subtle undertone to secular ideologies not always acknowledged by those who pronounced or enacted it. Nearly all revolutionary visionaries of modern times, such as Karl Marx, entertained utopian visions brimming over with millennial aspirations of one form or another. Even more so, apocalyptic images and motifs influenced those artists, writers, and futurists who, by invoking millennial fears and hopes, challenged the norms of their own time and searched for alternatives.

As has often been noted, the passing of the *fin de siècle* at the turn of the twentieth century was welcomed by Western intellectual and artistic communities with a mix of despair and optimism. Their fears, more than their hopes, were soon to be realized through the horrors of the new century. As it turned out, the twentieth century was better equipped than any other time in human history to simulate a catastrophic End. The artistic and literary sensibilities, as reflected in the *decadence* mood of the time, were highly prophetic of the imminent calamities. The two highly destructive world wars were followed by the fearsome anxieties of the nuclear age, the ideological revolutions with poignant utopian programs, and with authoritarian regimes to brutally implement them. They all resuscitated apocalyptic paradigms.

The victims of many acts of genocide and mass violence in the twentieth century perceived their own experiences in apocalyptic terms. Most notably, European Jewry and other victims of the Holocaust placed in apocalyptic terms their experiences of round-ups, killings, concentration camps, gas chambers, dislocation, and exile. And, ironically, so did the Nazi perpetrators of the Holocaust – they, too, pursued an apocalyptic End in their crimes of the Final Solution, with the necessity to arrive at the pure and mighty utopia of the "thousand-year Reich". It was as though this most harrowing episode in contemporary history epitomized for generations to come an ultimate apocalyptic encounter between the vulnerable, the weak and the defenseless on the one hand, and the diabolic might of political ideologies on the other. Whether secular or otherwise in its origins, the roots of the anti-Semitism of the Nazi era lay in a long tradition of such sentiments in millenarian Europe of the Middle Ages and early modern times.

Desire for the absolute and the final through sacrifice of expendable minorities, a program of chiliastic scale, was shared by other ideologically driven leaders of the twentieth century. Stalin's classless paradise of collective communes, Mao Tse-Tung's Great Leap that aimed to rapidly transform rural China into an industrial utopia, the Cambodian genocide perpetrated by Pol Pot and his associates to restore the state of peasant purity, the Cold War obsession with nuclear attacks and pre-emptive attacks, and later the Islamic Revolution in Iran and Khomeini's fierce vision of pristine Islam versus the Great Satan, and the atrocious Iraq war against Iran, all qualify as modern apocalyptic interludes. Mao capitalized on China's rich millennial tradition to present himself as a messianic prophet whose launching of a Marxist revolution and the Cultural Revolution were necessary stages on the way to a millennial utopia. Khomeini relied on a long Shi'i Iranian millennial legacy to portray himself as the Imam, only a short step away from the Mahdi, to demonize the shah as a pharaonic power, the old elite as idol-worshipers, and his greatest ideological enemy, the United States, as the Great Satan.

As a revolutionary ideology Marxism fully accommodated millennial aspirations. The doctrine of historical determinism offered a certain inevitability parallel to apocalyptic prophecies of any religious traditions. It promised an egalitarian paradise of plenty and freedom of choice in which the divine was substituted with dialectical materialism and its progressive course in history. In articulating a utopian future, Marxism relied as much on German philosophical idealism, with its roots in Protestant millennialism, as on the socialist idealism of Saint Simon and other nineteenth-century utopian prophets conscious of their Christian millennial past. In the writings of the young Marx especially, and before the days of "scientific" socialism, a passionate tone of millennial utopianism is audible even though he sharply dismissed as "philistine" most other socialist trends of his time.

If anything in the Western bloc, and especially in the United States, could have matched the millenarian zeal of the communist revolutionaries, it was the anti-communist apocalyptic rhetoric of the Cold War, and its corollary, the fear of nuclear exchange. The imagery of Doomsday, Armageddon, and other biblical allusions readily available in the hellfire rhetoric of American Evangelical preachers were grafted onto the science fiction imagery of the Evil Empire by popular writers, filmmakers, military analysts, political commentators, conservative politicians, and ideologically bent nuclear scientists. Ironically, they shared their anxieties for the impending End of human civilization with advocates of peace and coexistence, who also viewed the arms race and the proliferation of nuclear weapons as a road to an inevitable doomsday. The fact that ancient fears and hopes could so placidly and effectively be transported into a new setting and be exploited for political and ideological ends, or for greater coexistence, testifies to the potency of apocalyptic motifs and their endurance in the face of a seemingly secularizing age.

The many cinematic expressions of the apocalypse clearly speak of the persistence of these anxieties. From German Expressionist masterpieces such as Robert Wiene's *Cabinet of Dr Caligari* (1919) and Fritz Lang's *Metropolis* (1927), in the aftermath of the First World War, to Ingmar Bergman's 1957 *The Seventh Seal,* Stanley Kremer's *On the Beach* (1959), Stanley Kubrick's *Dr Strangelove* (1964, based on Peter George's novel), in the Cold War era and Francis Coppola's *Apocalypse Now* (1979) of the Vietnam era, all conveyed powerful apocalyptic messages comparable to any visual imagery in biblical apocalyptic.

In the post-Cold War era and eclipse of ideologies (or lull, perhaps), apocalyptic anxieties hardly subsided. The field of future studies surely offers a variety of scenarios to bring out the worst apocalyptic fears but also our precious and soon expiring millennial hopes for human sensibility. Above all, a genuine fear of environmental catastrophe looms large. Global warming, deforestation, desertification and soil erosion, scarcity of water resources, toxic and nuclear pollution, and other ecological hazards are possibilities as grim as a nuclear exchange and nuclear proliferation and as horrifying as the images of the Book of the Apocalypse.

The growing economic gap between the rich and the poor, the "technomania" that reigns supreme in the age of global communication in cyberspace, and recurring ethnic and religious conflicts, surely unbalance, if they do not entirely spoil, the vista of new millennial hopes. Even more ominously since September 11, 2001, the U.S. "War on Terror," the labeling of anti-American countries as the "Axis of Evil," the ruinous U.S. invasion of Iraq, Israel's continuous occupation of the Palestinian Territories, the rise of Evangelical Zionism in the United States and its call to eliminate so called "Islamo-Fascism" and, finally, Mahmud Ahmadinejad's call for removing the State of Israel, all keenly correspond to the worst nightmarish apocalyptic scenarios the world has encountered, at least since the First World War almost a century ago.

It is reasonable to ask, therefore, if prospects for a new millennial discourse, rather than an apocalyptic disaster, are on the horizon. And, if so, whether the issues addressed in an academic context are likely to have any relevance. The answer is by no means unambiguous. It is possible to suggest that the same intrinsic fears of the unknown that in the past engendered comparable apocalyptic imagining in Jewish, Christian, and Islamic traditions are still very much in effect, and are likely to remain so as long as the future poses unsettling questions. Often, though, these anxieties are less reliant, explicitly at least, on a divine agency to intervene vengefully against the evil and compassionately on the side of the good and vulnerable. Responsibility for a felicitous or a disastrous future seems to rest more than ever on human shoulders than the dictates of the heavens. This gives a whole new meaning to the verse by the Persian poet Hafiz:

> Heaven could carry not the entrusted pain,
> My lot was the burden, me, the insane.

The experiences of the past hundred years have taken the confidence, and the passion, out of the modern rationalism of the Enlightenment – which once sneered at Christian millennialism, ironically only to pursue its own millennial happiness. Even in the prosperous and powerful West, where globalization has become a reassuring politico-economic currency, voices of deconstruction and the postmodernist critique of reason are questioning the validity of what was once considered as sacred and definite. And no doubt the events of the past seven years have given greater weight to such rethinking. At least in the realm of the humanities, attention to new cultural discourses, of imagining, unreason and uncertainty, the unaccounted and the subversive, of textual ambiguities, and of the persuasiveness of rhetorical argument have become more prominent. A call for an end to conventional study in venerable disciplines, the way they were categorized by positivist philosophies of the nineteenth century, may be seen as the intellectual ramification of the rethinking about the End. Could this be seen as what Heidegger, another apocalyptic thinker of our time, famously characterized as the "turnaround" in humankind's relation with Being?

In thinking about the End we may ask, in conclusion, whether it is tied to the very basic rhetoric of all salvation religions. And if so, does it sway a lasting hold over all cultural memories? It is enticing to think – though not very realistic – that the age of the literal interpretation of the apocalypse, of the horrors and hopes of the Book of Revelation and of similar texts, is at its ebb. For all but the most fervent enthusiasts and fundamentalists on the fringe, such prophecies no longer inculcate a "realistic" vision of the End. This is parting with a tradition of literal imagining, which endured surprisingly long. Increasingly, however, believers have found in the allegorical reading of the biblical and Qur'anic prophecies keys to the understanding of the troubling questions of their own times. Yet beyond the religious domain, though not necessarily detached from its memory, the paradigm of the End and the rhetoric of renewal seem to endure for as long as there are anxieties about moral and material troubles ahead.

CHAPTER 2

# *The Resurgence of Apocalyptic in Modern Islam*

Apocalypticism in the Islamic context primarily corresponds to the fundamental doctrine of resurrection *(qiyama)* and applies to eschatological speculations concerning the return of the dead, the Day of Judgment, the process of salvation and damnation, and their complex realizations at the end of time *(akhir al-zaman)*. In a broader sense it also encompasses preparatory events preceding the resurrection including the advent of the Mahdi (the [divinely] guided, the Islamic Messiah), symbolic re-enactment of the sacred past, and the ultimate triumph of the forces of Islam over disbelief. Though the evidence in the Qur'an and the hadith is employed as apocalyptic prophecies, apocalypse in the biblical sense – namely, revelatory dreams and visions – this rarely occurs in the Islamic tradition.

In historical reality, apocalyptic is applied to all speculative or redemptive experiences and movements aspiring to transform the normative Islam, the existing political order, and the ethics of the Muslim community, by claiming a new divine mandate and by declaring commencement of an era of rejuvenated faith. Such experiences, often triggered by messianic, utopian, and apocalyptic potentials embedded in the Islamic tradition and led by charismatic figures, punctuate the whole course of Islamic history. While the Sunni world witnessed numerous examples of shari'a-oriented Mahdism with a distinct desire to restore pristine Islam of Muhammad's time, the Shi'i world regenerated messianic impulses with distinct apocalyptic features aiming at a break with the shari'a and creation of a post-millennial order.[1]

Modern Islamic times have often been dated from the latter decades of the eighteenth century and the beginning of the nineteenth, when Muslim thinkers, statesmen, and reformers began to air a sense of anxiety for what they believed to be their communities' moral and material decline. In part the outcome of political disarray, or total disintegration, of the Muslim empires of earlier centuries, this sense of decline often equated with the decay of Islam as a religion. In the same period, Muslim societies, from Indonesia and India to Central Asia, the Middle East, and North Africa, began to experience the presence of the West through commerce and diplomacy. By the beginning of the nineteenth century the impact of Europe's colonial domination and its military, industrial, and later cultural and ideological manifestations became apparent not only to the Muslim states but to the Muslim peoples. These coinciding processes in turn contributed to the Muslim notion of modernity as an indigenous effort to revitalize religious, political, and social institutions. Concepts of renewal *(tajdid)* and reform *(islah),* though not foreign to Islamic thought from earlier times, were widely used by reformers, visionaries, prophets, and revolutionaries to transform Muslim culture and material life and to resist political subordination to the West.[2]

## *Sunni Frontier Messianism and the Prophetic Way*

The earliest of what may be called proto-messianic trends appeared in North Africa as part of a greater religious revival in the peripheries of the Islamic world. Inspired by such figures as Shaykh Ahmad Sirhindi (1564–1624), founder of the Mujaddidiyya Sufi order in India, and Muhammad ibn 'Abd al-Wahhab (1703–92), founder of the Wahhabi puritanical movement in the Arabian peninsula, the most significant among North African trends were the Tijaniyya and Idrisiyya neo-Sufi orders at the turn of the nineteenth century, followed by the Sanusiyya order a few decades later. Differences aside, all these orders were founded by charismatic figures with puritanical proclivities and with intuitive and visionary aspirations calling for the austere observance of a monolithic shari'a and repudiation of any monistic notion of the divinity.

Warning against alien infiltration into the domains of Islam and denouncing as heretical any form of "innovation" *(bid'a)* in religion, these mystic guides looked upon the pristine Islam of the Prophet's time as the only sacred model for emulation, a tendency that often was complemented by a claim to receive guidance from the Prophet himself. "The Muhammadan Way" *(Tariqa Muhammadiyya)* thus entailed a call against normative and popular

Islam and toward restoration of a utopian community on the model of the Prophet's time. Endogenous to North African Islam, this pattern of Mahdism went back in time to the Almohad movement of Ibn Tumart (*c*.1078–1130) and before.[3]

Although restoring the glory of the Islamic past in these trends could potentially trigger an apocalyptic scenario, in reality the idea of restoration of the prophetic way came closer to the Salafiyya, a trend that called for restoring the way of the forefathers *(salaf)*. It is important to note that, since Islam regarded Muhammad's revelation as complete and final and ruled out the possibility for future prophetic revelation of any kind, adherents to the Muhammadan Way could employ only intuitive experiences to restore the "pure Islam" of the early Muslim community and to strive for Islam's predominance through political power and, if necessary, by means of jihad. Developing in the stateless periphery of urban Islam and at a time when North Africa was experiencing the dwindling power of the Ottoman state and intrusion of the Western colonial powers, these movements were bound to acquire a political character. Although Tijaniyya and Sanusiyya began as purely Sufi revivalist trends with little overt political ambitions, they soon gave birth to political expressions that eventually, in defiance of European colonialism, led to the emergence of new states.[4]

The first among these visionary mystics with what may be called proto-messianic propensities was Ahmad al-Tijani (1737–1815), the Algerian founder of the Tijaniyya order. Experiencing visionary encounters with the Prophet in the state of wakefulness, al-Tijani arrogated to himself the status of the "master of masters" *(qutb al-aqtab)*, a position that implied supreme spiritual supervision over all contemporary Sufi orders. In his writings al-Tijani even hinted at a status of infallibility, a quality exclusively reserved in Sunni Islam for the prophets. He believed that his infallibility, a gift bestowed on him by the Prophet Muhammad, would enable him on the Day of Resurrection to intercede *(shifa'a)* with God on behalf of his followers in the spirit of the Prophet. On the Day of Judgment he and his followers will be saved whereas his enemies will be banished into hell.[5]

Ahmad Ibn Idris (1760–1837), a Moroccan peripatetic Sufi scholar and the founder of the Idrisiyya order (whose influence on the early development of neo-Sufism was felt throughout North Africa, Egypt, the Sudan, and as far as Yemen) also experienced prophetic visions. A co-citizen of al-Tijani, Ibn Idris claimed that the Prophet Muhammad appeared to him in the company of al-Khidr (otherwise known as Ilyas, the Hebrew prophet Elijah), who acted as an intermediary, instructing him with new Sufi litanies and prayers. Yet these mystical experiences barely took a messianic direction beyond allusions to the apocalyptic "signs of the hour," one of which he identified as the ignorance of the 'ulama of his time. No doubt the antagonism of the clerical establishments in Fez, then an active center for Moroccan scholarship, and in Mecca, where he spent some years during the Wahhabi presence, was influential in his rejection of the four traditional schools of Sunni law in favor of the exercise of *ijtihad* (the deduction of legal opinions on the basis of the Qur'an, the hadith, logical rudiments, and the consensus of the experts).[6]

The same desire for establishing direct spiritual communication with the Prophet can also be observed in the teachings of Muhammad ibn 'Ali al-Sanusi (1787–1859, also known to the Europeans as the Grand Sanusi), the founder of the influential Sanusiyya order of Cyrenaica in eastern Libya. A student of Ibn Idris and al-Tijani, he was influenced by the Meccan revivalist circle at the turn of the nineteenth century. He sensed an even greater urgency than his teachers in seeking a spiritual remedy to Islam's political and moral infirmity. Such a worldview no doubt was influenced by al-Sanusi's residence in Egypt, where he was denounced by the 'ulama of al-Azhar for his emphasis on *ijtihad* and for his strict adherence to the Muhammadan Way.[7]

Even more than the intellectual environment of al-Azhar and Fez, it was the threat of European domination that motivated al-Sanusi and his successors to undertake a largely peaceful missionary expansion of the Sanusi order among the mixed nomadic population and the peasantry of present-day Libya, Algeria, and Chad, as far south as equatorial Africa, and along the southern Mediterranean coast. In this endeavor al-Sanusi and his son and successor, al-Sayyid al-Mahdi (1844–1902), initially prescribed a course of moral reconstruction of the community on the Muhammadan model as an alternative to an outward jihad. Although Sayyid al-Mahdi was viewed by his followers as the Mahdi (and *mujaddid* at the turn of AH 1300 [1882–3]), he preferred to publicly play down the messianic attribute. He nevertheless drew upon the North African cult of saints and the dormant expectation of the advent of the Mahdi, especially among the Berbers, to preserve an aura of Mahdihood. In due course, the changing political climate in North Africa transformed the Sanusiyya's political quiescence into an outward revolt. By the turn of the twentieth century the movement took a definite anti-colonial bent as the Sanusiyya spearheaded a formidable force of indigenous resistance against French, and later Italian, occupation of Libya. The bonds of loyalty to the Sanusi leadership were upheld with messianic zeal, throughout the First World War and after. In the post-Second World War era the residue of the movement's charismatic past contributed to the legitimacy of the Sanusi monarchy of Libya.

Yet it was with the rise of the Mahdi of the Sudan, perhaps the most well known of the Sunni claimants to Mahdihood, that African neo-Sufism found its most intense expression of puritanical messianism. Muhammad Ahmad ibn 'Abdullah (1844–85), a *faki* (Sufi adepts were known as *faqir* in Sudanese Islam) from a family of boatbuilders in Donghola, on the southern edge of the Nubian desert, received formal madrasa education and rigorous Sufi training before settling in 1870 in the strategically located island of Aba, which served as a gateway for the slave trade of equatorial Sudan and for the Baqqara tribal confederacy in the adjacent Kordofan and the Darfur ranges. This was at a time when the Egyptian conquest of the Sudan in the 1810s had created a political vacuum in the region which the Egyptian Khedival administration had difficulty filling.

Along the frontiers of Nilotic Sudan with its complex and volatile tribal structure, the Egyptian attempt to enforce administrative control through a harsh taxation policy disturbed not only the agricultural and urban patterns of traditional life but the delicate tribal balance, which had already been upset by massive movements of population. Equally disruptive was the British-backed Egyptian attempt in the 1860s to enforce a ban on the lucrative slave trade of the south. Intrusive centralization measures, combined with the excesses of alien and haughty officials and a rapidly transforming economy aided by the introduction of modern communication aroused popular discontent at all levels, to which al-Mahdi's movement became an indigenous response.[8]

As one of the leaders of a Sammaniyya Sufi order, Muhammad Ahmad gained a reputation for being a deeply pious and observant man, a predictable precondition for claim to Mahdihood. The dissemination of neo-Sufi orders may be seen as a Sudanese response to the penetration of the madrasa-oriented Islam of al-Azhar sponsored by the Egyptian administration. Muhammad Ahmad first aired in secret his messianic claims around 1880, shortly after coming into contact with his most influential follower and later his successor, 'Abdullah ibn Muhammad of Darfur; a Sufi devotee suffused with Mahdistic longings. More explicit manifestation *(zuhur)* as the expected Mahdi *(al-Mahdi al-muntazar)* of the Islamic world came in June 1881, following his adoption of the title Muhammad al-Mahdi, which he claimed was conferred on him by Muhammad the Prophet.

In numerous proclamations *(manshurat)* dispatched in the course of the next four years, al-Mahdi defined his mission as one inspired through intuitive communication with Muhammad in which he was given the task of erasing the corruption and decay that plagued the Muslim community and restoring the unspoiled Islam of the Prophet's time. He drew upon Islamic apocalyptic prophecies as well as Sufi prognostications (such as Ibn al-'Arabi's) to justify his own prophetic "signs," both physical and behavioral, which he compared with those of the Prophet of Islam. He further viewed his manifestation at the impending end of the thirteenth Islamic century (which was to arrive in 1300 / 1883), not only as a divine will to "renovate" Islam but as a manifestation from the world of "concealment;" a notion closely associated with the Shi'i notion of Occultation *(ghayba)*. Al-Mahdi's emphasis on his sacred lineage from the "prophetic house" and the fashion in which he claimed to have received inspirations also pointed in a Shi'i apocalyptic direction.

Yet in carrying out his mission, al-Mahdi seldom, if ever, trespassed the bounds of a shari'a-restoring Mahdism. He believed himself to be the locus for the "prophetic lights," from the "niche of [Muhammadan] prophecy" and recipient of "divine voices" who was called upon to "revive" the essence of the prophecy and "return matters to their beginning," by "filling the earth with justice," as the famous messianic hadith prescribed, "when it is filled with oppression and tyranny." To rebuild the Prophet's shari'a, which has been "obliterated" by the enemies of Islam, and to restore the "true religion," like Muhammad he had to resort to the sword in order to remove not only the spurious four schools of Sunni law and to replace them with "pure Islamic rules" and "God's punishing limits," but also to declare jihad against the most virulent enemies of Islam.

The symbolic re-enactment of early Islamic history held sway over much of al-Mahdi's action. The infidels of his manifestation were the Turks, a generic term applied in his parlance to the Egyptian Khedival authority (after the assumed Turkish origin of the dynasty) and to all Egyptian and European officials, officers and troops in its service. It was even stretched to include the Ottoman state, the nominal suzerain of the Egyptian rulers, and the European powers supporting the Khedivate of Egypt. Al-Mahdi's profound enmity toward the Turks was probably rooted in the memories of the harsh treatment the northern Sudanese tribes, among them the Danghula, received at the hands of Muhammad 'Ali, the pasha of Egypt and his conquering armies earlier in the century.

Al-Mahdi moreover viewed the Turko-Egyptian domination and their modernizing measures as deviations from Islamic norms and thus tantamount to idolatry. In his messianic worldview the distinction between the forces of good and evil was sharp. Any deviations, whether advancing the madrasa-based Islam of the heartland, neglecting the Islamic "prohibition of the evil," relaxing restrictions on veiling of the women, or enforcing unlawful taxes, were all justifiable grounds for declaring a holy war. As evidence of Islam's subjugation, he pointed to state taxes alien to Sudanese society as a form *jizya* (Islamic poll tax imposed on religious minorities) which, he believed, was antithetical to Islam's sovereignty especially as they were imposed upon Muslims by Christian agents.[9]

Reconstructing his mission on the model of early Islam in late 1881, al-Mahdi embarked on the symbolic act of "immigration" *(hijra)* from Aba to Qadir to the safety of the Baqqara tribes in the Kordofan. He consciously portrayed his *hijra* as a replication of Muhammad's Hijra (departure to Medina in 622); a symbolic act of breaking with unbelievers and striking a new covenant with his "helpers" *(ansar)*. The capture of the provincial capital, al-'Ubayd, in 1883, at the turn of the fourteenth Islamic century, was the first of the victories affirming al-Mahdi's belief that he was repeating Muhammad's victories in the battlefield. Coinciding with the 'Arabi

Pasha's revolt in Egypt – which led to the British occupation of that country in September 1882 – al-Mahdi succeeded further in the battle of Shaykhan to annihilate another expeditionary force led by Colonel William Hicks.

Later, the fall of Khartoum to al-Mahdi's forces in January 1885, and the slaying of General Charles Gordon, to his followers was the pinnacle of the new prophet's victory and a prelude to successes beyond the Sudan. To the Western public, anxiously following the events through extensive press reports, the rise and the success of al-Mahdi were viewed as nothing but the resurgence of fanaticism, tribal savagery, and senseless resistance to the benevolent forces of white civilization.[10] To Muslims, who read about his successes with a reserved interest, he remained a pseudo-Mahdi *(al-Mutamahdi)*, even though he was sometimes praised for his defiance of the British. By June 1885 when al-Mahdi died, possibly because of an epidemic, he controlled most of the Sudan through conquest and tribal alliances and had laid the foundation for a theocratic state under his successor, Khalifa 'Abdullahi, and his lieutenants.

Thirteen years later, in 1898, a British expedition under General Kitchener routed the Khalifa's forces in the decisive battle of Omdurman, a brutal operation that led to the destruction of al-Mahdi's state. Winston Churchill, then a young war correspondent, was thrilled with the military action and welcomed British imperial reassertion but could not hide his disgust with the British command's vengeful retaliation for Gordon's death.[11] Al-Mahdi's messianic drive no doubt was regressive in its orientation and oppressive in its application, but it was, to the extent that it was realized, a formidable force consolidating desperate and divided tribal loyalties into a centralized political-religious entity.[12]

## *Shi'i Mahdism and the End of the Time*

Even in modern times expectations for the Mahdi were more prevalent in Shi'i Islam, particularly in Iranian Shi'ism, than in the Sunni world. Deeply ingrained in its belief system and, in turn, in the Shi'i psyche, the doctrine of Imamate ensured the continuity of divine inspiration. As designated descendants of the Prophet who inherited in a direct line the leadership of the community, the Imams' continued existence was considered "proof" *(hujja)* of the continuity of divine grace toward the "guided" Shi'i community. In Twelver Shi'ism the Mahdi is the Twelfth (and the last) Imam in the line, who is believed to have entered in the year 260 /873–4 into a state of Occultation and hence is invisible to believers through normal means.

Essential to the Shi'i apocalyptic beliefs is that the advent of the Hidden Imam *(al-Imam al-Gha'ib)* will set in motion a course of events ultimately leading to the destruction of the world and the end of time. Though no specific time was ever set for his advent, it was generally believed that his revolt *(khuruj)* would occur at the turn of a millennium after his Occultation. As the Lord of Time *(al-Sahib al-Zaman)* and the Riser *(Qa'im)* of the House of the Prophet, he will restore justice and equity to the world when it is filled with evil and oppression. This sense of restoring justice was tied in Shi'i prophecies with reinstalling the right to political leadership of the House of the Prophet, vengeance against the usurpers of that authority, and consequently expansion through jihad and the Imam's world domination.

This millennial scenario, elaborated and embellished over centuries in a vast body of apocalyptic literature, presented the advent of the Imam and his accomplishments against the forces of the Dajjal, the false Messiah, as the prelude to the resurrection and the final judgment. Contrary to the Sunni Mahdi, whose advent was aimed to enhance the foundations of Islam on a periodic (centennial) basis, Shi'i Islam essentially strived to invoke the Imamate paradigm so as to bring about the resurrection and an end to the prevailing dispensation. The Imam's advent will differentiate the forces of good from evil in two confronting armies and establish the sovereignty of the House of the Prophet, but his kingdom was predicted to be ephemeral and only a preparatory stage before the cataclysmic end of the material world, the commencement of the day of judgment, and thereafter the final departure of the saved to paradise and the damned to hell.[13]

Despite this rich and dynamic apocalyptic tradition, however, during the period of expectation *(intizar)* for the Lord of Time to bring relief from oppression, no course of action was prescribed for believers except vigilance and, if need be, dissimulation of true beliefs in the face of danger. Although, almost immediately after the Occultation, Shi'ism began to develop an elaborate body of formal religious sciences crowned by the study of jurisprudence, the question of political leadership of the community during the interregnum of the Imam's absence remained essentially unaddressed. A long tradition of madrasa education, reinforced under the patronage of the Safavid dynasty (1501–1732), led to the emergence of a community of jurists (mujtahids) who claimed a collective vicegerency *(niyaba)* on behalf of the Hidden Imam while condoning the shahs' vague notion of political vicegerency. Partially independent from the state, these 'ulama, who assumed for themselves the task of preserving the "essence of Islam" as experts in the holy law and its sole implementers, became increasingly self-conscious of their status after the fall of the Safavid state in the early eighteenth century.

By the time the Qajar dynasty (1785–1925) had been consolidated, the 'ulama of the predominant Usuli legal school presented a socio-religious force to be reckoned with in the domain of the judiciary and of education. They seldom, however, in theory or practice, laid any claim to political authority in the state beyond occasional challenges to its conduct. The clergy–state equilibrium, a legacy of the Safavid period, had the natural tendency to relegate the advent of the Hidden Imam to a distant future and in turn dismiss as unorthodox, if not heretical, all such speculations. The actual messianic aspirations were tolerated even less, having routinely been labeled as fraudulent and heretical.[14]

Yet Shi'ism never fully dissociated itself from messianic aspirations, even though preoccupation with jurisprudence and supplementary sciences steered mainstream learning in a non-messianic direction. No less important a scholar than Mulla Muhammad Baqir Majlisi (1628–99), the celebrated theologian most responsible for popularizing Shi'ism, dedicated a substantial portion of his famous *Al-Bihar al-Anwar* and a number of his Persian works to the subject of the Hidden Imam, the circumstances of his manifestation, the struggle against the Dajjal, and the consequent eschatological occurrences leading to the return *(raj'a)* of the past prophets and Imams, the raising of the dead on the Plane of the Gathering, the Final Judgment, Heaven's bliss, and the torments of Hell. The apocalyptic literature produced by Majlisi, and later writers up to the twentieth century, was influential not only in keeping alive debates about the advent of the Imam in madrasa circles but, more significantly, in the popular imagination. Beyond the calm and stern surface of formal Shi'ism there continued to surge a mass of millennial yearning, often with revolutionary potential in contrast to the prevailing religion of the 'ulama and the institutions of the state.[15]

Speculative Shi'ism also elaborated on Shi'i eschatology and, more specifically, on the circumstances of resurrection. The immortality of the soul, modes of existence in the hereafter, and, most troubling of all, the doctrine of the corporal resurrection *(al-ma'ad al-jismani)* came to preoccupy such philosophers as the Sadr al-Din Shirazi, better known as Mulla Sadra (d. 1640), the greatest of Muslim philosophers of the post-classical period. In contrast to Sunni Islam's relinquishing serious philosophical discourse, learned Shi'ism preserved a thriving and highly diverse philosophical tradition and articulated within the framework of mystical philosophy notions of time and modalities of being essential for innovative conceptualization of the End.

Unlike the historically static worldview of the shari'a-minded 'ulama, Mulla Sadra and his students, known as Muta'allahin (theosophists), envisioned a dynamic view of time that in final analysis was at odds with the conventional notion of the *eschaton* as the permanent point of termination. Sadra'ians essentially remained loyal to a blend of peripatetic and Neoplatonic philosophy expounded by classical Muslim philosophers, but their notion of beings' everlasting motion in time was a breakthrough. In what Mulla Sadra defined as the "essential motion" *(al-haraka al-jawhariyya)* of all things, the universe "is ceaselessly being renewed and passing away, originating and ending." Unlike the theory of the fixed cycles or the ahistorical approach of mainstream theology, the Sadra'ian concept of "essential motion" (or transubstantiation) pointed to an unending spiral, if not linear, course of humankind's spiritual and material progression. Even in its dormant philosophical rendition, this concept challenged conventional interpretation of the End and cast doubt on its occurrence as a providential cataclysm destined to bring the world to a permanent end. Yet Shi'i philosophical speculations remained essentially loyal to the doctrine of Islam's perfection and finality.[16]

With the emergence of the Shaykhi school and the visionary theology of its founder, Shaykh Ahmad Ahsa'i (1756–1826), Shi'ism generated a new mystical-philosophical synthesis that was highly influential in shaping later millennial trends. A peripatetic and widely read scholar from al-Ahsa' (northeastern province of the Arabian peninsula), Ahsa'i was preoccupied not only with the theosophist school of Isfahan (though he violently denounced Mulla Sadra) but also with the speculative Sufism of Ibn al-'Arabi and the illuminist philosophy of Shihab al-Din Suhrawardi, both known for their apocalyptic propensity. Ahsa'i's speculative contribution was in areas corresponding to three principle issues of Shi'i eschatology. On the question of the Hidden Imam's physical endurance in the state of Occultation, Ahsa'i proposed a celestial visionary space, which he called *Hurqalya,* where the Hidden Imam resides until his return to the physical world. Speculating on the metaphysical means of communicating with the Imam, Ahsa'i emphasized an intuitive experience. Furthermore, he redefined the corporal resurrection as a complex process that aimed at humankind's spiritual recreation to be accomplished at the time of the Hidden Imam's return to the physical world.

The luminous *Hurqalya* – a purgatory through which all beings must pass before being finally judged on the Day of Resurrection – was perceived as a world whose "state was neither the absolutely subtle state of separate substances nor the opaque density of the material things of our world." In this liminal space the Imam, who endured in a refined frame, could be encountered by the believers through intuitive visions, holy dreams, and occult sciences. This placement of the Imam in the visionary space of *Hurqalya* in effect rescued him from the timeless, confused, and inaccessible tangle to which he was relegated by Shi'i prophecies. Instead it subjected his existence to the dictates of historical time and space. Ahsa'i further maintained that so long as the Imam was in Occultation and while the world was still undergoing pre-resurrectional preparation, only one person could acquire perfect awareness of the Imam at any moment of time. The belief in this Perfect Shi'a *(al-shi'a al-kamil),* the one who can visualize the Imam in an all-embracing state of intuitive experience, became the Fourth Principle *(al-rukn al-rabi')* of the Shaykhi school and the central point for its messianic speculations.

Ahsa'i's chief disciple and successor, Sayyid Kazim Rashti (d. 1844), who further elaborated on his teacher's philosophy and created an organizational rudiment for Shaykhism, was viewed by his followers as that Perfect Shi'a and thus the gate *(bab)* through which the Imam's presence could be grasped. Yet beyond the circle of the adepts such identification was never made explicit. Employing the same idea of celestial conservatory, Ahsa'i conceived a fourfold human existence which goes through a complex process of quintessential overhaul before being refashioned in its original form at the final judgment.[17]

Under Rashti, a small but active group of Shaykhi seminarians, trained in the madrasas of the Shi'i holy city of Karbala in Iraq, preached Shaykhism in mostly Iranian urban and rural communities. As Shaykhism gradually evolved from a theological school into a messianic movement with followers among the lower- and middle-rank clergy, members of the urban guilds, merchant families, local government officials, and some peasant communities, it was increasingly perceived as a threat by its opponents in the clerical establishment. By the end of Rashti's time, the persecuted Shaykhis nurtured a sense of expectation for some form of messianic advent, which they hoped could redeem them from the harassment and denunciation of their opponents.

With this sense of expectation there also emerged among the Shaykhis a more humanlike picture of the Lord of the Age and of his mission. He no longer was perceived as superhuman with fantastic powers that allowed him, according to Shi'i prophecies, to survive a thousand years. He was seen, rather, as a human being born to mortal parents. Nor was his divine mission for universal conquest to be accomplished through a set of bizarre and confused apocalyptic events that would ultimately lead to the destruction of the world. His main task, to restore justice and equity, was seen no longer as mere vengeance for the long-standing feud with the historical enemies of his holy family but as a gradual process whose success against his enemies depended on the support and sacrifice of his followers.

## *The Babi Movement and the Baha'i Faith*

The rise of what came to be known as the Babi movement in Iran in the 1840s and 1850s was an outgrowth of a wide range of messianic speculations of which Shaykhism was the most prevalent. In May 1844 the founder of the new movement, Sayyid 'Ali Muhammad Shirazi (1819–50), a self-educated young merchant with

Shaykhi leanings from Shiraz (capital of the Zand dynasty, Fars province, ousted by the Qajars in the late eighteenth century), declared that he is the *bab* (gate) to the Hidden Imam and the sole source of legitimate moral authority on his behalf. Though the Bab adopted the early Shi'i notion of "gateship," as revived by Shaykhism, and came to be known by that title by the general public, he was nevertheless even in his earliest declarations equivocal about his exact claim. The Bab gradually confided to Mulla Husain Bushru'i – an ardent student of Rashti who became the Bab's first convert and one of the most influential in the shaping of the movement – and to a group of mostly Shaykhi clerics who constituted his circle of early believers, that he was not merely a gate to the Hidden Imam but the very manifestation of the expected Imam, the Qa'im himself, whose appearance the Shi'is expected for a thousand years.

Preoccupied with numerology and hermeneutical interpretation of the Qur'an, the Bab drew on the fact that his "manifestation of the [divine] cause" occurred in the year AH 1260, a thousand years after the presumed Greater Occultation of the Twelfth Imam, Muhammad ibn Hasan al-'Askari, in the year 260 /873–4. He also drew on the fact that he was a *sayyid,* a descendant of the house of the Prophet, from which the Mahdi will appear, while stressing his own intuitive experiences and visions, his purity of character, and his ability to utter holy verses similar to the Qur'an. Yet implicitly denying the doctrine of Occultation, he further stated that his manifestation was a historical necessity that only symbolically fulfilled the return of the Lord of the Age and not the flesh-and-blood reappearance of Muhammad ibn Hasan al-'Askari, who had died a millennium earlier.[18]

What was also remarkable about the Bab's claim, as it evolved in the course of the next five years, was that he considered his call not as a reassertion of Islamic shari'a, as was the case with the Sunni Mahdist movements, but as the beginning of an apocalyptic process that was destined to bring the Islamic dispensation to its inevitable cyclical end. His call, he claimed, was to inaugurate instead a new dispensation *(dawr)*, which he called the era of *Bayan* (lit. explanation, the title of his most important work). Relying on a hermeneutical reading of the Shi'i prophecies, for the first time in the history of modern Islam, he claimed that with his advent the age of Resurrection has started and the End of Time is at hand.

This he stressed should not be taken literally but as the resurrection of Islamic age and the end of the past prophetic cycle.

Employing the ancient Iranian tree metaphor and its seasonal renewal, he explained in the Persian *Bayan* that religious dispensations come in cycles so as to revitalize for humankind the moral essence of divine emanation. This he called "pure religion"; a concept with a long history in esoteric *(batini)* trends in Islam. In his theory of progressive revelation, he compared the successive dispensations to the lifecycle of a tree with a spring of inception and early growth, a summer of strength and maturation, an autumn of gradual decline and decrepitude, and a winter of barrenness and death. This key notion of continuity in revelation not only legitimized the Bayan religion but recognized and anticipated future prophetic claims after the Bab. Contrary to the prevailing Islamic notion of Islam's finality and Muhammad as the "seal of all prophets and messengers" and the cataclysmic end to the material world, the Bab believed that the "time cycle is in progress."[19]

Beyond the theme of progressive revelation, Babi theology brought to the surface new anthropocentric potentials deeply rooted in Perso-Islamic apocalyptic thought. His manifestation, the Bab asserted in the *Bayan,* was not only the fulfillment of Shi'i expectations for the Qa'im and the beginning of a new prophetic dispensation but also a new stage in humankind's continuous spiritual elevation in the process of reunification with the Creator. Though wrapped in a complex and convoluted language with much neology, the Bab's emphasis on humanity as a corporal mirror reflecting the essence of the sun of divine truth offered a new outlook. Here believers were held collectively responsible for the success or failure of the new dispensation rather than serving individually as passive agents to the will of Providence.

This sense of collective enterprise was apparent from the start in the nascent organization of the movement and in the beliefs and conduct of early Babis. The Letters of the Living, as the Bab named the inceptive Babi Unit of nineteen consisting of himself and eighteen early believers, was at the heart of the renewed dispensation. In his conception of the new religion, the Bab was influenced also by the story of Jesus and his disciples as narrated in newly accessible printed translations of the New Testament. In his religious scheme, the Bab constituted the Primal Point *(Nuqta-yi Ula)* of a scriptural universe in which each convert was considered a building block, a symbolic point, in the Bayan revelation. They were thus also letters in the book of *Bayan*, which was uttered not only in letters and words but in their human equivalents of the sacred text in the physical world. At the same time the Bab's assumed epithet, the Sublime Lord *(Rabb-i A'la)*, was close to the Christian characterization of Jesus as the *logos*, Son of God and the Savior, whose account of life and sufferings was appreciated by the Bab. Yet it was Imam Husayn's martyrdom that left the greatest imprint on the Bab's self image and his sense of fatal end.

In the Bab's scripture-oriented worldview, the Europeans, whose increasing presence was felt in Iran around the middle of the nineteenth century, were recognized as the "Letters of the Gospel." They were praised for their material advances and their savvy but were frowned upon for their unsavory intrusion into the land of the believers – a reflection, one may surmise, of the growing European commercial and diplomatic dominance. Indeed, the Bab, himself from the ancient province of Fars, expressed in his writings a nascent national awareness exemplified not only by his ban on Christian intrusion into the land of Bayan but by the use of Persian (along with Arabic) as a scriptural language of the new revelation. His fierce criticism of the conventional Islamic madrasa education of his time, which was exclusively in Arabic, brought him to the point of banning the study of jurisprudence and scholastic philosophy and calling for a burning of all books that were contrary to the essence of the *Bayan*. He also adopted a new solar calendar (in part based on ancient Iranian time reckoning) in place of the Islamic lunar calendar and marked the date of his own manifestation as a beginning of a novel *(badi')* era.[20]

Yet the new Babi identity still carried a powerful Shi'i component that was best discernible in the re-enactment of the Shi'i apocalyptic paradigm. Based on the sufferings of the Shi'i saints of the early Islamic period and aimed at redressing them, the apocalyptic myth was invoked as the Babis faced harassment and persecution. Following the arrest and incarceration of the founder of the movement and experiencing a number of humiliating episodes, the initial Jesus-like program for peaceful propagation was surpassed by the ever-present Husayn paradigm of martyrdom in the battlefield. In this shift of paradigms the Bab saw his own fate as being identical with the fate of the Lord of the Age as foretold by prophecies. He was to be killed at the hand of the Dajjal of his time in the same way that the Third Imam, Husayn ibn 'Ali, was martyred at the hand of his Umayyad adversaries in the battle of Karbala.

The Babis, too, reflected this convergence of the Persian and the Shi'i identities. The socio-geographic composition of the Babi movement revealed national characteristics consonant with Babi beliefs but in contrast to the compartmentalized structure of the society in which it appeared. Babism was perhaps the first movement in the modern Muslim world that brought together a wider spectrum of converts, including a few Jewish believers, from different walks of life and across a vast geographical span. Confrontations with the forces of opposition, first the Shi'i clerical establishment and later the Qajar state, further reinforced this national fusion. In the siege of Tabarsi in Mazandaran province in northern Iran, when in 1848–9 the Babis put up a stiff and bloody resistance against the government forces and their clerical allies, there came together converts from all over Iran, as well as from Herat (in today's Afghanistan) and from southern Iraq, of different social classes with diverse occupational background, education, and religious leanings. The Tabarsi resistance, like a number of other Babi armed struggles around the same time in Zanjan and Nayriz, embodied the anticlerical and anti-state sentiments that were combined at times with indigenous communistic proclivities, giving expression to urban and rural grievances and ethnic strife.[21]

In addition to lower ranks of the clergy and members of the bazaar guilds, a number of women also joined the movement. Most notable among them was Zarrin Taj Baraghani (1814–52); better known by her titles Qurrat al-'Ayn (the solace of the eye) and later, Tahira (the pure one). An ardent Shaykhi scholar and orator from a well-known clerical family, she was a mystic and a poet. She probably was the first Muslim woman in modern times to remove her facial veil in public – reportedly while preaching to a male audience.

Among the early Babis, moreover, she was the chief advocate of the independent nature of the Babi dispensation. In the important gathering of Badasht in 1848 she held that the ongoing Age of Resurrection had put an end to the Islamic shari'a and that during the interregnum *(fatrat)* between the old religion and the birth of the new one, such obligations as prayers and fasting and even institutions of marriage and divorce are abolished. Her very act of removing her facial veil was as much an expression of protest against women's inferior position as it was a symbolic declaration of the age of apocalypse and the time of revolt (*fitna;* also meaning revolution, sedition and civil war). She declared that the age of "delivering the word" has only brought abuse and persecution and that no option was left to the Babis but to resort to the sword.[22]

By 1848, as Babi armed resistance came to a head, the government's attitude hardened toward the Babis. The new premier, Mirza Taqi Khan Amir Kabir, who viewed the movement as a revolutionary threat to the very survival of the state, with much trouble managed to suppress the revolts, and subsequently, in 1850, with the backing of the 'ulama of Tabriz, he ordered the Bab's execution in that city, then the most important urban center in Iran. As a result of confrontation with the state, the leadership of the movement suffered badly, and large numbers of Babis were killed in action or were massacred and their families enslaved. Two years later the remnant of the movement's elite was executed or lynched in the aftermath of a Babi assassination plot against the new shah, Nasir al-Din Qajar (1848–96).

A few of the leaders, most significantly Mirza Husain 'Ali Nuri, better know as Baha'ullah (1817–92), were sent in exile to Ottoman Iraq. The suppression of Babi millennialism at the hands of a reform-minded premier, with the full blessing of the 'ulama, symbolized the triumph of one vision of modernity over another, namely, that of state-sponsored secular reformism over an indigenous grassroots messianic revolution. The Babi movement, perhaps the most intensive example of apocalyptic aspirations in modern Islam, was thus militarily defeated and driven underground.

Despite disillusionment and persecution, the new Babi creed survived and even thrived in the following decades as the most prominent force of religious and political dissent in Iran. Despite horrifying mistreatment at the hand of government officials, the fierce animosity of the 'ulama, and frequent mob attacks and scenes of gruesome lynching, known as *Babi-kushi,* and despite serious internecine conflicts, conceptual divisions and rivalry within the exiled leadership, the Babis continued to attract converts from discontented elements of all ranks. Baha'ullah led the Babi majority faction which later came to be known as Baha'is. In exile in Baghdad, then Ederna, and later 'Akka in Palestine, he was supported by converts mostly from among merchants and other sectors of the emerging middle classes. A member of the bureaucratic elite, Baha'ullah renounced Babi militancy in favor of a more pacifistic approach based on a doctrinal reassessment of the Babi teachings. The minority Babis followed Mirza Yahya Nuri, Baha'ullah's younger half-brother, and later came to be known as Azalis. They remained theoretically loyal to the Babi non-revisionist stance and the notion of revolt against the state and the 'ulama and refused redefinition of the Babi scripture.[23]

The emerging Babi-Baha'i faith represented a religious outlook based on Bayani religion but in many respects, particularly in its socio-moral message, was distinct from it. Baha'ullah, who first claimed in 1864 to be "He whom God shall manifest," the awaited savior of the Bayani dispensation, combined in his teachings aspects of Sufi mysticism with a utopian discourse of possible European origin while preserving the Babi messianic outlook and communal vigor. In the spirit of the Babi theophany, he claimed to be the manifestation of the divine word uttered in the day of encounter with God. His ecumenical call drew upon Islam as well as Judaism and Christianity as he claimed to be the messianic fulfillment of all monotheistic religions, a manifestation aimed at elevating humankind to the status of cognition while Baha'ullah himself was to be the ultimate pinnacle of this divine manifestation. Baha'ullah viewed the arrival of this apocalyptic moment, God's Day, as a sign of maturation of human moral and civil potentials. The call for the "unity of humankind," the ultimate goal of the anticipated "universal peace," reflected the Baha'i wish to break with the ethnic, racial, and gender norms and loyalties prevalent at the time.

Baha'ullah's later writings emphasized racial and gender equality, rejection of slavery, economic harmony, constitutional monarchy, and religious toleration. His doctrine of "truth liberation" *(taharri-yi haqiqat)* as the guiding principle for personal enlightenment independent from conventional beliefs also dismissed religious conviction on the bases of ancestral, communal, or scriptural identities and instead underscored a shade of modern individuality. "Universal maturation" was thus viewed as the prelude to a new age of cognition, rather than abiding dogma, and individual responsibility, rather than collective rituals. The Babi teachings were further modified so as to remove relics of the Islamic past in the areas of devotional acts, legalistic provenance of the 'ulama, women's segregation, strictures in dealing with nonbelievers, and dietary rules. More importantly, as a post-apocalyptic faith, Baha'i Faith sought to disengage from Islam's preoccupation with the hereafter, at least in its heaven–hell dichotomy, and to highlight instead the gradual elevation of the human soul in the afterlife.[24]

The unfolding of the millenarian potential of Iranian Shi'ism in the Babi movement, and its later Baha'i and Azali manifestations, occurred at a critical juncture, when Islamic societies had begun to encounter the threatening and yet luring West. The Babi movement thus represented a novel answer to the question of religious modernization by breaking with Islam while preserving the continuity of the Middle East's prophetic tradition.

## *The Ahmadi Movement and Reconciling with Islam*

In contrast to the Babi trend to break from Islam, the Ahmadiyya movement of the Indo-Muslim prophet Mirza Ghulam Ahmad Qadiyani (1839–1908), demonstrates the foreboding obstacles in the way of movements of messianic renewal that strived to remain within the pale of Islam. Mirza Ghulam Ahmad, a Sufi-oriented advocate of continuity in prophethood, viewed divine revelation as the only remedy to Islam's evident doctrinal ailment and intellectual decrepitude. Being part of the Muslim (and Hindu) eclectic modernism of colonial India and having been exposed to messianic Christian missionary literature (mostly by American Presbyterians), from around 1880 Ghulam Ahmad claimed to be the locus of divine revelation and the advent of both the Islamic Mahdi and the second coming of Jesus Christ *(Masih)*.

Rejecting the doctrine of crucifixion (as does the Qur'an*)*, Ghulam Ahmad made the extraordinary claim that in reality Jesus recovered from his wounds and left Palestine for Kashmir, where he died a natural death and was buried. He believed that just as Jesus' ministry transpired 1,400 years after Moses, so Ghulam Ahmad's divine mission occurred 1,400 years after Muhammad's divine mission; a juncture that corresponded also to the beginning of the twentieth century of the Christian era. Yet his claim that he is the "likeness" of Jesus, who now in him confesses Islam, did not entail the approach of the apocalypse. Nor was his claim to Mahdihood to be understood as waging an apocalyptic jihad. As he eventually asserted after facing bitter opposition from the Sunni 'ulama, Hindu reformers, and Christian missionaries, he was a *nabi* (prophet) whose peaceful advent was to revitalize true Islam and reveal the secrets of its scripture. This claim, with its insistence on remaining within the pale of Islam while striving to revitalize it through prophetic inspiration, was not in essence altogether different from that of the Mahdi of the Sudan, whom Ghulam Ahmad had attacked for his militancy, nor was it essentially distinct from North African intuitive Mahdism.[25]

Under Ghulam Ahmad's son and successor, Bashir al-Din Mahmud Ahmad Masih II, the majority of the Ahmadiyya, known as Jama'at Ahmadiyya, came even closer to an Islamic revisionist creed. Despite its exclusive sense of community and its missionary drive, Jama'at Ahmadiyya still fully complied with the doctrine of Islam's finality and its superiority. The troubling Qur'anic assertion in respect of *khatam al-nabi'in* (the seal of the prophets) (33:41) thus was rendered by Ahmadiyya, based on semantic variations, as an affirmation of Muhammad's superior virtue, hence being the "seal of the prophets," and not the "last of the prophets." Ghulam Ahmad viewed himself as a prophetic manifestation under the aegis of Muhammadan shari'a and not an end to it. For the Ahmadiyya the hereafter was a continuous journey of the soul toward spiritual perfection, an interpretation distinct from literal Qur'anic rendition of heaven and hell. The rival Anjuman Ahmadiyya, led by Mawlana Muhammad 'Ali, reverted to the Islamic fold even more than the majority Jama'at Ahmadiyya by recognizing Ghulam Ahmad not as a prophet but as an Islamic centennial renovator *(mujaddid)*.[26]

## *Modern Shi'ism and the Islamic Revolution*

The desire to create a "true" Islamic community found in modern Shi'ism a resonance no less intense than in the Sunni world, albeit with an undercurrent of messianic deliverance and apocalyptic motifs. Though Shi'i Islam was generally less exposed than Sunnism to religious modernization, in the decade leading to the Islamic Revolution of 1979 in Iran there were some efforts to reassess such themes as the nature of the hereafter, the coming of the Mahdi, and the Utopian order he will establish. Likewise, topics such as the duties of believers during the Occultation of the Hidden Imam were more assertively linked to questions of political legitimacy and clerical leadership on behalf of the expected Mahdi. Evident in these premessianic reflections was a gradual distancing from the traditional narrative of the apocalyptic end in favor of portraying the Imam's return as an all-embracing revolution *(inqilab)* with this-worldly causes and consequences. This new tendency may be detected first in polemical responses to Marxists, secularists, and Baha'i critics who denied the validity of the doctrine of Occultation and the literal understanding of corporal Resurrection and the Last Judgment.

One such advocate of rational and scientific exposition of eschatological questions was Mehdi Bazargan (1907–95), a French-educated university professor of thermodynamics and an Islamic activist who later became the premier of the Islamic Revolution's provisional government. In several of his works Bazargan, a prolific writer on Islamic themes from a "scientific" angle, questioned the very existence of the human soul *(rawh)* and its provability. Yet he did not deny the existence of the hereafter, which he argued could be explained by means of modern science. Though his use of science, which he avidly applied to all aspects of Islamic beliefs and practices, was not entirely novel to contemporary Islamic discourse, it did stir in the mid-1970s some controversy in conservative Shi'i circles and in turn encouraged further debates about the circumstances of the Hidden Imam's apocalyptic advent. His explanations for the Hidden Imam's millennial longevity, in particular, rested on farfetched biological theories and outlandish applications of modern theories of physics. He speculated, for instance, that, unlike matter and energy, a "third element" endures after death, and will be reanimated at the time of the resurrection.[27]

The reflections of 'Ali Shari'ati (1933–77) on the subject of expectation, on the other hand, clearly illustrate how modern Shi'i activists, influenced by Western ideological trends, grappled with the central themes of messianic advent and the *eschaton*. In a pamphlet entitled "Expectation, a school of protest," Shari'ati, a major ideologue of revolutionary Shi'ism and one of the forebears of the Islamic Revolution, regarded the End of the Time as an "ultimate revolution" for humanity. The "Mahdi's revolution" *(inqilab-i Mahdi),* as he called it, could not happen without Muslims first arriving at a new understanding of expectation *(intizar)* of the return of the Imam as a way of acquiring social responsibility, working toward a just and equitable order and rejecting political oppression and cultural degradation.

Complying with Shi'i prophecies, he repeated that the Lord of the Age will come when "the entire life of humanity reaches the lowest ebb of corruption" but until that time, he recommended, the community of believers should settle on the leadership of a democratically elected jurist *(faqih)* to serve as the "general deputy" *(na'ib-i 'amm)* of the Hidden Imam. The true understanding of the end, he stated, will advance only when Muslims abandon troubling theological entanglements on the circumstances of the Resurrection (and in effect, the rationally perplexing doctrine of Occultation) and instead develop a perspective conforming to modern "social and human sciences" and grounded in a sociological analysis of class conflict.

Shari'ati's "ideological" dimensions of expectation went only so far in endorsing a Marxist-Socialist-inspired Islamic revolution. His Islam, he asserted, was an "imperishable and lively religion" that has been misunderstood and misapplied by obscurantists who exploited the doctrine of Occultation to compromise with corrupt worldly powers. This "negative expectation" for the Imam, as he labeled it, stood in contrast to his "positive expectation," during which the "disinherited of the earth" will hasten the coming of the Mahdi through vigorous resistance to the "corruptor of the earth" and triumph over "satanic forces." Led by their "Imam-type" *(imam-gunih)* leader, who is the elected vicegerent of the Imam, the "disinherited of the earth" actively bring about a "revolution of universal scale," destroy the satanic superpowers and realize the "dictate of history." True expectation, Shari'ati concluded, is "believing that in the life of humankind on this very earth and before death, not in the Resurrection after death, history will bring about the triumph of the oppressed and destruction of the oppressors."[28]

A conscious effort to transform Shi'i messianic expectations into a worldly revolution thus reduced the Hidden Imam's place to a merely nominal one. Interestingly enough, Shari'ati's rendition was not entirely oblivious to a modern understanding of messianism from a sociological perspective. He acknowledges that the "yearning instinct" for a savior is a universal phenomenon in all human cultures and that Islamic yearning for the Mahdi is identical to the expectation in Christianity of Christ's Second Coming and to a universal hope for establishing a "golden age." *Messianisme* and *futurisme* (both terms cited in original French spelling) in his view were the outcomes of a "synthesis between the ideals and the realities" of Islam, an ambition to restore the ideals of 'Ali's just rule and to redress his defeat in reality at the hands of his enemies.

To reconstruct such an idealized past, Shari'ati believed, the "disinherited *(mustaz'afin)* of the earth" should strive for a "classless society" in which justice and equality will triumph over exploitation, imperialism, and tyranny. Though there is no explicit reference to contemporary political regimes, Shari'ati's treatise, *Intizar,* like his other works, was suffused with implicit hints to the ruling Pahlavi monarchy as a contemporary embodiment of the corrupt and oppressive rule of the Umayyad dynasty of the seventh century; the historical (and apocalyptic) enemies of Shi'ism and the killers of the most celebrated Shi'i martyr, Imam Husayn ibn Ali, whose martyrdom is to be avenged by the Mahdi. In the true spirit of the prevalent radicalism of the 1960s and 1970s, Shari'ati also portrayed Muhammad Riza Shah Pahlavi's most ardent supporter, the United States, along with its ideological rival, the Soviet Union, as the "world-devouring" *(Jahan-khwar)* superpowers who exhibit the diabolical powers of the Dajjal.[29]

Shari'ati's revolutionary messianism had a resonance in the rapidly radicalizing environment of Iran of the 1970s and no doubt influenced debates on the question of communal Islamic leadership in the absence of the Hidden Imam. The gradual articulation of these themes may be observed among such radical clerical thinkers as Murtaza Mutahhari, a prominent student of Khomeini, a teacher of philosophy and a public figure of some popularity among university students. In his essay on the uprising and the revolution of the Mahdi, he treated the advent of the Lord of the Age no longer as a sudden and cataclysmic event outside the pale of history, but as the final stage in an ideologically driven revolution to establish Islam's "ideal society." Mutahhari conceived the coming of the Mahdi, this "eminent and holy personality," as the climax of a revolutionary struggle that, in its primary stages, requires believers' active involvement.[30]

According to Mutahhari, unlike the secular theory of revolution, the Mahdi's revolution was divinely inspired yet was still contingent on the alertness and action of the community. The "great expectation" for the coming of the Mahdi by itself was to sketch out the forthcoming Islamic utopia, optimism for humanity's salvation. It promised the triumph of morality, justice, and freedom over unscrupulous capitalism and political arrogance, the establishment of world peace and global government, material development and the utilization of the earth's natural resources. Moreover, it motivated humanity's maturity and liberation from bestial and barbaric bonds, equality of wealth for all, the elimination of all moral depravities, and harmony with the natural environment.[31] Though wrapped in an Islamic guise, such utopian Mahdism was a far cry from the customary Shi'i view of the Mahdi's return and in some respects was close to the Babi-Baha'i ideals a century earlier as well as to the very Marxist utopianism against which Mutahhari proposed his "Islamic ideology." Establishing a "just state" thus became for Mutahhari and like-minded activists a legitimate first step toward the final revolution of the Mahdi.[32]

The publication in 1971 of Ayatollah Khomeini's well-known work *Wilayat-i Faqih* (The Authority of the Jurist), otherwise known as *Hukumat-i Islami* (Islamic Government) was clearly meant to render an answer to the most urgent of these concerns.[33] In this work, which almost coincides with Shari'ati's *Intizar,* Khomeini unequivocally, and in sharp contrast to the traditional Shi'i view, advocated the necessity for instituting an Islamic government in the absence of the Hidden Imam. Other theological considerations aside, his argument with regard to the Occultation revolved around a bold (and in many respects contradictory) interpretation of the doctrine of *wilayat* (guardianship, vicegerency, authority) whereby the jurists were called upon to preserve the "essence of Islam" from chaos and to defend its sacred values at a time when it had fallen into a state of alienation. It stands to reason, Khomeini argued, that while the Imam is in the state of Occultation, these tasks are to be accomplished by an Islamic government under the aegis of a "Guardian Jurist" who, though not infallible, by virtue of his position is to be upheld as the "vicegerent" *(na'ib)* of the Hidden Imam and hence superior to all other temporal powers.[34]

Identifying a set of pre-apocalyptic "signs" generally associated with the advent of the Imam and offering them as evidence for the necessity of forming an Islamic government, Khomeini in effect appropriated the function of the Imam to himself though staying short of claiming divine inspiration and infallibility. In support of this doctrine, Khomeini cites, among other evidence, one of the Hidden Imam's decrees in which the 'ulama were upheld as "proofs" *(hujaj)* of the Lord of the Age – who himself is "the proof of God" – and assigns to them the right to interpret the "events of the time." Both terms, *hujjat* and the "events of the time," implied a clear apocalyptic undertone. He paralleled these upheavals with the perceived malaise of his own time including "dissemination of vices," such as prostitution and drug addiction, by the "corruptor of the earth" and mischievous idol-worshiping *(taghuti)* rulers who allied themselves with the satanic superpowers to destroy Islam, to isolate and humiliate its 'ulama, and to corrupt and violate its women.

These vices were part of a conspiratorial scheme in which the threat of "Jewish domination" over the Muslims, exemplified by Israel's occupation of the Muslim holy lands, was complemented by perceived distortion of Islam's sacred text by agents of colonialism, anti-Islamic propaganda by the Baha'is and the Christian missionaries, and the evil designs of the British and other colonial powers to exploit Muslim natural resources and to ensure Muslims' material and cultural backwardness. The United States, in particular, occupied a prominent place in this house of Western demons not only for conducting an unjust and brutal war in Vietnam and for supporting the heinous policies of the Zionist state but also for re-imposing the colonialist capitulatory rights over the Iranian people, backing the Pahlavi dictatorial regime, conspiring to deprive Muslims through its espionage agencies, and above all for tempting believers to imitate the vilest immoralities of the West. This anti-American rhetoric was further embellished during the Revolution and confrontation with the United States. Khomeini labeled the United States the Great Satan *(shaytan-i buzurg)*, an epithet probably adopted from Marxist-Leninist propaganda of earlier decades in an Islamic guise and with an apocalyptic undertone.[35]

The vehemence with which Khomeini called for destruction of the monarchical shambles and for erecting in its place an Islamic government under the guidance of the Guardian Jurist displayed an unmistakable messianic resolve. Complemented by his single-minded sense of mission to rescue Islam from the ebb of disgrace and humility, his shrewd yet ruthless maneuvering against all other reformist and revolutionary forces, and his uncompromising stance in dealing with domestic and international opposition, he loomed large as a prophetic figure in late twentieth-century Islam – in the eyes of his supporters, perhaps larger than any other in Islamic history. He was not merely a "vicegerent" of the Imam, as he theoretically claimed to be, but an *imam,* as he was universally addressed in the Islamic Republic, an unprecedented honorific exclusively reserved for Shi'i Imams and not assumed by any Shi'i figure since the Occultation of the Twelfth Imam in the ninth century. The fact that the victory of the Islamic movement and Khomeini's rise to power in November 1979 coincided with the beginning of the fifteenth Islamic century only added to his prophetic aura, which in the popular mind was further embellished with tales of supernatural feats.[36]

With the establishment of the Islamic Republic, the debate about the Mahdi's revolution was partially cast aside. The vigor with which the Pahlavi monarchy was overthrown created a certain momentum and a confidence in the totality of the revolution among its religiously motivated supporters. Dramatic events such as the hostage crisis and subsequent damming of the United States, massive human casualties and material destruction in the war with Iraq, and the struggle to acquire a monopoly of power in the face of domestic opposition further prompted Khomeini's followers to view the revolution as an end in itself. The Islamic Republic was no longer regarded as the fulfillment of the "positive expectation" for a Mahdi-like revolt but came to supplant the authority of the Mahdi with the "authority of the jurist," as Khomeini stated.

Pivotal though the doctrine of the "authority of the jurist" was for the Islamic Republic, it was not accepted by all parties even within the revolutionary spectrum. In the years following the revolution, the secular opposition and the Islamic modernists questioned its validity because of its antidemocratic presumptions, while some of the high-ranking 'ulama implicitly took issue with its juristic soundness. A more vociferous objection to its unrestricted authority, however, came from the members of the Hujjatiyya Society, a splinter religious organization dedicated, as it claimed, to the Twelfth Imam, after whom it was named. Led by Shaykh Mahmud Halabi, an old preacher and an extreme anti-Baha'i activist with an expressed messianic bent, the Hujjatiyya acknowledged, at least in public, the collective "authority of jurists" within its legal bounds but only as an interim to the impending advent of the Hidden Imam. Hujjatiyya's position, in contrast to those who defended the jurists' total authority, is best illustrated in competing slogans: while the Hujjatiyya party exclaimed "Until the Mahdi's Revolution the movement continues," its opponents replied "Khomeini! Khomeini! You are the Imam's manifestation." Partly isolated for its antiwar position during the Iraq–Iran war, the Hujjatiyya Society was banned in 1983 by Khomeini's order.[37]

There were ample "apocalyptic" manifestations in the unfolding of the revolution itself, both in theory and in practice, to ward off the endemic resistance to the doctrine of the "authority of the jurist." Protracted war with Iraq with its horrendous scenes of bloodshed and destruction, set the stage for the characterization of the war in the official media as a cataclysmic "struggle of truth against falsehood," which could be won only by martyrdom, as Khomeini reassured armies of ill-equipped and untrained teenage volunteers who were dispatched to the fronts only to serve as fodder for Iraqi guns. By means of dramatic war murals the cult of martyrdom was perpetuated throughout the war, reminding all Iranians that "all days are Ashura, all lands are Karbala." This was a deliberate and highly effective use of an old Shi'i mourning chant invoking Husain's tragic fall in the battle of Karbala on 10th Muharram (Ashura) 61/10 October 680.

The messianic undertone of the story of Karbala, the ultimate paradigm for martyrdom, is evident, for it is this event that serves as the chief motive for the Mahdi's vengeance in his final showdown with the forces of Dajjal, now reincarnated in the Iraqi leader, the "infidel" Saddam Hussein. The messianic myth was further reinvoked by frequent citations on the war front of the Mahdi himself exhorting the "warriors of Islam" to sacrifice in the way of true religion; by the prosaic yet moving "testimonies of the martyrs," invariably aspiring to "adjoin the face of God," an ostensibly apocalyptic yearning; and by the equally innocent wearing of a plastic "key to paradise" around the neck. In the battlefields of southern Iraq, the scene of Shi'i apocalyptic prophecies, the warriors of the revolution were assured on makeshift signsposts that "the road to Quds [Jerusalem] was through Karbala." The celebration of martyrdom as a shortcut to eternal salvation was reinforced by public displays of ornate *hijla*, replicating the wedding chambers of martyrs who were about to taste the sensual recompenses of paradise, and by the tinted water gushing from the fountains of Tehran cemetery reminding visitors of the martyrs' ever-flowing blood, which nurtures the Islamic Revolution.

Revolutionary rage and righteous martyrdom could not thrive without their antagonist, no longer an apocalyptic beast or a hated tyrant from early Islamic history but a contemporary superpower or its perceived subordinate. As the Hidden Imam now was effectively replaced by his modern revolutionary vicegerent, so the old enemies were to be replaced with new ones. Khomeini and his propaganda machine labeled the United States the Great Satan, lurking in the shadow of the revolution, conspiring, seducing, and devouring. Insatiable in its appetite for the flesh and blood of martyrs, Khomeini assured his crowd, the Great Satan was to be revoked by hysterical calls of "Death to America!" almost as if it were a demon-repelling chant.

Most Islamic militants shared the Islamic Republic's anti-Western sentiments. In the post-Cold War era hard-line fundamentalists, from Algeria, Egypt, and the Sudan to Saudi Arabia, Lebanon, Palestine, and Afghanistan chastised the United States not only for supporting anti-Islamic dictatorial regimes or for backing Israel's aggression against its neighbors but for disseminating what they believed to be a culture of immorality and materialism. Anti-Westernism proved to be a potent weapon in the hands of all preachers of radical Islam who grudgingly admired the West for its scientific and industrial achievements but were anxious to resist its cultural and political influences. An idealized image of the Islamic revolution in Iran thus became for many throughout the Islamic world a prototype of steadfastness against the temptations and mischiefs of the West, and Khomeini, regardless of his Shi'i identity, a renovator of modern Islam if not its prophet.

With the end of the eight-year Iraq–Iran war in 1988 and the death of Khomeini, soon after in 1989, the tides of revolutionary zeal began to subside as though an exhausted nation was ready to bury with the militant prophet the decade-long memoirs of a Mahdi-like revolution. Post-Khomeini Iran quietly cast aside the myth of martyrdom, along with the urge to restore power and privilege to the disinherited of the earth. Even calls to confront the Great Satan no longer moved the masses as they once did, though such tiresome rhetoric still comes to the aid of the clerical elite anxious to regain their waning popularity. The Party of God *(Hizbullah)*, once a dreadful force of Islamic reprisal, turned for the most part into a political tendency occasionally flexing its muscles in mob action and within the Army of Defenders of the Islamic Revolution (the Revolutionary Guards) and retreated to the barracks, acting as a shadow of the regular armed forces. A set of new Islamic institutions emerged to define and preserve – and if need be to modify – the constitution of the Islamic Republic, but as yet a crucial question concerning the theological justification for the central doctrine of the "authority of the jurists" hangs in the balance. Khomeini's successor, often referred to as the leader *(rahbar)* of the revolution, strives to adhere to his predecessor's charismatic image by stressing the divinely ordained nature of his office; yet Khomeini's messianic charisma as the supreme master of the revolution defies routinization.

As Islamic militancy is now moving in the direction of a monolithic outlook and ideology, the messianic characteristics of both Shi'ism and Sunni Islam seem to embrace a common pattern. Belief in the hereafter and in the events of the last day remain strong and continue to generate messianic impulses for salvation, though such impulses often find expression in "fundamentalist" trends with predominantly regressive paradigms of glorious early Islam and revival of Muhammadan shari'a. Yet at the same time most of these trends are not devoid of utopian paradigms for moral renovation. The revolution in Iran no doubt was permeated by such motifs, though the Shi'i legacy that motivated Khomeini and his followers maintained its urge to break with the past – which, one may argue, is unique in the contemporary Islamic experience. The mixing of these paradigms is symptomatic of Islam's dilemma in an enlarging world system and is likely to bring new synthesis with latent or manifest apocalyptic characteristics. The rise of Osma bin Laden and al-Qaeida is one such manifestation of fundamentalist apocalypticism.

# PART 2

# *Millennial Cycles and Commemorating Martyrs*

CHAPTER 3

# *The Nuqtavi Movement of Mahmud Pasikhani and his Persian Cycle of Mystical Materialism*

In the year 1002 of the Islamic era (AD 1593–4), at the height of the Safavid persecution of the Nuqtavi heresy, a certain Darwish Kuchak, a *qalandar* (a wandering dervish liberated from the strictures of normative Islam) from Qazvin, committed suicide by consuming a large dose of opium. Pursued by Safavid henchmen for his heretical beliefs, just before his death the Nuqtavi leader told his fellow guards: "We leave until we return in another cycle" *(raftim ta dawr-i digar biya'im)* and then covered his head with his robe.[1] Darwish Kuchak's confidence in his personal reincarnation, if that is what he had in mind, may or may not have proved warranted. The spirit of millenarian renewal, however, which motivated him and many others like him, persisted as it had endured for many centuries in Persian heterodox milieu. In that respect there was a symbolic truth in Darwish Kuchak's word.

The destruction of Alamut castle and other Nizari Isma'ili strongholds at the hands of the Mongol armies and the dispersal of Nizari communities after 654/1256 marked a turning point in Islamic history no less significant than the simultaneous demise of the 'Abbasid caliphate in Baghdad. The deep-rooted tradition of dissent that for centuries was kept alive by various Isma'ili trends had now lost its organizational core and its confined fortress community. Pockets of Nizari resistance in Iran were forced to adopt a cryptic existence, often in the garb of Sufi orders. Our knowledge of the post-Alamut Nizari Isma'ilis and their communal endurance in Iran remains scanty, but enough is known to believe that in most cases Nizari activism was turned into a parochial acquiescence typical of all sectarian religions in their post-revolutionary phase. Not before the end of the twelfth/eighteenth century was there a noticeable change in this pattern.

The dynamics of dissent inherent in Isma'ilism could not have remained dormant infinitely, however. The eighth/fourteenth and ninth/fifteenth centuries witnessed one of the most intense, yet diffuse, phases of "heterodox" resurgence in the Iranian world, with doctrinal features and political consequences akin to Nizari Isma'ilism. Ranging from Ni'mat Allahi and Nurbakhshi Sufi orders to Hurufi and Nuqtavi heresies, these movements shared a doctrinal pattern founded on the ideas of cyclical renewal of sacred time, anticipation of a messianic advent, and hermeneutical *(batini)* interpretation of the text. The Safavid movement in part owed its making to this vibrant messianic milieu. The Safavid state (907–1135/1501–1722), on the other hand, ultimately suppressed and discarded the same messianic spirit in favor of a normative Shi'ism presided over by the Twelver Shi'i 'ulama. Official Safavid repression helped the diffusion of these movements into the religiously more receptive environments of Mughal India and Ottoman Anatolia and beyond.

The Nuqtavi movement was one important, and largely overlooked, product of this dynamic fermentation. By resorting to a nascent materialism with its roots in ancient Greco-Persian beliefs, Nuqtavism represented a rare example of a conscious departure from Islam. Moreover, an incipient sense of Persian "national" awareness complemented this Nuqtavi doctrinal departure. The former characteristic may be seen as a culmination of Qarmati Isma'ili (and certain Shi'i *ghulat*) aspirations to extend the cyclical renewal beyond Islam. The latter characteristic, on the other hand, anticipated the Safavid movement and its Perso-Shi'i particularism, which was destined to constitute the core of Iran's national ethos. With a religious latitude that was missing in the state-sponsored Shi'ism of the Safavid era, Nuqtavism, similar to its parent Hurufi movement, provided a crucial link between the religious dissent of the classical Islamic era and its development in the age of Muslim empires in the early modern period.

## *Early History*

That precious little that is known about the early history of Nuqtavism and the life of its founder, Mahmud Pasikhani, is based on evidence recorded almost two centuries later. Like other post-Islamic movements of the Iranian world, the history of Nuqtavism is largely lost to posterity and may never be recovered. Until such time that new Nuqtavi texts in Iranian and Indian collections (if extant) come to light we are bound to rely for the most part on literary and historical accounts by non-Nuqtavis. By piecing together the meagre evidence and applying a critical treatment we can retrieve a hazy picture of the movement's early history and its founder, just enough to highlight the need for further research.[2]

Born in the village of Pasikhan in the vicinity of Rasht in the Gilan province (on the southern shores of the Caspian Sea) in the second half of the eighth/fourteenth century, Mahmud Pasikhani, as he came to be known, began advocating his new religion around 800/1397–8. We know that the village of Pasikhan was the battleground between the two feuding regions of the Biya-pish, dominated by the warlords of eastern Gilan (based in Lahijan and Langarud), and their western Gilani rivals of the Biya-pas (based in Fuman and Rasht).[3] A border situation such as this may have had some effect on Mahmud's attitude toward political power and its temporality.

It is not clear to what extent, if at all, Mahmud's movement was a conscious effort to break away from his contemporary and presumably his mentor, Fadl Allah Astarabadi, the founder of the Hurufi movement. To be sure, Mahmud seems to have owed to Fadl Allah much of his cabalistic symbology and hermeneutics. It is possible that after Fadl Allah's execution in 804/1401–2 at the hands of the Timurid prince Miranshah, Mahmud was involved in a power struggle with other leaders of the movement. He may have tried to introduce into Hurufism, then popular throughout northern Iran, the Caucasus and Anatolia, a new chiliastic impetus.[4] Mahmud's messianic pronouncements at the turn of the ninth Islamic century were not accidental. Similar to those of Fadl Allah, Mahmud's call may have been inspired by a popular prophecy attributed to the Prophet Muhammad which anticipated the advent of an Islamic renewer at the outset of every century *(mujaddid ra's mi'a)*. In a pattern familiar to many messianic trends in Islam, Mahmud seems to have set out to advocate a message more radical in substance than the existing antinomian movement of Hurufism. Such a dramatic move away from its parent movement may have been the reason why a Hurufi source labeled him as the "excommunicated Mahmud" *(Mahmud-i matrud)* for his presumed egocentricity *(ananiyat)*. This disparaging title may convey more than personal ambition, however, given the fact that, according to another Hurufi source, Mahmud was one of the four closest companions of Fadl Allah.[5]

Mahmud's motives for rupture with Hurufism are indeed evident in his cabalistic doctrine. In contrast to Hurufism, which emphasized the secrets of the letters, Mahmud elaborated a system based on points. As one source puts it, "he created a system based on a point" *(az nuqta karkhanih pardakht)*. In his sixteen books and reportedly his thousand and one treatises he expounded the centrality of the point *(nuqta)*, an effort which in spite of its popularity among the Nuqtavi adepts *(umana')* was viewed by a pro-Hurufi author as "embellishments" *(zakharif)* worthy of eternal damnation.[6] The title of Mahmud's most important work, *Mizan* (balance), which so far has remained lost, also implies a clear cabalistic connotation. We may surmise that he saw his book as the apocalyptical balance by which good and the evil are reckoned on the Day of Resurrection, a concept similar to the *furqan* (distinguisher), one of the names of the Qur'an denoting its eschatological property. It is possible that in the *Mizan*, the reckoning for salvation or damnation, was determined by means of *jafr* (the science of occult prognostication), a practice common to all Shi'i movements.

Our information about Mahmud's reclusive retirement on an unspecified locale on the bank of the Aras River on the frontier of Adharbayjan and Arran (the Caucasus), where he died around 831/1427–8, is meager. One may surmise that Mahmud's departure from his home province was due to the fact that his guide, Fadl Allah, was residing in the Shirwan region on the northwestern Caspian coast not far from the banks of the Aras River. Mahmud's residence was also in the general vicinity of Ardabil, the convent of the celebrated Shaykh Safi al-Din Ardabili (d. 735/1334), the founder of the Safawi order which during the course of the ninth/fifteenth century became openly Shi'i. Throughout the Ilkhanid period the capital city of Tabriz in northwestern Iran was one of the largest metropolises of the Muslim world. Through its commercial outlets to the Black Sea, such as the Byzantine port of Trabzon, it thrived from trade with the principalities of Anatolia, the Armenian and Georgian centres in the Caucasus, and with venturing Mediterranean city states such as Venice. The impact of this diverse and bustling environment may also be seen in the departure of the

Gilani "prophet" from Muslim norms. He practiced celibacy, which he regarded as the highest status in the hierarchy of his religion, an act of asceticism reminiscent of Byzantine monastic tradition. Yet reincarnation themes in Nuqtavi doctrine, along with celibacy, may point to an eastern Buddhist (or even Manichaean) influence that was rampant under the religiously tolerant Mongols.[7]

## *Doctrine and Worldview*

The idea of cyclical renewal of prophetic revelations was an ancient Zoroastrian legacy present in Islamic Persia and particularly prominent in Isma'ilism. With Nuqtavism, however, it took a dramatic turn, essential for the understanding of Persian religious thought in the Timurid era and beyond. Loyal to the basic theory of cyclical renewal, Nuqtavism viewed human history as a series of consecutive prophetic cycles each running its course before being superseded by the advent of a new one. The cycles followed an identical pattern in their commencement, duration and termination but this did not mean, at least in its Nuqtavi rendition, that their renewal was devoid of a forward progression in time.

For Nuqtavism, however, the doctrine of renewal did not imply an Islamic messianic manifestation in the conventional sense. The advent of the Islamic Mahdi, who often was expected to consolidate the quivering pillars of the faith rather than to dislodge them, was not what Mahmud had in mind. Rather, the advent of the new prophet in the Nuqtavi scheme was to bring to an end the Islamic cycle *(dawr)* altogether and replace it with a new cycle initiated by Mahmud himself. Such a departure from one of Islam's most fundamental creeds, namely the eternal nature of the Prophet Muhammad's divine mission and his status as the "seal of the prophets" *(khatam al-nabiyyin)*, should be seen as a rare phenomenon in Muslim history. The early Isma'ilis, for instance, came to see their messiah as inaugurating a complementary phase within the Islamic cycle rather than a new era beyond it.

More significantly, this break from Islam was explicitly linked in Nuqtavi writings with the ethnic origin of the new prophet and his teachings. The end of the "Arab cycle," which was initiated by the Arabian Muhammad, was superseded in the new religion by the "Persian cycle" (*dawr-i 'ajam)* of Mahmud Pasikhani, who was the "Persian soul" *(nafs-i 'ajami)* and the "unique person" *(shakhs-i wahid)* of the new cycle. This aspiration to divorce the Arabian religion is traceable, for example, in a verse by an anonymous Nuqtavi poet who seemed to be stirring the Shu'ubi sentiments of the bygone times:

> Now is the turn for the fortunate sceptics *(rindan-i 'aqibat mahmud)*,
> The time is now gone for the Arabs to scold the Persians.[8]

The Persian cycle was the latest phase of a broad cosmological process. According to the Indo-Persian author of the *Dabistan-i madhahib,* who in the eleventh/seventeenth century provided the most succinct exposition of Nuqtavi doctrine, Mahmud viewed the entire lifetime of the world in terms of four super cycles of 16,000 years each, covering the era between the creation of the world and its termination. Mankind was now still in the first of these super cycles, which itself consisted of two successive shorter cycles: the first eight thousand years, Mahmud believed, was the Arab cycle which began with Adam, continued with six other prophets, and ended with Muhammad. The second eight thousand years of the Nuqtavi cosmology, the Persian cycle, on the other hand, begins with Mahmud and would continue after him with seven consecutive manifestations, identified as explicators *(mubayyin)*. The first cycle of eight thousand years he defined as super-terrestrial *(fawq-i thara),* apparently because it was divine in origin and inspiration and thus above the physical world. The Persian cycle on the other hand, was regarded as a sub-terrestrial *(taht-i thara)* cycle, presumably because it originated in the earth and conceived of human substance. "When the Persian cycle prevails," declares the *Dabistan,* "people will discover the truth and worship man and hold the human essence to be the truth."[9] This contrast between the super-terrestrial and sub-terrestrial may be traced back to Zoroastrian doctrines.

The dichotomy between Muhammad's and Mahmud's respective cycles was further highlighted in the Nuqtavi sources by celestial symbolism, also akin to Zoroastrian metaphors. Muhammad is the full moon *(badr)* in the prophetic heavens, but he is also viewed as a herald for the advent of Mahmud, who is defined as the prophetic sun. The celestial contrast between lunar chaos and the solar cosmos has long been employed in Iranian belief systems to explain the state of the human microcosm. In Nuqtavi belief this metaphor was also tied to the difference between the Arabian/Islamic lunar calendar and the Iranian solar calendar or the "ancient zodiac" *(burj-i qadim),* as a Nuqtavi source recognizes it. Muhammad's lunar calendar, asserts Mahmud, is inferior to the Persian solar calendar. Because the latter is based on twelve fixed months, it is "accurate and unchangeable and is not like lunar months which are based on full moon, half-moon and crescent."[10] Whereas Muhammad is the "lord of the twenty eight," the cycle of a lunar month, Mahmud is the "lord of the twelve" *(sahib-i ithna'ashar)* solar months, an idea which at the same time hints at a veiled affinity with the twelve imams of Ithna 'Ashari Shi'ism (believers in the Twelve Shi'i Imams often translated as Twelver Shi'ism). Not only was the rotation of the zodiacal cosmos to be measured by the solar calendar, but Mahmud also sought to restore the navel centre of his religious universe. The Nuqtavis' special prayer was to be set in the direction of the sun as opposed to the Islamic *qibla,* an act of worship clearly pointing to the Zoroastrian veneration of *mihr.*

Needless to say that emphasis on time reckoning went far beyond its practical function. Adoption of the Persian calendar denoted the end of the Islamic era and the beginning of Iranian times. The alternating lunar calendar indeed provided Mahmud with a chance to extend his criticism to other aspects of Islamic religion, with the aim of accentuating the superiority of his own. In the same celestial vein the contrast between the two prophets found other allegorical dimensions familiar to the Persian worldview. Whereas Muhammad is the night, like the dark hair of the beloved, Mahmud is the day, like the beloved's countenance *(wajh).* While Muhammad is created *(jadid)* as a "centennial prince" *(mir-i sad)* and a herald *(mukhbir),* Mahmud is uncreated *(qadim)* and is precursor to the "millennial king" *(padishah-i hazar).* Mahmud's mission is to be an explicator *(mubayyin)* of the mystery of creation.[11] The nocturnal temporality of Islam, like the dark entangled hair of the divine beloved, shall end in the dawn of her face. The mystical allegorism of Mahmud hints unmistakably at the eighth/fourteenth-century poetry of Hafiz, a contemporary of his who also was engaged with Zoroastrianism.

The most dramatic aspect of Nuqtavi doctrine, however, was its materialist cosmogony and the way it interpreted the course of man's intellectual evolution. In the view of the Persian prophet, all existence primarily originated in the earth (*khak*, literally, soil), which according to Nuqtavis was the source of the other three essential elements. The earth, in Nuqtavi thought, was the origin of an evolutionary process that occurs over the course of successive cycles. In spite of its seemingly modern attributes, Nuqtavism shared this pantheistic outlook with the Sufism of the Persian school. From the earthly matter *(jamad)*, so Mahmud advocated, emerged plants, and from plants came animals and from animals grew human beings; a reminiscent of the famous verse by Rumi:

From the matter I died to become vegitative,
From vegetation I died to become animalistic,
From animal I died to become human,
Until a time when I transcend humanity.

But in contrast to mainstream Sufism, Nuqtavi eschatology viewed man as an earthly being retractable to his earthly origin. "Once a human being dies and is buried, his bodily organs will revert to material and vegetational modes. Then vegetation is consumed by animals or human beings to appear [once again] in human guise." Yet the essence of human existence is not all lost. "All dispersed elemental parts of the body which are worthy of knowledge *('ilm)* and action *('amal)* will come back together and will not decompose, whether in the material (non-organic), vegetational, animalistic, or humanly states, even if their composition is broken up."[12] It is difficult to determine the origin of this reincarnatory eschatology. It may very well be the outcome of a later Indian environment when Nuqtavism interacted in the Mughal period with Hinduism and Janism.

The Nuqtavi emphasis on earth as the elemental origin of all beings is significant because it corresponds to the status of man as the earth's ultimate objective and outcome. It may be argued that such a view of man's elemental endurance was forged in order to resolve the problem of corporeal resurrection in Islam. In obvious contrast to the monotheistic religions of the time, which held mankind as a unique creation of God, Nuqtavism considered man as purely earthbound though still created by God. The statement attributed to Mahmud: "I am the manifest composite" *(ana murakkab al-mubin)* has an agnostic tone typical of his mystical materialism. Man is no more than an earthly composite *(murakkab)*, endowed with a manifest *(mubin)* mission, a concept reminiscent of a famous verse by Hafiz:

> Last night I dreamed the angels knocked on the tavern's door,
> Mixing man's clay and casting it out in a cup.

The idea of man's earthly origins is further reinforced by a sense of self-reliance, which is epitomized in the Nuqtavi motto "Seek help in yourself for there is no god but he" *(ista'in bi-nafsik al-ladhi la ilah illa hu)*. The enigmatic pronoun *hu* (or *huwa*) in the Nuqtavi context seems to point to man's divine status at the center of creation. Nuqtavi anthropocentric materialism thus seems to depart from the sceptic outlook latent in Persian fatalism *(dahriyya)* and is closer in substance to the modern notion of man. Emphasis on knowledge and action, reliance on the self *(nafs)*, and belief in an earthly evolution that culminates in man while believing in his composite perishability, point in that direction.

The Nuqtavis shared messianic yearnings with other "extremist" movements, but for them speculation with letters or written characters *(huruf)* took a peculiar, essentialist turn. Unlike the Hurufis, they were not so much concerned with the magical values of letters and thus, so far as we know, did not practice *abjad* numerological calculations. Instead, following earlier cabalistic trends in Sufism (as in Jewish mysticism), Mahmud emphasized the significance of the point *(nuqta)* as the building block of his symbological system, from which first alphabetical letters and then words were constructed. Thus follows the conscious recognition of his new religion as *Nuqtawiyya* (Pointism), his cabalistic speculations as the "science of the point" *('ilm-I nuqta)*, and his followers as the "People of the Point" *(ahl-i nuqta)*.[13]

The symbolic adoption of the *nuqta* to signify the four essential elements: earth, water, air, and fire seem to be unique to Nuqtavism. The quadrangular compound, represented by four dots ⁞ as in Nuqtavi texts, was at the basis of Mahmud's cosmology. Identified as the "quadrangular essence" *(zat-i murabba')*, this cosmology only acquired a structural completion in the Nuqtavi cycle when the "fourth essence" *(zat-i rabi')*, which is the earth element, gained its primal place. Devoid of the "fourth essence" the remaining "triangular bond" *('iqd-i thalith)*, represented with three dots ∴ epitomizes the Muhammadan cycle. The Muhammadan versus Mahmudian binary is thus played out in full and much to the benefit of the latter. The essential quadrangle (::) once perfected in its human form, represented by four vertical dots ⁞ denoting the original man, Adam, who is constituted of the four elements, is the fourth and final stage of creation above things, plants and animals. In its most perfect form, however, the original man appears in Mahmud himself. He stands in contrast to Muhammad, who is the embodiment of the "triangular bond" and, therefore, represented in Nuqtavi symbology with three vertical dots ⁝. The disparity of one point between the two figures translates in Nuqtavi doctrine to a whole range of other differences, which again corresponds to its author's evolutionary view of prophethood.[14]

Beyond an encounter with the "fourth essence" *(zat-i rabi')*, which in Mahmud's thought is tantamount to an earthly manifestation of a cyclical resurrection, however, Nuqtavi doctrine denies the conventional eschatology of Islam, including Paradise and Hell as conventionally understood. The Nuqtavi anthropocentric Resurrection is tied closely with the progression of man in the course of time and is geared toward understanding his own earthly essence, an association which turns Resurrection into a this-worldly event within the grasp of humanity. Resurrection is an event brought about by man's own deeds in his own lifetime rather than an event beyond his control that will only occur after his death. Likewise, the residents of Paradise are none but the "People of the Point," who earn their sublime recompense in this world not because they followed the shari'a but because they recognized the truth of Mahmud's religion. In contrast, Mahmud's opponents were relegated to the abyss of a this-worldly Hell because they ignored the advent of the new prophet. Emphasis on virtue rather than observation of the dogma (as in Christian Protestantism) was dormant in Nuqtavism. The fulfilment of the earthly Paradise was also bound up with a certain emphasis on Persian cultural identity.

## *Nuqtavism under the Safavids and the Mughals*

Beyond the internal evidence of Nuqtavi catechisms, whatever external evidence is available on Mahmud and the early history of Nuqtavism comes from the Safavid and Mughal sources written almost two centuries after the movement's inception. The noticeable absence of the Nuqtavis from the late Timurid and post-Timurid accounts implies that prior to the early decades of the tenth/sixteenth century they were viewed as offshoots of Hurufism or had failed to attract any attention. During the reign of Isma'il I (907–30/1501–24) and Tahmasp I (930–84/1524–76), however, for the first time references are made to Nuqtavism as a heresy harassed and persecuted by the Safavid state. Only after Tahmasp's death, during an interregnum of political instability and conflict prior to 'Abbas I's accession to the throne in 996/1588, do we witness a revival of Nuqtavism as a widespread movement with a millenarian message. It is not unlikely that this revival benefited from the policy of religious tolerance of Isma'il II (984–5/1576–8).

One of the earliest known references to the resurfacing of the Nuqtavis is found in the late tenth/sixteenth century *Ta'rikh-i alfi* (literally, "the millennial history", for it chronicled the events at the turn of the first Islamic millennium). Under the year 983/1575-1576, it records a revolt by the followers of Mahmud (whom the author misidentifies as Mahmud Fasakhani) in the villages surrounding the city of Kashan. Interestingly, this revolt occurred in conjunction with an uprising in the Isma'ili village of Anjudan in the Malayir region led by a certain Murad, a young Nizari imam with followers in Sind and Makran. The Nuqtavi revolt was put down by the Qizilbash governor of Hamadan, Amir Khan Mawsillu, who acted on Shah Tahmasp's order.[15] The coincidence between the two revolts, which carried over to the period after Tahmasp's death, is not accidental. Although Tatawi is vague about the connection between the two revolts – even though his father directly took part in suppressing the Kashan revolt – he seems to be suggesting that the followers of Mahmud were collaborating with the Isma'ilis of Anjudan. It is not unreasonable to assume that a revival of Nuqtavism "one hundred and fifty years after the death of Mahmud," as Tatawi points out, was part of a millenarian awakening that grew upon a network of Isma'ili and other older religious communities in central and northern Iran.

Nuqtavi aspirations persisted, however, after the accession of the greatest of the Safavid kings, 'Abbas I (996–1038/1588–1629), four years before the end of the Islamic millennium. Nuqtavi activism is often played down by pro-Safavid chronicles, yet it must have been acute enough to attract the young 'Abbas' attention at the shaky start of his reign when he was still grappling with the Qizilbash hegemony. Evidently fascinated by Nuqtavism and its potential to counterbalance Shi'i "orthodoxy," on several occasions he visited in disguise the convent *(tikkiya)* of a prominent Nuqtavi leader, Darwish Khusraw Qazwini. The shah's favorable leaning toward the Nuqtavis, whether out of curiosity or expediency, reflects the growth of the movement among certain segments of the Persian urban population.

Around the year AH 1000 (AD 1591–2) the movement seems to have reached the height of its popularity. Darwish Khusraw, whose views had previously brought him into trouble with the 'ulama and who repeatedly was the subject of inquisitorial examinations and harassments, is blamed by Iskandar Beg Munshi, author of the *'Alam-ara-yi 'Abbasi,* for luring to his convent the "low-minded commoners" *(kutah-khiradan-i' awam)* and the "penniless villains among the Turkmen and the Persians *(Turk va Tajik)*." Yet it is as though he reserves some secret praise not only for Khusraw's taste for the good life, his "well-kept gardens" and his taste for "colorful dishes" prepared in the convent's kitchen, but also for the facility with which he had long negotiated his way through theological and juristic ambushes laid for him by the ever-anxious 'ulama. A Hafizian *rind,* perhaps, he knew how to sit with the prince and the pauper at the same table. Many nights he entertained 'Abbas in his convent during the shah's nocturnal outings around the capital. Yet in spite of his accomplishments and apparent popularity, it was the need for "implementing the rites of the luminous shari'a," as Iskandar Beg puts it, that finally obliged the shah to pay back Khusraw's hospitality by ordering his arrest together with his followers. Conveniently, "wine jars" were found in his convent and the 'ulama lost no time in discovering that Khusraw's "open-mindedness and ill-beliefs *(wus'at-i bad-i tiqadi va)* had reached such a level that he is not observing the obligations of the shari'a." Condemned to death by the shah, who now was convinced of Khusraw's Nuqtavi adherence, he was tied by the neck to a camel's saddle and dragged along the streets of Qazvin.[16] Earlier on in Fars a certain Abu'l-Qasim Amri, a Sufi poet with Nuqtavi tendencies who had already been blinded by the order of Tahmasp for his heretical beliefs, was lynched in 990/1582 after the 'ulama pressed against him charges of "major sedition and rebellion."[17] But it was Khusraw's murder and the events related to the shah's temporary abdication that set off in earnest the "hereticide" *(mulhid-kushi)* of 1002/1593–4.

In a seemingly bizarre move in the year 1000/1591–2, upon the occurrence of an ominous celestial conjunction at the turn of the millennium, 'Abbas I abdicated in favor of a Nuqtavi adept, Ustad Yusufi[-yi] Tarkish-duz, a master quiver-maker as his name implies. Only three days later the shah was restored to his throne and Ustad Yusufi was killed by royal executioners. This temporary investiture was apparently patterned after an ancient Persian annual rite of spring renewal known as *Mir-i Nawruzi,* whereby on the occurrence of the spring equinox a carnival king presided over the symbolic shift from chaos to cosmos. In reality, however, the episode was symptomatic of 'Abbas' concern with Nuqtavi millenarian prophecies. It aimed at preventing celestial misfortunes from falling on the real shah, a pre-emptive measure against a millennial calamity propagated by the Nuqtavis and awaited by the public. Even through the pro-Safavid accounts of Iskandar Beg Munshi and Mulla Jalal Munajjim Yazdi, the royal astrologer and the chief instigator of the anti-Nuqtavi campaign who oversaw the shah's temporary sidestep, it is possible to see flashes of Nuqtavi popularity among the urban guilds and the dervishes. "It became apparent," writes Iskandar Beg, "that in the guarded realms [of Iran] the number of these people who strive for heedlessness has greatly increased."[18]

In the ensuing wave of persecution and mass killing that was championed by the shah and blessed by the 'ulama, a large number of leading Nuqtavis were slain and communities of the Nuqtavis in Kashan (particularly in Nasrabad), Isfahan, Istahbanat (in Fars), and Qazvin were massacred. Darwish Yusufi himself, as Iskandar Beg euphemistically puts it, "was stripped from the garb of life and fell from the throne onto the mortuary board." The fate of another prominent Nuqtavi, Mawlana Sulayman Sawuji, a physician from Sawa who was "the most learned" of the Nuqtavis, was referred to the 'ulama. Fearful of the "backlash of the heedless ruffians", no doubt a reference to his supporters among the city inhabitants, the 'ulama opted for his temporary detention but the "shari'a-nurturing" shah who regarded his elimination equal to a *hajj* pilgrimage insisted on his death. Likewise, Mir Sayyid Ahmad Kashani, another Nuqtavi leader, captured in the village of Nasrabad in the vicinity of Kashan, was cut in half on the spot by the shah's own sword.[19]

Driven away from the "guarded domains" of the Safavid empire many Nuqtavis immigrated to the neighboring Mughal (Indo-Timurid) empire even before the massacre of 1002/1593–4. There they found a refuge in the court of Emperor Akbar (963–1014/1556–1605) and an enthusiastic listener in the person of his celebrated adviser, Abu'l-Fadl 'Allami, author of *Akbar-nama*. Thus the Nuqtavi revolt in Iran was crushed in its inception but its intellectual residue endured and contributed to the court culture of Mughal India. The Persian Nuqtavis and their Indian sympathizers found the great emperor a more plausible candidate for the "millennial king," whose court became a venue for debates among representatives of different religious traditions (including Zoroastrian Parsis and Portuguese Jesuit missionaries) and inter-confessional innovation.

'Abd al-Qadir Bada'uni, the chief chronicler of Akbar's era and himself a staunch Sunni, holds the Nuqtavis in Akbar's court responsible for the dissemination of millenarian prophecies. The emperor was so influenced by Nuqtavi views, Bada'uni implies, as to declare himself the prophet of what came to be known as the "divine religion" *(din-i ilahi)* and advocate the doctrine of "universal conciliation" *(sulh-i kull)*. Indeed, a prominent Nuqtavi scholar and a refugee at the Mughal court, Mir Sharif Amuli, seems to have been a source of intellectual inspiration for Akbar and his minister Abu'l-Fadl 'Allami, the architect of "universal conciliation." Amuli and other Nuqtavis in Akbar's court drew upon Mahmud Pasikhani's prophecies to speculate on the advent of a "remover of falsehood" in the year 990/1582 which, as they saw it, implied the abrogation of Islam by Akbar at the end of the millennium. Khwaja Mawlana Shirazi, a Nuqtavi specializing in *jafr*, offered to Akbar a treatise (*risala*), presumably from the *sharifs* of Mecca, which, on the bases of the Islamic hadith, predicted the impending doomsday and the advent of the Mahdi at the end of the seventh millennium from the time of Adam. Corresponding to Mahmud's super-cycles, the idea of seven millennial cycles was long popular among Isma'ilis and other Shi'i communities. Similarly, among other "Shi'i superstitions," so Bada'uni puts it, the Nuqtavis relied on a chiliastic quadrant attributed to the Isma'ili poet and philosopher Nasir-i Khusraw:

> In the year nine hundred and ninety by the ordinance of the fate,
> Gather all the stars in one place.
> In the year Leo, month Leo, day Leo,
> Walks out from behind the curtain the God's lion.

Bada'uni believed it was such insinuations that persuaded Akbar "to claim prophethood *(nubuwwa)* in all respects but name," for he was the "lord of the age" *(sahib al-zaman)* and "God's lion" *(Asad-Allah)* who, as Nuqtavis insisted, removed the communal barrier between the seventy-two nations *(haftad u du millat)* of Muslim and Hindu persuasions.[20]

After Akbar, court patronage of Nuqtavism gradually subsided before finally turning into open hostility under Awrangzib in the middle of the eleventh/seventeenth century. Sarmad Kashani, a Persian Sufi poet of Jewish origin who later seems to have adopted Janist views and practices in India, is the last important Nuqtavi known to us. A protégé and companion of the celebrated Mughal prince and scholar Dara Shukoh, son of Shah Jahan, he was executed when the 'ulama issued a *fatwa* condemning him to death soon after the prince's defeat by his half-brother Awrangzib and his subsequent murder in 1069/1659. This marked the end of the Nuqtavis' unhampered activities in India for close to a century. It was also an end to a remarkable age of religious innovation and communal tolerance under the early Mughal emperors.[21]

The diffused Nuqtavi impact on the Perso-Indian environment was not depleted altogether. In the middle of the eleventh/seventeeth century, the author of the *Dabistan-i madhahib,* himself presumably a Parsi priest *(mu'bad)* and a product of the confessional syncretism of Mughal India, could still meet Perso-Indian Nuqtavi writers and poets in the North Indian intellectual capital, Lahore, and record a summary account of their beliefs as a distinct "sectarian" creed. Even as late as the middle of the thirteenth/nineteenth century from time to time the wandering dervishes of Jalali and Khaksar with eclectic *qalandari* tendencies entertained views reminiscent of Nuqtavism. No reference to their hierarchical or communal existence however has come to light.

Nuqtavi texts may have also continued to be read in mystical and "heterodox" circles up to the thirteenth/ninetenth century. The striking resemblance between the ideas of Sayyid 'Ali Muhammad Shirazi, the Bab (1236–66/1821–50), the founder of the Babi movement, and the beliefs and practices of Nuqtavism is too explicit to be attributed solely to the diffuse esotericism *(batini)* of the Persian "heterodox" milieux.[22] Nor could such an affinity be solely assigned to the Shaykhi school whose founder, Shaykh Ahmad Ahsa'i (d. 1241/1825), was indirectly influenced by Isma'ili-related themes, as was his successor, Sayyid Kazim Rashti (d. 1259/1844).

During the tenth/sixteenth and eleventh/seventeenth centuries, some poets and literary figures of the "Indian" school were inspired by Nuqtavi themes even at the risk of harassment by the 'ulama. Their lives and works deserve independent examination, but even as early as the late-Timurid era traces of Nuqtavi themes may be detected in the poetry of Iran and in no less a prominent contemporary of Mahmud Pasikhani than Hafiz of Shiraz (d. *c.*792/1390). Hafiz's allusions may indeed be counted among the earliest evidence of the popularity of Nuqtavi themes. The author of the *Dabistan* recognizes Hafiz as a Nuqtavi sympathizer. For this claim he relies on the word of an anonymous Nuqtavi, possibly a Shirazi friend of the author in Lahore. To buttress his claim he also quotes a famous, and indeed enigmatic, verse from the poet:

> O, zephyr *(saba)*! When passing by the banks of River Aras,
> Kiss the soil *(khak)* of the plain and sweeten your breath.[23]

Whether this is an allusion to Mahmud, who was residing on the bank of Aras in northern Adharbayjan, so that Hafiz symbolically salutes Mahmud's veneration of the earth, is a matter of interpretation. There are enough references in Hafiz's poetry to *nuqta*, the change of cycle, man's earthly creation and resurrection, and enough skepticism about the Islamic hereafter to merit a separate study.

The paucity of data makes it difficult to determine the connections between Nuqtavism and Isma'ilism. What evidence remains is circumstantial. Nuqtavism, one may conjecture, absorbed certain values dormant in later Isma'ilism: millenarian aspirations based on cyclical renewal, preoccupation with occult sciences, and symbolic explanation of Resurrection. Hierarchical grading and missionary appeal to the non-elite urban and rural populace as well as to the intelligentsia were also common between the two. The geographical distribution of Nuqtavism may also have matched the pattern of the crypto-Isma'ili centers in post-Mongol Iran. Yet there are fundamental differences. Nuqtavism did not conceive the inward–outward *(batin-zahir)* dichotomy in the same fashion as Isma'ilism, which never departed from the boundaries of Shi'i Islam. This can be explained by the Nuqtavi movement's aspirations to bring about in this world a millenarian Utopia free from the concealment of the *batin* or the auspices of a hidden or revealed imam. To achieve this, the Nuqtavis seem to have favored a benevolent ruler who could merge political and religious legitimations. In this context Nuqtavism anticipated incipient Safavid Shi'ism.

The time-honored cord that tied the twin siblings, the "just ruler," and the "good religion," and keystone of social order in the Perso-Islamic system, was too strong to be ruptured with the Nuqtavis' millenarian agnosticism. What seemed in another time and place, for instance Europe of the Enlightenment, a plausible proposition for reshaping human thoughts and societies, was destined to be labeled a heresy in its own world and witness suppression while the religious conservatives of the Safavid and late Mughal eras closed their ranks.

CHAPTER 4

# Meadow of the Martyrs: *Kashifi's Persianization of the Shi'i Martyrdom Narrative in Late Timurid Herat*

In the vast Shi'i literature commemorating the martyrs of Karbala, few texts have been as influential as Husayn Wa'iz Kashifi's *Rawdat al-Shuhada* (*Meadow of the Martyrs*).[1] The Shi'i biographer Muhammad Baqir Khwansari, writing in the nineteenth century, considers *Rawdat al-Shuhada* "as the first book to be written in a fashion distinct by its order and lavish style and in such admirable method." So successful was this early sixteenth-century book of martyrs that the "narrators of the sufferings" of Karbala, who often recited it verbatim, came to be known in Iran as *rawda-khwan* (reciters of the *Rawda*).[2] Beyond the melodic recitation over the pulpit, *Rawdat al-Shuhada* was highly influential in the development of the Shi'i passion play *(ta'ziya)* and the mourning verses *(nawha)* of the Muharram procession.[3] It is not an exaggeration to suggest that no medium has helped to shape popular Shi'ism so much as *rawda-khani* and *ta'ziya*, either in Iran or in Shi'i India, southern Lebanon, or elsewhere. The enduring memory of recitation and performance of the tragedies can be seen in every instance of Safavid and post-Safavid Iran, and even as late as the Islamic Revolution.[4]

Despite its profound impact there has been little study of the *rawda* tradition, and even less of Kashifi's work. This is all the more remarkable in that *Rawdat al-Shuhada* was produced in a seemingly Sunni environment at a crucial historical juncture, coinciding with the rise of the Safavid dynasty and the establishment of Shi'ism as the official creed of the newly founded state. This coincidence lends itself to intriguing questions. The circumstances leading to the production of the book are as relevant as the author's religious loyalty and the possible political motives behind his Timurid patron. In presentation and style, and in the characterization of heroes and villains of the upheaval of Karbala, the book's main theme, we may detect a subtle subtext, one which corresponds to the rapidly shifting political realities of Kashifi's time. *Rawda al-Shuhada* thus may be read not only as an allusive commentary on the sinking fortunes of Timurid rule but perhaps as a means of forging new political bonds by appealing to dormant Shi'i sentiments. This was at a time when Kashifi's princely patron had moved closer to a pro-Shi'i position, perhaps in response to the impending Uzbek threat, which has already reached the walls of Herat. Playing on the old narrative of Shi'i martyrdom, and relying on his remarkable preaching and performing skills, Kashifi transformed the Arabic *maqatil* narrative and created instead a Persian drama of vividness and emotional impact.[5] Punctuated by apt poetic references and employing Persian musical scales, Kashifi as the author/performer shrewdly played on the collective grief of his growing audiences. Some contemporary sources consider him a suspect Shi'i not only because of his Shi'i background but because of the sentiments he expressed for the House of 'Ali in his sermons. Yet his ancestral Shi'i creed allowed him to practice dissimulation *(taqiyya)*, a religious license necessary in securing success in a cosmopolitan climate such as that of Herat.[6]

## *From Periphery to Cosmopolitan Herat*

Born *c.*840/1436 in Sabzivar, a stronghold of Twelver Shi'ism, Kamal al-Din Husayn Sabzivari, better known as Wa'iz Kashifi, was the son of a local Shi'i preacher. During his childhood the memory of the Shi'i Sarbidari rule of Sabzivar and Nishabur (737–808/1335–1405) had not entirely faded. Only a generation earlier, in 808/1405, the Sarbidari leader Sultan 'Ali Khwaja Mas'ud was captured by Timurid forces and executed in Herat after his failed uprising in Sabzivar. Two decades earlier still, Najm al-Din 'Ali Mu'ayyad, the last effective Sarbidari leader, had died after twenty-seven years of rule over the Bayhaq province. He had accepted Timur's suzerainty, quashed the messianic dervish wing within the Sarbidari movement, and promoted a ritualized orthodox Twelver Shi'ism interlaced with Karbala eulogies.[7]

This Sarbidari legacy is likely to have inspired Kashifi and influenced the rendering of *Rawdat al-Shuhada* both in style and substance. As early as a the middle of the fourteenth century the Sarbidari ruler, Khwaja Nizam al-Din Yahya Kurabi (r. 753–59/1352–57), commissioned Persian works by Shi'i writers on the sufferings of the Imams.[8] Among the works of the prolific Kashifi one can also consider *Futuwwat-nama-i Sultani*, a commemoration of the Sarbadari age. This extensive account of the chivalrous traditions and rituals of the *futuwwa* brotherhood was promoted by the Sarbadaris, whose leadership was closely associated with the urban guilds and their *futuwwa* network. Parallel to *Rawdat al-Shuhada,* Kashifi's objective in *Futuwwat-nama* is to introduce the popular Shi'i-Sufi legacy of his homeland into the cosmopolitan environment of Herat.[9] The very dedication of this work – to the Eighth Shi'i Imam, 'Ali ibn Musa al-Rida, who is identified in the preface as the "king of the saints" *(sultan al-awliya')* – verifies Kashifi's Shi'i-Sufi affiliations.[10]

The dedication of this work may not be unrelated to Kashifi's years of study in Mashhad, the shrine of the Eighth Imam, before departing for Herat, presumably in 860/1455. The chain of "reporters of the hadith" *(ruwat)* to which Kashifi was affiliated went back through his father all the way to the Eighth Imam himself.[11] Yet the Shi'i affiliation did not prevent the young Kashifi from seeking patronage in a predominantly Sunni Herat. In 860/1455 in a dream he saw himself stepping out of the shrine of the Eighth Imam in Mashhad only to encounter a saintly figure clad in white who introduced himself as Sa'd al-Din Kashghari, the renowned successor to Baha' al-Din Naqshbandi. The shaykh invites Kashifi to join his Sufi convent, but does not specify the location. In search of the shaykh in the world of reality, Kashifi abandons his studies in Mashhad and heads for Herat, where he realizes that the Kashghari of his dream had died shortly before his arrival.[12]

Kashifi's dream, most likely apocryphal, can be taken as a revealing symbol of his shift from the parochial Shi'i world of his hometown to a promising Sunni Timurid capital. He manages this shift to outward cosmopolitanism through the medium of Sufism. Shortly after his arrival, he became associated with the circle of Shaykh 'Abd al-Rahman Jami (817–98/ 1414–92), the celebrated master Sufi, poet, scholar, and teacher of the fifteenth century and a former disciple of Kashghari. His marriage to Jami's sister fortified affiliation with the influential master and paved Kashifi's way toward a successful public career and prolific authorship. Yet even in the guise of a Naqshbandi Sufi, Kashifi never fully escaped the charges of harboring Shi'i loyalties, nor of being blamed by his own countrymen. When years later he was appointed chief judge of the Bayhaq district (whose center was Sabzevar), he was not immune from charges of betraying his Shi'ite heritage by the local population. Predictably, his career as a judge did not last long and he returned to the bustle of Herat where he could better maintain a liminal identity.[13] A later Shi'i biographer, Qadi Nurullah Shushtari, assigns the subtle blame of "worldly expediency" *(masalih-i dunya-dari)* as Kashifi's motive for abandoning his real Shi'i identity.[14]

Yet Herat of the late fifteenth century was not devoid of pro-Shi'i sentiments. Most Sufi orders revered the House of the Prophet and recognized 'Ali as a patriarchal saint. The passion of Husayn also served as a powerful sacrifice paradigm across communal and sectarian loyalties. It is not therefore unlikely that the ranks of the "preferential Sunnis" *(Sunniyan-i tafdili),* as the sympathizers of the house of 'Ali among the Sunnis were known, included such notables as Jami and other Naqshbandi luminaries. In his poetry and prose Jami praised 'Ali and his sacred progeny and lamented in passing the tragedy of Karbala though without ever denying the legitimacy of the four "Rightly Guided" caliphs.[15] The last effective ruler of Herat, Sultan Husayn Bayqura (r. 875–912/1470–1506), and some members of the Timurid royal family, also harbored Shi'i sympathies. Kashifi's *Rawdat al-Shuhada,* after all, was commissioned by Bayqura's son-in-law, Sayyid 'Abdullah Mirza, also known as Sayyid Mirza.[16] Such was the attitude of many Herat notables, even though Amir 'Ali Shir Nava'i (845–907/1441–1501), the most influential statesman, patron, and literary figure of the late Timurid period, stood out for his strong Sunni proclivities.

'Ali Shir Nava'i's concern for the growth of Shi'ism was more likely occasioned by the rising Shi'i-Sufi activism and especially the success of pro-Safavi propaganda in the eastern Timurid lands. Earlier on, the proto-messianic teachings of the Shah Qasim Anwar (757–837/1356–1433), a Sufi poet and propagandist, had caused anxiety among the Timurid authorities. Anwar promoted the cause of the lords of Ardabil six decades before the rise of the Safavid dynasty. As part of the fifteenth-century Shi'i symbiosis, Anwar's message struck a sympathetic chord not only with the wandering dervishes and with the general public but, seemingly, with Timurid prices and patricians. His popular preaching no doubt was the cause of his expulsion from Herat in 830/1426. These measures, however, did not diminish support for Shi'ism. By the very end of the fifteenth century throughout the Persian-Islamic world, from Kashghar, Delhi, Samarkand, and Herat to Shiraz, Tabriz, and Brusa, prospects for the Persianized Sufi-Shi'i orders, often with subversive agendas, were improving. This was at a time when the days of the Timurids of Khurasan were numbered.[17] Kashifi's measured crypto-Shi'i sermons in the praise of the House of 'Ali and of the martyrdom of Husayn appealed to these Sufi-Shi'i sentiments without posing a threat to the Timurid establishment.

## *The Crumbling World of Timurid Herat*

The real threat to Timurid rule, however, came not from Shi'i-Sufi orders but from the rising Sunni Uzbek nomadic power of the neighboring Central Asian steppes. In his biography of Amir 'Ali Shir Nava'i, the celebrated Timurid historian Ghiath al-Din Khwand Mir offers a fascinating account of the growing anxieties of the Herat elite in the face of the rising Uzbek threat. In Muharram 906/July 1500 so much was the survival of the Timurid state at stake that even after Nava'i eventually acquired Sultan Husayn Bayqura's permission for a Hajj pilgrimage, the notables of the city pleaded with him to once more cancel his journey. Kashifi was among the notables of Herat who argued that:

> The reason for the stability of the cities of Khurasan and the tranquility of their peoples is your benevolent presence. Now that this land is devoid of the residence of the auspicious sultan [who was campaigning against the Uzbeks], if your light-emitting presence also descends, it is possible that many troubles *(fitna-ha)* occur which cannot be conceivably mastered, particularly since the king of the Uzbeks, who has gained mastery over Mawira' al-Nahr (Transoxiana), is aiming to cross the Amuyya (Amu Darya or Oxsus) river. Now that Iraq and Sham are also in the state of utmost anarchy, and roads are extremely unsafe, according to the dictates of the noble shari'a

> the *hajj* pilgrimage is not obligatory. Our humble appeal is that once again you spare the souls of the people of Khurasan and cancel your journey since your stay this year equals the reward of seventy Hajj pilgrimage on foot.[18]

Out of concern for the "welfare of the people," Nava'i complied with the request. He did not live long enough however to undertake his pilgrimage. His death a year later in 1501 was a blow to Timurid rule and ushered in a period of unrest that plunged Herat into a decade of tumultuous upheaval. In 905/1499 the Uzbek chief, Budaq Khan, had defeated Husayn Byqura in Balkh. Two years later, in 907/1501, his son, Muhammad Khan, better known as Shaibak Khan, consolidated Shaibanid conrol over Samarkand, hence effectively ending the fragile Timurid presence beyond the Oxsus. The loss of Timurid principalities to the conquering Uzbeks, which followed by the flight of the Timurid princes to Khurasan, was viewed in Herat with horror. Driven out of his ancestral home, Babur Mirza (the future founder of the Mughal empire of India) captured Kabul in 909/1503 and soon after entered into an alliance with Husain Bayqura in Herat against their common Uzbek enemy. But three years later, in 911/1506, the death of Sultan Husayn Bayqura sealed the fate of the Timurid dynasty. In Muharram 912/May 1506 Shaibak Khan captured Herat and, after crushing the meager resistance offered by the late sultan's two sons, he extended Shaibanid control over the rest of Khurasan. The Uzbeks' Mongol ancestry, which brought back memories of past brutalities, and their vigorously enforced Sunni orthodoxy were not welcomed by the Herat elite, which was accustomed to the refinements of a vibrant cultural life and its subtle complexities.[19]

It was within this critical timeframe that in 908/1502 Kashifi composed his *Rawdat al-Shuhada*, just two years before his death in 910/1504.[20] The symmetry between the course of events and the subject matter of Kashifi's book cannot be entirely coincidental. The compatibility is all the more remarkable in that soon after orthodox Sunnism was imposed across Herat by the Uzbek conqueror, the city was captured by an even more zealous Shi'i conqueror. In 916/1510 Shah Isma'il I (r. 907–30/1501–24) defeated the Uzbeks in the battle of Marv, in the course of which Shaibak Khan was killed. In the same year Isma'il captured Herat, the greatest prize of his Khurasan campaign. Following the Timurid model, Herat became the eastern capital of the newly founded Safavid empire. The capture of the city by a Shi'i messianic king-prophet came only eight years after the composition of *Rawdat al-Shuhada*, a Shi'i narrative commemorating the the tragedies of Karbala.[21]

It is quite conceivable that by 1502, a year after Isma'il's conquest of Tabriz and the proclamation of Ithna Ashari Shi'ism as the state creed, Kashifi and the pro-Shi'i Herat elite were already aware of the decisive events in western Iran.[22] It is plausible that, at this brief juncture before the Uzbek invasion, the Timurid prince Sayyid 'Abdullah Mirza, a prominent Shi'i sympathizer in Herat, felt it necessary to patronize Kashifi's work in order to honor the memory of his own Shi'i descent. By doing so the prince may have intended to enhance his prospects for succession shortly before Bayqura's death, at a time when mobilizing the public through Shi'i message was in vogue.

That Kashifi's book was meant to enhance Sayyid Mirza's stature among the patricians of Herat is evident in the epilogue, where he praises the prince for his dual noble descent. He admires him for his high rank in the royal lineage *(sumow martabat dar nasab-i saltanat)* but, more importantly, for being of noble descent through the house of the Prophet *('uluw-i nasab dar siyadat)*. Sayyid 'Abdullah Mirza, who was married to Sultan Husayn Bayqura's daughter, Maryam Sultan Baygum, was a nephew of the Timurid ruler and an influential figure in Herat politics. Kashifi traces the prince's paternal genealogy in the Hasani line back to Imam Hasan, the Second Imam, and his maternal ancestry to the *sayyid*s of the Husayni line. To complete the prince's noble position, he then traces Sayyid Mirza's maternal Timurid genealogy to Timur himself.[23] As such *Rawdat al-Shuhada* served the purpose of glorifying the political ambitions of a Timurid prince and enhancing his status among the pro-Shi'i public.

Sayyid Mirza's career, to the extent that it is known, only confirms such a political program in the final days of Timurid rule. During the internecine rivalries of the last days of Bayqura's rule and immediately after his death, which eventually brought about the Timurid collapse, Sayyid Mirza may have underscored his own Shi'i lineage in order to secure support among the urban population of Herat. In 906/1500 he had fought for the defense of Herat against Prince

Badi' al-Zaman Mirza, the eldest son of Sultan Husayn Bayqura, who had rebelled against his father. Having been defeated in the battle, Sayyid Mirza had taken refuge in Bayqura's camp. Later, in 911/1506, in the wake of Bayqura's death, his ambitions for power seem to have revived. Though he was obliged under pressure from Timurid royal women, including his own wife, to pay his allegiance to Badi' al-Zaman Mirza, he did not seem to have actually succumbed to the new ruler's ephemeral reign. In the last days of Timurid rule, however, he escaped before the Uzbek armies reached Herat and in Mashhad joined the forces of the same Badi' al-Zaman Mirza whom he had earlier opposed. The desperate resistance against the Uzbek army ended in total defeat. Yet shortly after, Sayyid Mirza took part in another desperate counter-offensive, this time in the city of Sabzevar, where he must have relied on the sympathies of the Shi'i population. There he was killed in battle in 913/1507.[24]

## *Remaking of a Martyrdom Narrative*

The final composition of *Rawdat al-Shuhada,* we may thus safely assume, was facilitated by the patronage of a prince who pursued a political end. Yet it is very likely that its content, and even organization, was long rehearsed during the sermons delivered in the month of Muharram. Khwand Mir, who provides us with Kashifi's weekly preaching schedule, specifies his Friday morning sermons from the pulpit of Herat's Dar al-Siyada-yi Sultani (the royal hall of the *sayyids*).[25] After-preaching, Kashifi would lead congregational prayers in the Herat Friday Mosque. His busy schedule also included preaching on Tuesdays in the Sultani madrasa and Wednesdays in a Sufi shrine.[26] This diverse lecturing and preaching may very well underline not only Kashifi's popularity, as Khwand Mir insinuates, but his ecumenical appeal to mainstream Sunnis, as well as Sufi and Shi'i sympathizers. Large segments of these sermons, rehearsed in the pulpit and finetuned before large congregations, were to appear in his copious works, ranging from his popular commentary on the Qur'an, *Mawahib-i 'Alliya* (the Blessings of the Sublime) to the more mystically inclined commentary *Jawahir al-Tafsir* (the Jewel of the Commentaries).

Kashifi's broad appeal is also evident in his vast scope, which made him something of a "universal man," and almost unique in the Persian literary world of the late medieval period. A great popularizing author, he was conscious to utilize all the potentials of a dramatic language to reach his Persian-speaking audiences. His objective in *Rawdat al-Shuhada* was to produce, according to the wishes of his patron, a readable Persian account that superseded existing narratives in comprehensiveness and accessibility. Kashifi has already shown, to the delight of his vast readership over many centuries, his great expertise in rendering, revising, compiling, and popularizing a wide range of Persian classical texts.[27]

The rationale for the production of a Shi'i popular narrative, however, becomes more apparent if we look at similar Sunni hagiographies about the Prophet and the early caliphs, accounts that Kashifi apparently aimed to emulate, incorporate, and even supersede. It is possible that he organized his book, and even named its title, in conjunction with the work of a contemporary Persian preacher in Herat, Jamal al-Din 'Ataullah Dashtaki Shirazi, better known as Jamal Husayni (d. 927/1521).[28] An influential minister and later chief of the city's nobles, he came to play a part in the transitory period between the fall of the Timurids and the Safavid conquest of Herat.[29] His popular hagiography in Persian, *Rawdat al-Ahbab fi Sirat al-Nabi wa'l-Al wa'l-Ashab* (the Garden of Friends on the Biography of the Prophet, the People of the House, and the Companions) was commissioned by 'Ali Shir Nava'i in 888/1483 but was later revised and completed in 903/1497. It consists of three parts in a typical Sunni format, covering biographies of the Prophet, the Companions *(ashab)*, the adherents *(tabi'in)*, and the early transmitters of the hadith.[30] Frequently in the *Rawdat al-Shuhada* Kashifi quotes Jamal Husayni, highlighting prevailing 'Alid sentiments in the Sunni hadith source.

The creation by two celebrated preachers of Herat of texts with similar themes and titles may not be a coincidence. It is likely that Nava'i's death reduced Timurid enthusiasm for official Sunnism and opened the way for the open expression of Shi'i sentiments. Such a shift obviously included the writing of the already well-developed oral repertoire of Karbala, an essential component of Shi'i collective identity. The rise of a new Shi'i state in western Iran hence may have promoted the cult of Husayn as a mobilizing strategy against the imminent Uzbek threat. Admittedly, there is no explicit evidence to suggest any ideological urgency for production of Kashifi's account.

Yet, unmistakably, there is an air of confidence in his unfettered Shi'i presentation of the story of the House of 'Ali and especially the account of Husayn's martyrdom and the lives of the Twelve Imams and their descendants, which suggests a renewed boldness in uncovering Shi'ism as a communal memory.

Competing for a larger audience, Kashifi possessed performing techniques suitable to such an appeal. He no doubt acquired these in his Shi'i homeland. A seasoned preacher known for his good voice and for mastery of classical Persian musical modes, he employed both in his recitations of Karbala sufferings. His prose was frequently interlaced with vivid verses, which were either borrowed from classical and contemporary poets, or his own. Following an old Shi'i tradition, Kashifi insists on the importance of the Karbala narrative to induce tears. He assures his reader that "whoever sheds tears for Husayn, or [even] make himself weep *(tabaki)*, he is bound to enter paradise."[31]

Amir 'Ali Shir Nava'i, who praises Kashifi as an unequaled preacher, cares to emphasize his extraordinary popularity. During his sermons, "no matter how spacious the place, there is such a huge crowd that most people cannot find seats. At times the crowd was so dense that people were in the danger of being trampled on." The chief reason for his appeal, Nava'i observes, was that Kashifi's "voice and presentation *(sawt wa insha')* were extremely melodious and tender. In truth, the voice of David, peace be upon him, has emanated in him. Throughout the Muhammadan community there is not a single person equaled to his perfect Davidian quality."[32] Such a strong endorsement was of course qualified by casting some doubt on Kashfi's adherence to Sunnism. He is from Sabzivar, Nava'i consented, "but he is clear of their [Shi'i] heresy *(rafd)* and free of their false creed, although he is not free of such an accusation."[33] A subtle qualifier such as this from a great statesman with strict Sunni beliefs seemed to have been necessary so as to eliminate any guilt by association.

Kashifi's sermons surely brought an accusation of Shi'i heresy. It has been said that on one occasion in Herat someone in the audience who routinely lampooned his sermons handed him a note with this famous verse from Hafiz: "Preachers who shine in the [prayer] niche and on the pulpit; once in private, they engage in that other act."[34] Kashifi was reportedly so incensed that for two months he stopped preaching.[35] Ironically, not only lampooners in his Sunni audience troubled Kashifi but even his own Shi'i countrymen from Sabzevar were not convinced of his Shi'i loyalties. The staunch Shi'i author Qadi Nurullah Shushtari, who pities Kashifi for being "condemned to the painful companionship" of 'Ali Shir Nava'i and for being "trapped" into becoming Jami's "brother-in-law," relates an anecdote demonstrative of the level of Shi'i suspicion of Kashifi's sincerity.[36]

Sentiments such as these, however, did not seem to dampen public enthusiasm for his sermons or diminish patronage such as that of Amir 'Ali Shir himself. Kashifi's much-appreciated art of narration, as witnessed by his contemporaries, was not confined to his oratorical skills: his *Anwar Suhayli* was destined to become one of the most widely read Persian prose works before the twentieth century,[37] second only, perhaps, to Sa'di's *Gulistan* (which is the product of another successful *wa'iz*). Not surprisingly, the works of Kashifi exerted a lasting influence on Persian popular culture largely because they struck powerful emotional and moral cords. His use of a discursive style in an accessible language was polished and finetuned by many years of experience and practice. His mastery of Persian narrative prose is perhaps best demonstrated in *Rawdat al-Shuhada*. Here we witness the emergence of a new genre of Persian prose that aims to break the strictures of formal secretarial or theological styles.

Contrary to the ornate literary prose of the Timurid period, and the tedious digressions of much of historical writing of his time, and contrary to the consciously Arabized prose of the jurists and theologians (if they ever wrote in Persian), Kashifi's narrative almost deliberately simulates the spoken Persian of his time. It is direct, easy to comprehend, intimate, and emotional and is garnished with frequent poetic references. Its passionate, almost sentimental tone is designed to play on the melancholic mood of its audience during the month of Muharram and bring tears to their eyes. Its frequent references to historical sources, on the other hand, was meant to generate authenticity and trust. It is not an exaggeration to suggest that in its scope and emotional impact *Rawdat al-Shuhada* supersedes earlier Shi'i eulogies in Arabic, Persian, and Turkish, above all because it successfully managed to construct a tragedy almost in the classical sense.[38]

On the events of the Karbala, for example, Kashifi points out that "in most treatises that deal with this tragedy, the details of the struggles of Husayn and his companions are not recorded." The earlier sources often "sufficed mentioning a name and a verse." Kashifi claims that he "carried out extensive investigation and research in order to report in these pages the details of this upheaval in the best of styles." He further states that he has omitted especially the Arabic battle poems *(rajaz)*, which were of no benefit to the Persian-speaking audience, so as to avoid the break in the flow of the story. Instead he added Persian verses suitable for the occasion.[39] Yet we know that a vast portion of *Rawdat al-Shuhada* is reconstructed by the author either based on existing legends or figments of Kashifi's own imagination. In this respect he elevated the much-appreciated art of storytelling onto a new plane. Here, most notably in the account of the martyrs of Karbala, and especially Husayn and his relatives, we witness the full blown genre of the historical novel. More purposefully than any history text, this medium was able to arouse emotions and carry the message of mourning and lamentation to its audience.

Though essentially a historical drama, *Rawdat al-Shuhada* utilizes an array of Arabic and Persian sources ranging from hagiographies and eulogies to general histories, biographical dictionaries, collections of hadith and Qur'anic commentaries, as well as poetry, didactics, and Sufi aphorisms which are quoted at every instance with scholarly caution so as to avoid charges of sectarian propaganda. Among its frequently quoted sources is 'Abd al-Rahman Jami's *Shawahid al-Nubuwwa li-Taqwiyat al-Ahl al-Futuwwa* (Signs of Prophecy in Support of the [Sufi] brethren). In this mystical account of the life of the Prophet, Jami cites miraculous dreams and visions of the Prophet forecasting the martyrdom of his grandson, Husayn. A chapter on the "consequent punishments of the enemies" *('uqubat-i a'da)*, on the other hand, anticipates the fate of the killers of Husayn in this world and the next. Kashifi's frequent citing of this source reveals the mystical influence of his brother-in-law. It also underscores the author's strategy to safeguard against charges of deviation.[41]

Jamal Husayni's *Rawdat al- Ahbab* is another frequently quoted source, and perhaps used for the same reason, of shielding the author against accusations.[42] Likewise, Shi'i sources such as Shaykh Mufid's *Rawdat al-Wa'izin* and Ibn Babuya's *'Uyun Akhba al-Rida* were counterbalanced with Sunni canonical texts such as Ahmad ibn Hanbal's *Musnad* and Tarmadhi's *Sunan,* and with standard histories such as al-Tabari's *Ta'rikh al-Rusul wa'l Muluk*.[43] Yet when he describes the pivotal events of Karbala and the slaying of Husayn and his close relatives, Kashifi is rarely shy of political license, which is often highlighted by a masterful rendering of ambiance.

On the occasion of 'Ali Akbar's death on the day of Ashura, Husayn seeks him in the battlefield and once he has found him mourns his loss:

> "O, my beloved son where are you? Why no longer can you turn your lovely face toward your heartbroken father? My son, I am injured by the enemy's mischief. Yes, my heart's injury deserves the salt of parting." Meanwhile Imam Husain's eyes fell on 'Ali Akbar's horse but he did not find its rider. He followed the horse into the battlefield until it stopped at the spot where the Imam encountered his fallen son. Like a decapitated bird he was throbbing unconsciously in blood and dust. Imam immediately dismounted and sat beside his son, laying his hand on his forehead. 'Ali Akbar opened his eyes and saw his father's splendid countenance. He said: "Do you see, father?" The Imam replied, "See what my son?" He said: "Here, look! This is my great-grandfather, the Prophet. He holds in his hands two bowls of heavenly drink. He offers one to me. I ask: 'give me the other one too because I am extremely thirsty.' He replies: "Ali! drink only this one; I have prepared the other one for your father. He too will join me with blistered lips and bloody heart.'" Soon after 'Ali Akbar uttered these words, he passed away. The Imam fastened his body on the horse and brought him to the camp where his mother and sisters began crying and serenading elegies . . . Alas, the shining new moon of the sky of *wilayat* which has dawned from the horizon of the guiding *Imamat* was eclipsed behind the veil of darkness before reaching its full light and high place in the sky and the heavenly like tree from the orchid of charity which was grown on the bank of the river of courage and chivalry, was killed off by the windstorm of death before reaching its bloom and offering its fruits.[44]

The desire to render a Persian work accessible to the public aptly places Kashifi in Herat's cultural landscape of the late fifteenth century. He states that "at the outset of composing these pages it was resolved that no Arabic verses are to be included, unless necessary, since listening *(istima')* to these [verses] in the midst of [historical] reports will cause the Persian-speaking audience *(Farsi-zabanan)* to lose concentration."[45] While this is not an unusual concern for a popular preacher, his text instead is punctuated with Persian verse citations by Sana'i, Attar, Hafiz, Sa'di, and some of Kashifi's own. To maximize the emotional impact on the audience, these verses were to be recited melodically and with the requisite theatrical intonations.

Moreover, the *Rawdat al-Shuhada* narrative was organized as a tragic cycle. Divided into ten chapters, corresponding to the first ten days of the month of Muharram, each chapter was designed to build up toward the martyrdom of Husayn on the tenth day, the day of Ashura. Chapters one to three portray prophetic sufferings, including Muhammad's own at the hands of his opponents, as an unavoidable consequence of any divine mission beginning with Adam. Chapters four to six describe the sufferings of the members of the Prophet's House: Fatima, 'Ali and their son, Hasan ibn 'Ali, the Second Imam. Chapters seven to ten are on the life of Husayn and the tragedy of Karbala and its consequences. This section is completed with short biographies of the Twelve Imams and their descendants.

This structure holds together as a controlled dramatic narrative with a central plot, which consists essentially of the circumstances leading to the paradigmatic martyrdom of Husayn and its redemptive underpinning. The protagonists (*awliya'*, lit. the friends) are 'Ali and his sons, Hasan and Husayn, and his family, companions, helpers, and sympathizers. The antagonists (*ashqiya'*, lit. the villains) are the ruling house of Umayyad, most notably the usurper of the office of the caliphate, Yazid ibn Mu'awiyya, followed by the governor of Kufa, 'Ubaydullah Ibn Ziyad, and his agents, including Husayn's murderer, Shimr, and the carrier of Husayn's severed head to Damascus, Khuli. It begins with a prologue on the sufferings of the prophets of the past and ends with an epilogue on the eschatological consequences of Husayn's murder and the fate of his supporters and his enemies.

Suffering, Kashifi affirms, is the touchstone of the human condition and God's love for those "on whom He dispatches armies of suffering and grief," an allusion, no doubt, to adherents to the Shi'i faith. Indeed, the very essence of humanity in the author's eye is ingrained with grief, and the prophets are to be seen as the enduring epitomes of such pains. At the time of creation, by divine order, Kashifi opens his narrative: for thirty-nine days the clouds arising from the sea of grief rained on the clay of Adam and only on the fortieth day a few drops from the sea of happiness were sprinkled on that clay.[46] The theme of mankind's inherent grief, no doubt influenced by Jami's mystical hagiography, is followed up in the stories of Noah, Abraham, Jacob, Joseph, Job, Zachary, and John the Baptist (though, oddly enough, not Jesus) before recounting the sufferings of Muhammad and his House.[47]

Accounts of Muhammad's sufferings are particularly important, however, because Kashifi aims to graft them onto the sufferings of the holy family and especially onto the forthcoming tragedies of Karbala. This blending of Shi'i metahistory with the accepted Sufi narrative of the Prophet's life is a subtle strategy.[47] Repeatedly, the reader is reminded of the Archangel Gabriel's revealed prophecy to Muhammad that his beloved grandson, Husayn, will be wronged by the enemies of his House and eventually be martyred. Through dreams and visions 'Ali and Fatima also grasp the same bitter reality about their son when he is still an infant, and they too lament his seemingly irrevocable fate. Upon his birth, we were told, Gabriel is revealed to Muhammad, congratulating him and yet offering his condolences. The archangel warns the Prophet, while he is playfully wooing his grandson: "The throat that you kiss now will be slashed by the saber of injustice." When Fatima and 'Ali are informed of what fate has stored up for their son, they too join the Prophet, weeping bitterly at the imminent tragedy. The holy parents and his grandparent, Muhammad, never question this irreversible destiny.[48]

Also in the manner of true tragedy, the element of pity is largely assigned to a female figure, Fatima, daughter of the Prophet. As much as Muhammad and 'Ali exemplify submission to divine will and forbearance in the face of trouble, Fatima epitomizes motherly compassion. In one scene in the book Fatima appears on the Day of Judgment carrying Husayn's bloody shirt on her left shoulder, the poison-contaminated gown of her other son, Hasan, on her right shoulder, and the bloody turban of 'Ali in her hands. She pleads with her father, Muhammad, who is sitting on the pulpit, to redress the repeated injustices to her family. The Prophet though fully sympathizing with his daughter, nevertheless reminds her of his own task on the Last Day to intercede *(shifa'a)* on behalf of the weak and the oppressed rather than to avenge. The blood of Husayn and the martyrs of the House, the Prophet stresses, is an atonement to redeem the sins of all those Shi'i believers who wept for the sufferings of the holy family.[49] Husayn thus shares with the Prophet the eschatological function of serving in the Day of Judgment as intermediary *(wasila)* for the salvation of the believers.[50]

The above images of Fatima are among many scenes throughout the book engendering intimacy and empathy with the holy family. As a skilled preacher Kashifi uses the digression devise (*guriz*: literary "escape") to switch to the tragedy of Karbala so as to sustain the attention of his audience and build up toward a final upheaval. At the heart of this discourse is a desire to share a tragic experience, whether as an individual reader, or more likely an audience listening to it (or eventually viewing it as a *ta'ziya* play). The vivid imagery depicted in highly sentimental language and melodramatic tone, was intended to reinforce bonds of loyalty among the "partisans" *(shi'a)* of 'Ali's House. Kashifi embellishes a sentimental image of Fatima. As the daughter of Muhammad, wife of 'Ali, and mother of Hasan and Husayn her sufferings were bound to arouse tremendous sympathy among his readers and listeners. The presence of an enthusiastic female audience must have encouraged Kashifi in assigning to Fatima such a central role. Quoting Ja'far Sadiq (the Sixth Imam), Kashifi gives Fatima special treatment as one of the five great weepers of history.[51] This is one of many reminders to the reader that weeping as a collective catharsis is blessing with a redemptive quality. It also underscores the role of Fatima as a paradigm of familial agony.[52]

Kashifi's account of the People of the House is indeed saturated with agony. The fate of the sacred offspring, Husayn, in particular, has been dramatized through a prism of miracles, marvels, saintly visions, dreams, and prophecies in order to impress upon the reader the mysteries of his preordained sacrifice. Like any other tragedy, here too blind fate overshadows prudence, reason, and reality. These elements admittedly are not missing from the *Rawdat al-Shuhada*, but they are ultimately overridden by the forces of destiny. The tension between the martyrdom myth and historical reality is well evident in Kashifi's semi-historical account of Husayn's life and the circumstances leading to Karbala. But more than being history in the modern sense, it is a rendition of Shi'i collective memory.

The Husayn of the *Rawdat al-Shuhada* is deeply aware of his own impending end and of the triumph of worldly villains. Despite tantalizing incentives to compromise and against the dictate of common sense, he too, like his older brother Hasan, who compromised with the Umayyads, succumbs to his destiny. Yet he is portrayed as a human being. He does not shy away from power-seeking and at times is hostage to his own doubts and trepidations. Nor is he immune from indecision and fear, and ultimately fails to save his own family and companions, aspects of character which were almost always glossed over in Kashifi's rendition, with its luster of saintly innocence. Yet by highlighting these human sentiments, Kashifi aims to demonstrate the inefficacy of human will in reversing the forces of destiny. Husayn's fall in the battle of Karbala is a dictate of heaven over which neither he, nor his parents nor the Prophet, nor archangels have any control. On the way to Kufa, for instance, he is repeatedly forewarned by his supporters of the great dangers ahead. But his response reiterates his grandfather's dream and his mother's anguish: that he will encounter the inevitable martyrdom because "destiny can not be defeated by sagacity" *(daf'-i taqdir bi-tadbir nashayad kardan)*."[53]

Yet Husayn's martyrdom on the day of Ashura (10th Muharram AH 61/ 10th Oct. 860) implies a symbolic meaning in the *Rawdat al-Shuhada* beyond its dramatic and redemptive contexts. In a broader scheme, Husayn's fate, as repeatedly prophesized in the text, is to depict a Shi'i moral struggle of the righteous and the innocent against the overwhelming forces of evil and injustice. Here, the martyr is not acting by his own volition, but as part of a cosmic battle between the forces of good and evil, an overarching theme in Persian culture. It is as though in Kashifi's rendering the old Persian notion of Time *(ruzgar, zamanih)* as the ultimate trickster has been successfully grafted onto the story of Karbala and Husayn as its martyr hero. We may wonder if this is Kashifi's own devise or, more likely, whether he is dramatizing and standardizing the existing narrative of Husayn and Karbala inherent in the Shi'i past where martyrdom, or more specifically the act of self-sacrifice, is offered as the only means of prevailing over the superior evil power.

The striking parallels between the legend of Siyavus, the martyr-heroes of pre-Islamic legend (as in the *shah-namih*) and Husayn in the narrative of Karbala, in plot and character, suggests an ancient link going back to the formative centuries of Shi'ism. Siyavush, a victim of a family plot fueled by old ethnic conflict, succumbs to an unavoidable tragic end. The Zurvanite undertone in this story, as in Husayn's story, is unmistakable. As has been observed for long by a number of scholars, the similarities between the ceremonies of Muharram and the rite of Suvashun (literary *Siyavash-kushan*) or *kin-i Siyavush* (vengeance of Siyavush), commemorating the mournful death of the Persian hero at the hand of Afrasiyab, the Turanid king, is not coincidental.[54]

What Kashifi has done, we may conclude, is to rarefy and dramatize this ancient narrative for popular taste while reinforcing its doom-laden message. Whether deliberately employed or simply a poetic devise, this encoded message came to reflect an impending political reality of Kashifi's own time – a message that anticipated the capitulation of the rightful to the power of the usurping villain. We may speculate that recording this narrative of Husayn and Karbala made particular sense in late Timurid Herat because it resonated the impending disasters that threatened Kashifi's own world and the world of his audience. Are his antagonists the usurping Uzbeks who were about to destroy the legitimate kingdom of Husayn Bayqura's as the Umayyads of *Rawdat al-Shuhada* destroyed Husayn ibn 'Ali and his claim to rightful accession? If so, what role may we ascribe to the rising power of the Safavids and the king-prophet figure of Isma'il and his messianic revolution? Is he the savior who will eventually redress the wrong, as the Mahdi will avenge the martyrdom of Husayn? Kashifi is silent. His perspective is decidedly unapocalyptic. In his concluding remarks, he gives a brief standard account of the Twelfth Imam, Muhammad ibn Hasan, the anticipated Shi'i Mahdi, adding the well-known hadith: "He will render justice when the earth is filled with oppression and injustice." But he then adds, "and some say that in the extreme western lands *(aqsa-yi maghrib)*, there are cities in his possession and he is confirmed by his children and offspring. But God knows the apparent and the hidden." If *maghrib* is to be understood, even allegorically, as lands west of Herat, then we may take this as a faint allusion to Isma'il and the rising house of the Safavids.[55]

However speculative, the very production of *Rawdat al-Shuhada* on the eve of the Shi'i rise to political power cannot be viewed as sheer coincidence. As a text celebrating the cult of martyrdom, perhaps the most central myth of Shi'ism, *Rawdat al-Shuhada* rendered an important dual function. It "Persianized" the Twelver Shi'i myth as much as it prepared the ground for "Shi'itizing" the Persian world of Safavid and post-Safavid times. This dual function, already underway through Isma'il's campaign for establishing a Shi'i state, is anticipated, and audibly echoed, in Kashifi's work and scripted in his narrative of the People of the House.

For generations after Kashifi, writers of Persian Shi'i eulogies were influenced by *Rawdat al-Shuhada*. Its preacher-friendly style, mixing of Persian prose and poetry, dramatic depictions of tragic scenes, intimate tone, and emotional appeal to idealized moral values acting as an instrument of collective catharsis produced an enduring genre which contributed widely to the shaping of a complex Persian Shi'i psyche.[56]

## CHAPTER 5

# *The Persian* Bayan *and the Shaping of the Babi Renewal in Iran*

In the history of modern reform movements in the Muslim world, the Bayani religion of Sayyid 'Ali Muhammad the Bab (1819–50), otherwise known as the Babi Movement holds a unique place. It is the only religious current which consciously and concretely broke away from Islamic beliefs and Islamic community and initiated a new prophetic cycle with its own scripture, sense of community, and vision. The Babi religion nevertheless was the product of the religious environment of Shi'i Iran, and was deeply influenced by the inherent esoteric culture and apocalyptic vision embedded in that tradition. Some features of Babi thought may also be traced back through the Shi'i sectarian milieu to the religions and heresies of pre-Islamic Iran.

Yet in many respects the Babi movement was a new phenomenon. This novelty can be observed in its social composition and historical development, but more so in the apocalyptic urgency by which it meant to transform the prevailing religion of its time. As the Bab put it, his religion was "a new prophetic creation" *(khalq-i badi')* that had come to advance the cycle of human perfection. "The grand cycle is in progression" *(kawr dar taraqqist)*, he declared at a time when Iran, like the rest of Muslim world, was beginning to experience a sense of despair in the face of Western hegemonic presence and its material and technological advances. The Bab's call for progression in time thus offered an endogenous "modern" answer to the crisis of confidence which has lurked behind the political, economic, and moral fabric of Iranian society.

Such a perspective could perhaps only be entertained in an esoteric *(batini)* worldview with apocalyptic dynamics of its own and with historical precedence in movements ranging from Isma'iliyya and Hurufiyya to the Shi'i-Sufi movements of the early modern period. Yet "esoteric" they all remained, at least in their articulation of new prophetic cycles beyond Islam. The idea of the "Perfect Man" in Sufi thought perhaps is the closest alternative to the problem of terminal prophecy in Islam. The only exception in recent centuries, however, is the fourteenth–seventeenth century-Nuqtavi movement and its advancing of the doctrine of a new "Persian cycle" *(dawr-i 'ajam),* which intended to abrogate Muhammad's mission and terminate Islam.[1] Most esoteric texts, whether speculative or popular, however, externally conform to the overarching primacy of Islam as a system of norms and reference, even though internally they may subvert the sacred text beyond the pale of accepted Islam. The Shi'i doctrine of the Imamate, too, provides a sacred continuity through the line of the Imams only within the frame of Islam. Yet, here, too, the apocalyptic Mahdi in the Final Day, arguably abolishes the rule of the shari'a and effectively ends what may be defined as normative Islam and instead establishes the post-millennial heavenly order.

What sets the Babi movement apart from this Shi'i esoteric tradition is that it eventually escapes the binary of inner *(batin)* versus outer *(zahir)* scheme, hence actualizing what may be called the progression of the "divine sacred" of the inner truth into the outer reality. This attempt to "reveal" the inner sacred beyond the perimeter of the adept *(khawas)* into the world at large set Babism at odds both with the 'ulama, as guardians of the external world of the shari'a and with the guardians of esoteric truth. The Shaykhi school, out of which the Babi movement first emerged, meticulously negotiated the accepted boundaries of the Islamic inner truth and outer reality. The *Bayan*, the Bab's most important text after which the Bayani religion was named, thus denotes "revelation" (*bayan*; lit. explanation) and with a Qur'anic connotation that implies divulging the secret truth, presumably to all people.[2] The Bab applies the term not only to the *Bayan* but to the entire body of his writings, which he considers as key to the secrets of past scriptures. The existential truth that he reveals is for all people to grasp. It is a direct appeal beyond the medium of the elite, whether the mystically adept or the 'ulama of the shari'a.

The *Bayan* thus is primarily a manifestation in words, a written text, signifying the ancient Middle Eastern and Indo-European preoccupation with the scripture that culminated in the Qur'an. Muhammad's "proof" *(hujja)* and "evidence" *(bayyina)* as repeatedly pointed out in the Qur'an is primarily the miracle of his words.

This emphasis on the miraculous quality of words also appears in the writings of the Bab. He not only deliberately imitates the Qur'anic style in his Arabic writings but he suggests that his speed in uttering words and verses as proof of his divine inspiration. Furthermore, he is preoccupied with the cabalistic quality of letters and words. This, too, is part of an ancient esoteric tradition that stretches from ancient Babylonian, Judaic and Greek to Sufism and folk Shi'ism. The Bab hence employs the Qur'an, and especially the esoteric reading of it, as a point of reference for creating his own innovative text.

This revelatory quality of the *Bayan* can be better understood in the context of the Qur'anic commentaries that the Bab produced throughout his short prophetic career. Esoteric Shi'ism upholds the view that the existing Qur'an is incomplete and has been corrupted, especially on the issue of 'Ali's succession and the legitimate right of the House of 'Ali. The true Qur'an was believed to be in the Heavens and only to be revealed by the Mahdi on the Day of Resurrection. Thus the *Bayan* of the Bab, who himself was a *sayyid* (i.e. a descendant of the House of the Prophet), and the entire body of his work were perceived as an apocalyptic revelation meant to bring down the heavenly book in its entirety and offer it to the people as the true test of their loyalty.[3] Hence the term *furqan* (the separator), which is one of of the Qur'an's attributes, in the writing of the Bab is used for the *Bayan* as a text that distinguishes between believers and unbelievers.

The Islamic "occult sciences" *(al-'ulum al-ghariba)*, specifically the cabalistic *jafr-i jam'* and its corollary the numerological *hisab al-jammal*, were viewed as tools to discover the apocalyptic secrets of the scripture and to sort believers and unbelievers. Similarly, belief in the magical quality of *awrad* (incantations) and *adhkar* (prayers) placed great emphasis on the recitation and chanting of divine words. The talismanic images and composition (and by extension their calligraphic production) were of equal significance. As evident in the writings of the Bab, including the *Bayan*, neither oral nor written texts are exclusively, or even primarily, valued for their functionality as a means of communication.

As a meditative tool, remembrance *(dhikr)* in the Babi writings, as in Sufi tradition, served an entirely different purpose of intuitively revealing to the reader the divine sacred. The author of divine words, in this case the Bab, as well as those who utter them, hence all become part of the magical practice of incantation *(dhikr*; same word as "remembrance" mentioned above). That the Bab calls himself the *dhikr* therefore implies that he is an inseparable part of his own text, more specifically his own *Bayan* manifestation.[4] This discourse between the text, the author, and the reader is one of the remarkable features of Babi writings.

## *The Bayan as Discursive Scripture*

To better appreciate the innovative character of the *Bayan* and its place in the Babi corpus we must first look at the circumstances of its authoring and highlight some of its pertinent themes. The *Bayan* was viewed by the Bab and his followers as even by his opponents as the most consistent exposition of Babi theology, law, and the Babi worldview. Begun in 1263/1847 in Maku, where the Bab was incarcerated in a frontier fortress in northwestern Azarbaijan, the *Bayan* received relatively wide publication within Babi circles even during the Bab's own short life. Before his execution in 1266/1850 his followers possessed copies of the yet incomplete *Bayan* and already were speculating on the identity of the Babi-promised messiah. The so-called "He Whom God Shall Manifest" *(man uzhurullah)* had received an extraordinary preferential treatment in the *Bayan* as the forthcoming "manifestation" who will complete, alter, enforce, and even abrogate the laws of the *Bayan*.[5]

Yet, as a text consciously conceived as a scripture, the *Bayan* barely provides a comprehensive social program or even a coherent vision of communal life. Rather, it is a curious blend of speculative theology with shari'a-orientated legal and pragmatic instructions. Its organization is governed by a sacred numerological order that is replicated beyond the text in the community of believers and further through the entire divinely ordained universe. The *Bayan* originally perceived of having nineteen units *(wahid)*, each consisting of nineteen chapters *(bab)* to constitute the total of 361 chapters (19 x 19 = 361). According to the *abjad* numerical system the number 361 equals the Qur'anic phrase "all things" *(kullu shay')*, a highly charged mystical notion often rendered as the Being *(wujud)*.[6]

In reality, the *Bayan*'s divine structure remained incomplete. For uncertain reasons the Bab did not proceed beyond chapter 10 of unit 9 of his book. He may have abandoned it because of lack of inspiration, as a result of his captivity, homesickness, and grief *(huzn),* sentiments that mark the writings of the Maku period. No doubt the looming threat of harsher treatment and even execution were in his mind, especially after the 1848 inquisition in Tabriz when he was interrogated by the 'ulama, humiliated, and physically punished. Later, in his testimony, the Bab assigned the task of completing the remaining units of the *Bayan* to his successor, if suitable conditions prevail. This was interpreted by later Babis as the task of the He Whom God Shall Manifest.[7]

The Bab produced two versions of the *Bayan*, one in Persian and another in Arabic, presumably during the same time period. Though not entirely compatible, they were intended to serve the same objective. Whereas the Arabic *Bayan,* a summary of Babi doctrine, aimed to emulate the Arabic Qur'an, the Persian *Bayan* intended to offer all believers direct access to the canon of Babi theology and law free from any human intermediary and linguistic obstacles. This drive toward the "democratization" of the scripture, reminiscent of vernacular translations of the Bible during the Reformation, was in sharp contrast to Islamic learned culture of the time and the Shi'i 'ulama's textual monopoly. Even by the middle decades of the nineteenth century, very few works of religious scholarship were written in Persian.[8]

The principle of *ijtihad* further reinforced the legal monopoly of the dominant Usuli elite and in effect made lay access to the sources of the sacred law more formidable. The 'ulama's reluctance to employ Persian carried a certain cultural bias in favor of Arabic as the language of religious scholarship. Persian works by the 'ulama were not rare, ranging from Islamic fundamental creeds to the literature of Muharram eulogy and anti-Sufi and anti-missionary polemics. Yet, by the time the *Bayan* was composed, there was little public access to any sacred text, including any Persian translation of the Qur'an. The printed Persian translation of the New Testaments, first published in 1815 and reprinted three times by 1834, was the first widely printed scripture available to the Persian-speaking public. The *Bayan,* which intended to address this cultural lacuna, may have been influenced by the message and tone of the New Testament – there are numerous references in the text to Jesus and the Gospels. Yet, in the main, the *Bayan* came in a long line of such inspirational literature either of Sufi or apocalyptic character, including Isma'ili, Hurufi, and Nuqtavi texts.

The fact that the Bab recommends the printing of the *Bayan* and other Babi writings only confirms his intention for making his works more widely available. In the *Bayan* he specifies:

> About printing *(chap)* and that it is ordained. The summary of this chapter is that printing is permitted in the *Bayan* and whatever is written under its wing and according to it, until the manifestation of He Whom Shall God Manifest. By that time if all [people] are empowered in a manner that they could preserve the divine words in a good writing hand, he then will order it [to be done in long hand]. Otherwise, whatever necessitates his generosity and grace, he will permit. And after that there will be no excuse for any single person before God for not having a [copy of the] *Bayan* so as to remember He Whom God Shall Manifest. It is [to be produced] in best of the hands, not like what is customary today, to the extent that they print whatever bad writing they can lay their hands on. It has reached a stage that the gift price of the Qur'an has been reduced to 28 *nukhud* of silver. If it was not out of concern for the poor [financial] capacity of most believers, no doubt this [i.e. printing] would not have been permitted but now [i.e. in the future] that all live in the shadow of the essence of God's grace, by his permission whoever can write the *Bayan* best, it is favorable for his own being rather than possessing even a well printed copy.[9]

The above passage demonstrates the Bab's pragmatic recognition of printing as an invaluable tool of mass communication in the wake of a new era of greater literacy, even at the expense of condoning the decline of his beloved art of calligraphy. Yet, typical of the *Bayan,* the same passage betrays some of the peculiarities of the Bab's style, which made it difficult to understand, even for educated believers. As noted above, his fascination with speed in uttering "verses" *(ayat)*, no doubt in the manner of the fragmented style of the Qur'an, may have seriously affected his style and tarnished its public appeal. His Persian is often hurried, convoluted, and repetitive, and grammatically leaves much to be desired.

The peculiarities of the *Bayan*, which makes the text at times disjointed and even incoherent, at least by the standards of conventional Persian of the twentieth century, nevertheless betray a certain originality. It is possible to argue that the *Bayan*'s inspirational style was uttered in the form of a discourse with an amanuensis, or more likely, as an expression of the Bab's inner dialogue with his believers. Frequent use of the intimate second person singular and colloquial pronoun *un* (that), instead of the more correct *an*, and similar features of colloquial speech, also illustrate a desire to break away from the formalities of classical Persian so as to incorporate features of the spoken language. His unhappy experience with madrasa education and his consistent resistance to the conventional learning process must have also contributed to his improvised style. Many instances in the *Bayan*, as in his other works, betray an artistic search for a new medium of expression, in language as in calligraphy and in talismanic images, mostly in his favorite *shikastih* (broken) style.

This use of plain Persian in the *Bayan* is often blended with advanced, and at times obscure, technical terms from *hikmat* and *fiqh* literature that carry complex textual references to philosophical and esoteric Shi'ism. This admixture of the colloquial and technical, with philosophical and legal references all wrapped in the Bab's liturgical style, gives the *Bayan* a certain surreal quality which may best be called "postmodern," in the vogue of our time. It is this intuitive quality that invites the reader to experience with the author the esoteric dimension of the text, and through the text experience its unifying context in the external universe, a context that becomes readable through the numerological key of verses, words, letters, and numbers.

This numerological organizing principle of the *Bayan* in its external expression divides mankind into the believers and non-believers, or in the Babi idiom, to the letters of light and the letters of fire *(huruf-i nar wa huruf-i nur)*. The cornerstone of this communal order is the "point of the *Bayan*" (*nuqta-yi bayan*), or the "primal point" *(nuqta-yi 'ula)*, associated with the Bab himself. Emanating from this primal point are the building blocks of the community, the letters *(huruf)* of believers, who are to be organized in words and chapters, identical with the structure of the *Bayan*. The eighteen "Letters of the Living," as the Bab designated his early believers, together with the primal point, constituted the foundation of the Babi community and its revitalizing force. The units *(wahid)* that are to be generated by the Letters, symbolically were to create the Babi community, the so-called all things *(kullu shay')*. The same divine principle is also at work in the organization of time. The new solar Babi calendar of 365 days consisted of nineteen months of nineteen days each plus four extra days known as the days of *ha*. The new year is to be celebrated at the vernal equinox, the Iranian festival of Nouruz. Through numerological equivalents the Bab thus defines as a text the Babi community and Babi time, a symbolic order that is waiting to be read.

The Neo-Platonic binary of microcosm and macrocosm, long enduring in Islamic esoteric circles, is also evident in the Bab's preoccupation with talismans and amulets, which are recommended in the *Bayan*. The production of a series of pentagram figures known as *haykal*s and of circular tables known as *dawa'ir*s were intended to connect the sacred text with its human and universal context.[10] This esoteric symbolism may be viewed as an expression of worldly empowerment and a desire to control the material environment by a thaumaturgic manipulation of words and numbers. In its popularized application, the amulets (s. *harz)* and talismans (s. *tilism)* possess protective and remedial qualities which shield their wearers against bad omens, whether physical or metaphysical. The emphasis on this magical power of words is not accidental. At the time, we may speculate, the Bab, his followers, and countrymen had many reasons to seek a measure of control over intrusive forces that appeared in their surroundings. Among them we may include Europeans.

Indeed, the bipolar division between believers and non-believers in the *Bayan* is further complicated, or perhaps modified, by the presence of a new category of people, that is, Christians. The "letters of the Gospel" *(huruf-i Injil* or *huruf-i alif)* may primarily be read as a reference to Europeans, toward which the *Bayan* remains essentially ambivalent. They are a potential threat to the land of the *Bayan*, and are therefore to be expelled if they pose an actual danger to the security of the community. This assertion may be taken as a relic of the long-standing Islamic prohibition on the entry of the infidel into the abode of Islam, reinforced here, no doubt, because of the menacing European presence. This threat became more tangible to the Bab in Maku, where he could witness Russian advances in the north after two rounds of war with Iran. Between 1805 and 1828 Persian defeats resulted in major loss of territory, a sizable population of Caucasian Mulism émigrés *(muhajirs)* in Azerbaijan province, and a great loss of Islamic confidence and the Qajar state prestige. Earlier, in his carreer as a merchant in the southern port of Bushehr on the Persian Gulf, the Bab also witnessed the growing British commercial and strategic presence in his homeland, the Fars province.

Yet the Bab's entrepreneurial background in part counter-balanced his understandable concern about the foreign presence. He states in the *Bayan* that the letters of the Gospel are not to be entirely avoided, especially if they are "merchants and engage in useful professions." In these cases they are allowed to settle among the believers, even though trade with them is subject to certain regulations. Moreover, Europeans are praised in the *Bayan* for their demeanor and public conduct, their cleanliness, and technological advances. Reference to Europe's printing of books and its regular postal service may also be seen as his recognition of the place of mass communication in the spread of the new religion. He seems to be anticipating the emergence of print culture as the defining character of a modern national community.

On another level, the Bab's frequent references in the *Bayan* to Jesus and his mission demonstrate a deep engagement with the figure of the Christ whom he reportedly rediscovered in the printed Persian translation of the New Testament. This preoccupation evidently goes beyond the Muslim polemical response to the Christian missionaries on the validity of the Gospels and absorbs the Bab on a personal level. He identifies with the story of Jesus and with his forbearance, suffering, and sacrifice. Such an affinity seems to be particularly fitting to the Bab's nonviolent disposition and his denouncing in the *Bayan* of resorting to violence as means of spreading his message. Desire for peaceful growth, in contrast to the dominant paradigm of jihad and military conquest, placed the word, rather than the sword, at the center of *Bayan*'s engagement with power.[11]

In challenging the prevailing norms of his time, the Bab also encouraged greater inclusion of women in the Babi community. He refers to women in the *Bayan* with the talismanic name of "possessors of the circles" *(dhawat-i dawa'ir)*, presumably a gender signifier in contradistinction to men as pentagram frames *(hayakil)*. They are both needed for the building of the primeval letters of the Babi community. Reaffirming women's legal personality in a way similar to Islamic law, the *Bayan* further facilitates more communication between the sexes and imposes fewer gender restrictions, though it does not altogether escape the patriarchal mores of its time. An indication of the Bab's favorable view of women's public role can be observed in the case of Fatima Zarrin-Taj Baraghani, better known as Qurrat al-'Ayn and Tahira. The Bab conferred on her the title of *Tahira* (the pure) in defiance of the charges of immodesty brought against her because of her attempt to remove her facial veil. Furthermore, he recognized her equal rank among the Babi primal rank of the Letters of the Living, an unprecedented position in the Bab's communal sacred scheme.[12]

Other features of an endogenous communal awareness are evident in the *Bayan*'s designation of Shiraz, the Bab's birthplace and capital of the Fars province, as the "mother of all cities" *(umm al-quar')* and a place of pilgrimage for all believers. This significant shift of the center of the sacred from Mecca to Shiraz, especially after the Bab's disillusioning Hajj pilgrimage in 1261/1845, displays a doctrinal autonomy that set him apart from the prevailing Islamic identity of his time. Even though the shadow of Shi'i culture was never lifted from the *Bayan*, there was an urge for what may be called a constructive disengagement from Islam by inventing a new Bayani shari'a tradition.

A number of revolutionary injunctions in the *Bayan*, including the obliteration of all non-Bayani books *(mahw-i kutub)*, aimed at that doctrinal break. The *Bayan* unabashedly commands believers to destroy all books that are not "in support of God's faith *(amr Allah)* and His religion." The Bab's aversion to Islamic madrasa schooling, which he considered as a futile exercise in sophistry and fallacy, may be responsible for this ruling. Yet the severity of this apocalyptic injunction has been softened, as in virtually all similar cases, by placing the final judgment in the hand of He Whom God Shall Manifest.[13] It is as though the Bab viewed his own *Bayan*, and the religion it represented, as a transitory stage in the establishment of a more mature and balanced social order in the future. How close a future remains a mystery, but most assertions in the

Bayan imply an impending appearance of the Babi messiah. It is as though the Bab's disillusionment with prospects of mass conversion and his own incarceration and suffering persuaded him to project into the future the creation of a utopian order.

The messianic hope for this utopian order did not diminish what may be called the divine absolutism of the *Bayan*, and by implication, the mystico-theocratic order it envisioned. The Bab's political vision no doubt acknowledged the believers' collective responsibility, even collective leadership and a shared destiny for the Bayani community. The Bab's own peaceful and nonviolent disposition was also inclined toward the delegation of power to a hierarchical leadership. Yet the *Bayan,* even more than the Qur'an, required from the believer total absorption into the will of a monistic and yet omnipotent God. Every page of the *Bayan* acknowledges the all-embracing power of this divine source and humanity's sheer powerlessness before it. In this community of hermeneutical symbiosis, the Bab does not arrogate great power to the 'ulama or to kings, though both parties do appear in the *Bayan;* rather, ultimate power rests with the unknowable truth *(haqq)* that emanates only in the mirror of all people *(khalq)*, but not through the media of kings and priests. Instead, he manifests himself through successive prophetic "manifestations" *(zuhurat)* that appear at the renewal of each cycle and will appear in future cycles of divine revelation. They are in effect the masters of the universe insofar as they actuate the unequivocal divine will at their own time.

This unsettling landscape of absolute theocracy in the *Bayan,* however, is sharply modified, even undermined, by frequent emphasis on the changing will of God and the impermanence of the human condition. This divine will, the *Bayan* insists, requires successive manifestations and frequent changes of the shari'a according to the needs of the time – an idea that is at heart of the Babi theory of prophecy. The laws of the *Bayan* itself, the Bab constantly reminded believers, will be subject to abrogation upon the appearance of He Whom God Shall Manifest. Believers were repeatedly forewarned that they should anticipate, and indeed welcome, the impending coming of this messiah. Reflecting on his own persecution, the Bab admonishes his own believers for opposing any claim, even if false, lest they impede the appearance of the true messiah. This state of perpetual manifestation borders on a form of pantheistic prophecy whereby any human being can claim to be a manifestation of God.[14]

This democratization of the sacred is one of the most important features of the *Bayan* and directly corresponds to the Babi theory of progressive revelation. The very apocalyptic dynamism that the Bab set in motion was a quest for future human improvement. The ever-growing "tree of the truth" *(shajara-yi haqiqat)* with its seasonal turns, a favorite image of the Bab, demanded that the course of prophetic revelation should continue and even accelerate, with the ultimate aim of human spiritual perfection. This perfection, as the *Bayan* alludes, comes with He Whom God Shall Manifest, that is, not only a person but a state of human development.

The *Bayan* presents a fully fledged version of the Babi theory of prophecy. Like the Qur'an, it considers and recognizes the Abrahamic chain of prophets from Adam on and traces among them a certain historical continuity and doctrinal affinity. Yet, unlike normative Islam, which considers Muhammad as the "seal of the prophets" and interpret that as meaning the end of the prophetic revelation, the Bab, and especially in the *Bayan*, views divine revelation through the prophets, or rather divine "manifestations," as an open-ended and unavoidable process. In an ingenious symbolic interpretation of the eschatological doctrine of the Resurrection *(qiyamat)* in Islam, the Bab considers each prophetic cycle as the end of the old cycle and the beginning of a new one.

The "tree of the truth," which in its Babi interpretation stands for divine interaction with humankind, goes through seasonal turns. Each prophetic revelation and religious tradition that it generates has it own cycle, with the spring of birth, summer of development, autumn of maturity, and winter of decay and death. But instead of the end of each cycle in this theory of progressive prophecy terminating the life of the "tree of truth," the spiral process of cyclical progression in fact leads to its growth and further maturation. The Bayani manifestation, in the Bab's views, is one more in the chain of gradual perfection of human truth (or human wisdom: *ilm*), but with an important exception. The *Bayan* seems to suggest that the advent of the He Whom God Shall Manifest is not merely another cycle of prophecy, like those of the past and even that of the Bab. Rather, it is a divine manifestation that brings mankind into its full maturation, free from any future prophets, and subsequently, of any shari'a-orientated tradition.

## Conclusion

As a text intended as a "revelation" (or *apocalypse*), divulging the esoteric meaning of the Qur'an (and past prophetic revelations as a whole), the *Bayan* came to mark the final stage of the Babi break with Islam. In attempting to establish a new relationship between humankind and the divinity, between the profane and the sacred, the Babi movement thus in a way put an end to the long-held Sufi-Shi'i taboo of differentiating the esoteric form the exoteric. By declaring an independent cycle of revelation, the *Bayan* demonstrated a genuine desire to generate in content and language a new scripture. Yet it did not free itself from the very Islamic (or monotheistic) shari'a model that it set out to abrogate in the first place. In contrast to the Islamic clerical emphasis on Arabic, the Bab's opting for Persian as the sacred language signaled a budding sense of national awareness. Its message of cyclical yet progressive renewal was rooted in Shi'ite as well as Manichaean and Zoroastrian traditions. Both these features, the new language and the message of renewal, presented a discourse of indigenous modernity unique to the modern Iranian religious experience.

It may be argued that it was only through revealing this esoteric culture of Shi'i Islam that a self-educated layman like the Bab could improvise a crucial crossing from traditional religion to an endogenous form of modernity. The essentially progressive, rather than regressive, historical perspective presented in the *Bayan* offered revolutionary potential for the moral and material transformation of Iranian society, a potential that remained unfulfilled even in the twentieth century.

# PART 3

# *Clerical Encounters with Modernity*

## CHAPTER 6

# *Mujtahids and Missionaries: Shi'i Responses to Christian Polemics in the Early Qajar Period*

Among the few cultural encounters between Iranians and Europeans in the early part of the nineteenth century, none perhaps is as remarkable (and so far under-studied) as the Christian–Muslim controversies instigated by the young and fiery English evangelical preacher and proto-Orientalist Henry Martyn (1781–1812). During his relatively short stay in Iran between 1811 and 1812, mostly in Shiraz, Martyn became something of a celebrity and a formidable theological challenge to the Shi'i 'ulama and, in turn, to the Qajar state. While in Iran he also entirely revised, with the help of a member of the Persian literati, his new translation of the New Testament (which was published shortly afterwards in St. Petersburg and in Calcutta). In addition, he wrote a number of polemical tracts refuting Islam, and engaged in disputation with a mujtahid of the city, which resonated in Iranian clerical circles then and later. As his poor health deteriorated – he was suffering from tuberculosis – he headed back to England but died en route in the Armenian town of Tukat in Eastern Anatolia in 1812.

Virtually a martyr for the Church Missionary Society, which initially had sent him off to India, Martyn was portrayed as a champion of Evangelical Christianity who spread the "good word" among Hindu and Muslim "heathens" in India and, more importantly, "prevailed" over Muslim divines in Iran and earned their grudging respect. Nearly two centuries later this episode deserves to be revisited not so much because it throws light on the largely futile Christian missionary endeavors among the Muslims (an exhausted and altogether uninspiring topic), but because of the cultural make-up of Martyn and his Shi'i interlocutors, and the context in which his refutations and the Shi'i rejoinders were produced. The untapped wealth of the available material makes this case an anomaly in an otherwise poorly documented area of Qajar cross-cultural encounters. Martyn's journal and correspondence reveals in particular some aspects of Shiraz intellectual life. The refutations of Shi'i scholars then and later in response to Martyn's polemics engendered a new theological genre known as *radd-i padri* (refuting the padre, as Martyn and other missionaries were known to the Persians); despite the predictable pitfalls of this genre there were also innovative strategies which help us better understand their perceptions of Islam vis-à-vis the all-encompassing presence of Christian Europe. Equally important, the dissemination of the printed version of the New Testament in Persian, one of the earliest examples of Western print culture to appear in Iran, left an enduring mark, though not so apparent, on the Iranian cultural consciousness.

## *An Evangelical Preacher Abroad*

Henry Martyn was a curious mix of scholarship and evangelical zeal, the "right stuff" for the task to which he was recruited jointly by the newly established Church Missionary Society and the East India Company. Son of a local clerk with puritanical persuasions, he was brought up in the austere Cornwall countryside before entering Cambridge, where he studied Mathematics but also excelled in languages. He learned Greek, Latin, and Hebrew, and shortly after graduation, in preparation for his translation and missionary tasks, he learned Arabic, Persian, Bengali, and Urdu, though judging by his many linguistic inaccuracies, he never really mastered Persian.

At the time Cambridge was a fertile ground for recruiting missionaries, often from among country folk who felt out of place in the increasingly agnostic environment of the university. Martyn in turn fell under the spell of the Reverend Charles Simeon, vicar of Holy Trinity Cambridge and a leader of the Evangelical Movement, who was one of the founders of the Church Missionary Society. Founded in 1799, the Society grew rapidly during its first decade, quadrupling its budget between 1803 and 1806, to serve as the proselytizing arm of British colonial advances in India, Southern Africa, and the West Indies, and with a millennial zeal fitting to its task. To encourage missionary activities abroad, Simeon solicited active support from influential quarters in England; his patrons included Charles Grant, Chairman of the Board of Control of the East India Company.

After four unhappy years as a tutor at St. John's, Martyn was ordained as a priest and first assigned to a village in Cambridgeshire. But his hellfire rhetoric soon proved too strong for the homey parishioners. Even when he was employed as the chaplain of the East India Company and dispatched to Bombay in 1805, neither his mentor, Simeon, nor his employer, Grant, or his admirers, believed that his overzealous sermons would go down well with British officials in India. His anti-alcohol preaching to English sailors during his crossing to India, which almost caused a riot aboard, proved the point. Yet it was hoped that his missionary labor among the "natives," and his translation of the New Testament into Persian, then still the lingua franca of India, might give weight to the Christianization of the subcontinent and its cultural assimilation. Ambitions such as this were at variance with the East India Company's official policy of religious non-interference. Yet years of residence in India (1805–11), first in Calcutta and then in the newly annexed frontier lands of Patna and Cawnpore, proved the futility and the hazards of his aggressive approach in the face of Hindu and Muslim hostility and indifference. "Here every man I meet is an enemy," he wrote. A Brahman or a shrewd Muslim secretary, Martyn entered in his diary, "being an enemy of God... is [also] an enemy to me. But he is an enemy too because I am an Englishman." The "four-faced devil" he was convinced, was none other than "the heathen [by whom he meant Hindus], the Mohammedans, the Papists, and the infidels."[1] It is small wonder that the printing of some of his tracts led to a riot in India and in turn precipitated his departure.[2]

Failing health only added to Martyn's frustration. He took the advice of friends and missionary colleagues to visit Iran, not only in the hope of recovery but to revise his obviously less-than-adequate translation of the New Testament. The governor of Bombay, Sir James Mckintosh, had told him that "in order that the Gospel might spread over the world, ... the Oriental world [must be] made Greek by the successors of the Alexander in order to make way for the religion of [the] Christ."[3] Major General John Malcolm, who had just returned from Iran, had more prudent advice when, in Bombay, he warned Martyn about the hazards of "preaching to the Persians or of entering into any theological controversies." He admired Martyn nonetheless for his Arabic as being "superior to any Englishman in India" and his "constant cheerfulness." In his letter of introduction to Sir Gore Ouseley, the British Ambassador Extraordinary, then on his way from London to the Persian capital, Malcolm remarked, "I told him I thought you would require him to act with great caution and not allow his zeal to run away with him. He declared he will not, and I must believe him."[4] Martyn, on the other hand, must have had his own apprehensions, since Malcolm had asked him to make some queries while in Iran on matters unspecified by Martyn, presumably for the compilation of Malcolm's famous *History of Persia*. In a half-serious tone Martyn noted: "perhaps I shall be taken up and hanged as a spy."[5]

Malcolm's concern about Martyn's possible activities in Iran reflected British apprehension (both on the part of the Government of India and the Foreign Office) in allowing missionary propaganda at a delicate time when an improper move could jeopardize the good relations recently resumed between the two countries. Indeed, whether because of coincidence or design, Martyn's visit to Iran acquired a sensitive political dimension. By May 1811, when he arrived in Bushehr, the British envoy, Sir Harford Jones (resident between 1809 and 1811), and John Malcolm from the EIC (who arrived on his second visit in 1810) had just managed to secure the confidence of the Persian government and persuade them to replace Napoleonic France (represented by the Gardane mission) with Britain as a reliable ally in the war against Russia. Unlike France's initial plans, British policy was to act largely as a mediator, rather than to assist Iran, in the first round of the Russo-Persian wars (1805–13). This policy ultimately aimed at securing the defense of British India against France; hence the dispatch of Sir Gore Ouseley and his mission to Iran (1811–14) to strengthen relations and to mediate on behalf of Iran with Russia. As it turned out, Martyn's presence strengthened the hand of the astute English aristocrat to indirectly pressurize the Iranian authorities to comply with British positions.

## *Facing the Mujtahids*

During his eleven-month stay in Shiraz (June 1811 to May 1812) Martyn primary task was the revision of his Persian translation of the New Testament but he also engaged in private discussion and public debate with the city's religious elite, some of which were more frustrating for Martyn than those he had experienced in India.

Many pages of his journal, and much of his correspondence, are filled with disparaging remarks about the "immoral Persians." One almost senses that his tortured evangelical mind had great difficulty in coming to terms with the *bon vivant* Shirazi lifestyle. He wondered that with such degenerated "moral state in Persia... how is it that their nation is not blotted out from under heaven."[6] He began to deliver "the message of the Christ" to "devilish Mohammedans" but soon was "completely disgusted with the land of Fars and with men thereof" because he "lost hopes in ever convincing Muhammedans by argument."[7] Oddly enough, however, despite his disillusionment, Martyn was able to discern among the same Persians a "far more unprejudiced and inquisitive people than the Indians, and not standing quite so much in awe of the Englishman, as their timid natives of Hindoostan."[8]

This grudging compliment to the Persians, made at the expense of insulting the neighboring Indians, was rooted in Martyn' s experience both with the defiantly Shi'i 'ulama and his encounters with latitudinarians among the Sufis and others on the fringes of the Shiraz intelligentsia. One of the earliest Europeans appearing on the Persian horizon, Martyn was received with curiosity, even amusement, for his charm and his linguistic abilities. To the Persians the *padri-yi farangi* was a "man of God" *(mard-i khuda)* who, unlike European diplomats, soldiers, and merchants, was interested in debates and disputes about familiar issues of religion, however daring and even offensive his style might have been. Even if to the urban elite he was an overzealous polemicist, he could be tenderly challenged, even with a certain skepticism or candor, or questioned as a source of information to satisfy their growing thirst for things European or even to confirm their agnostic doubts about their own religion. Whatever was the case, he was an enigma who revealed Persian fears of European imperial intentions toward their country. He confesses that:

> The prevailing opinion concerning me is that I have repaired in Shiraz in order to become a Mussulman. Others more sagacious, say, that I shall bring from India some (5,000) or more under pretence of making them Mussulmans, but, in reality, to seize the place. They do not seem to have thought of my wish, to have them converted to my religion; they have been so long accustomed to remain without proselytes to their own.[9]

Such xenophobic speculations, childish though they may sound (if indeed we believe the accuracy of Martyn's statement), is more understandable if one notes the strains on the frontiers of the not-so-well Guarded Domains of Persia both against the Russians in the north and against the rapid expansion of British India in the southeast. From the Persians' perspective Martyn's polemics provided convincing proof of British ambitions. His challenge touched the very religious integrity of Qajar Iran which, as a Shi'i society, was even more conscious of its exclusive identity than neighboring multi-confessional India or the Ottoman Empire. Yet Iran proved to be more responsive to Martyn's challenge than both its neighbors, perhaps because of the deep chasms and religious-moral crisis that existed within its seemingly unanimous Shi'i identity.

While in Shiraz, through his host Ja'far Khan Nawwab (originally of the Indian family of Nawwabs [anglicized as *nabob*] of Masulipatam) and one of Malcom's contacts, Martyn first met some of the students of the chief mujtahid of the city, Mirza Ibrahim Fasa'i. Finding it difficult to give up his evangelical missionary habits, Martyn did not miss the opportunity to enter into familiar debates about the validity of Islam and Muhammad's prophecy. It was as a result of these preliminary discussions with members of the Nawwab family that he was invited a number of times to meet with Fasa'i himself. The outcome of these interviews was the exchange of four polemical tracts, the first of which was written in Arabic by Fasa'i in response to Martyn's verbal objections. Martyn countered Fasa'i's *risala* with two of his own in Persian, spelling out his refutation of Islam and specifically the Qur'an. The third tract by Martyn, again in Persian, highlighted the points of convergence and divergence between Christianity and Sufism and was the outcome of long hours of debates with a number of mystics and philosophers in Shiraz.

Engaging in these debates was not always spontaneous. On his way to Iran, Martyn has already collected a number of anti-Islamic polemics then in circulation in Europe. They were mostly based on earlier polemics from the Renaissance and of the early Middle Ages.[10] In Bombay he even had produced an Arabic tract for the benefit of his friend and colleague the Jewish convert Joseph Sabatiani, to be incorporated into his new Arabic translation of the New Testament. Sabastiani, known as Yusif Padri, himself had engaged in polemical debates in Isfahan shortly before Martyn's arrival. The questions and answers in the exchange between Fasa'i and Martyn betray a distinctly scholastic flavor borrowed from medieval Christian and Muslim polemical sources. Yet, if the objections were familiar, or redundant, the response strategy was new; which makes the exchanges and the literature produced around them particularly valuable.

Mirza Ibrahim Fasa'i, an Usuli jurist of great influence in the Fars province, had studied in Najaf under such prominent scholars as Sayyid 'Ali Tabataba'i. He did not however share the habitual Usuli disregard for philosophy *(hikmat)*, and being from Shiraz, almost by default he had some leanings toward Mulla Sadra's theosophical school. In the first decades of the nineteenth century Shiraz was not yet entirely conquered by Usuli jurists, and mujtahids such as Fasa'i faced lively competition from Ni'matullahi and Zahabi Sufis, not to mention closet agnostics. Fasa'i's interest in *hikmat*, moreover, was complemented with a spirit of revelation which contrasted not only with Martyn's zeal and arrogance but the haughtiness of many of Fasa'i's Usuli colleagues.[11] At the beginning of his *risala* Fasa'i noted:

> Since a certain Christian priest has requested me to set down the proofs upon which I rely respecting the mission of our Prophet Muhammad after Christ, upon our Prophet and him be peace, it became my wish to write the following pages, hoping they may be of advantage to him, or to others who are in quest of the truth: and should he think proper to reply, it is hoped he will refrain from a mere strife about words, which is at best, but the offspring of folly: "for God direct whom he pleased into the right way." And may he grant to both him and us a disposition to justice, as well as an aversion to prejudice and mere dispute.[12]

Fasa'i's Arabic *risala*, in contrast to the author's oral philosophical discourse with Martyn, was produced in the conventional scholastic fashion on the theme of "specific prophecy" *(nubuwwa khassa)* and carried all the signs of theological tedium associated with such literature. As opposed to "general prophecy" *(nubuwwa 'amma)*, which argued the general benefits and proofs of divine prophecy as a whole, "specific prophecy" argued the veracity of Muhammad as the prophet of Islam and offered "proofs" *(hujaj)* and demonstrations *(bayyina)* in support of his divine mission.

Theologically this debate fell under the principle of "prophecy" *(nubuwwa)*, one of the fundamental articles of the Muslim faith that argued Muhammad's superior status as the "seal of the prophets" *(khatam al-nabi'in)*. Such doctrine had interested theologians often in the Islamic past whenever Muhammad's prophetic authenticity or his finality was challenged by religious subversives from within the community or from those outside. The cross-confessional debates of the Umayyad and early Abbasid periods and disputations in Islamic Spain set the tone for much of polemical literature on the subject and governed scholastic strategies in response to Christian, Jewish, and Zoroastrian refutations of Islam.[13]

To the early nineteenth-century Shi'i mujtahid*s* of Iran, Fasa'i among them, these debates, and the polemics produced about them, were merely academic. Having been preoccupied most of the time with the study of jurisprudence *(fiqh)* and the "roots of jurisprudence" *(usul al-fiqh)*, the mujtahids' familiarity with theological points such as the doctrine of "specific prophecy" was merely an academic tool often used to demonstrate their scholarly ecumenicity *(jami'iyya)*. Even though, at least since the seventeenth century, there were new challenges to the Iranian 'ulama, most notably from the Portuguese Jesuits based in Goa, by the nineteenth century these memories had largely faded in the isolating world of legalistic scrutiny of the Qajar period. The most significant Safavid response to the Jesuit challenge was the Persian *al-Lawami' al-Rabbaniyya fi Radd al-Shubha al-Nasraniyya* by Ahmd ibn Zayn al-'Abidin 'Alawi 'Amili, a learned descendant of Karaki. This work was barely known to the nineteenth-century Iranian 'ulama.[14]

Indeed, before the arrival of Martyn and Sabastiani there was little incentive for the Shi'i 'ulama to engage in anti-Christian polemical debates even though they produced a large body of anti-Sufi, anti-Jewish, and later anti-Babi refutations. Even the threat of Russian intrusion during and after the first Russo-Persian wars (1805–13) – which led to the first compilation of a series of *Jahadiyya*s by the leading mujtahids of the time at the request of the Qajar states and under the auspices of Mirza Buzurg Farahani Qa'im-Maqam I – triggered little, if any, anxiety or urgency to try to prove the status of Islam as a superior religion.[15] For Shi'i society, at least within the parameters of official theology, the question of "specific prophecy" of Muhammad was a given fact unchallenged and unchallengeable. From the official standpoint of the Shi'i 'ulama, there were other urgent threats to be dealt with, challenges that defined more clearly the boundaries of formal Shi'ism, ranging from defiance of Sunnism to the more familiar adversity toward Sufis. On the surface, none of these "heresies," as the non-shari'a currents were labeled, manifestly questioned the doctrine of "specific prophecy," at least not before the emergence of the Babi movement in the middle of the century.

Fasa'i's mode of argument against Martyn thus revisited some neglected areas in the Shi'i theology and hence mirrored the Shi'i mujtahids' obvious weaknesses in debating anything beyond mundane points of jurisprudence. The *risala* addressed to Martyn primarily relied on the Islamic definition of miracle *(i'jaz, mu'jiza)*, as proof of prophetic authenticity, in contradistinction to "extraordinary feat" *(kharq 'adat)* and to magic *(sihr)*. The differentiation was necessary in order to argue Qur'anic eloquence *(fisaha)* as Muhammad's greatest miracle. In this regard, remarkably, Fasa'i emphasized the relativity of prophetic miracles and qualified them according to their time and location. Muhammad's miracle, he argued, could only happen among Arabs who could appreciate his eloquence. Yet despite such an assertion, he urged his reader to consider Muhammad's miracle as perfect and thus timeless. In contrast to the miracles of past prophets, Fasa'i wrote, Muhammad's was not based on ephemeral impressions *(hissiyat)* but on rational discernments *(idrakat 'aqlaniyya)* as recorded in the text of the Qur'an. Other miracles attributed to Muhammad on the basis of a single or frequent reporting *(tawatur)*, he believed, could be viewed favorably only if they collaterally confirmed the miracle of the Qur'an. "If you examine this question for yourself, turn to the illustrious Qur'an, there you will find his miraculous powers so established as to remain unimpaired till the Day of Resurrection."[16]

Martyn's first Persian responses to Fasa'i were systematic in argument yet decidedy less tolerant in tone and approach. He disputed not only the relativity of time and circumstance as criteria for miracles but doubted the Islamic notion of Qur'anic eloquence as proof of Muhammad's divine mission. Instead he defended frequent reporting as a legitimate method for accepting Christ's miracles, as reported in the Gospels.[17] This no doubt was a reaction to a criticism implicit in Fasa'i's argument that, unlike the Qur'an, which was a "revealed" text, the Gospels were merely reports about Christ and could not be relied upon without corroborating textual evidence. As in other instances, here Shi'i critical assessment of the Bible was closer to modern biblical study, then in its inception in Europe, than to Martyn's evangelical proclivity, even though he was equipped with a Cambridge degree in mathematics.

In his following tract, the second in Persian, Martyn's tone is distinctly poignant and irritated; an indication perhaps, as his journal reveals, of a change from the dignified mood of the earlier discourses. He began the tract by dwelling on the familiar polemical charges against Islam's historical advances by sword, coercion, and booty and Muhammad's fashioning of Islamic doctrine based on his own "selfish desires" *(khwahish-i nafsani)*. As an example, Martyn resorted to the charge of Muhammad's unbridled urge for women (complete with stories of Mariyya, the Coptic wife of Muhammad's adopted son) which, he argued, was the ground for allowing polygamy in Islam. Yet the crux of his attack was on the Qur'an itself, which he characterized as a humanly manufactured text devoid of eloquence, unsystematic, repetitious, contradictory, and brimming over with platitudes, historical errors, and plagiarized biblical stories. Moreover, he denounced Muslim criteria for Qur'anic eloquence as self-serving and argued that its presumed unmatchable quality is nothing but an age-old Muslim illusion.[18]

## *Context, Controversy, and Subtext*

So far as the content was concerned, little new was to be found in the above exchange, either in Martyn's attack or Fasa'i's response. With a few exceptions aside, the exchange could have taken place centuries earlier, in Baghdad, Andalus, or Damascus. Yet what made the debate significant, and controversial, was not so much the text as the context. Martyn represented a European movement of religious awakening reacting to the unsettling forces of industrialization and enlivened by the new possibilities of an expanding colonial empire. Fasa'i, and many of his Iranian co-religionists, who then and later tried to refute Martyn, represented a religio-national community, at least on the surface confident of its own identity, even complacent about its place in the world and not yet fully aware of the waves of Western military, diplomatic, and eventually cultural intrusions that were soon to arrive.

Almost immediately following the Martyn–Fasa'i exchange, whether because of Martyn's own claim that he had "prevailed" over the mujtahid, or more likely because of anti-Usuli sentiments in the city that wished to see Fasa'i subdued, there was a sense of religio-cultural anxiety. The call to respond to the Christian polemist soon spread beyond Shiraz and led to the production of a number of refutations that aimed to address Martyn's objections more comprehensively and from angles different from those of Fasa'i. One of the earliest was entitled *Nur al-Hidaya fi Ithbat al-Risala* (the guiding light in proof of [Muhammad] mission); it was written by another Shirazi mujtahid, Mirza 'Ali Akbar Mudarris Shirazi (with the penname *bismil*) of the Nawwab family (and presumably a relative of Fasa'i),[19] as a catechism in response to Martyn while he was still residing in Shiraz.

Mirza 'Ali Akbar first resorted to the predictable logical tedium of frequent reports to validate – in contrast to Fasa'i – the non-textual miracles of the Prophet. Relying on such works as Majlisi's *Hayat al-Qulub*, the author offered an amusing litany of popular Shi'i beliefs about Muhammad's, and the Imam's, miracles, ranging from the better-known story of splitting the moon *(shaqq al-qamar)* to the more grotesque account of a half-eaten broiled chicken: Abu Jahl denied the validity of this miracle as testimony of the Prophet's veracity. The Prophet eventually restores the consumed half of the chicken and transforms it into a heavenly bird. Even more than Fasa'i's solemn, and concise, yet scholastic high ground, Mirza 'Ali Akbar's hurried and innocuously mundane rejoinder was a visible embarrassment to the leading 'ulama and government authorities. These inadequacies were viewed as a scandal for the clerical establishment, and in the long term as incentives for the public to convert to the religion of the Europeans.

Immediate efforts to commission comprehensive rejoinders were proof of such concerns. At least seven major rejoinders were produced over the next five years, reflecting a wide spectrum of theological approaches. With few exceptions, however, they did not substantively add to existing Shi'i theological positions. By the end of Fath 'Ali Shah era (1834) there were at least twenty-eight "refutations of the padre" by Shi'i jurists, philosophers, Sufi scholars, and lay writers. The earliest, and in many way the most significant, were commissioned by the Qajar state and patronized by the influential Mirza Buzurg Qa'im Maqam Farahani (father of Mirza Abul-Qasim), minister to the crown prince 'Abbas Mirza in Azarbaijan. The first, by the Sufi scholar, Mulla Muhammad Riza Hamadani, entitled *Irshad al-Mudillin* (Guide to the Erroneous), was compiled in 1227/1812 while Martyn was still in Iran. Hamadani also produced at least two other related works before 1815. Simultaneously, another important Ni'matullahi Sufi from Isfahan, Zayn al-'Abidin Husain 'Ali Shah, produced a rejoinder in response to both Martyn and Sabatiani. More than a year after Hamadani, Mirza Abul-Qasim Qumi (better known as Mirza-yi Qumi), the influential Usuli jurist, produced his *fiqh*-orientated *Radd-i Pardri* at the request of the shah. This work remained incomplete. Shortly after, in 1230/1814, the contentious scholar Mirza Muhammad Akhbari also wrote his *A'inih-yi 'Abbasi* (or *Amali 'Abbasi*) at the request of 'Abbas Mirza (and possibly in competition with his Usuli rivals such as Mirza Abul-Qasim Qumi). The teacher of philosophy in Isfahan, Mulla 'Ali Nuri, felt enough urgency to temporarily suspend his teaching circle and devote his time writing *Hujjat al-Islam* (the proof of Islam) in 1232/1816 in response to missionary attacks and more specifically to Sabatiani. In 1233/1817 the influential jurist and theologian Mulla Ahmad Naraqi produced his voluminous *Sayf al-Umma va Burhan al-Milla* (the Sword of the Community and Proof of the Nation), the only one of the early rejoinders to be published in Iran thirty-three years later, in 1267/1850. A number of Najaf jurists, among them Sayyid Muhammad Karbala'i, better-known as Mujahid, also produced anti-missionary polemics though not directly against Martyn.[20] Moreover, Mirza Buzurg Qa'im Maqam Farahani himself produced a rejoinder, summarizing other responses as he had earlier produced a similar *jihadiyya* compendium in 1805.[21] By the middle of the century refutations of padre, now a genre of polemics, were commonplace. Even the eccentric historian Mirza Muhammad Hashim Asaf, better known as Rustam al-Hukama, produced a "*radd-i padri.*"[22]

Though much of this literature was a reworking of medieval arguments, at least in three salient points there were breakthroughs in polemical discourse. First was a new strategy in *usul al-fiqh* devised by Shi'i jurists in questioning the prophethood *(nubuwwa)* of Jesus, what came to be known as "scriptural argumentation" *(ihtijaj kitabi)*. Second, and perhaps the most remarkable, was an emphasis, mostly among the Sufi writers, on the evolutionary *(takwini)* nature of prophethood as proof of Islam's validity. Third, was a more thorough reading of the Bible, both the Hebrew Bible and the New Testament, by Shi'i scholars not only in search of prophecies regarding Muhammad's revelation but to highlight what they considered discrepancies, contradictions, corruption, and divinations *(tahrif)* in the Christian holy scriptures. In all there was a certain rhetorical robustness in the literature, different from the tedium of the juristic and theological texts, but still barely crossing the permitted boundaries of Islamic orthodoxy.

From the methodological point of view, the "scriptural argumentation," first set forth by Mirza-yi Qumi, gave Muslim scholars the necessary logical tool to question the legitimacy of Christ's prophecy and engage in a wider biblical criticism in defense of their positions. In what might be called a "phenomenological" approach, Qumi argued that since the "evidence" (or "validity," i.e. *hujjiyat*) of the Qur'an is denied by Christians, it is logically impossible for them to expect Muslims to believe in past prophets, including Jesus, on the basis of the Qur'anic evidence. This, he proposed, was what was inferred in Martyn's refutations. Relying on Qur'anic advice to resort to the "the best method of disputation" *(tariq-i mujadila bar wajh-i ahsan)*, he virtually set aside "transmitted proofs" *(hujjiyat-i naqli)* based on Qur'anic evidence in favor of the "sound evidence of reason" *(hujjiyat-i 'aql-i qati')*. As a good Usuli he then relied on the principle of "preferential reasoning" *(istihbab)* to set forth a complicated argument against the "continuity" *(istimrar)* of Jesus' "absolute prophecy" *(nubuwwat-i mutalaqa)*. Even if the "very prophecy" of Jesus, what Qumi defines as "*mutlaq-i nubuwwat*," is accepted by Muslims as an assumption (or supposition, i.e. *zann*), based on "preferential deduction," it is impossible to prove it unconditionally *(bila-qayd)* based on the available textual evidence. But prophecy, Qumi argued, being one of the articles of faith, required certainty *(qat')* and not mere assumption *(zann)*. Despite some scholastic acrobatics, implicit in this argument was a sense of relativity, which though not denying Jesus' prophethood, subjected it to the condition of time and circumstance. Yet Qumi was careful not to extend this argument too far, since he must have been aware of its applicability to the Islamic doctrine of Muhammad's "finality" *(khatamiyat)*. The rest of Qumi's incomplete *risala* employed familiar attacks on the Trinity and other Christian doctrines long disputed by Muslim polemicists and, inevitably, he fell into all the familiar scholastic pitfalls which for centuries characterized such works.[23]

Whether explicit or, more often, implicit, "scriptural argumentation" was evident in most later Shi'i rejoinders. Mulla Ahmad Naraqi's *Sayf a-Umma,* offered a perfect example. "Muslim's confession of Jesus' miracles," he argues, "rests on the prophecy of the seal of the Prophets [i.e. Muhammad]." He argued that not only the "transmitted" *(naqli)* evidence of the Qur'an but the evidence of reason *('aql)* dictate that the advent of the prophets should follow a certain rational "order" *(tartib)* whereby every new revelation abrogates *(naskh)* the "laws and dogmas" *(ahkam va shari'at)* of previous prophets. Naraqi's mystical *('irfani)* proclivities are more evident is his articulation of the notion of prophetic progression. Here he resorts to the doctrine of "divine favor" to argue that, since mankind is social by nature *(madni al-tab'),* God invariably shows his favor by sending prophets for guidance of communities. These are endowed with divine inspiration, leadership, and an abiding shari'a.[24] Further, Naraqi's Usuli training leads him to an extensive reassessment of the New Testament in which he widely relies on the Hebrew Bible to refute the Christian orthodox doctrines of the Trinity and Christ's miracles, and also the textual distortions in Christ's message introduced by his disciples (and in particular Paul).

Naraqi, who lived in Kashan, and was readily helped in his task by the city's rabbis, frequently quoted Old Testament passages in Hebrew is support of his points. Throughout he showed a measure of anti-Jewish scorn and abuse, presumably to protect himself against charges of collaboration with the Jews. Yet he particularly dwelt on the Jewish messianic prophecies regarding the advent of the Messiah *(Mashiah).* Without hesitation Naraqi recognizes the subject of these prophecies as no other person than *Ahmad*, the name by which Islamic theology detects Muhammad in the Bible.[25] He must also have had access to European anti-Catholic polemics. In several instances he quotes passages in Latin (transcribed in Persian) in order to demonstrate, predictably, distortions *(tahrifat)* in Christ's original prophecy about the advent of Muhammad.

Before Naraqi, and arguably a more articulate response, was produced by Mulla Muhammad Riza Hamadani. He was the author of the above-mentioned 1812 *Irshad al-Mudillin* (the abridged translation of this work is the core of Lee's *Controversial Tracts,* perhaps is the first work by any living Iranian to be translated into a European language).[26] He employed the same doctrine of divine grace, or the "principle of [divine] favor" *(qa'ida-i lutf)*, to argue the continuous need for prophetic revelations and, in turn, for Muhammad's prophecy. A Ni'matullahi Sufi originally from Hamadan with the *tariqa* name of Kawsar 'Ali Shah, he was a disciple of the martyr Sufi saint Nur 'Ali Shah and later a leading scholar in the Tabriz circle patronized by 'Abbas Mirza and his minister Mirza Buzurg Farahani.

Hamadani is specific about humankind's need not only for prophets but for vicegerents *(wasi-yi nabi)*. "He is considered as one of those means by which divine intentions may be accomplished ... And divine intentions are that men may advance towards perfection by the cultivation of every virtue, both practical and theoretical (material and intellectual) and avoid extremes in both camps." Unmistakably Shi'i-Sufi in his outlook, Hamadani's almost Mutazilite regard for God's obligation to guide humankind no doubt is a variation on both

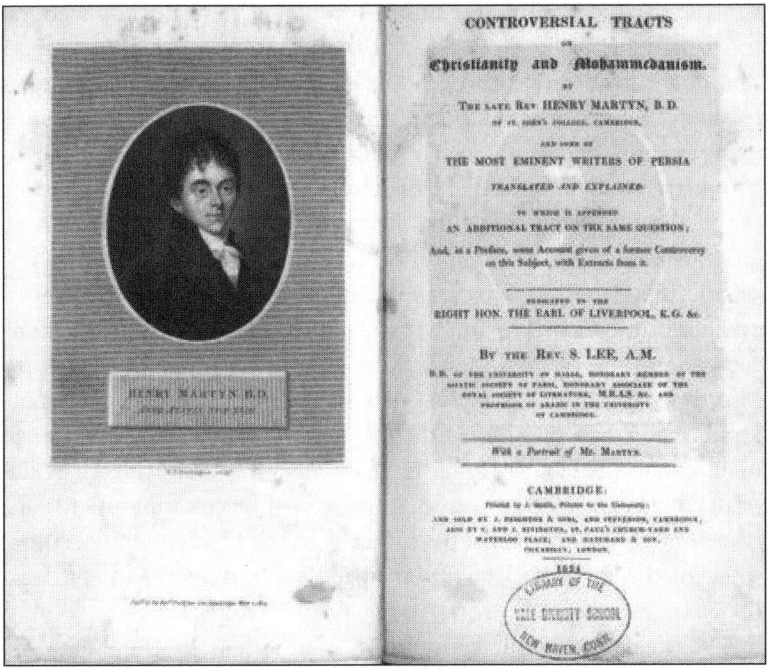
CONTROVERSIAL TRACTS

Christianity and Mohammedanism.

The late Rev. HENRY MARTYN, B.D.

THE MOST EMINENT WRITERS OF PERSIA

TRANSLATED AND EXPLAINED

AN ADDITIONAL TRACT ON THE SAME QUESTION;

And, in a Preface, some Account given of a former Controversy on this Subject, with Extracts from it.

RIGHT HON. THE EARL OF LIVERPOOL, K.G. &c.

By the Rev. S. LEE, A.M.

With a Portrait of Mr. Martyn.

CAMBRIDGE:

1824

**Figure 1.** Title page of Lee's translation of the collection of treatises written by Martyn and his adversaries (Cambridge, 1824).

themes of Imamate in Shi'ism and *wilayat* of the Perfect Man *(insan-i kamil)* in Sufism.[27] Such a leader, Hamadani argues, "who has in his power either to execute or dispense with divine counsels, without the danger of mistake, is in the language of theologians termed a prophet, or his vicegerent." From the days of Adam to those of Muhammad, "the necessity of such an instructor must, in the process of time, have become more and more apparent because those whose religious habits were exercised daily would necessarily become more and more prepared for further information." This progression *(takwin)* of divine revelation for the perfection of humankind comes even through more clearly when he underlines the historical relativity of prophecy. "When the time of his [i.e. any prophet's] departure shall have arrived, another charged with the same commission of mercy may supply his place. In this case, should the circumstances of the times be such as not to call for the abrogation of existing laws, the vicegerent of the prophet would suffice, but should there be otherwise, one charged with powers sufficient for that purpose should become necessary." Arriving at such conclusions, namely the necessity for the renewal of revelation, Hamadani recommends recourse to "reasoning faculty" *(isti'dad 'aqliya)*, a course which convinces him of the absurdity of the Sunni practice of following the founders of the four legal schools *(madhhabs)*.

A natural conclusion to the thesis of the necessity of continuous prophetic guidance brings Hamadani dangerously close to denying the finality of Muhammad and the eternal perfection of Islamic revelation for all mankind at all times – the standard doctrine of Islamic orthodoxy. He wisely avoids the debate, as did many speculative Sufis and philosophers before him, yet as a Shi'i he can not avoid addressing the issue of the Hidden Imam. Why, he asks rhetorically, should the "Lord of the Cause" *(sahib al-amr)*, who is in Occultation and inaccessible, be thus considered as an effective source of guidance for mankind, as the Shi'is believe? Here his answer relies on all the pedestrian solutions to the lasting Shi'i problem of Occultation. As the last resort, he considers the people rather than the Hidden Imam responsible for the Imam's Occultation since people lacked, and still lack, the capacity to benefit from God's grace.[28]

The weakness of such a position is not clear to Hamadani, no doubt because in the absence of the Imam he resorts to the Sufi doctrine of *wilaya* as the living proof of God's grace. Yet, understandably in an official refutation to a Christian missionary, he never claims anything more explicit than a *wasi*. The same theological impasse and fear of contradicting the doctrine of the finality of Muhammad is also evident here. Underneath the ornate surface of sound reasoning, there existed in the literature a sense of anxiety and, at times, even desperation. Judging by Martyn's *Journal*, even a high dose of skepticism can be sensed, especially among those in Shiraz who conversed with Martyn rather than responding to him in writing. Even though we should allow room for Martyn's exaggerations, biases, and unfamiliarity with Islamic philosophical and mystical debate, there still exists enough evidence to convince the reader of the depth of such an anti-orthodox discourse.

That is why, in contrast to the mujtahids and theologians, Martyn finds a certain affinity in his dialogue with the Sufis, clearly apparent in his third tract, which was essentially written in response to their doctrinal objections. Some of the Sufi leaders who conversed with Martyn, among them Mirza Baba, a leader of the Zahabi order, and the celebrated Mirza Abul-Qasim known as Sukut, a Ni'matullahi with heterodox views, interpreted Christianity, and particularly the doctrine of the Trinity, in the light of the doctrine of the "unity of being" *(wahdat-i wujud)*. Within such a framework, they claimed that the differences between God and man, and in effect between prophets and the rest of the humankind, pale. Moreover, Sukut even seemed to imply that organized religions, and the Islamic shari'a in particular, are of no eternal validity. When it came to Martyn's aide and co-translator of the Gospels into Persian, Sayyid 'Ali Nawwab Shirazi, a poet and calligrapher (whose penname was Niyaz), such skepticism turned into agnosticism, even "contempt for revelation," and criticism of organized religions and their representatives. One can even speculate that Martyn's whole engagement with the mujtahid of Shiraz was first instigated by Mir Sayyid 'Ali, a relative and former student of Fasa'i. "Persians," Sayyid 'Ali asserted, are "very far from thinking the eloquence of the Qur'an [as] miraculous, however the Arabs might think." Instead, he thought merit should be given to prophets for their "example and instruction." Sufis, Martyn regreted to admit, were "delighted in everything Christian, except in being exclusive."[29]

Martyn was further impressed with the Persians' enthusiasm and curiosity to know not only about the New Testament and the message of the Christ but about contemporary European philosophy, mathematics, physics, and astronomy. The latter subject, predictably, caused some bewilderment among his audience when Martyn drew diagrams to demonstrate the Copernican system of planetary motions. Yet Martyn's own attraction to the exact sciences carried a deep mystical and messianic undertone. With a mixed bag of Newtonian mathematics, which he picked up in Cambridge, and Evangelical millennialism and expectation for an imminent Second Coming, Martyn found a curious affinity with his Persian audience. In particular he shared with them a preoccupation with numerology and the science of letters. He makes a passing reference to an unnamed scholar in Yazd who "has fallen into the same way of thinking as myself about letters, and professes to have found out all the arts and sciences from them. I should be glad to compare notes with him." One is tempted to think that this is a tantalizing reference to the theologian, philosopher, and practitioner of numerology Shaykh Ahmad Ahsa'i, the founder of the Shaykhi school, who at the time lived in Yazd.[30]

## *Translating the New Testament*

Conversing with the Shirazi literati, and amusing them, made Martyn the talk of the town. It is not surprising therefore that the state authorities and the mujtahid establishment began to sense a potential threat in his activities which, if left unchecked, could trigger irreligiosity and dissent. In this context, the Shi'i rejoinders to the English missionary aimed to save those believers who, if left to themselves, could be lured by the skepticism of a small but influential minority of indigenous dissenters who had resisted the hegemony of the Usuli 'ulama and their allies.

The Qajar authorities seem to have realized that "the Martyn phenomenon," may have been effective not only in deflating the mujtahids' egos, but also in potentially damaging Qajar prestige. Martyn no doubt was conscious of the fact that he was protected by the British envoy and that political circumstances favored the ascendancy of his country. This must have been an important factor both in his daring criticism of Islam and in his endeavor to translate and publish the New Testament. The British Ambassador Extraordinary to the Persian court and his brother, William, were both Persianists of some repute. On a number of occasions Ouseley, and the secretary of his mission, the celebrated James Morrier, met with Martyn in Shiraz and again in Tabriz, and in each case Martyn benefited from their moral support.

While in Shiraz he completely revised his Persian translation from the original Greek with the help of Mirza Sayyid 'Ali Shirazi. His co-translator was largely responsible for the style and choice of Persian equivalents. Martyn tells us that in the process of revision Sayyid 'Ali consciously tried to follow the simple Persian style favored by the literary circle patronized by Fath 'Ali Shah. This no doubt is a reference to the "royal society" (Anjuman-i Khaqan) whose members were responsible for the development of the "new style" based on the so called tenth-century Persian poetry of the school of Khurasan. Despite obvious shortcomings, the appearance of the Persian translation of the New Testament was a turning pointing in the Persian religious and literary scene which has remained largely unacknowledged by modern scholarship. It is important to note that the new translation for the first time made available an alternative scripture to the Qur'an. The widely accessible and easily comprehendible Persian translation by Martyn appeared at the time when the Arabic Qur'an was largely outside the reach of average Persians and even rarely studied by the 'ulama as part of their madrasa curriculum.

In 1815, less than three years after Martyn's death, a lavish edition of his translation appeared in St. Petersburg under the supervision of Sir Gore Ouseley. In 1813 on his way back from Iran he visited the Russian capital to mediate the conclusion of the Gulistan peace treaty between Russia and Iran. It is probable that the availability of the Arabic/Persian typeface in St. Petersburg encouraged the British envoy to arrange for this edition for immediate dissemination. It is also likely that the Russian authorities found in Martyn's direct translation from Greek into Persian an affinity with Russia's Greek Orthodox creed.[31] A year later, Mir Sayyid 'Ali, who may have secretly converted to Christianity, went to India (perhaps with the support of the Church Missionary Society) and helped publish in 1816 another edition of the *Payman-i Jadid-i Khudavand va Rahanand-yi Ma 'Isa Masih* (i.e. the New Testaments of our Lord and Savior Jesus Christ) in Calcutta in *nast'aliq* typeface. His efforts as Martyn's assistant were acknowledged on the title page. Copies of this and later editions, printed in the *nast'aliq* typeface familiar to the Persian eye, was published in London by the British and Foreign Bible Society. They were widely distributed in Iran and India throughout the nineteenth century. By 1837 a forth edition was issued.[32]

The publication of the Persian translation in St. Petersburg came at a time when Ouseley was in the Russian capital mediating a peace treaty between Iran and Russia at the close of the first round of the Russo-Persian wars. While in Iran the envoy no doubt had used his newly gained influence with Fath 'Ali Shah to seek permission for the distribution of Martyn's polemical tracts and his translation of the New Testament. It is not hard to gauge the reaction of Fath 'Ali Shah and his ministers, who must have shuddered at the prospect of any such publication. When presented with Martyn's refutation tracts the shah had reportedly said "the Farangis' government and [the] army, and now some of their Mullahs [have] come to the East," a sobering and perhaps truncated remark reflecting the growing fear in the Qajar court of European domination.

Indeed, it was the prospect of printing the Persian tracts and

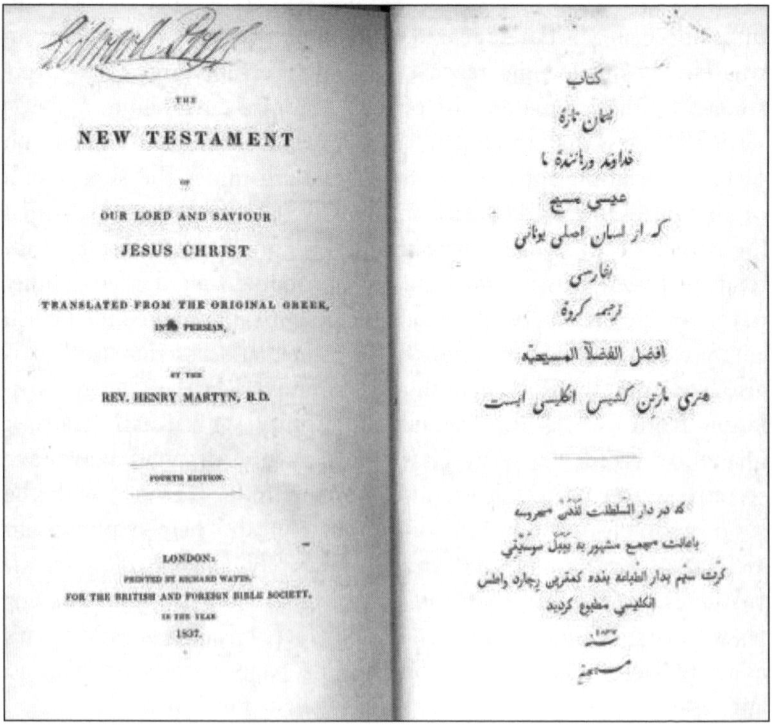
THE
NEW TESTAMENT
OF
OUR LORD AND SAVIOUR
JESUS CHRIST
TRANSLATED FROM THE ORIGINAL GREEK,
INTO PERSIAN,
BY THE
REV. HENRY MARTYN, B.D.
FOURTH EDITION.
LONDON:
PRINTED BY RICHARD WATTS,
FOR THE BRITISH AND FOREIGN BIBLE SOCIETY,
IN THE YEAR
1837.

کتاب
پیمان تازهٔ
خداوند ورهانندهٔ ما
عیسی مسیح
که از لسان اصلی یونانی
بفارسی
ترجمه کردهٔ
افضل الفضلاء المسیحیه
هنری مارتین کشیش انکلیسی است
که در دار السلطنت لندن محروسه
باعانت مجمع مشهور به بیبل سوسیتی
کرت سیم بدار الطباعه بنده کمترین ریچارد واطس
انکلیسی مطبوع کردید
۱۸۳۷
مسیحیه

**Figure 2.** Title page of Martyn's translation of the New Testament, 4th edition (London, 1837).

their widespread dissemination in Iran that persuaded the shah to order Mirza Buzurg to urgently "prepare an answer" to them. This in turn explains the palpable sense of anxiety in the above-mentioned rejoinders by the Shi'i scholars.[33] At the same time the shah also issued a *farman* in 1229/1814, at the request of his "dear friend, the worthy and respectable Sir Gore Ouseley," acknowledging receipt of a manuscript copy of the new translation of the New Testament. The *farman* further stated that the shah has read the entire text in the company of his attendants and found it a "source of satisfaction" to his "enlightened mind."[34] Though the *farman* did not refer to the publication of the New Testament, it is not impossible that Ouseley and later the Bible Society used this decree as an authorization for distributing the printed edition.

By 1815 the postmortem impact of Martyn's challenge must have been truly felt. In his preface to Mulla Riza Hamadani's second refutation of Martyn, called *Miftah al-Nubuwwa* (the key to prophecy), Mirza Abul-Qasim Farahani, son of Mirza Buzurg and the celebrated Qajar statesman and literary figure, is explicit in his condemnation of the 'ulama and praise for Hamadani, his Sufi guide. The new work, which was a supplement to the earlier *Irshad al-Mudillin*, was compiled in 1232/1815. Qa'im Maqam asserted that Hamadani's work, through "envoys of the Christian nation," has reached Europe and "like fear of majestic splendor has spread in all quarters of the land of infidelity, shaken the pillars of idolatry and antagonism, and demonstrated the incapacity of Christian scholars to criticize or refute it." Yet such claims sounded more like empty boasts by a master of wordplay indulging his own Persian readership at a time when Iran was defeated in war and tricked in peace.[35] By 1828, when Qa'im Maqam wrote his famous letter to the 'ulama of Tabriz, presumably on behalf of 'Abbas Mirza, accusing them of worthlessness and betrayal, he twice alluded to the mujtahids' incompetence in responding to European padres, a clear reference to the inefficacy of many rejoinders produced by the 'ulama.[36]

By way of conclusion, two observations may be made corresponding to the above criticism. First, facing the challenge of a Christian missionary (with obvious Orientalist proclivities), Shi'i writers of early nineteenth century Iran were willing partners in polemic debates. They counter-argued Martyn's refutation with refutations of their own. Their strategies were at times novel, and were coupled with an agile rhetoric. Martyn's challenge was within their theological sphere and something to which they could relate. Yet their responses were almost entirely irrelevant to the political realities of Iran and they themselves were uninterested and, most likely, unaware of the context in which Martyn presented his challenge. They viewed him as no more than an exotic European phenomenon and failed to see him as a representative of a pervasive culture with potent modern tools. Most telling, Martyn's publication of the New Testament demonstrated the advantage his printed words held over his Shi'i opponents in narrating to a wider Persian audience Christ's fascinating story of life and death, until then barely known to Iranians beyond the Qur'anic references and Islamic apocryphal texts. In 1817, when Naraqi wrote his *Sayf al-Umma*, he did not seem to have a word for printing. Instead of the Perso-Indian verb *chap kardan* he used *qalib zadan* (presumably from woodblock printing on fabric). He could only urge Muslims, especially the "adventurous, the youth, and people of passion and desire" to refrain from following the behavior of Christians, "for those [Muslims] who follow their desires and whose sense of religiosity is not strong, will be inclined to follow such habits."[37]

Second, Shi'i responses to Martyn, especially the non-clerical ones, revealed a nasent inclination to view consecutive prophetic revelations as historical phenomena confined to their time and place. Such historical relativism, embedded in the Shi'i sense of historical time, could potentially question the suitability of Islam for all ages and of Muhammad as the seal of the Prophets. Though not new in Sufi circles, exposure to Christian polemics at a time of political crisis could encourage Muslims, and Shi'is in particular, to look for not only a messianic (or more correctly Mahdistic) manifestation but for an occurrence of a prophetic renewal. One can almost detect in such polemics the intellectual origins of Babi doctrine, and later the message of progressive revelation. It is not sheer accident perhaps that such a movement of indigenous modernity should originate in Shiraz. Despite tantalizing traits, however, the doctrinal impasse evident in these Shi'i rejoinders points at the acute problem of scholastic Usuli Shi'ism to modernize its theological discourse; perhaps all the way to the Islamic Revolution of 1978–9. After all, Ayatollah Khomeini's ideology of *wilayat-i faqih* is rooted in Naraqi's concept of jurists' *wilayat*, possibly an answer to the issue of prophetic leadership articulated in his response to Martyn.

## CHAPTER 7

# *In-Between the Madrasa and the Marketplace: The Designation of Clerical Leadership in Modern Shi'ism*

"The order of the clerical community *(ruhaniyat)* is in its disorder." Whether genuine or apocryphal, this dictum, popular in clerical circles, expresses the cynicism of those who saw the lack of a well-defined Shi'i hierarchy as an inherent blessing.[1] This anarchic discipline – if such contradiction in terms can be employed – is an important clue for the study of clerical leadership over the past two centuries.

The theory of *ijtihad* as first introduced to Shi'ism in pre-modern times, and elaborated in the Safavid and post-Safavid eras, established a functional relationship between the *mujtahid* (one who applies limited deductive methods to arrive at reasonably practical legal norms) and the *muqallid* (one who emulates/follows the mujtahids in his legal rulings).[2] By the late eighteenth century, mujtahids were distinguished as a religious elite, and qualifications for acquiring the status of *ijtihad* were formulated in some detail. Most notable among these were three qualities: *'ilm* (knowledge of law; more specifically *usul* [jurisprudence] and *furu'* [branches or the actual body of law]); *'adl* (justice in the practice of law); and *wara'* (piety) or *taqwa* (godliness).[3] Such formulation was sufficient to designate a body of mujtahids with substantial juristic authority, but it was barely adequate to create an ecclesiastical hierarchy.

## *Ansari and Qualities of the Supreme Exemplar*

To compensate for this structural handicap, first the concept of *marja'-i taqlid* ("supreme exemplar"; in Twelver Shi'ism, superior judicial status) and then the notion of *marja'iyat-i taqlid-i tamm* (complete authority [of one mujtahid] over the community, the supreme exemplar) were proposed in the latter part of the nineteenth century. In turn, the respective nuances of the three moral qualities mentioned above – knowledge, justice, and piety – were highlighted to demonstrate not only the relativity of *ijtihad* but the superiority of one mujtahid over the others. Thus *a'lamiyat* (superiority in learning) was held by most later jurists as the key prerequisite for *marja'iyat-i tamm,* though no practical set of criteria was ever established for determining its definition.[4]

Indeed, the theoretical obstacles inherent in Imami Shi'ism posed a serious obstacle to any clear definition of superiority in learning and, in effect, to the fuller institutionalization of the religious authority. The inescapable presence of the Hidden Imam made any attempt at theoretical elaboration of a supreme authority a matter of controversy and conflict. The theological grounds for the designation of leadership, therefore, remained inherently limited. The fact that the degree of such legal knowledge could not be determined by any empirical means may not have facilitated the follower's difficult task of choosing a marja', but it clearly established one point: There was no theoretical justification – even in the jurisprudence *(fiqh)* of the dominant Usuli school – for absolute legal authority. Even the greatest of the nineteenth-century legal scholars, Shaykh Murtaza Ansari (d. 1864), who is often regarded by posterity as the first *marja'-i taqlid-i tamm,* is careful to interpret *a'lamiyat,* without ever clearly defining its boundaries, as a comparative quality. Several commentators of Ansari also agree with him on this issue. Ansari delineates this point in his *Sirat al-Najat:*[5]

> What is intended by [the term] *a'lam* (superiority in learning), is the one who is more skillful *(ustadtar)* in deducing God's law *(hukm)* and comprehending it from the lawful evidence *(adalla-yi shar'iya).* For recognition of the *a'lam* and obligation of referring to him, testimony of a single just man *('adl-i wahid)* who is one of the people of insight is sufficient to provide reasonable presumption *(zann).*

In their commentaries on Ansari's tract, none of the seven juristic authorities of later generations challenge the main premises of the above statement. The first of these commentators, Mirza Hasan Shirazi (d. 1896), remarks that, in the absence of positive knowledge *('ilm)*, any degree of presumption *(zann)* would suffice. Even if there is a slight probability *(ihtimal)* that one mujtahid is superior to another, it is not unreasonable to honor that probability.[6] Isma'il Sadr Isfahani, on the other hand, maintains that "the sufficiency of a single just man is open to doubt," presumably implying that two just men *('adlayn)* are needed.[7] Mulla Muhammad Kazim Khurasani sustains the same position: presumption is acceptable "where positive knowledge and proof *(bayyina)* is absent."[8] In contrast, Muhammad Taqi Shirazi maintains that, at this juncture, *zann* has absolutely no validity.

What is at issue is the relative rather than absolute superiority of the jurist. Even though some disagreement does exist on the validity of presumption *(zann),* there is no dispute on the literal meaning of *a'lam* as more learned (*ustadtar* rather than *ustadtarin,* the most learned). Nor is there any major difference regarding the method of observing priorities in choosing a marja'. Except for Muhammad Taqi Shirazi, who denies the validity of *zann* (an un-Usuli position), all three major figures – Ansari, Shirazi, and Khurasani – admit that presumption *(zann),* and even probability *(ihtimal),* which is based on the testimony of one just man would be adequate to establish the *a'lamiyat* of a mujtahid.[9]

The basis for designation of the *a'lam* is thus laid on such shaky grounds that even the most scrupulous followers can make a choice of marja' by merely relying on the testimony of one or two just men. It is difficult to exaggerate the vulnerability of such a formulation. The main guideline for the lay follower is to follow the rule of priority as Ansari states and others agree (with minor variations in Muhammad Taqi Shirazi). The follower is left at the discretion of just men who may recommend diverse choices of *maraji'*. Beyond this, there is little to guide the laity in its choice, nor is there a precise definition of "the people of the insight" beyond its conventional meaning. In effect, the process of observing the priorities and thus choosing one *a'lam* is entirely delegated to the individual follower *(muqallid).* Even other conditions of *marja'iyat,* namely, justice *('adl)* and godliness *(taqva),* are subordinated to prime quality of knowledge. Echoing Usuli jurists before him, Ansari maintains "a more learned [but less] just [mujtahid] is preferable to a more just [but less] learned [mujtahid]."[10] The same rule applies to the quality of godliness.[11]

Though in theory the order of priorities are knowledge, justice, and piety, in practice the determination of these priorities is made by the follower and his "just consultants." Besides the above conditions, no other prerequisites for becoming an eligible marja' have been set except that of being a fully recognized mujtahid *(musallam al-ijtihad)* or fully qualified mujtahid *(jami' al-sharayit)* – a quality which is implicit in the notion of *a'lamiyat*. There is no institutional scheme, as for instance in the Catholic Church, to govern the choice of the supreme clerical authority.

Two conclusions may be drawn. First, based on the evidence in the work of Ansari and later experts, there is no logical ground for constituting a systematic line of juristic authority. The three theoretical prerequisites are subjective ideals which are open to arbitrary interpretations. There are no institutional authorities, such as the church or the state, to verify these prerequisites or to designate their possessors. The ultimate arbiter, therefore, is the follower *(muqallid)* who decides upon, and thus presents his loyalty to, the mujtahid of his choice. This allows the follower considerable room to maneuver; to shift from one *marja'* to another as he pleases (e.g. upon the necessity of obtaining favorable opinions) and to direct religious dues and other funds to the appropriate recipient. The marja' is in effect the willing dependent of the *muqallid*.[12]

Second, the evidence presented in Ansari and others in fact tends to remove the justification for the emergence of a supreme *marja'* on doctrinal grounds. This has more to do with the limitations of Shi'i hierarchical theory, Usuli or otherwise, rather than the failure of prominent experts. Usulism no doubt encouraged rationalization through deductive premises of conventional logic and thus legitimized clerical elitism by distinguishing a body of mujtahids for their expert knowledge. However, it never developed an institutionalized process for creating a complete pyramid. The emergence of a supreme authority, which seems the logical culmination of any hierarchy in pre-modern times, was thus held back, at least in theory, by the presence (more accurately, the material absence) of the Imam. It can be asserted that in no time during the history of post-formative orthodox Shi'ism, prior to Khumeini's doctrine of the Guardianship of the Jurist *(Wilayat-i Faqih)*, were the doctrinal barriers crossed to create a centralized leadership in the same way that *ijtihad* was institutionalized a century before the death of Ansari. The rudimentary regulations for *taqlid* (as they appeared in treatises for public consumption) never indicated – let alone assumed – that "the order of priority" *(al-a'lamu fi al-a'lam)* should be taken to its logical conclusion. What emerged in the second half of the nineteenth century and later came to be known as *marja'-i taqlid* was therefore an informal status based on the practicalities of leadership rather than on doctrinal grounds. Interestingly enough, the most renowned holders of this office, Shaykh Murtaza Ansari and Mirza Hasan Shirazi, were cautious not to attach a doctrinal justification to their own seniority.

Shaykh Murtaza Ansari has often been considered the first recognized *marja'-i taqlid kull* (the supreme source of emulation). But a closer examination of the available historical evidence would pose a question as to the very existence of such a notion at the time of Ansari. The author of *Rawdat al-Jannat,* one of the more reliable biographical dictionaries, who was a contemporary of Ansari, gave a typical description of the celebrated scholar when he distinguished him as the one "to whom at this time came the leadership *(riyasat)* of the Imamiyya:"[13] a title by which the author refers to at least three other immediate predecessors of Ansari.[14] The first explicit reference to Ansari's supreme authority, however, appears much later, in the sources of the twentieth century, where, somewhat retrospectively, his leadership was taken synonymously with the later-coined *marja'iyat-i taqlid tamm.*[15]

The absence of the *marja'iyat,* therefore, stands against the later assumptions that, from the time of Ansari onwards, there existed a unified leadership with unchallenged jurisdiction over the whole community, both mujtahid and lay. But if *a'lamiyat* in its theoretical context is not a decisive criterion, what else has determined the course of evolution of clerical authority over the past century? In other words, what factors have influenced the designation of certain leaders and allowed them to maintain a certain prominence over the rest of the mujtahids? We have already mentioned the mandate of the laity as a major factor. Such a mandate could hardly materialize in isolation from a social context. Rather, it was the outcome of a process in which a set of social, economic, and political factors permitted a prominent figure to stand above others.

Though much has been said in the writings of the jurists on the qualifications and functions of the mujtahids, almost nothing has been mentioned about the status of *riyasat*, a fact which strongly confirms the practical nature of this status.[16] Indeed, the evolution of *riyasat* before Ansari was due to several important elements in the prevailing historical climate. Perhaps one of the most evident features of *riyasat* was the transformation of the mujtahids' function from mere teachers of the madrasa to powerful figures in the life of urban centers. Consequently, the actual situation which emerged in this period was far from the scholastic seniority of the Usuli elite of the 'Atabat in the closing decades of the eighteenth century.

## *Collective Leadership to Individualized Authority*

The Usuli school, even from the early days of its formation in the last decades of the eighteenth century, had nurtured the seed of a more organized clerical body; but even after the eclipse of the rival Akhbari school, it could not overcome traditional Shi'i resistance to institutionalization. Teachers such as Aqa Muhammad Baqir Bihbahani and his early colleagues rose to prominence primarily because of their effective control over the teaching circles of Najaf and, later, Karbala and Kazimayn.[17] Bihbahani (d.1205/1790–1) was posthumously singled out by the 'ulama of later generations as the renovator *(mujaddid)*, the unique *(wahid)*, the master of all *(ustad-i kull)*, and he was addressed as the *aqa* (sometimes *agha*) not only to reflect reverence and gratitude towards the founder *(mu'assis)* of neo-Usulism but more significantly in order to create a patron saint for the emerging clerical "corporation."[18] The professional designation was complemented by some degree of support from the Shi'i merchants of Baghdad who presumably found the Persian Usulis more cooperative and useful for their business than the Akhbaris. The pro-Shi'i Mamluks of Iraq, sometimes in rivalry with the Zand rulers of Iran, were also willing to extend their patronage to the Usuli 'ulama.

Prior to the turn of the nineteenth century, therefore, the Usuli group in Iraq was content with academic independence. The ambitions of senior mujtahids hardly ever exceeded their scholastic means. After the establishment of the Qajars, and especially after the accession of Fath 'Ali Shah (1797–1834), royal patronage became more frequent, and the attention of the Usuli 'ulama further tilted towards Iran. The Wahhabi sack of Karbala (1802) and the Ottomans' brief restoration of direct rule in Iraq (1810), and the ensuing decades of power struggle, tribal conflict, and insecurity (up to 1843), changed the political climate. Moreover, the diversion of Persian supply routes from Basra-Baghdad-Kirmanshah to the Persian Gulf ports of Bushher and Muhammarah dried up local commercial resources, thus affecting the self-sufficiency of the 'Atabat community.[19]

The flow of funds from Iran, India, and elsewhere required a more robust and determined mujtahid with a stamina for dealing with the laity *('awamm)* and the despotic monarch *(sultan-i ja'ir)*. A prototype for such jurists was Shaykh Ja'far Najafi (d. 1228/1813), a disciple of Bihbahani and the famous author of *Kashf al-Ghita'*, the first comprehensive Usuli work of *fiqh* in modern times.[20] Tours for collection of pious alms through Iran, the warm reception and generous gifts from the monarch, Fath 'Ali Shah, and by princely governors and notables, gave a special veneer to the image of this flamboyant Arab mujtahid.[21] Najafi is often considered as the first to have contemplated the *niyabat 'amm* (general deputyship) of the Imam primarily as the collective function of the 'ulama body. The re-emergence of the old Shi'i notion of "deputyship" in a new context, and at times even with an undertone of specific deputyship *(niyabat-i khass)*, consolidated the mujtahids' status and helped to legitimize the regular reception of religious dues. The revival of the *sahm-i Imam* as a regular pension assigned to the 'ulama became a necessary component of deputyship.[22]

Thus, the diffuse leadership was shared among a number of Bihbahani's students. Sayyid Muhammad Mahdi-Bahr al-'Ulum (Tabataba'i) was renowned for his comprehensive learning *(jami'iyat)*; while a son-in-law of Bihbahani, Sayyid 'Ali Tabataba'i, and Mirza-yi Qumi specialized in the methodology of jurisprudence *(usul al-fiqh)*. Others such as Najafi and Muhammad Tabataba'i (son of Sayyid 'Ali) became prominent owing to their control of teaching circles and reception of funds. For more than half a century, close family ties, often with remote but vital genealogical links to the Majlisis of Isfahan, guaranteed the domination of three families – Bihbahanis, Tabataba'is, and Najafis – over the clerical establishment. At least up to the third decade of the nineteenth century, this collective leadership maintained its scholastic facade predominantly as a body of learned men engaged in jurisprudential studies. The founding of new endowments, especially in Najaf, and increasing pilgrimage enhanced the 'Atabat as the academic center of Shi'ism, with a large turnover of works on Usuli themes and a larger body of mujtahids authorized by scions of the 'Atabat.

With all the reverence these teachers enjoyed, from the early decades of the nineteenth century onwards they were overshadowed, at least in some respects, by their own students who returned to Iran after completing their studies. A reverse process to that of the eighteenth century brought many mujtahids back home where relative security and a recovering economy provided attractive alternatives to the overcrowded circles of the 'Atabat. Benefiting from the patronage of central government and local powers, mujtahids like Mirza-yi Qumi in Qom and Mulla Mahdi Naraqi in Kashan were among the first to achieve national prominence. In contrast to the 'Atabat clerical elite, these were representatives of a new generation of 'ulama, often with a humble peasant background, who had risen in rank chiefly as a consequence of their cooperation with the government and of their mediatory functions at a time when Qajars were still consolidating their urban base.

The treatment of Mirza Abu'l-Qasim Qumi (d. 1231/1815–16) by Fath 'Ali Shah demonstrates the latter's efforts to maintain amicable relations with celebrated 'ulama. Qumi, an expert in *usul al-fiqh,* was chiefly responsible for revitalizing teaching circles in the old pilgrimage town of Qom.[23] The shah's support was extended to him mostly by means of cash consignments delivered as religious dues. In one instance, a royal decree specified payment as a "lawful portion of the gift *(pish-kish)* received from the rulers of Farang and agent of frontier provinces of Rum (i.e. the Ottoman empire)."[24] Other forms of patronage included construction and agricultural projects to revive Qom and its environs. Precious gifts to the shrine of Fatima and frequent visits enhanced the shah's image as a protector of Islam and supporter of its venerable representatives. Mirza-yi Qumi was addressed by the monarch as "the refuge *(marja')* of the East and the West," "the mujtahid of the age," "the most learned *('allama)* of the time," "the source of emulation to the people *(muqtadi al-anam),*" and "the refuge of Islam."[25]

The respectful tone with which the Shi'i mujtahid was addressed demonstrates the shah's intention to foster a cooperative religious leadership in Qom. His use of the titles *marja'* and *muqtadi al-anam* seems to have been calculated to promote Qumi and to deliberately undermine the authorities of the 'Atabat at a time when many prominent mujtahids, including some of the latter's teachers, were still active. This is also apparent in the royal contributions Qumi was assigned to distribute among the distressed, the needy, and the *sayyids* of Qom, for which receipts were to be produced. Part of the contributions, however, was allotted to Qumi's own personal use. Implicit in his responsibilities was his mediatory role between the state and its domestic adversaries, sometimes to prevent political crises (as in the case of Husayn Quli Mirza's revolt against his brother Fath 'Ali Shah) and endemic urban riots.[26]

Cooperation over a broad range of juristic and political issues guaranteed mutual legitimacy for the shah and the mujtahids, and it is largely in this context that their veneration by the state can be fully understood. The designation of prominent mujtahids by the early Qajar state proved to be a successful adoption of late Safavid policy. With slight variations, the 'ulama of the early Qajar period upheld positions and discharged duties not wholly dissimilar to those of their late seventeenth-century predecessors. One major difference, however, became more apparent during the reigns of Fath 'Ali Shah and his successor, Muhammad Shah (1834–48). The gradual consolidation of the Persian mujtahids' socio-economic base in effect made them less dependent on the state patronage and more assertive in the pursuit of their own vested interests. This is not unrelated to the apparent decline in the authority of central government during the second quarter of the century. The growing sphere of the mujtahids' power is particularly visible in the latter years of Fath 'Ali Shah and throughout the years of Muhammad Shah. Symbolically, this falls between the second round of Russo-Persian wars (1826–8), when high-ranking mujtahids for the first time made their collective presence felt in the political arena, and the accession of Nasir al-Din Shah, when the dual effect of the state's centralization policies and the rise of the anti-clerical Babi movement engendered some noticeable setbacks for clerical power.

## *Building a Network*

By the second decade of the century, the emergence of a new generation of mujtahids made some kind of collective leadership desirable. Mujtahids such as Sayyid Muhammad Baqir Shafti and Hajji

Ibrahim Karbasi in Isfahan, Mulla Ahmad Naraqi in Kashan, the Baraqani brothers in Qazvin, and others in Tabriz, Tehran, Yazd, and Shiraz created a vast network of jurists who boasted their years of study under Najafi teachers and held a sense of "old boy" solidarity. What allowed them to hold sway over the major urban centers of Iran, however, was not merely their academic credentials or their pragmatic application of Usuli jurisprudence to the needs of their constituencies. The key to their success was more the timely exploitation of the growing political vacuum in the provinces. Even more significant was their direct participation in the economic market. Former peasant youths from remote villages in Gilan, and later impoverished *tullab* of the seminaries of Najaf and Karbala, gradually turned into major investors, landowning magnates, and moneylenders. The flow of pious bequests, alms, and the newly revived *sahm-i Imam* (the portion of the income received by prominent 'ulama as lawful de facto deputies of the Imam), the resumption of the trusteeship of endowments, and even direct participation in the economic market turned some of Ansari's predecessors from humble teachers of the madrasas into significant financiers and investors.[27]

Benefiting from the mujtahids' financial support, numerous seminarians *(tullab)* crowded their teaching circles. A large student body was considered an indispensable asset, since the dispersal of the students after the completion of their studies broadened the mujtahids' network of patronage and influence, and boosted the mujtahids' public image. Equally essential was the ability to maintain amicable relations with the government while at the same time publicly demonstrating a combination of austerity and independence in legal judgment. In this respect, the support of some urban groups, among them merchants, was vital and in some instances decisive in the 'ulama's political behavior vis-à-vis the state. Furthermore, the ability of some of the mujtahids to patronize and protect the *sayyids* and the *lutis* (the urban brigands) put at their disposal an effective force. With such support, control over the pulpits of the mosques was secured and old accounts with the government, notables, and other mujtahids were settled; heretics were punished, mobs incited, and city quarters divided.

The most notorious example of the rapid social mobility of the new generation of mujtahids was Muhammad Baqir Shafti (d. 1260/1844), who owed his fortune and position in Isfahan in the 1820s and 1830s to his skillful blend of juristic acrobatics and economic speculation. The widening gap between the Isfahan government and the central authorities, and the efforts of a semi-autonomous class of bureaucrats, merchants, tribal chiefs, and notables to seek clerical support, provided golden opportunities for Shafti to exploit the delicate balance of power in the city and to forge ephemeral alliances with ultimate advantage to himself.[28]

Yet Shafti was not alone amongst the mujtahids of his time in benefiting from the generous interpretation of jurists' functions. The restoration of Safavid *waqfs* under Fath 'Ali – the reverse of Nadir's policy – brought a large portion of *raqabat-i Nadiri* under clerical control. Skillful justification for the repossession of unclaimed property *(ghasb-i bila-sahib)*, as well as actual participation in trade and agriculture, gave them a substantial economic base.

These successes enhanced the authority of the mujtahids resident in Iran. Though the teachers of the 'Atabat were still regarded as their nominal superiors, real power rested with the former. In addition to their reliable economic resources, the advantage of the Iranian 'ulama over their 'Atabat counterparts was their control of the judiciary – especially under Fath 'Ali when they were given a virtually free rein. Moreover, there was the proximity to large constituencies, the direct supervision of endowments, and an ample supply of local students. Close contact with the government and its provincial agents, however, was a mixed blessing. On the one hand, this furnished the 'ulama with funds, titles, and functions; and on the other, it obliged them to comply with the government's wishes, either by persuasion, coercion, or by fostering rivalries.

A reflection of the growing importance of the 'ulama of Iran can be seen in the adoption of more grandiose titles. Shafti, who probably was the most significant among them, was addressed as *Hujjat al-Islam* (the Proof of Islam), an epithet apparently with no precedent in the history of Shi'ism.[29] Use of this title suggests a degree of reverence reserved for a de facto head. Shafti created an appealing image of a leader who combined material wealth and power with utterances of devotion and independence. Yet his authority did not remain unchallenged even in his home base, Isfahan. Sayyid Muhammad Khatun-abadi, the *imam jum'a* of the city, who carried an equally pompous title of Sultan al-'Ulama, was a sufficient match to Shafti's power.[30] The government's desire to counterbalance the influence of major mujtahids often meant the appointing or reinstating of rival jurists to the semi-official office of *imam jum'a* in the hope of preventing full autonomy from state control.

Diverse as they were, all the above elements – a growing body of high-ranking mujtahids, the accumulation of wealth, and inherent competition between 'ulama – were instrumental in the division of labor and the emergence of a collective leadership. While the high-ranking 'ulama of Iran primarily enjoyed wealth and socio-political influence, the teachers of the 'Atabat were reputed for their scholarship and teaching abilities, even after the eclipse of the "aristocratic" clerical families in the middle of the century. This naturally encouraged competition for public followings and government attention. The Qajar rulers fostered such diversity with some success, hence avoiding the rise of a major clerical figure outside their reach. For them, the hazards of the 'ulama's minor insubordinations at home were still surmountable. Occasional conflict of interest could result in spasmodic turmoil (as in the case of the Shafti and Isfahan riots of the 1830s and 1840s), but most of the time the bulk of the 'ulama remained loyal to, albeit not uncritical of, the Qajars.

Most mujtahids, whether in Iran or the 'Atabat, were aware of their limitations and thus willing to comply with a diffuse leadership. The *esprit de corps* was particularly strong whenever the clerical community was threatened and its legitimacy challenged. Responding to the claims for spiritual guidance of Ni'matullahi leaders – who even during their gradual decline in the 1830s still posed a threat to the 'ulama – Shafti held the "concillium of the 'ulama of the time *(qatib-yi 'ulama-yi zaman)*" solely responsible for "delving into the roots *(usul)* and the branches *(furu')* (i.e. jurisprudence and applied law) until the day of Resurrection." He made it incumbent upon believers to refer all matters of religion to "the righteous 'ulama *('ulama -yi abrar)*" and denounced other claims of religious guidance as "abrogated, void, corrupt, and futile." He further asserted that "the rightly guided 'ulama are the trustees of the illustrious creed and vicars *(khulafa')* of the virtuous Imams.[31]

The sense of monopoly and exclusive clerical rights apparent in Shafti's statement was fundamentally the reassertion of the doctrine of *taqlid* and the duty of the followers to comply with the mujtahids in order to avoid the danger of schism. This standpoint was defended with greater clarity and vehemence during the Babi resurgence of the 1840s and 1850s, when the 'ulama faced serious defection within their own ranks. Curiously, with all its vigorous denunciations of the Babis in this period, which would logically have implied unification of the leadership, the clerical establishment barely departed from its pattern of diffuse leadership. Instead, the "synodic" consensus achieved among the leading mujtahids resulted in further stratification of the religious body along socio-economic lines. Such division, however, was not devoid of a strong ideological content. The lower and middle ranks already exposed to Shaykhi revisionism became increasingly critical of the privileged Usuli mujtahids. Their grievances eventually erupted into radical tendencies that denied the very basis of the mujtahids' legitimacy and in effect weakened the solidarity of the clerical class.[32]

The reign of Muhammad Shah was particularly critical in the polarization of the clerical community. Under Hajji Mirza Aqasi, a self-styled Sufi adept with profound influence over the shah, the Qajar government reduced its support for the mainstream Usuli school and even sought to curb its influence. This in turn facilitated, somewhat unintentionally, the growth of anticlerical tendencies at a time when the unusually rapid loss of the high-ranking leaders made the collective leadership more vulnerable.

## *Epidemics and Challenges of the Babis*

During the 1840s – in less than a decade – the death of a number of eminent jurists created a vacuum not immediately filled by a younger generation. In Isfahan, the alliance of prominent jurists, already weakened during the governorship of Manuchihr Khan Mu'tamid al-Dawla, came to an end with the death of Shafti in 1844 and that of his ally, Hajji Muhammad Ibrahim Karbasi, in 1845. Another prominent mujtahid, Sayyid Sadr al-Din 'Amili, died in 1846, giving Mir Sayyid Muhammad Imam Jum'a (d. 1874–5) an obvious advantage over Asadullah Shafti (d. 1873), son of Muhammad Baqir, and other heirs to clerical positions. In the 'Atabat, the leader of the Shaykhi school, Sayyid Kazim Rashti, died at the end of 1843; his notorious opponent Sayyid Muhammad Mahdi, the last of the influential Tabataba'is, died in 1844. Shortly thereafter, Sayyid Ibrahim Qazvini, one of the leading authorities in

Karbala and another opponent of the Shaykhis, died in 1846. His counterpart, Shaykh Hasan Al-i Kashif al-Ghita', the leader of the Arab Shi'a of Iraq, died in the same year. The leadership *(riyasat)* of the two latter figures had been acknowledged particularly by the Ottoman *pashaliq*, who held them responsible for the religious affairs of the Shi'a in Iraq. After them, the only significant survivor of the older group, Shaykh Muhammad Hasan Najafi Isfahani (the author of *Jawahir al-Kalam*, d. 1850) rose to *riyasat* in the late 1840s.[33] In other centers, Shaykh 'Abd al-Vahhab Qazvini, a respected leader with Shaykhi leanings, died in 1847; his rival Mulla Muhammad Taqi Baraqani, an arch-enemy of the Shaykhis, was assassinated in the same year by Shaykhi-Babi elements. Also in the same year, Mulla Muhammad Ja'far Astarabadi, another troublesome opponent of Shaykhis, died in Tehran.

The death of these leading jurists, partly because of the plague of 1845–7 in Iran and Iraq, had serious repercussions. Their successors – inheritors of their fathers' wealth, pulpits, and religious courts – could not rapidly master the political arena. Not infrequently they were victims of local intrigue and the target of sharp criticism. The absence of prominent figures in the Usuli camp gave a new dimension to the deep-rooted Shaykhl-Usuli schism which, since the 1820s, had polarized the religious community. After the death of Sayyid Kazim Rashti, the younger and more radical students of the Shaykhi school were reorganized under the banners of the Babi movement and began an all-embracing campaign against the very foundation of orthodox Shi'ism.

The Babi movement advocated a messianic revelation – the externalization of Shaykh Ahmad Ahsa'i's theory of *Shi'a Kamil* – in the person of the Bab Sayyid 'Ali Muhammad Shirazi as the only legitimate source of spiritual guidance. The Babis criticized the mujtahids for their moral conduct, their usurpation of the Imam's authority, and their worldly attachment. Recruiting most of its ardent supporters from Shaykhi ranks, the movement's rapid growth was accelerated by defections from the clergy and the conversion of middle rank merchants, guilds, and peasantry. Though the ratio of the active Babis to the entire population of the country was relatively small, the potential for a Babi breakthrough alarmed the 'ulama. This jeopardized, at least temporarily, the position of the juristic elite. The supply of newly authorized mujtahids – products of Shaykhi teaching circles – could hardly be absorbed in the clerical establishment so long as inherited positions and privileges were closely guarded by the established mujtahids and their heirs.

Faced with the prospects of internal revolt, the jurists and their allies had little choice but to turn to a government that was essentially unsympathetic to their plight, and yet was equally apprehensive of the Babis' popularity. The outcome of this realignment with the state was as fateful to the Babis as it was disheartening to the 'ulama. The Babi experience proved to the jurists their precarious dependence on the state and made the government more conscious of its vital role. The decades following the final episode of the Babi movement (1848–52) thus witnessed the gradual diminution of clerical prestige in Iran and the reversal of the earlier autonomous trend. Though the mujtahids still exercised considerable influence (e.g. the Najafi family in Isfahan, Shaykh al-Islams in Tabriz, and Razavis in Mashhad), the clerical elite throughout Nasir al-Din's reign was evidently more prone to Qajar pressure. Not until the time of Mirza Muhammad Hasan Shirazi and the Tobacco protest (1891–2) did the mujtahids of Iran stage a united stand against the state. Nor did they venture a major confrontation with the government on policy measures and their implementations.

Thus, the evolution of clerical leadership from the late eighteenth century to the middle of the nineteenth century could be best summed up as a vigorous move from the madrasa to the marketplace. In this process, academic seniority was transformed into collective leadership, with no ultimate place reserved for a supreme authority. The 'ulama grew more autonomous, but serious perils from within compelled them to remain loyal to the state.

## *The Ascendancy of Ansari*

The new climate in state–'ulama relations and the conciliatory mood that resulted from the defeat of the Babis and the fall of Mirza Taqi Khan Amir Nizam (posthumously known as Amir Kabir, d. 1851) was bound to find a reflection in the conduct of the later jurists. The earlier generations of the mujtahids of Iran could not always convince the public of their overall moral purity, judicial impartiality, and material detachment – hence the aspiration for a morally reformed leadership, both among the 'ulama and the public at large, found expression in the idealized image of a religious figure distant from the familiar market environment. The recognition of religious headship *(riyasat-i shar'iya)* in Shaykh Murtaza Ansari in the late 1850s was not a mere coincidence. Earlier in the century, public desire for nonclerical saintly figures had already given rise to a wide range of charismatic personages. The Ni'matullahi Sufi Nur 'Ali Shah, theosophist Shaykh Ahmad Ahsa'i, the ascetic-scholar Sayyid Mahdi Bahr al-'Ulum, and above all the prophet-mystic Sayyid 'Ali Muhammad the Bab, are only a few examples. Such aspirations, as well as the denunciation of unacceptable practices among the 'ulama, heightened the veneration of Ansari's public image at a time when all alternative heterodoxies were effectively suppressed.

The circumstances that led to Ansari's ascendancy pose two interrelated problems. First, what elements in his background and personality qualified him for this exceptional reverence? Secondly, to what extent did he symbolize a shift from the collective consensus of earlier times to the leadership of a single individual with which he was associated? The answer to the first question is perhaps best summed up by his contemporaries, who repeatedly praised him for two distinct qualities: piety *(wara')* and scholarship (*'ilm*).[34] The reassertion of traditional values – already defined in the Usuli literature of earlier decades – had a peculiar resonance in the religious milieu of the time and was symptomatic of a moral crisis within the Shi'i establishment. There seems to be a direct relation between emphasis on Ansari's piety and his growing popularity. The image of a serious scholar with the austerity of an ascetic and the sagacity of a statesman needed a certain dissociation, though not total isolation, from worldly affairs. He was particularly admired for avoiding any accumulation of personal wealth.[35] His reluctance to issue controversial legal opinions[36] and his efforts to depoliticize the clerical community[37] made him an advocate of political acquiescence and nonintervention, often in sharp contrast to the entrepreneurial image of some earlier mujtahids. Impartiality and fairness, underscored by frequent references to his justice *('adl)*, permitted him to enjoy the support of influential groups – merchants, landowners, and other contributors to religious funds – who preferred to see more judicial cooperation and less hindrance and competition. The reverence shown toward Ansari in Najaf thus may be seen as a sign of discontent with the Iranian mujtahids' economic ventures and the extravagance of their private lifestyles.

Equally crucial was the support of the Qajar government. The growing independence of Nasir al-Din Shah after the fall of his prime minister, Mirza Aqa Khan Nuri, in 1858 required greater cooperation and coexistence between the state and the 'ulama. Interdependency made the latter more accommodating, and Ansari's political quietism was a timely reflection of such a mood. This policy did not remain unrewarded as the flow of funds – alms, *sahm-i Imam,* and bequests from private and government sources – flooded Najaf. At one stage in the late 1850s, the figure of two hundred thousand *tumans* has been given for the lawful funds *(vujuhat-i shar'iya)* annually received by Ansari;[38] a substantial figure, taking into account the government's total revenue of about three million *tumans* for the same period – and this, in spite of Ansari's reported disapproval of the concentration of funds in Najaf.

The administration of the incoming funds and methods of disbursement proved to be formidable, as Ansari strongly disapproved of the private use or investment of such funds. The alternative was immediate distribution among Najaf's growing number of deserving recipients. Barring relatives and proxies from misappropriation was not an easy task, especially as bureaucratic procedures were kept to a bare minimum. Haphazard and irregular as it was, the payment of pensions and alms created a large following for Ansari in Najaf and beyond. The large number of students attending his classes were the prime beneficiaries. According to one witness, at one time as many as five hundred attended his lectures,[39] though the number of students who systematically studied under him over a period of two decades may have been in excess of one thousand.[40]

The reputation of Shaykh Murtaza as a serious teacher and his academic prominence made every student in Najaf keen to obtain his authorization *(ijaza).* Popularity and large attendance in turn gave wider circulation to his works.[41] His collection of treatises and his work on the laws of commerce became textbooks in the Najaf curriculum. His systematic discourses of *usul al-fiqh* in *Fara'id al-Usul,* a complex subject which for long baffled students of the madrasas, was a noticeable improvement compared with the works of Bihbahani and Mirza-yi Qumi.[42] His *Makasib* was equally attractive for the *tullab,* who considered it a useful exercise for their future careers.[43] Though the theoretical speculations of these works were not easily applicable to the rapidly changing economic market, they nevertheless witnessed the author's awareness of the role of the jurists vis-à-vis their mercantile clients.

The reassertion of all three qualities – piety, justice, and knowledge – contributed, each in its own way, to the widespread acknowledgement of Ansari's status of leadership *(riyasat).* The root of his success lay in his ability to attract funds and divert them for the upkeep of his educational and social network – almost the functions of a rudimentary welfare system – both to the satisfaction of the contributors and the recipients. This *riyasat* was a modest step beyond the collective leadership of "the concillium of the 'ulama of the time" which nonetheless did not undermine the inherent diversity of the institution of *ijtihad.* It remained an informal status reserved for one or several prominent mujtahids whose social conduct, popularity, and assured moral qualities qualified them to supervise the practical affairs of the clerical community.

In this respect, Ansari followed what had already been laid down by his immediate predecessors. Both his teachers, Shaykh Muhammad Hasan Najafi and Shaykh 'Ali Najafi (Al-i Kashif al-Ghita', d. 1838), exercised the same *riyasat* over Persian and Arab Shi'i communities of Iraq, respectively.[44] The ethnic division – at times, rivalry – among the *tullab* as well as among merchants, the notables, and nomads often determined loyalties. The Ottoman *millet* system, for all practical purposes, honored such diversity and recognized Shi'i leaders of Arab and Persian origins as the heads (*ra'is*) responsible for their constituencies. Ansari, being originally from Dizful, a region with a mixed Perso-Arabic background, enjoyed an advantage over his predecessors. Teaching in both vernaculars, his appeal lay partly in his ability to bridge the ethnic division and merge, as Muhammad Hasan Najafi put it, "the point of union between two rivers and the choice of two factions" *(majma' al-bahrayn wa pasandida-yi fariqayn).*[45]

Initial hesitation on the part of Ansari to assume the *riyasat* and be responsible for receiving and distributing funds in Najaf does not seem to have come purely from prudence *(ihtiyat)* or modesty, but also from fear of internal revolt in the highest ranks. Perhaps it is not a coincidence that he first invited the chief mujtahid of Mazandaran and an old school mate, Mulla Sa'id Barfurushi (Sa'id al-'Ulama, d. *c*.1270/1854–5), to assume *riyasat* of the 'Atabat.[46] The latter made a career for himself out of vigorous persecution of the Babis during the uprising of Tabarsi (1848–9). He was a remarkable example of the mujtahids whose active clamp down on the heretics secured them both prominence among the 'ulama and amicable relations with Nasir al-Din Shah.[47] By securing Barfurushi's approval, Ansari defused a potential source of opposition. Yet he remained aware of the limitations of his status. Once questioned as to the lawfulness of the Friday congregational prayer – an issue heatedly debated among jurists – he reinstated the non-Usuli disapproval but went as far as to state that Friday prayers can only be performed with the authority of the ruler (*sultan,* presumably the Ottoman sultan) and possessors of authority *(ulu'l-amr)*.[48]

In his overcautious judicial conduct Ansari seems also to have deliberately swum against the mainstream of Usuli practice by showing reluctance – almost to the point of refusal – to issue a legal opinion *(fatwa)* on matters of such seemingly obvious consensus as the refutation of the Babis.[49] In refraining from issuing a *fatwa,* Ansari followed his predecessor, Shaykh 'Ali Kashif al-Ghita', in distinguishing between the scholarly elaboration of law and the actual passing of legal judgments. Highlighting the former as the essential undertaking of his career, he seems to have recommended a return to scholarly pursuits within the walls of the madrasa. It is in this context that his discourse on *a'lamiyat* can be better understood. These exegetical and deductive skills were confined to the madrasa and did not account for the universality of *marja'iyat.* He was highly praised as the "Seal of the mujtahids" *(khatam al-mujtahidin)* and "the Chief of the Party [of the Shi'a]" *(shaykh al-ta'ifa)* but even his keenest eulogists did not include *marja'iyat* – whether relative or absolute – in their long list of honorifics.[50]

## *Shirazi and "Headship" of the Community*

By the time Ansari died in 1864, the Shi'i *riyasat* had acquired a more scholarly form. The collective leadership was transformed into a single headship with far greater acceptance among Arabs and Persians and with financial backing chiefly diverted towards the 'Atabat. The supremacy of Najaf over other centers was firmly established, and amicable relations with the state were achieved.

Yet Ansari's success was in many ways ephemeral. The struggle that started in the wake of his death and continued for almost a decade (1864–74) demonstrated the precarious nature of *riyasat*. The struggle meant a return to traditional plurality. This in due course challenged the hard-earned superiority of Najaf. The ethnic divisions – this time more significantly between the *tullab* of Azarbaijan (and Caucasus) and the Persian-speaking students – polarized the 'Atabat and led to the emergence of an independent *riyasat* for Turkish-speaking followers in the person of Hajji Sayyid Husayn Kuh-Kamara'i (d. 1299/1881–2), who, reputed for his systematic teaching of *Usul*, increased attendance to more than six hundred.[51]

Such popularity understandably reduced the *riyasat* of his chief contestant, Mirza Hasan Shirazi, and restricted the latter's sphere of influence to predominantly Persian-speaking students and followers.[52] Shirazi's credentials as a teaching assistant and aid to Ansari were impeccable. Reportedly, he was praised by the late teacher, together with Mirza Habiballah Rashti, as the most promising of his students.[53] He was also admired by his biographers, particularly for his endeavors in facilitating the livelihood of the *tullab*, the needy, and the distressed. Manifestation of such public concern during the famine of 1871, and the setting up of an emergency relief center, boosted his reputation.[54]

Competition in Najaf nevertheless proved to be too intense. Though Shirazi had already secured the blessing of many ex-classmates, he evidently lacked total support and saw little chance of wider recognition.[55] In 1874, when he "emigrated" from Najaf to the nearby Sunni-dominated Samarra, he reportedly intended "to resign his *riyasat* and relieve himself from its restraints" in order to pursue the life of an ascetic.[56] Whether he was testing the loyalty of the student body or was genuinely frustrated with being one of many in Najaf is difficult to know. What is certain, however, is the effectiveness of this move. A faction of Persian-speaking students who followed him to Samarra later became the most prominent 'ulama of the next generation. Among them were Mirza Husayn Nuri, the author of *Mustadrak*, and his son-in-law Shaykh Fadlullah Nuri; Muhammad Kazim Khurasani; Muhammad Tabataba'i; and Sayyid Husayn Sadr.[57]

The growing popularity of the new center overshadowed Najaf, particularly after the death of Kuh-Kamara'i in 1882. Yet Najaf survived as a center of learning and even thrived through the last quarter of the century. The Azarbaijanis found a new marja': Shaykh Muhammad Hasan Mamaqani (d. 1905–6), a student of Kuh-Kamara'i.[58] Meanwhile, Mirza Habibullah Rashti emerged as the most scholarly-minded teacher of the 'Atabat.[59] Though neither of the two matched Shirazi, the diversity in leadership continued to contrast with the unanimity of Ansari's time. Mirza Habibullah Rashti is quoted as having said that of Ansari's three distinguished qualities, the learnedness *(a'lamiyat)* was inherited by himself (i.e. Rashti) and the leadership *(riyasat)* by Shirazi; but the piety, Habibullah believed, Ansari took with him to the grave.[60] Such a remark is particularly revealing, as it reflects a division of labor which had emerged as a result of clerical competition. Rashti denies exemplary piety for himself and Shirazi, perhaps to contrast the idealized purity of Ansari's time with the shady realities of his own. At the same time, he draws a distinction between leadership and scholarship. Indeed, if the volume of written works could be a standard for *a'lamiyat,* Shirazi's meager record as a writer could hardly have qualified him as the *a'lam.*[61] He was nevertheless successful in drawing the support of a large portion of contributors – primarily merchant-landowners of Fars, his home province – who sought in his *riyasat* a reassertion of the traditional bonds between 'ulama and the merchants.[62]

Throughout the 1880s, the fame of Shirazi surpassed that of any other mujtahid, chiefly because of his more systematic endeavors to achieve two objectives: first, to attract merchant support and funds, and second, to expand his own network of students. Most effective in his first task was Shirazi's own mercantile background. He came from a Shirazi family of petty clerics with long-established links with the closely woven network of merchants of southern Iran. From the same family came the *imam jum'a* of Kirman, Sayyid Javad Shirazi (d. *c.*1264/1848), and more significantly, Sayyid 'Ali Muhammad the Bab, a paternal second cousin of Shirazi.[63] The merchant connection almost automatically put Shirazi in an advantageous position, making him an ideal candidate of Persian *tujjar* and their counterparts in India and elsewhere, as the recipient of large sums. The flow of religious dues and bequests, which probably included the Oudh bequest administered by the British Consul-General in Baghdad, symbolically materialized in various building projects under his auspices in Samarra. A bridge over Tigris at the cost of ten thousand Turkish golden lira, two madrasas in Samarra, and a new market *(suq)* financed by some Indian bequests testify to Shirazi's success in generating funds for the improvement of his educational center.[64]

The fruits of thirty years of teaching generations of students and often funding their long years of study, on the other hand, finally ripened by the late 1880s, when these students occupied high places throughout Iran, Iraq, India, and the Caucasus. Such a network of mujtahids with prime allegiance to Shirazi secured him a more comprehensive and powerful *riyasat.* Both of these factors contributed to what his student Sayyid Hasan Sadr calls "the monopolization of the *riyasat* of the Ja'fari denomination throughout the world." In the latter part of his life, Sadr asserts, "the death of the [previous] heads and sources of public emulation all over the [Shi'i] lands left amongst that denomination no head *(ra'is)* except him."[65]

If the above factors paved the way for the wider recognition of *riyasat,* the participation in the tobacco protest of 1891–2 sealed its unanimous acceptance. More crucially, it also furnished the *riyasat* with a political dimension without precedent since the *jihad* proclamation of 1825–6. The shift in the policy of non-interference did not come without a great deal of hesitation. Any political commitment would have meant the abandonment of the neutrality of *riyasat* and a disturbance of the equilibrium achieved under Ansari. But if the pressure exerted upon Shirazi by the prominent mujtahids of the major cities during the Regie episode was resistible, he could not afford to ignore the unmistakable signals from his financial backers – the merchants and landowners of Fars, Isfahan, Tabriz, and elsewhere. The implementation of the 1891 Regie Concession, which granted the sale and export of Iran's tobacco production to a British company, was a direct threat to the prosperity and financial viability of this class. The gloomy prospects of the Regie intrusion, reflected in the merchants' petitions and repeated inquiries, compelled Shirazi to cast off his customary prudence and to side with his constituency against the Qajar's sale of the concession.[66]

This decision was only a prelude to what became a familiar characteristic of *riyasat* in the following decades. The reciprocal interdependency demonstrated in the tobacco protest had far-reaching consequences for both parties. It became increasingly in the merchants' interest to support a united *riyasat* rather than merely to back local mujtahids in their hometowns. Greater centralization of the government brought further pressure upon the mercantile community through the sale of concessions, taxation, and customs, and intervention in the market. On the other hand, the growing volume of foreign trade in the latter part of the century made long-distance merchants more dependent on the export of cash crops (more precisely, cotton, opium, and tobacco), and, in turn, on heavy investment in the production of these commodities. The organization of production and exports brought handsome profits to some, but it also increased their exposure and vulnerability to the government's arbitrary measures. The merchants' allies and beneficiaries, the local mujtahids, were effective so far as government intervention was within the recognized boundaries of coercion and compromise. The odds against the merchants increased gradually as the state resorted to the sale of concessions on a national scale. In response, investors in land and trade sought a more potent agent of influence and protection, a source of authority more immune from the state which could, if need be, reflect their grievances and speak out on their behalf.

This gradual shift to the universal *riyasat* was further facilitated by the need for arbitration by a superior authority in cases of disputes between the mujtahids and their chief clients, the merchants. In the absence of an overall state judiciary, the mujtahids of cities had at their disposal the only available judicial machinery and the registry of contracts and deeds, without which the merchants could hardly operate. A constant charge in the otherwise amicable relations between the two groups was the merchants' complaints at the mujtahids' lack of impartiality in judicial proceedings and their contradictory rulings. These charges were not helped by the notoriety some 'ulama acquired for receiving double bribes in litigations to rule in favor of one party and then to overrule their first verdict in favor of the other. These and other irregularities, particularly in the guardianship of minors, orphans, and imbeciles, and the supervision of their assets, harmed the already tarnished image of religious courts. Privileged groups were critical of local mujtahids for the increasing price of their favor and influence, which, in any case, could not be secured for long if a higher bidder emerged. The gradual shift to a superior arbiter in the 'Atabat may be explained in terms of this crisis of confidence as reflected in the shift of religious funds to Samarra. The mujtahids in urban centers were thus overshadowed by the grand mujtahids of Iraq. By the end of the century, many of them performed the role of agents for the 'Atabat leadership.

Other external elements also facilitated the prominence of the 'Atabat. The expansion of trade networks and better means of communication (including the expansion of the telegraph system) ensured regular funds as well as regular contact with followers. More convenient means of transport brought pilgrims to the holy cities who previously visited local shrines. The memories of the 'Atabat pilgrimage, which often included visits to the prominent divines, helped to spread their fame to remote places. Even prior to Regie, the government preferred to see a moderate and uncontroversial head in the 'Atabat in order to ensure the subordination of the other mujtahids at home.

This more direct relation between the public and the *ra'is,* with other 'ulama serving as agents, created a new setup in which the aspirations of the contributors were reflected more clearly than ever before in their choice of the head. The conspicuous presence of a patron–client relationship is unmistakable, but what makes such a relationship especially important in this context is the way it acquired a pronounced expression in the concept of universal juristic authority *(marja'iyat-i tamm).* Even prior to the Regie episode, the official Qajar almanac, *al-Ma'athir w'al-Athar,* in 1888 defines Shirazi not only as "the proof of Islam" *(hujjat al-Islam),* "the Deputy of the Imam" *(na'ib al-Imam)* and "the renovator of [Islamic] ordinance *(mujadid-i ahkam)* whose prior status is recognized by other mujtahids" but as "the most learned of mujtahids whose opinions *(fatawi)* are the standard of sound practice by Shi'i emulators." One can hear an echo of public reverence augmented by the government's desire to create a shadow authority superior to any mujtahid at home – a necessary step to bring the prominent jurists into rank.

The aspirations of the followers are more clearly evident in the way Shirazi's prohibition of the use of tobacco during Regie was interpreted as a "ruling" *(hukm)* binding on all Shi'is rather than a legal opinion *(fatwa)* binding only on the mujtahid's emulators.[67] Throughout the Regie episode – from the first petitions of the merchants and dealers of tobacco, agitations in Shiraz, Isfahan, and Tabriz, and correspondence between the 'ulama to rumors concerning Shirazi's issuance of the prohibition and finally his confirmation of the ban on the use of tobacco – it is possible to detect a clear attempt by the merchants, the 'ulama, and the radical laity, all for their own varying reasons, to increase Shirazi's involvement. Either by persuasion, pressure, or by unsolicited delegation on his behalf, Shirazi was obliged to throw his support behind the movement of protest against the concession.

The network of merchants throughout Iran and Iraq – among them, tobacco producers from Lar as well as merchants and dealers of Shiraz – was the first to urge clerical involvement by inducing popular preachers like Sayyid 'Ali Akbar Falasiri, a son-in-law of Shirazi, to appeal to public sentiment.[68] Later on, after his exile to Iraq, Falasiri was instrumental in providing the link between his father-in-law and the other opponent of Regie, Sayyid Jamal al-Din Asadabadi (al-Afghani). In Iran, the clerical-merchant family network worked hard to promote Shirazi and to widen the significance of his objection to Regie. Shirazi's letters to Nasir al-Din Shah clearly reflect his prime concern with the fate of the merchants and their trade:

> In spite of the fact that for centuries the guardians of religion, the kings of the Muslims – pray to God for their endeavors – sacrificed souls and spent fortunes towards promotion of the cause of Islam, why is it that today, for the sake of trifling profits and regardless of its corrupt consequences, they allow the infidels to dominate the livelihood and commerce *(ma'ayish va tijarat)* of the Muslims? It was uncharacteristic of your royal prudence to permit your subjects, who indeed are abundant treasures of the state, to be deprived of controlling their own trade and business, and instead to bow to the subjugation of the infidels.[69]

Shirazi's letters reflected the merchants' concern but also the exhortations of the religious activist, Sayyid Jamal al-Din Asadabadi. After his disgraceful expulsion from Iran by the order of Nasir al-Sin Shah, Jamal al-Din, who was enraged with humiliation, found in Shirazi a tactical ally and an effective platform against Nasir al-Din and his policies. The implicit elevation of Shirazi by the merchants soon found explicit acknowledgment in Jamal al-Din's famous letter to the grand mujtahid. The impact of this letter upon Shirazi's action should not be exaggerated; yet the endorsement of Shirazi and the magnification of his position must have given the mujtahids some reassurance. Moreover, the fact that it was widely circulated in Persian translation must have raised Shirazi's position in the eyes of the Iranian population. The modernist Afghani seems to have had no hesitation in conferring upon the traditional mujtahid the ultimate religious authority and in showering him with honorifics.[70] Addressing him as "the pontiff of the people, the ray of Imams' light, the pillar of the edifice of religion [and] the tongue attuned to the exposition of the perspicuous law,"[71] Afghani, with a flattery close to adulation, attributes to Shirazi "the vicegerency of the Most Great Proof *(niyabat al-'uzma 'an al-hujjat al-kubra),* "the throne of general leadership" *(arikat al-riyasat al-'amm),* and "supremacy over people" *(siyadat 'ala khalqih).*[72] He goes even further to say what amounts to recognition of Shirazi's universal authority.

> Thine is the word which will unite them [i.e. people of Iran] and thine the proof which shall decide, that thy command is effective, and that none will contest thy wits by a word on thy part.[73]

Afghani therefore should be credited with being the first to realize the potential of Shi'i *riyasat.* He reminded the 'ulama of the possibility of utilizing such leadership, not for limited and often personalized gains but for explicit political ends.

The chief mujtahids of Iran – among them Mirza Hasan Ashtiyani (d. 1319/1901–2) in Tehran, Muhammad Taqi Najafi (Aqa Najafi) in Isfahan, and Mirza Javad Mujtahid in Tabriz – viewed Shirazi's direct involvement as a mixed blessing. It has been said that Ashtiyani himself composed the text of the famous declaration prohibiting the use of tobacco in the name of Shirazi, thus obliging the latter to confirm what amounted to be a *fait accompli.*[74] Whatever the circumstance, Shirazi's involvement greatly improved the mujtahids' overall stance vis-à-vis the government, and for a while returned unity to their ranks. Yet, as far as the long-term interests of these mujtahids were concerned, such involvement could potentially undermine their position not only as champions of anti-government action but as the only religious authorities present in their constituencies. Ashtiyani, an old classmate of Shirazi and a prominent commentator of Ansari's discourses in *usul al-fiqh,* was well aware of this threat. He was canny enough to use the occasion to attract Shirazi's confidence and at the same time to dictate his own objectives through that channel. This collaboration worked throughout the Regie period, but it collapsed soon after the cancellation of the concession, when the government gained enough confidence to buy back the loyalty of Ashtiyani and others. Once the major crisis was over, disagreement over the future course of action between Shirazi and Ashtiyani, and between the latter and more junior figures, may be taken as symptoms of fragmentation.[75]

In the years following the death of Shirazi in 1312/1895, the problem of *riyasat* remained unresolved. The sole *riyasat* of the Regie episode was once again changed to plurality in leadership. The absence of an influential head brought a number of leading mujtahids into the limelight. While Mirza Hasan Ashtiyani relied on his connections with the court and the notables in the capital, Shaykh Muhammad Sharabiyani (d. 1905) in the 'Atabat attained considerable authority chiefly for being an effective mediator between the Turkish-speaking populace and governments in Iran and the Ottoman empire.[76] Mirza Husayn Tihrani (ibn Mirza Khalil) was widely followed by the Persian-speaking population. Shaykh Hasan Mamaqani (d. 1905) and Shaykh Muhammad Kazim Khurasani (d. 1911) both relied on their *tullab* support, the latter being the mentor of Persian-speaking students and for a while the recipient of the Oudh bequest. As the constitutional revolution brought Khurasani to the forefront of pro-Constitutional forces, Sayyid Kazim Yazdi (d. 1918) emerged as the representative of the anti-Constitutional tendency.[77] As a whole, they represented a broad spectrum of religious leaders with limited jurisdiction.

What survived from Shirazi's time, however, was the legacy of political *riyasat*, which became more explicit under his successors. In the wake of the Constitutional Revolution, the *maraji'-i 'uzam* (grand authorities) is the most common reference to these high-ranking mujtahids, often with extended legal authority in the political sphere. The collective action of the senior 'ulama and the joint issuance of *fatwas* on matters of national significance would confirm the tendency to maintain a facade of unity.[78] For a brief period, a pronounced political dimension became the determining factor in the process of designating a clerical leader. But during the Constitutional period, in contrast to Shirazi's time, no unanimously accepted leadership emerged. What was apparent, however, was that political participation rather than customary practice became the norm in the way funds were located and students were attracted.

During the Constitutional period, the widening rift within the ranks of religious leaders can best be explained in terms of their willingness to represent conflicting interests and divergences in their followers' political views and actions. Though ideological disagreement regarding the nature of the Constitution cannot be overlooked, for the most part it was the contest for popularity and support of the laity that determined the political orientation of the 'ulama. Faced with the challenges of secular Constitutionalists and popular preachers of lower ranks, the maraji' were hardly able to maintain their unanimity. Unlike the Babi episode, where the 'ulama preserved their unity and survived the revolt of the lower ranks, the Constitutional Revolution had a far larger mass appeal and could not be safely ignored or rejected. Even after the split in the 'ulama's ranks became apparent in 1907, the Constitutionalists continued to receive not only the backing of the lesser mullas but that of a few celebrated jurists such as Khurasani and Tabataba'i.

Yet political disagreements and defections weakened the hard-earned unity of Shirazi's time. The bulk of the 'ulama either withdrew their earlier support for the constitution and abstained from politics, or else actively backed the absolutist monarchy. The best example of the polarization of the 'ulama in this period is the secret war waged between Khurasani and Yazdi during 1909–11.[79] Ironically, the shift from non-intervention to activism not only resulted in internal division but also in a long-term social decline and loss of popular support. Unable to keep pace with the accelerating secularization of the Iranian polity, the prominent mujtahids after the Constitutional period quietly returned to their scholastic retreat.[80] Save for sporadic attempts, the majority of the surviving *maraji'*, bitter with the memories of the Constitutional experience and cautious not to endanger their dwindling financial and public backing, chose to maintain a low profile and to watch jealously from the safety of their madrasa the rising tides of anticlerical modernity and the gradual loss of their monopolies and privileges.

## *Conclusion*

The interaction between the Shi'i scholarly milieu, on the one hand, and the economic, social, and political forces that shaped nineteenth-century Shi'i society on the other hand, was subject to a complex set of factors. First, whenever the adverse forces of political anarchy (as in the first and the second interregnum in the eighteenth century), state opposition (as under Hajji Mirza Aqasi's regime), or anticlerical revolt (as in the Babi movement) posed a threat to the religious leadership, it tended to retreat to the madrasa and undertake the safe practices of teaching and scholarship. Greater involvement in the affairs of the marketplace, however, came whenever there was a relative degree of social and economic stability, state cooperation, and royal patronage (as in Fath 'Ali Shah's reign), or when there was a willingness on the side of the interest groups, most notably the merchants, to offer the mujtahids non-academic functions, whether judicial, financial, or political. The alternating shifts of leadership between the 'Atabat and the religious centers of Iran may also, to some extent, be explained in terms of this changing climate. The 'Atabat leadership, with its emphasis on legal scholarship, gained ground at times when direct involvement in worldly affairs was not desirable. On the other hand, the mujtahids resident in Iran, as the actual representatives of the religious law, enhanced their position at times when the overall conditions for this worldly involvement were suitable.

Second, the informal hierarchy that evolved within the 'ulama establishment recognized an equally informal status of *riyasat* with almost caretaker responsibilities towards the clerics and the laity. In the second half of the century, this status gained prominence under the mujtahids, who were able to combine successfully the support of the community with the backing of the state, to enhance their popular image as the models of piety and knowledge, and to strengthen their control over teaching circles. Contrary to conventional interpretations, the transition from plural to singular leadership during Ansari and Shirazi was not the result of the community's recognition of the most learned *(a'lam),* which, at any rate, was institutionally inconceivable. Nor was it at the outset the result of the mujtahids' greater involvement in political affairs. Rather, it was the mechanics of the madrasa-bazaar interaction that allowed the designation of a senior mujtahid as the sole head; one who could best monopolize the academic and non-academic spheres by having the largest constituency of followers and agents. Such a supreme authority thus enjoyed the greatest access to financial resources and the endorsement of the state and the other mujtahids.

Third, the notion of the *riyasat* gained further substance only when the changing political situation in the last decade of the century obliged the religious leaders to take a markedly anti-governmental position in the interest of their lay clients. In the period between the Regie protest and the end of the Constitutional period, the position of *marja'iyat-i taqlid* came to represent not only the traditional *riyasat* but also a supreme religious authority with marked political concerns on behalf of the entire community. Though the sole *marja'iyat* received almost universal recognition during the Regie episode, this development proved to be ephemeral. The institutional provisions in the doctrine of *taqlid* made it practically impossible for any future clerical figure (except perhaps Ayatallah Burujirdi in the 1950s) to claim undisputed authority. During the Constitutional period, the diverse choices of the followers remained the determining factor in the rise of the competing exemplars *(maraji');* a fact which contributed to the exhaustion of clerical power and the hasty return of the *maraji'* to the previous non-political position in the aftermath of that revolution.

Therefore, it is not unrealistic to suggest that in no time before the establishment of the Islamic Republic of Iran and the institutionalization of the Guardianship of the Jurist, was the designation of the religious leadership, be it *riyasat* or *marja'iyat,* made by the mujtahids themselves. Rather, it remained at the discretion of the followers – more the laity than the lower-rank clerics – to employ the loosely defined provisions for *taqlid* and to bring the *marja'* in line with their own diverse wishes. From this historical perspective, Ayatollah Khomeini's thesis of the Guardianship of the Jurist is an innovation as much in revolt against the authority of a secular ruler as it is against the hegemony of the followers.

## CHAPTER 8

# *From* ijtihad *to* wilayat-i faqih: *The Evolving of Shi'i Legal Authority into Political Power*

In November 2002 Hashim Aghajari, an Iranian teacher of history and a veteran of the Iran–Iraq war, was sentenced to death by the Islamic revolutionary court in Hamadan for questioning the practice of blind "emulation/ following" *(taqlid)* of the mujtahids in matters of belief and practice. His sentencing led to several days of widespread university protests fueled by Aghajari's refusal to appeal against his death sentence. What incensed the Iranian court, which accused him of blasphemy, was that by implication Aghajari was denying the "authority/guardianship of the jurist" (*wilayat-i faqih*), the very founding principle of the Islamic Republic. Aghajari's objection focused not merely on the practice of *taqlid* but the legitimacy (if such existed) of the "guardian jurist" *(wali-yi faqih)*, the "supreme leader" of the Islamic Republic. For the ruling elite of Iran, *wilayat-i faqih* is the prime source of their political legitimacy. The idea of the "Guardianship of the Jurist" over the political processes in Shi'i Muslim society goes back to Ayatollah Khomeini (1902–89), who first published on the subject in the late 1960s. Hashim Aghajari's criticism thus was a new anti-clerical quest which was bound to excite much interest among younger generations of Iranians.

Aghajaris' speech commemorated 'Ali Shari'ati (1933–77), the renowned revolutionary reformist. Invoking Shari'ati's notion of "Islamic Protestantism" as the only way to liberate society from the impasse of "traditional Islam," Aghajari was striving to arrive at a historical understanding of the Shi'i heritage. Though still grounded in the Qur'an and hadith, this new reading appeared to be engaged more deeply with individual choice, human rights, and a plurality of ideas. It called for social justice, economic democracy, and openness in politics, though Aghajari distanced himself from Shari'ati's firebrand rhetoric. He did not of course remain entirely untouched by Shari'ati's exhortations to be the prophet of Protestant Islam, a claim made by a number of Islamic reformers going back to Jamal al-Din "al-Afghani" (1838–97) and earlier. Yet he did go so far as to criticize the Shi'i establishment for its culture of condescension, especially in the exercise of *ijtihad*:

> People who merely imitate are not monkeys. The pupils understand and react, and they try to expand their own understanding, so someday they will not need a teacher. The relationship that the fundamentalists seek is one of master and follower; the master must always remain master and the follower will always remain follower. This is like shackles around your neck. We must understand that the master is not a holy, divine being, and we cannot grant him that status. They [i.e. the Shi'i authorities in positions of power], however, want to exercise total power. Shari'ati did something about it; he told the religious leaders: "You are not imams, you are not prophets, [you] cannot consider the people a subhuman species."[1]

Such critique of the abiding authority of *ijtihad* and that of the so-called "source of emulation" *(marja'-i taqlid)* inevitably brings to light the much debated issue of legal authority in Shi'i Islam and, more specifically, the problem of the institutionalization of *ijtihad*.

Aghajari naturally does not address the *wilayat-i faqih* openly, but his reference to the "Imam" in the above passage, as other allusions sprinkled throughout his speech, signifies the obvious to his sensitive audience. He deliberately seems to have touched on a sore point since the doctrine of the "guardianship of the jurists," it can be argued, stands on shaky legal grounds. Shi'ism never historically or institutionally made the necessary leap from loosely defined *ijtihad* to a centralized *marja'iyat*, let alone ever developing the theoretical ground for creating a universal judicial authority.

Before the time of Ayatollah Khomeini Shi'i legal thought never seriously engaged in the sphere of public law and consequently never articulated a coherent theory of government. Even in the safety of the madrasa, Shi'i law remained largely preoccupied with articulation of civil and private law as practiced in mujtahid-run civil courts. Practice of *ijtihad* was never systematized or, one may venture to say, never subjected to clear and universally accepted norms, almost by choice. The Shi'i law on which the mujtahids relied remained a matter of interpretation and scholastic scrutiny largely within the madrasa environment rather than through the actual practice of the law. Throughout the Safavid and the early Qajar periods (sixteenth to nineteenth centuries) Shi'i law acquired a remarkable level of sophistication, especially in the theoretical field of the so-called roots of jurisprudence (*usul al-fiqh*). Yet both in the study of the individual rulings *(furu)* and in the methodology of *usul al-fiqh*, Shi'i scholarship resisted systematic codification beyond what was determined by earlier jurists between the tenth and fourteenth centuries.

Even the "emergence" of the status of the "supreme exemplar" (*marja' taqlid*, lit. "the source of emulation)" in the nineteenth century remained largely an informal practice. No set of objective standards developed for designating such a leadership and no specific legal privileges were arrogated to this office. The *marja'iyat* was meant primarily to address the need for communal leadership rather than a supreme legal authority. No *marja'* ever claimed his legal opinions to be universally binding. Nor did any of the marja's claim to be standing at the apex of a judicial hierarchy or was accepted as such by the mujtahids or the community at large. Whenever they effectively exercised their legal power, as in the tobacco rebellion of 1890–1 or during the Constitutional Revolution of 1906–11 or the banning of the drinking of Pepsi Cola in the 1950s, the *marja'* relied on their popularity and prestige rather than any legal precept. The three preconditions for a marja' being the most learned *(a'lam)*, the most judicious *(a'dal)*, and the most pious *(atqa)*, were qualities barely measurable by legal or academic standards. No institutional procedure was ever set to determine such preconditions. What in reality determined the success of a *marja'*, or for that matter any mujtahid, was his popularity and the size of his follower constituency (or congregation).[2] The question thus remains as to what process, historical and legal, transformed this informal and democratically chaotic form of diffuse judicial leadership into the binding, all-embracing, and authoritative office of the *wilayat-i faqih* with claim over the judicial and political authority.

## *The Usuli Interpretation of Judicial Authority*

As early as the tenth century the Twelver Shi'i (*Ithna* Ashari) jurists recognized the Occultation *(ghayba)* of the Twelfth Imam, the state of his invisible (yet indirectly effective) existence in the physical world, as the chief postulate for denouncing any form of temporal power (in the absence of the Imam) as inherently unjust and therefore illegitimate. Only the return of the Imam in an undetermined moment in future, it was believed, could establish on earth the ultimate values of justice and legitimate rule. This messianic belief in the Imam's eventual establishment of a perfect utopian order has often been viewed as the chief obstacle in the way of articulating a legal public space in Shi'ism. The same rationale also barred in theory any legitimate collaboration between the jurists and the state. Every government was in theory seen as inherently oppressive. The same principle of avoiding political collaboration was conducive to the flourishing of the Shi'i study of hadith, as a means of emulating the models of the Prophet and the Imams, and the early development of jurisprudence *(fiqh)* focusing on civil and contractual law as well as on devotional acts and obligations.[3]

In practice, however, the quietist tendency among Shi'i jurists, as opposed to the powerful messianic trends of the Shi'i past, encouraged compliance and even collaboration with the "unjust" and "tyrannical" *(ja'ir)* state especially if and when the state was accommodating the Shi'is. This de facto acceptance of the temporal power was, needless to say, in full agreement with the ancient Persian notion of the "sisterhood" of religious and state institutions, an interdependency perceived to be essential for the endurance of both sets of institutions and the stability of the social order against the corrupting influence of "bad religion." While the state maintained peace and order, upheld the shari'a, defended the domain of Islam, and in effect guarded the jurists' vested interests, the jurists were in turn expected to maintain good relations with the state and even serve in the state-controlled judiciary.[4]

Already by the fourteenth century Shi'i jurists developed an elaborate legal system of private law based on *ijtihad*, the exercise of logical reasoning by utilizing the sources of the law to form qualified legal opinions within a specific timeframe. The exercise of *ijtihad* in turn led to the development of an elaborate methodology of jurisprudence, the science of the *usul al-fiqh*. Some of the best legal minds articulated complex linguistic debates on legal semantics and phenomenological discussions on the authority of the text. Yet, strangely, *usul al-fiqh* avoided the practical dimensions of *ijtihad*, such as the mujtahids' qualifications and hierarchy, and failed to discuss such seemingly mundane issues as the madrasa curriculum. Nor did it address the inconsistencies and ambiguities of Islamic law or question the rationale behind its archaic classification.[5]

Even the establishment of the Safavid state (1501–1736) and the declaration of Shi'ism as its official creed (in obvious contrast to the rival Ottoman empire's expressed upholding of "orthodox" Sunni Islam) did not substantially alter the mujtahids' resistance to institution development – and this in spite of the state's active sponsorship of the clerical establishment and heavy-handed patronage of teaching circles. Immigrant jurists from the Arab Shi'i communities of Jabal 'Amil (in today's Syria and Lebanon), Qatif and Bahrain in northern Arabia, and Najaf in southern Iraq were incorporated into the judiciary of the Safavid empire. These mujtahids and their Persian counterparts, many being converts from Sunnism, considered the Safavid shahs as legitimate defenders of the faith and their empire as the guarded Shi'i domain. For the "learned" ('ulama) community it was therefore permissible to assume judicial office, as the majority did, collect alms and the so-called share of the Imam (see below) and even to set the congregational Friday prayer.[6]

The jurists' failure in this period to solidify their gains and to implement a judicial leadership independent from the state is not surprising. Their reluctance to better define the boundaries of *ijtihad* was in part because the Safavid rulers successfully recruited the mujtahids as state functionaries. Although the office of *shaykh al-Islam* was held by a high-ranking jurist, this was not understood to be a legal supervision over the entire judicial community. Nor did it mean administrative or financial control, a task that the Safavid state consistently conferred on a non-clerical bureaucrat with the title of *sadr*. Moreover, the Safavids did not hesitate in the late seventeenth century to patronize the alternative Akhbari school, which rejected *ijtihad* and its logical rationalization, in contradistinction to the Usuli school.

The debate between the two schools in the late seventeenth and eighteenth centuries weakened the development of *usul al-fiqh* as a discretionary methodology in favor of the wholesale validity of all the hadith. More specifically, the Akhbari school held that all reports *(akhbar)* from diverse Shi'i hadith sources which are attributed to the Prophet *and* to the Imams are valid with little respect for their historical authenticity. Akhbari resistance to independent reasoning was congruent with the Safavid state's aversion to allow the emergence of an independent mujtahid-dominated judiciary.[7]

After the collapse of the Safavid empire in 1722 and the ensuing political instability, the Usuli school re-emerged as the predominant legal school, a position it retained during late eighteenth and throughout the ninteenth century. In contrast to most scholars of the rival Akhbari camp, Usuli jurists practised *ijtihad* by employing analogical deduction *(qiyas)* in order to infer opinions from the text of the Qur'an and the hadith. The analogical method was no doubt a far more effective strategy than Akhbarism in dealing with the judicial issues of Shi'i society at a time when the mujtahids often found themselves as leaders of their communities. In the early decades of the nineteenth century they made evident gains in socio-economic and educational areas by laying the foundations of a clerical establishment that has continued up to the present with little interruption. They monopolized the madrasas and the pulpit of the mosques, controlled vast charitable endowments *(awqaf)*, and collected religious taxes. The latter included the so-called portion of the Imam *(sahm-i imam)*, paid by pious followers to the mujtahids who received it as legitimate deputies *(na'ib)* of the Hidden Imam. They developed amicable though somewhat distant relations with the early rulers of the Qajar dynasty (1785–1925), an arrangement that was mutually beneficial to both sides and which therefore led to the apogee of Usuli *ijtihad*.

The growth of religious circles first in Najaf, where the Akhbari school was soundly defeated, and later in Iranian cities, was supported by a large student body and with a closely-knit network of teacher–pupil patronage.[8] Impressive numbers of legal works were produced both on the specifics of the law *(furu')* and on the methodology of the *usul al-fiqh*, with implicit emphasis on the role of the mujtahids not only as legal scholars but as judges and social mediators. The growth of congregations in mosques also strengthened jurists' ties with other social groups in search of legal support, most noticeably the merchants of the bazaar who backed the mujtahids and financed their teaching activities.

Yet with all their success in developing a semi-independent legal network and a solid lay constituency, the jurists of the Qajar period did not seek to reconstruct the theory of *ijtihad* and its application to public law. Despite occasional "turf wars" with the state over privilege and sphere of influence, or later in defiance of the state's Westernizing policies, they continued to honor the dichotomy of the religious law (shari'a), as it concerned jurists, versus the customary law *('urf)*, as exercised by the state. Customary law generally covered penal law such as that punishing criminals, dealing with public order, land use and agrarian arrangements *(nasaq)*, military, civic and government affairs, taxation and even family and business practices. It was based on historical precedents and though some laws were applicable across the land, most varied from region to region and even from town to town. They ran parallel with shari'a law but operated in a more fluid environment and were seldom documented. Moreover, the jurists frequently draw on *'urf* as an important source to argue legal points or to determine actual cases in the shari'a courts.

Neither side, jurists nor state (at least before the rise of European-inspired reforms), attempted to define the spheres of shari'a and *'urf* or to demarcate their boundaries through codification, let alone to breach the informal boundaries between them. The *usul al-fiqh* remained essentially concerned with its theoretical debates on the fine points of legal methodology. Voluminous works, commentaries, and glosses on commentaries were produced by Usuli scholars on intricate details of semantics and epistemology. Yet the jurists simply did not see the need for a centralized corporate identity or for disturbing the delicate balance with the state upon which they continuously negotiated their power. The state, in turn, preferred ambiguity, whereby through consent and coercion it hoped to persuade the jurists to comply with the its otherwise waning power and prestige. By the end of the century while the mujtahids were more than ever present in the public space, they were intellectually stagnant within the world of the madrasa and the arcane judicial practices of the shari'a courts. Accordingly, the curriculum of the seminaries was substantially truncated to focus solely on the roots of jurisprudence and the *furu'* at the expense of non-religious and especially non-legal topics. Even such traditional fields as mathematics, astronomy, and philosophy were no longer part of the jurists' general education.[9]

Voices of protest at the jurists' monopolies and their intellectual petrifaction further moved the mujtahids toward conservatism and distaste for new approaches. Most significantly, the messianic Babi movement in the middle decades of the century questioned the very legitimacy of the clerical community, its theoretical premises, educational methods, and legal practices. The Babi religion (later to be transformed into the Baha'i Faith) denied the long-held position of the jurists that they collectively represent the Imam of the Age in Occultation. As the Babi apocalyptic movement grew in popularity not only did it seek leadership in the new "Imam of the Age" but declared the end of the historical cycle of Islamic shari'a by ushering in a new cycle of prophetic manifestation. In response to the Babi challenge, the jurist community closed ranks and came closer to full collaboration with the state. In no other area did the jurists heed the Babi call for fundamental reform, though in the longer term the clerical community did produce a new form of communal leadership. The status of the marja' was first recognized in Shaykh Murtaza Ansari (1799–1864) in the late 1850s, and coincided with the growth of clandestine Babi anticlerical subversion. Ansari's emergence as the "supreme exemplar" no doubt mirrored the public desire for a clerical leadership committed to higher standards of morality, learning, and social justice. Ansari came to represent these values for a growing constituency of seminarians in the madrasas and among the lay followers.

The idea of *marja'iyat* continued in the second half of the century and through the Constitutional Revolution (1906–11) as a communal leadership with an increasing claim over political process. Perhaps the height of such politicized *marja'iyat* came with Mirza Hasan Shirazi (1815–95), the influential jurist and teacher whose access to funds and his ever-growing teaching circle placed him ahead of his competitors as the most widely recognized *marja'*. His general ban on the use of tobacco during the Regie protest of 1890–1 for the first time demonstrated the marja's' power and its potential for channeling public discontent into political channels. This came to be particularly true during the Constitutional Revolution. Several mujtahids simultaneously recognized as marja'*s* in this turbulent period appealed to diverse constituencies with contrasting political agendas and tendencies. This breakdown of a singular leadership more than ever demonstrated the crucial role of the jurists' constituencies in promoting the cause of one leader and demoting the other. Greater political polarization of the clerical community during the Constitutional Revolution vouched for this multiplicity of leadership.

## *From marja'iyat to wilayat-i faqih*

Only the latter part of the twentieth century, however, witnessed the gradual shift back to a centralized *marja'iyat* under Ayatollah Husayn Burujirdi (1875–1962). He should be viewed as the first to hold a united leadership not only in the management of the Qom seminaries, the collection of the religious taxes and distribution, and orchestrating a rigorous anti-Baha'i campaign but a certain degree of legal authority over the clerical community that resulted from these measures. It goes without saying that the "emergence" of this form of centralized *marja'iyat* was a belated, albeit inevitable, response to the state's intrusion into the judiciary – the rise of Pahlavi secular autocracy from the mid-1920s and the growth of modern educational institutions; the abolition of the mujtahids' civil courts and their replacement with a state-controlled judiciary; state-regulation of the use of charitable endowments; and other measures meant to undermine the 'ulama's social status.

The growth of the secularized or semi-secularized middle classes and the popularity of a variety of religious and ideological challenges, from Baha's, Marxists, secularizers, religious modernists and Islamic radicals of various sorts persuaded the demoralized and shrunken clerical community to reorganize the madrasa and solidify their network at the national level. Most importantly, they gradually moved away from the state–'ulama alliance that was founded on the ancient principle of preserving social equilibrium through guarded collaboration. In due course the new *marja'iyat* reconstituted its base not only in the bazaar community, where it was traditionally strong, but among a new class of urban and urbanized poor. They offered a pool for clerical recruitment and an enthusiastic mosque congregation.[10]

Greater solidarity and group identity, however, did not result in a reconsideration of Shi'i legal thought or any serious attempt to institutionalize the informal *marja'iyat* leadership. The study of *fiqh* in the seminaries of Najaf, Qom and elsewhere remained almost entirely loyal to traditional precepts and practices of Shi'i law and its obsessive preoccupation with devotional acts *('ibadat)* and contracts *('uqud)*. The striking persistence of legal archaism among Shi'i jurists can be explained in part by the inherent conservatism of the legal curriculum and in part by isolation from society's secular discourse. Left out of the new state-run judiciary, Shi'i teaching circles in Najaf and Qom made almost no attempt to address new issues of public law or even offer a modern reading of the old legal texts. The reconstituted Qom *hawza* continued to operate along the informal teacher–pupil patronage and produce growing number of jurists and/or preachers in need of new congregations.[11]

A number of marja's that "emerged" after the death of Burujirdi in 1962, including Ayatollah Khomeini, were no doubt more organized in their teaching and charitable operations. Yet there was no attempt in clerical circles to revisit the nature and conditions of *marja'iyat,* let alone arrive at a consensus about criteria for such leadership or the hierarchy. As much as the lay constituency of the marja' grew and the funding sources improved, no equivalent of an ecclesiastical hierarchy emerged even though there was a fairly coherent 'ulama network throughout Iran, southern Iraq, and Lebanon.

The diffuse *marja'iyat* leadership of this period relied heavily on both lay and clerical "followers." To mark their place in a complex game of prestige and popularity the marja's depended on their followers for higher standing. At times they were naturally bound by their whims and wishes. In this popularity contest no marja' could survive without his constituency's financial and moral backing, as Murtaza Mutahhari (1920–79), a prominent follower of Khomeini and a leader of the future Islamic Revolution, pointed out in the early 1960s. In a conference organized by religious modernists on the theme of *marja'iya,* the largely modernist lay, among them Mahdi Bazargan (1907–95) joined hands with the new generation of activist clerics, such as Mutahhari, to urge the marja's to bring some order into the notoriously chaotic world of Shi'i clerical leadership.[12]

The greater politicization of the clerical community, and especially the clerical clique around Khomeini from the mid-1960s, responded positively to this call. Among the marja's of Qom and Najaf, Khomeini represented the most radical political position. His open anti-Pahlavi platform caused as much trouble for him as it gained him popularity, especially among the lower and middle rank 'ulama disillusioned with other marja's and their collaboration with the shah's regime. Modernity thus came to the clerical establishment with political radicalization rather than as a fundamental revision of the Shi'i legal system and reconsideration of its curriculum and judicial premises. Even prominent students of Khomeini such as Husayn 'Ali Muntaziri (b. 1922) and Murtaza Mutahhari seldom called for a reconsideration of Islamic legal tradition or new teaching methods or the adoption of a modern legal philosophy. For them legal reform equaled succumbing to an alien secular modernity.[13] Those who did attempt in the Pahlavi period to reinterpret Shi'i theology and exegesis, among them Muhammad Hasan Sharia't Sangilagi and 'Ali-Akbar Hakamizada, were marginalized or soundly defeated by the jurists of Qom.[14]

The majority of the new seminarians and clerical followers of Khomeini came from among the underprivileged in small towns and villages. Increasingly in the late 1960s and 1970s they were drawn into political dissent and political activism, partly because they resented the wealth and privilege of the secularized urban middle classes. Further, they were critical of the Pahlavi legal system that replaced the old 'ulama-dominated judiciary with lay judges. Moreover, they also resented the subservience of the higher clerical ranks to the wishes of the state. Khomeini and his prominent students capitalized on these factors to promote his leadership as superior not necessarily because of his juristic qualifications, which were meager, but because of his uncompromising political stance.

In the tense environment of confrontation with the shah and his secret police, this message of political dissent was better transmitted to the layman by recalling the Shi'i narratives of defiance and self-sacrifice, as in the commemoration of the martyrdom of 'Ali ibn Abi Talib (d. 661) and that of his son, Husayn ibn 'Ali (d. 680). Laboring over the obscure and mostly redundant details of Shi'i law and the theoretical intricacies of *usul al-fiqh* appeared secondary, if not entirely obsolete. Even Mutahhari, the most promising intellectual product of Qom in the 1970s, preferred to delve into Western philosophy or Islamic reformism and revolutionary rhetoric rather than adopt a novel approach in *fiqh* and *usul.*[15]

In a climate of state-driven secular modernity versus the 'ulama's legal redundancy, Khomeini's gradual shift in the late 1960s toward the doctrine of juridical sovereignty was a solution to the prolonged problem of unregulated leadership. He borrowed from the Sunni reformist milieu the notion of the Islamic government, long debated by the likes of Muhammad Rashid Rida (1865–1935) and later Abu l-'Ala Mawdudi (1904–79), in order to set the legal ground for what he defined as the "authority of the jurist" (*wilayat-i faqih* [also rendered as Guardianship or Governance of the Jurist]). More of a teacher of Greco-Islamic philosophy than a teacher of jurisprudence, Khomeini was the right candidate to break through the inhibiting cobweb of juristic tedium. His theory no doubt had an unmistakable mystico-philosophical core that was externally colored by Shi'i legal trappings. On a personal level it was the work of a reluctant jurist who was anxious to overcome his marja' rivals through the philosophical backdoor; namely the charismatic leadership of the *wali,* long debated by the mystics and Shi'i theosophists.

The concept of *wilayat* upon which Khomeini propounded his theory is a complex and theologically charged term. Variably read as *wilayat* (Arabic *wilaya:* authority, guardianship) and *walayat* (Arabic *walaya*: bond of friendship), for Shi'is it was the hereditary status primarily arrogated to 'Ali and his Imam descendants as true successors to the Prophet; a status of sovereignty over his true believers. In Sufism *wilayat* implied friendship with God, a saintly status of proximity to Truth, even according to some on a par with prophethood.

For the Shi'i jurists, however, *wilayat* was a purely legal term denoting the state of guardianship often assumed by the jurist over the legal minor *(saghir)* and mentally retarded *(mahjur)*, hence *wilayat al-faqih*. Although in theory the guardianship of the jurist could be extended to the public sphere, in reality no jurist of any substance did consider as viable the jurist's "authority to rule" *(wilayat al-hukm)*. In the absence of the Hidden Imam, who is the just and legitimate enforcer of the *wilayat*, few jurists even condoned the "authority to judge" *(wilayat al-qada)* beyond mere issuance of opinions *(fatwas)*, but without the necessary power to enforce them. The notion of "general deputyship" (niyaba *'amma)* on behalf of the Imam, as claimed by some jurists in the Safavid and early Qajar periods, was never extended to the authority to govern, though it did reserve for the jurist certain prerogatives, such as declaring *jihad* under the auspices of the state.

In the latter part of the twentieth century, however, the prevalence of the idea of *marja'iyat* seldom allowed the doctrine of collective deputyship of the mujtahids to attract attention. The semantic shift in referring to the jurists also indicates a change in focus. Khomeini's use of *faqih* (jurist), rather than mujtahid or marja', in his own articulation of "guardianship" underlined sheer proficiency in *fiqh* rather than any acquired clerical status based on vague qualifications. His *wilayat,* in theory at least, could be extended to any jurist and not the one that is publicly recognized as the most important marja' or even a mujtahid. Such definition no doubt served Khomeini well while languishing in the exile of Najaf away from his constituency.

As defined by Khomeini, the doctrine of the "Guardianship of the Jurist" was applicable to public law as well as civil law. In the absence of the Hidden Imam, he argued, the jurist presents the least oppressive form of authority compared to temporal rule because it is founded on Islamic principles. The jurist is the most qualified in matters of Islamic law, which according to Khomeini is inherently superior to any secular body of law, and he is obliged by the same Islamic legal principles to uphold and enforce it. It is therefore incumbent upon the jurist, as an "individual duty" *(fard 'ayn)* to strive for political authority in order to form the Islamic government. Khomeini's doctrine was a revolutionary interpretation of the authority of the jurist even though he tried in his *wilayat-i faqih* (later *hukumat-i Islami*) to strengthen his theory with precedent from classical legal texts and citations from such Usuli jurists as the nineteenth-century Mulla Ahmad Naraqi (d. 1829). No Shi'i jurist before him ever extended the very limited application of legal *wilayat* to include public affairs, let alone the assumption of political power.[16]

Legal articulations aside, Khomeini's doctrine was driven by the requirements of his constituency not only to defy the legitimacy of the Pahlavi state, and whatever it stood for, but to bring coherence and unanimity to clerical leadership. The *wilayat-i faqih* promised not only the ascendancy of the jurists to positions of political power but a virtual end to clerical resistance to institutionalization. The rise of the *wilayat-i faqih* as an institution harbingered the eclipse of the *marja'iyat* and all the ambiguity that was inherent in qualities of the *mujtahid.*

Moreover, throughout his lectures Khomeini remained critical of the clerical establishment for its narrow understanding of *ijtihad* as mere preoccupation with devotional acts and other conventional categories of the Shi'i jurisprudence:

> In order to demonstrate to some degree how great the difference is between Islam and what is presented as Islam, I would like to draw your attention to the difference between the Qur'an and the books of hadith, on the one hand, and the practical treaties of jurisprudence *(risalaha-yi 'ilmiya)*, on the other. The Qur'an and the books of hadith, which are the sources of commands and ordinances of Islam, are completely different from the treatises written by the *mujtahids* of the present age both in breadth of scope and in the effect they are capable of exerting on the life of society.[17]

Khomeini goes on to say that issues related to society, including Muslim political affairs, occupy the greatest portion of Islamic teachings in the Qur'an and the hadith in comparison to a very small section dedicated to ritual acts *('ibadat)* and duties of man toward his creator. The thrust of the *Hukumat-i Islami* thus was to shift the emphasis back to Islam as a social agency and as a political power, and the responsibility of the Shi'i jurist to restore this vitality. This was in direct contrast to the traditional understanding of the role of the jurists as legal experts who were solely concerned with the pragmatic aspects of shari'a *(furu')* and was thus received as such by conservative jurists in Najaf and Qom.[18]

However, the assumption of political power by Khomeini and his 'ulama backers, which came with the revolution of 1979, imposed a bureaucratic regime on the Shi'i 'ulama more rigid than the chaotic madrasa system of Najaf and Qom had ever done. Even the honorary clerical titles, inflated over time, gained a new hierarchical connotation. While *ayatollah* (*ayat-Allah*; a sign of God) applied to the higher clerical figures, the *hujjat al-Islam* (a proof of Islam) signified the rank below. The highest status however was Khomeini's own. As the "Guardian Jurist" *(wali-yi faqih)* he assumed the title of *imam*, the first time this was ever used in the history of Shi'ism in a context other than that of the Twelve Imams. Although the office of Guardian Jurist was considered one and the same as the "deputy of the imam" *(na'ib-i imam)*, more in vogue in the nineteenth century, in practice a consensus was reached on the universal and sole reference of the term *imam* to the founder of the Islamic Republic, hence "*Imam* Khomeini."

The application of this honorific first appeared in Arabic works by Khomeini and about him published by a younger generation of his students in Najaf in the early 1970s. It is possible that the honorific was inspired by the Sunni notion of *imam* in the Arabic-speaking world (a leader of prayer, and more commonly, a clerical figure of certain prestige). With the rise of Khomeini's popularity in radical circles in the early 1970s, the term *imam* gained wide usage in Persian. The first known reference in Persian appears in a panegyric *(qasida)* dated 10 Tirmah 1349/July 1st 1970 by an unidentified poet:

> O, the true designated imam (*imam-i bi-haqq-i barguzidih*)
> You, the light of Islam's eye...
> You are the great imam that after the [Shi'i] Imams
> Islam has never witnessed like you a leader (*rahbar*).

Later, with the outbreak of the Islamic Revolution, the *imam* honorific was promoted by Khomeini's students and supporters (often intermittently with the more accepted notion of *na'ib-i imam*) to denote not only his superior authority over the Pahlavi monarchy but over the authority of the Shi'i marja's in Qom and Najaf. As the founder of the Islamic Republic, a certain semi-prophetic sanctity was also attached to the title, which was largely the work of propagandists in the revolutionary press but nevertheless was reminiscent of the recurring messianic tradition deeply embedded in Iranian Shi'ism.[19]

The constitutional authority and popular aura that Khomeini acquired as the guardian jurist and the *imam* denoted not only a desire for rationalization of the clerical community but also a drive toward clerical absolutism. The legitimacy and the mandate of the Guardian Jurist do not derive from his constituency of followers, as in the case of the marja‘, but from a sublime source. Despite the seemingly democratic trappings of the constitution of the Islamic Republic, the guardian jurist is answerable to no source but God, even though he is appointed by a Council of the Experts *(majlis-i khubragan)*; a select body of high-ranking 'ulama (and presumably impeachable by the same body).

The range of the guardian's institutional authority is vast and universally abiding even though the Islamic Consultative Council (*majlis-i shura-yi Islami*; i.e. the Iranian Parliament) tend to modify his ultimate power. Similarly, articles of the Constitution guaranteeing the inalienable rights and freedoms of the individual are at odds with the authoritarian power of the guardian jurist. Khomeini's charismatic aura in early years of the revolution glossed over the obvious contradiction in the constitution between democratic freedoms and the totalitarian power of the Guardian Jurist. In the post-Khomeini era, and three decades after the revolution, the contrast is glaring. The "supreme leader" *(rahbar)* as Khomeini's successor, Ayatollah 'Ali Khamene'i (b. 1939), is recognized in today's Islamic Republic, insists on these constitutional prerogatives to control, and if necessary quell, the legislative, the executive, and the judicial branches of the government and remains unaccountable to any elected body.

The authoritarian nature of *wilayat-i faqih* is no doubt indebted to the persistent culture of autocracy which the revolution denounced in theory but perpetuated in practice. But it also reflected the Shi'i judicial community's failure to rethink the precepts of Shi'i law and their applicability to pluralist values. The doctrine of the "Guardianship of the Jurist" was informed above all by a Shi'i legal mindset that was essentially alien to modern notions of plurality and democratic leadership even though, ironically, Shi'i *ijtihad* and *marja'iyat* operated on some form of popular representation. It was also colored, no doubt, by Khomeini's own mystical propensity for classical Sufism and specifically Ibn 'Arabi's (d. 1240) theory of *wilaya*.

Moreover, what historically informed "guardianship," as apparent in the rhetoric of the Islamic Revolution, was an imagined narrative of Islam's golden age, and especially 'Ali's pristine (though historically doomed) caliphate with great moral emphasis on leadership qualities of compassion *(walaya)* and self-denial *(ithar)* essential for creating a "classless" society. Added to the admix that shaped the "Guardianship of the Jurist" was the modern revolutionary urgency for assertive leadership harking back to the French Terror and the Russian "dictatorship of the proletariat." Such presuppositions were barely conducive to a progressive legal framework that separates legal authority from political power and religion from the state. What was crucially missing in this politico-legal vision of clerical leadership was a desire for re-examining traditional precepts of Islamic law in a new light of historical relativity.

The clerical community has largely come to constitute the backbone of the Islamic regime and actively seeks to monopolize positions of power. A minority of the jurists remained critical of the theory and the implementation of total authority of the jurist and faced the consequences of their criticisms. Yet opposition to *wilayat-*

*i faqih* further solidified the clerical hierarchy to an unprecedented degree. The Shi'i establishment now more than ever appears as an equivalent of a state-sponsored church with its ecclesiastical hierarchy, perhaps, as Said Arjomand observed, comparable to a Weberian "cesaro-papist" model of the state. The concentration of power in the hand of an oligarchy consisting of the Guardian Jurist and his top echelons of clerical allies inevitably triggered much resentment. The laymen and laywomen of the younger generation with revolutionary credentials now feel they have been left out by a clerical establishment that resorts to doctrinal repression to preserve its privileges and monopolies.

A whole body of literature that appeared since the revolution on the doctrine of *wilayat-i faqih,* ranging from progressives like Muhsin Kadivar to influential conservatives like Muhammad-Taqi Misbah-Yazdi, denote the yet undetermined parameters of the office of the Guardian Jurist in the Islamic Republic. In at least two of his works Kadivar examines *wilayat* within its conceptual and historical bounds. In *Hukumat-i Wila'i* (*wilaya* governance) he offers a framework of inquiry that relies on the Qur'an, the Shi'i hadith, as well as works of theologians, jurists, and mystics to define *wilayat-i shar'i* as a theocratic office irreconcilable with democratic values and essentially against the modern idea of social contact. "Guardianship over people is incompatible with deputation on their behalf," he concludes.[20] In his *Nazariyaha-yi Dawlat dar Fiqh-i Shi'a* (Theories of Government in Shi'i Jurisprudence) he traces the roots and development of the notion of government in the works of Shi'i Usuli writers of the nineteenth and twentieth centuries. Shi'i jurists, he argues, avoided a universal theory of government but went through four stages in accepting or denying the temporal authority of the state and its legitimacy. Though never explicit, Kadivar demonstrates conceptual contradictions within the Islamic regime and its constitution.[21]

At the other end of the spectrum Misbah Yazdi, in his *Nigahi Guzara bi Nazariya-yi Wilayat-I Faqih* (Brief Survey of the Theory of Guardianship of the Jurist) and a number of other works and collection of speeches, argues that the Guardian Jurist is solely designated by the Mahdi (the Hidden Imam) rather than by the people and that his command *(hukm)* is obligatory for all. The people's only prerogative is to "discover" *(kashf)* the guardian from among qualified jurists but they have no say in accepting or rejecting his decisions and have no right to participate in decision-making for the affairs of state. The Guardian Jurist consults only with experts in various fields in order to better govern but has no obligation to comply with their opinions. Misbah thus offers the most absolutist interpretation of *wilayat* even beyond Khomeini's earlier recognition of parliament as a legislative body and the constitutional right of the people to elect the Guardian Jurist through the Council of the Experts. In effect (and at times explicitly) Misbah thus questioned the very idea of an Islamic republic in that it is an eclectic innovation that is incompatible with the doctrine of the divinely guided Guardian Jurist and his rule on behalf of the Mahdi. As such he too, like Kadivar, acknowledges a fundamental contradiction in the foundation of the Islamic state.

The anticlerical content of Aghajari's speech and his call for an Islamic Reformation originates in this very contradiction. The younger generation of Iranians who are frustrated with the monopoly of power, heavy-handed treatment of dissident voices, and the obscurantist legal outlook of the clergy, are implicitly critical of the very existence of the office of the Guardian Jurist. Their disillusionment is even more evident after the repeated setbacks of the seemingly pro-reform wing of the clerical establishment as represented by the former President Muhammad Khatami (b. 1943) and his supporters. Such dissenter calls for reforming Islam are by no means rare in the history of antinomian Islam. Yet what distinguishes this post-revolutionary episode from earlier examples is that these voices of protest, especially since Khomeini's death in 1989, aimed at a consolidated clerical hierarchy with claim to infallible and comprehensive authority. The Guardianship of the Jurist is a far more explicit claim over religious hegemony in the public sphere and on behalf of the Imams than the old *marja'iyat* ever was. This is what makes the new criticism especially potent and enduring.

As for Aghajari's fate, he seems to have been the involuntary beneficiary of the inconsistencies that are typical of Shi'i legal practice. The same ruling of the Hamadan court that sentenced him to death for blasphemy also sentenced him to a total of eight years of imprisonment for three other related offenses and after that to a ten-year ban on teaching at any university. The seemingly ludicrous verdict of the court points to the ambiguities of a legal culture built on negotiations and compromise, a culture that still seems to be thriving three decades after the Islamic Revolution.[22]

# PART 4

# *Satan and Salvation in the Islamic Revolution*

## CHAPTER 9

# *Khomeini's* Great Satan: *Demonizing the American Other in the Islamic Revolution in Iran*

On November 5, 1979, Ayatollah Ruhullah Khomeini, then residing in Qom, made a highly publicized statement in support of the students who the previous day had taken hostage the staff of the American Embassy in Tehran. He reiterated their demand that the shah, who had been admitted for cancer treatment in New York, should be extradited. He also demanded that Great Britain should return Shapur Bakhtiar, the last premier under the old regime, who had taken refuge in Paris. While delivering his customary umbrage against the United States and Britain, he called the United States the Great Satan *(shaytan-i buzurg)*:

> In this revolution the Great Satan is America, which is gathering around it other satans by making loud noises – that included both the satans inside and outside Iran. You know that during the rule of those two evils [Reza Shah and Muhammad Reza Shah], whose rule was in contravention of the law, Iran was enslaved by Britain and then by America. The clamor being raised by the Great Satan . . . is because its hand has been cut off from our resources; it is afraid lest this amputation should become permanent, and so it is plotting. As for that center [the U.S. embassy] occupied by our young men, I have been informed it has been a lair for espionage and plotting.[1]

Khomeini's remarks contained all the major ingredients of his anti-Western concoction: the Western powers' long-standing interventions and conspiracy against Iran, Pahlavi rule as the embodiment of the *taghut* (the diabolical idol) subservient to the satanic powers, and the need for vigilance and closing ranks against further plots and support for the most extreme trends in the revolutionary melting pot. Little changed in his radical rhetoric over the next ten years.

Almost immediately the term "Great Satan" was adopted by the propaganda machine of the nascent Islamic Republic and became a staple of Iran's broadcasting services and editorials in revolutionary newspapers. It was heard frequently in Friday sermons, the slogans of the revolutionary rallies, and the war cry of the Revolutionary Guards in the battlefield of the Iraq–Iran war. It served as a complement to that other ominous slogan of the revolution, "Death to America." Cursing the Great Satan became a way of reaffirming solidarity to the revolution, as if by magical incantation exorcizing a ghost from the body of the revolutionary community.[2] Contrary to a vast corpus of revolutionary neologies coined during the revolution that were soon to be forgotten, the Great Satan endured and took on a life of its own, though never too far from the frowning face of its author. This was partly because the Great Satan became part of the hostage crisis, which was played out for more than a year over the international media to American audiences, almost to the point of becoming a raging obsession. The Great Satan became a kind of rude characterization that was meant to fuel anti-Iranian sentiments in the United States and to foment worse stereotypes of Iran and Islam, with lasting consequences.[3]

## *Conspiratorial Fears*

Khomeini's initial motivation for attaching a satanic label to the image of the United States was the exaggerated fear of U.S. covert operations following the collapse of Pahlavi rule. The remote possibility of Mahdi Bazargan's provisional government negotiating with American diplomats increased the chances of a U.S. coup similar to the one that had brought down Mohammad Mosaddeq in 1953.[4] After Khomeini announced his support of the Students Following the Imam's Path capturing the "Den of Spies" (as Khomeini labeled the American embassy), Bazargan's government collapsed. The immediate victim of Khomeini's shift to greater militancy was 'Abbas Amir-Entezam, a government spokesman who in December 1979 was charged with spying for the United States and later was sentenced to life imprisonment. The failed Nozheh coup in July 1980, organized by a group of middle rank army and air force officers, added to the revolution's paranoia.

Over time the Great Satan found new connotations beyond the hostage crisis. As the war with Iraq protracted in the mid-1980s, among many demonic labels that revolutionary Iran attached to Saddam Hussein and the Ba'thist regime was the "Lesser Satan" *(shaytan-i kuchak)*, with an obvious hierarchical implication. In some ways this was raising Saddam's status, for early on that epitaph was reserved for Britain. The Reagan administration's efforts to counterbalance Iranian revolutionary zeal by befriending the Iraqi regime changed the priorities in Iran's demonic hierarchy. By supplying Iraq with military hardware and intelligence and by encouraging the oil-rich Arab countries of the Persian Gulf to underwrite Iraq's crushing cost of the war, the United States reaffirmed its place in Khomeini's demonology.

Reagan's hard-line position against the Sandinistas in Nicaragua and against other anti-U.S. movements only broadened the usage of the satanic label. The Great Satan, however, received currency in Western circles critical of America's intrusive foreign policy. Even in the United States the label was recalled somewhat mockingly as a way of admitting the evils of American hegemony and its corrupting cultural influences, as if becoming satanic was the inevitable cost of being a superpower even after the 1991 collapse of the Soviet Union. More than twenty-five years later, the "Great Satan" seems to have made its way into the political jargon defining U.S. hegemonic power as exemplified by the invasion of Iraq and its enormous cultural lure all over the world. The *Oxford English Dictionary* included a second definition of the term "Great Satan" based on Khomeini's label: "The United States, viewed as an imperialistic and malevolent power, esp. in the context of U.S. policy in the Middle East."

It is difficult not to read in the title, and in the content, of Salman Rushdie's 1988 novel *The Satanic Verses* a deliberate allusion to Khomeini's Great Satan. The phantasmagoric portrayal of a Khomeini-like angry ascetic in the land of infidels may be taken as Rushdie's humorous – though, as it turned out, very dangerous – musings in the realm of modern demonology. If Khomeini wishes to indict the United States (and by extension the Western world) as the Great Satan, Rushdie seemed to imply, he should first look back at the phenomenon of extremist Islam and then specifically at the message alluded to in the Qur'an's so-called Satanic Verses. According to these verses and the apocryphal exegesis associated with them, while in Mecca the Prophet acknowledged the three female deities of the pagan Arabs. Coming to terms with his heathen adversaries, the Prophet openly compromised the doctrine of monotheism, the fundamental precept of his new religion (Qur'an 53:19–20). Relying on other Qur'anic verses, however, Muslim commentators tried to explain the flagrant inconsistency of these verses with the rest of the Qur'an's strict monotheistic teaching. The verses, so it was explained, were the outcome of a temporary lapse of prophetic inspiration that opened the door to Satan's temptation *(waswasa)*, and they were soon to be "abrogated" by solid affirmations of the oneness of Allah and denunciation of polytheism (Qur'an 22:52–3).[5]

Khomeini's declaration of war against the U.S. satanic power, Rushdie seems to have been suggesting, was a paradigmatic act of renouncing the polluting lure of the West after he has been compromised by it. Rushdie's subtle allegory, of course, was entirely incomprehensible to Khomeini, whose famous *fatwa* condemned Rushdie to death as an apostate not for his characterization of Khomeini, which he and his disciples probably never understood, but for defaming the Prophet of Islam and the imagined story behind the Satanic Verses. From Khomeini's perspective, the Great Satan primarily defined the conspiratorial capabilities of the United States as a superpower and its willingness to employ them in covert operations and in economic and cultural mischief.

Anyone who leafs through writings and pronouncements before and during the Islamic Revolution, especially Khomeini's 1970 *Wilayat-i Faqih* (later to be reprinted as *Hukumat-i Islami* and translated as *Islamic Government*), will encounter plenty of such allegations. References abound to British and American imperial designs for domination over Iran and the rest of the Muslim world and their regional agenda for economic exploitation and acculturation.[6] His Manichean characterization of the world powers is informed as much by politicized theology as by memories of nearly two centuries of often unhappy Iranian experiences with Western powers. The Great Satan thus was not a casual insult volleyed at the United States. Nor was it entirely formed outside Iran's self-image as persecuted and victimized, an image deeply embedded in Persian mythological, religious, and historical memories.

## *Who's Satan?*

Khomeini's demonology no doubt was heavily laced with Qur'anic terms and references even though the Persian adjective *bozurg* (great) for Satan appears to be without precedent in Islamic high literature. The standard Qur'anic references to Satan *(shaytan)* are numerous and have been the primary source for much discussion in the history of Islamic theodicy. Among the ninety-eight references to Satan in the Qur'an as the source of fear, slippage, precipitating hatred, and above all temptation, Satan does not stand at the top of a hierarchy of lesser demons. He does however have followings among the humans and the *jinn* who, according to the Qur'an (17:64), serve him as an army of "horsemen and foot soldiers." Even plural usage in the Qur'an of *shayatin* (devils), which occurs eighteen times, does not imply any hierarchical order either. No superlatives (such as *kabir* or *'azim*), moreover, are associated with him or even a relative supremacy (such as *akbar* or *a'zam*). References to *Iblis*, another Qur'anic term for Satan, often appear in the context of Adamic Creation and do not imply a clear sense of hierarchy either.[7]

Beyond the Qur'an, the Islamic exegetic also attributes to *shaytan* the paramount power of temptation, an almost diffuse but intelligent diabolical force who "invites" people to commit sins by appealing to their weaknesses but cannot compel them to do so. Contrary to Christian belief, which gives Satan a much greater role in shaping human character and society, the *shaytan* of Islamic tradition is at the most an instrument of testing human loyalties and devotion to God. His utterances on the Day of Judgment make it clear that he has been assigned by God to corrupt mankind (Qur'an 14:22). As a disobedient servant of God, presumably with status equal to the angels (although he apparently belonged to the jinn), *shaytan* is evidently limited to instigating a course independent of his creator. Indeed, the absence of an extensive demonology in the Islamic belief system may confirm the limitations on *shaytan*'s power, a demon working under divine license. The ritualistic throwing of seven pebbles at Satan in the Muna stage of the Hajj pilgrimage in Mecca, whereby the pilgrims target the Great Satan *(shaytan al-Kabir)* and his associates, implies, anthropologically speaking, a certain vulnerability on the part of Satan in the face of multitudes of Muslims.

Qur'anic ethics aside, Satan even gets a sympathetic treatment from some creative mystics. 'Ayn al-Qudat Hamadani commiserates with Satan's predicament, for he performs the arduous task of tempting humans in a course that ultimately serves God's purpose at the End of Time.[8] Perhaps he detects in Satan's work a certain commonality with the fate of human beings, for they too are instruments of a divine cause. In the *Masnavi* of Jalal al-Din Rumi, Satan's job is curiously elevated to a do-gooder of a sort. Once he even wakes Mu'awiya, the founder of the Umayyad caliphate, at dawn so that he does not miss his morning prayers, which in due course shall prevent him from committing sins, falling into Satan's trap, and jeopardizing the affairs of the community. This is hardly a diabolical figure capable of major mischief.

The apocalyptic association of the *shaytan* confirms his eternal servitude. He appears before God on the Day of Reckoning to witness his human followers being punished, though not to his chagrin. It is as if in this moment of turmoil and tribulation the reality of Satan's true divine mission is revealed to the damned and the saved. Once the work of resurrecting humans and judging them is over and they have been duly dispatched to wherever they belong, Satan's job is also done and, unlike his Christian counterpart, he has no business tormenting sinners or burning them in hellfire. For that purpose, in the Shi'i apocalyptic tradition there is a full squad of specialized agents headed by the Lord of the Hell, whose infernal tasks are hellish, so to speak, but not diabolical. Not surprisingly, the paradisiacal space does not have room for Satan either, despite all the carnal pleasures and sexual licenses freely available to the saved. Temptation, Satan's weapon of choice in the terrestrial war of good and evil, with all its sexual capability has no effect in the celestial bliss. Even purgatory remains outside his reach.

This corrective function of Satan as a deterrent has persuaded some recent Shi'i commentators to assign to him a role in the hearts and minds of believers, outside the physical space. Even among pious teachers of Shi'i ethics, Persian culture encourages adherence to a diffuse mystical *('irfani)* interpretation. We cannot miss the modernistic coloring, of course. If a personalized Satan is hard to prove in the age of modern science, it is more expedient to imagine him as an intrinsic force, one that still controls and corrupts but on a different existential plane. In this interpretation, as a metaphoric agency Satan acts inside people's hearts and minds, within an ethical frame. He tempts people to kill, steal, and deceive or to be the subject of angry outbursts. Yet he is not politicized, and ideologically he is not tied to actions attributed to an alien adversary. The leap from an ethical Satan to an ideological Satan is yet to come with the Islamic Revolution.

## *Pollutants of Body and Mind*

To understand how this transition came about, we should look at the broader issue of how Iranian Shi'ism positioned its "self" versus the alien "other." The Shi'i hadith is well aware of the *shaytan* and his mischief, particularly in the context of human bodily temptations and the means of combating them. This is a realm devoted mostly to folk religion: a set of prayers, invocations, and talismans as well as practical techniques and ethical advice to ward off the devil and his assistants. In the view of the master popularizer of Shi'i theology, Muhammad Baqir Majlisi (d. 1699), who is responsible for injecting a vast number of folk rituals into Iranian Shi'ism, the human body is susceptible to all kinds of satanic onslaughts and should thus be constantly guarded against his insidious plots. Majlisi's rather entertaining *Hilyat al-Muttaqin* (The Garb of the Pious) and other works offer some good examples of such hazards and the precautionary measures to remain safe. If appropriate invocations are not uttered, for instance, Satan will enter the body of the newborn through its anus or vagina. If proper measures are not taken, Satan can make his sorties in dark and unfrequented locations, such as corner niches of bathhouses and toilets, when the body is naked and exposed or during sexual intercourse or change of underwear. Even negligence as mundane as failing to put on both shoes may give Satan a chance.[9]

The believer's body, however, is most vulnerable to satanic incubation when defiled by outside pollutants. Far more than specific references to Satan himself and his corporal penetration, there exists in Iranian Shi'ism a preoccupation with bodily pollution and methods of combating it. The ritualistic cleansing of pollutants *[nijasat]* – a vast area in Shi'i jurisprudence – not only regulates bodily fluids and scatology, dietary laws, genitalia, and sexual intercourse but also regulates (prohibits) contact with nonbelievers, including the People of the Book. A typical work of Shi'i jurisprudence such as *Mustamsak al-'Urwat al-Wuthqa* by the twentieth-century Muhsin Hakim, which is a compendium based on all canonical works of Shi'i jurisprudence *(fiqh)*, devotes 281 entries to ritual purification *(taharat)* of which 185 are on ritual pollutants – one of the largest in the entire work (not to mention entries on pollutants in other chapters such as nullifiers of prayers or handling of corpses). Category nine of the section on pollutants deals exclusively with infidels and circumstances leading to ritual defilement as a result of contacting non-Muslims, apostates, and others with questionable beliefs.[10]

Much, of course, has been said about the influence of the Zoroastrian and Jewish notions of pollutants and laws of defilement on Islamic and especially on Shi'i law. The organizing principle of Zoroastrian religion is differentiation between the forces of good and evil personified in the eternal conflict between the supporters of Ahura Mazda and those of the Ahriman. The world is divided between pure believers and polluting infidels. Ahriman, the manifestation of evil, who is a powerful counterforce to Ahura Mazda, the Lord of Wisdom, is above all an Evil Thought, although he is also the master of all the polluting elements including evil animals and other beings. The cosmic battle that is waged between them through their human and superhuman agents shapes the course of human history that finalizes only at the End of Time. The feared Ahriman, who commands his own army of demons with specialized tasks, is often denoted in the Zoroastrian literature as being the Demon of the Demons *(divan div)*, a term strikingly comparable to the Great Satan. Contrary to the relatively docile *shaytan* of the Qur'anic tradition, Ahriman's scope of operation is wide and his powers immense. Unlike the Islamic Satan, Ahriman is not a fallen angel waiting to be rehabilitated but an independent agent as powerful, if not at times more potent, than Ahura Mazda. In the final cycle of the cosmic battle, Ahura Mazda and his army eventually destroy Ahriman and his army. Yet, until that final moment, the cosmic battle is continually waged with no certainty as to who will be the immediate winner.[11]

Establishing a link between the pre-Islamic notion of Ahriman and the Great Satan in the utterances of a revolutionary prophet in our time may seem alarmingly ahistorical and textually formidable (though not entirely impossible). Yet the affinity is startling. One may attribute the enduring presence of such cultural archetypes of good and evil in the Iranian Shi'i milieu to the absorbing and internalizing over the course of the early Islamic centuries of elements of ancient Zoroastrian theology and ethics, especially demonology. It is not a coincidence that the story of Karbala at a mythical level deeply resonates with the old Iranian notion of making a moral choice between good and evil. Giving support *(nusra)* to the apocalyptic Mahdi, the Hidden Imam of the Twelver Shi'ism, upon his advent is mandatory for every capable believer. This pre-apocalyptic battle with a host of anti-Shi'i villains – a vengeful re-enactment of the Karbala tragedy but with a reverse outcome – closely follows the Zoroastrian End of Time when Ahura Mazda and his followers confront his nemesis and defeat him.[12]

It can be argued that such a powerful archetype has persisted in the Iranian collective conscience (borrowing the Jungian notion) and hence in society's moral fabric. The ritualistic invocation of the Lord of Wisdom and the reinforcement of his worldly arsenal is the believer's lifelong duty. He is required to maintain bodily purity, preserving natural elements from *Ahrimanic* infiltration (water and fire in particular) and destroying evil creatures. Obsessive ritual cleansing of all taboos that defile the body and contaminate the community of believers thus ties distant Iranian memories to recent Shi'i beliefs.

Equally enduring in the binary between good and evil is the dichotomy between *iran* and *aniran* (non-Iran) as preserved in the Iranian legends. Firdawsi's *Shahnama* (Book of the Kings) differentiates Iranians from their Turanian (Turkic) enemies of the north-east. By implication, aniran includes other countries in the imagined geography of the *Shahnama,* although not always as enemies: China, Rum (the Roman/Byzantine empire), India, Yemen, and the Tazi people, who were identified with the Arabs of the southern Iranian frontiers.[13] This differentiation survived in Persian and Arabic cosmography parallel with the Greek notion of dividing the world into seven climes. With Iran in the center and the rest of the world as surrounding provinces *(ustans)* – mirroring the administrative divisions of the Sassanian empire – the presumed Iranian geographic centrality, and hence its ethnocentric exclusivity, re-emerges with greater vigor in Safavid Shi'ism. The notion of Shi'is as the "rightly guided nation" *(firqa-yi najiyya)* implied that non-Shi'is, presumably the "seventy-two" other denominations of Islam, are straying or misguided. The identification of the "rightly guided nation" as Iranians has been made at least since the sixteenth century when Twelver Shi'ism was declared the official creed of the Safavid state. It can be argued that this ethnocentric self-image helped Iran to survive a new *aniran*, that is, the territorial onslaughts and doctrinal hostilities of the Ottoman and Uzbek Sunni powers on its frontiers.

This Shi'i self-image persisted until the late nineteenth century and before the countering notions of decay and deprivation set in almost invariably in comparison with the West's material, military, and technological advances. Concurrently, modern geography and hemispheric mapping of the globe have modified and eventually obliterated Iranian ethnocentrism and relegated it, together with the rest of the Muslim world, to a marginal periphery. From the perspective of the non-Western people, the center of gravity in the new global map shifted to Europe – and more specifically to Western Europe – primarily because of that region's ability to kill more, colonize, dominate, and globally exploit economic resources. This paradigmatic shift in perception had long-term consequences in the way the new, feeble Iranian "self" perceived the non-Iranian "other."

## *Collective Myth and Individual Histories*

What do Iranian myths and legends or Shi'i rules of ritual purification have to do with the idea of the Great Satan as it was adopted by a revolutionary leader in reference to a twentieth-century superpower? The answer may lie in a modern discourse that governs the interplay between Iran as a community of memory and the imagined West as a new *aniran* – a hostile "other" comprising all the cultural lures and hegemonic instincts embedded in Western modernity. It also includes all the political, theological, and mythological devices employed by Khomeini and other Islamic radicals to demonize the United States as Islam's greatest adversary. Needless to say that, in the minds of its advocates, such a designation was essential to the contrast between the righteous community of the revolution and the dark forces of blasphemy and political deceit.

At a deeper level this did not preclude a subconscious preoccupation with the Qur'anic, Shi'i, and old Iranian archetypes of exceptionality. These paradigms may not consciously manifest themselves in the thoughts and actions of individuals but rather resonate in the cultural milieu in which Khomeini and likeminded revolutionaries operated. Even if most Iranians had forgotten the Ahriman of the *Avesta*, and the Manichean preoccupation with the irremovable residue of the evil in the material world is only a matter of academic interest, these archetypes remained alive and were reinforced by perceptions of disempowerment.

Khomeini's personal history – one that concurs aptly with Iran's troubled encounters with the potent forces of the Western modernity since the turn of the twentieth century – offers one such example. Iran's uneven road to modernity through Westernizing policies of autocratic reformers and the United States' geopolitical and economic presence in Iran left many Iranians with painful memories, real or reconstructed, of loss or perceived loss. This occurred at a time when the clerical classes to which he belonged had lost or stood to lose much of their prestige, public influence, and economic resources. From the perspective of Khomeini and a host of other Iranians of his background, the history of the twentieth century was an unfolding drama of swarming satanic spirits and polluting substances descending on pure and pious but helpless Muslim souls. It was a century of Western powers, specifically Britain and Russia and later the United States, hatching plots to defile Iranian dignity, exploit Iran's resources, and conspire against its sovereignty. In his view these powers enjoyed almost demiurgic knowledge of the world, especially cartographic and geological, and had access to technologies that could explore and exploit the resources of poor and naive nations incapable of controlling their own destinies. In his *Islamic Government,* as in numerous speeches and public remarks, Khomeini recalls Europeans exploring and utilizing Iran's riches with the aide of "maps" in their possession (presumably geological surveys).[14]

Reza Shah's era in particular (1921–41) left tormenting memories in Khomeini's mind. The founder of the Pahlavi dynasty was seen as a chief villain in Khomeini's frequent attacks on Iran's course of secularizing modernity. Born in 1900, Ruhullah Khomeini was brought up in an environment of violence and banditry in his hometown of Khomain, an environment typical of the post-Constitutional

Revolution and the First World War era. He lost both parents: his father was killed in a brawl when he was an infant, and his mother died when he was fifteen. As a young religious student who joined 'Abd al-Karim Ha'iri's seminary in Arak and then emigrated with him to Qom, he found relative calm and security in the madrasa environment (for which incidentally he should have been thankful to Pahlavi rule). Instead, like a few of his cohorts, he developed a profound dislike of the secularizing policies of the Pahlavi era and particularly of the imposition of various restrictions on the clerical establishment. These misgivings in later years – as early as 1943 – turned into sharp attacks on Reza Shah and his modernist project.

Khomeni's resentments were grounded in historical fact. The Pahlavi state had taken away from the clerical establishment its entire judicial power by means of creating a secular justice administration *(Vizarat-i 'Adliyya)*, codifying a modern legal system that skillfully incorporated aspects of Shi'i Islamic law but dismantled the arbitrary application of the shari'a as exercised by the mujtahids, and purged many of the clergy from positions of judgeship. Moreover, the state created a modern public educational system that vastly undermined the madrasa system and clerical control over it. The state imposed greater scrutiny over charitable endowments *(awqaf)* and their expenditure, monitored public preaching, and censured other activities in the mosques, introduced qualifying examinations for the members of the clergy, and restricted the use of clerical attire only to qualified individuals. The whole spirit of Westernization advanced by the state contrasted with the conservatism of the clergy and challenged their time-honored demeanor. From the intellectually isolated and socially fortified Qom madrasas, the outside world seemed hostile, ruthless, and godless, with evil forces setting out to destroy Islamic values, Muslim solidarity, and whatever Khomeini and his predecessors stood for.

Khomeini's sentiments reflected clerical defiance throughout the late nineteenth and early twentieth centuries against reformist imperatives initiated by the state or even innovations that came from within the Shi'i milieu. And greater defiance, of course, led to greater stagnation. This is evident in the arcane curriculum of the Shi'i madrasas, the tedious scholastic teaching methods, and the utterly outdated, irrelevant, and disorganized scholarship coming out of Najaf, Qom, and other religious centers in areas of law, ethics, theology, and philosophy. The Shi'i scholars of Khomeini's generation and their students simply refused to face the challenge of modernity not only in terms dictated by the secular state but in their own terms and within the bounds of their theological and legal specializations. Instead, they adhered to old shari'a notions of pollutants and purifiers, nullifiers of daily prayers, and complexities of sexual intercourse. Khomeini's *Tawdih al-Masa'il,* a conventional compendium on the practicalities *(furu')* of Islamic law, spends as much space on the above categories as any work of medieval Shi'i jurisprudence.[15] His other works on Islamic philosophy *(hikmat)*, ethics, and Qur'anic exegeses *(tafsir)* are no less traditional.

From the Qom perspective, the villainy of modernity, as the mullas experienced it, was not restricted to the Pahlavids (father and son) or to their ministers and administrators, beneficiaries, their police apparatus, and the secularized middle classes that thrived under the new rule. The Pahlavi modernizing program was seen as part and parcel of Western cultural hegemony, especially the new dress codes, secular education, advocacy of leisure and entertainment, drinking, mixing of sexes, and above all the unveiling of women. As early as the 1960s, intellectuals such as Jalal Al-e Ahmad in his *Occidentousis (Gharbzadigi)* offered much ammunition for this myopic and conspiratorial approach to the Western nemesis. Catchphrases such as "global arrogance" *(istikbar-i jahani)* and the "world devouring" *(jahan-khwar)* hegemony of the West, overused by Khomeini and the propaganda of the Islamic Republic, were borrowed in the early 1970s from the Shi'i radical intellectual 'Ali Shari'ati. *Taghuts* in the form of oppressive states, he believed, survived not only because of suppression at home but also because of subservience to foreign values and servitude to foreign powers.

In Qom, and later in his Najaf exile, Khomeini borrowed this fashionable terminology of the 1960s and 1970s from intellectuals such as Al-e Ahmad and Shari'ati who had long been enamored with radical Shi'ism. Moreover, he sufficiently fortified these terms with his politicized reading of the Qur'an and the Shi'i hadith. The contrast between the hegemonic West and the disempowered Muslim world was glaring. He portrayed the secularizing Pahlavi rule and its strong ties with the United States as the ultimate *taghut*, the demonic idol associated in the Qur'an with Satan. The *taghut* is, of course, the "corruptor of the earth" *(mufsid f'il-ard)* par excellence, whose oppressive rule, amassed wealth, display of opulence, and ultimately hollowed powerbase are exemplified in the Qur'an by Pharaonic rule. Yet beyond the story of Pharaoh and the Israelites, the *taghut* has an apocalyptic subtext, for he is ultimately destroyed in the cosmic battle at the End of Time.[16] The rich Shi'i apocalyptic tradition embellished this aspect to its fullest and made the *taghut* a precursor to the advent of the Imam of the Age. Placed in the politicized language of radical Islam, as articulated by Khomeini, the fall of the Pahlavi regime and the outbreak of the Islamic Revolution were seen as pre-apocalyptic events whereby the leadership of the deputy *(na'ib)* of the Imam of the Age, as "Imam Khomeini" was recognized in the course of the revolution, brought down the rotting pillars of the *taghut*.[17]

The demolition of the *taghut* on the pre-apocalyptic arena of the Islamic Revolution, however, was to be accomplished with the help of the "disinherited of the earth" *(mustad'afin fi'l-ard)* and for their sake. The "disinherited of the earth," another overspent rhetorical currency of the revolution, was a Qur'anic term with a strange history. It found its equivalent somehow in Frantz Fanon's 1961 postcolonial book *Damnés de la Terre* (English edition: *The Wretched of the Earth)*. Through Shari'ati or similar channels, it then re-emerged in the revolutionary parlance of the late 1970s to represent a kind of Islamic "proletariat," one that was assigned to fight the *taghut* and its satanic allies as the first step toward constructing the idyllic classless Islamic community under the sacred guidance of *wilayat-i faqih*.

## *Rediscovering the Great Satan*

Yet despite the Islamized cloak, the diluted dosage of Marxist ideology in the rhetoric and parlance of the Islamic Revolution is unmistakable. Through the same channels that the "disinherited of the earth" and their nemesis, the *taghut*, migrated from the pages of the sacred text to the plane of radical politics, so did the Great Satan. We may never fully uncover how this effective labeling was applied to the United States, but there is at least one curious piece of evidence that may help illustrate its origins. It goes back to the beginning of the United States' serious involvement in Iran in the aftermath of the Second World War, and it involves an illustrious (now slightly blemished) all-American public figure.

Supreme Court justice William O. Douglas (whose 1939–75 term was the longest in the history of the Court) was a Yale Law School professor before Franklin Roosevelt appointed him to head the U.S. Security and Exchange Commission. He was an avid traveler, mountaineer, and memoirist whose many adventures overseas included four visits to Iran between 1949 and 1957. A liberal in his domestic politics and a cold warrior in foreign affairs, he was preoccupied with the threat of Soviet communism in the Middle East. As a typical example of rugged American individualism, he took upon himself a mission to understand the peoples and countries of the Middle East and share his findings with the American people. It is not, however, entirely improbable that his visits to Iran also aimed to cultivate closer ties between U.S. government agencies (such as the Point Four Program under Truman and Eisenhower) and the Iranian government and individuals.

Douglas was friendly with a large number of Iranians, some rather influential, including army officers, politicians, and tribal khans. His first and second visits across remote regions of the country in 1949 and 1950 stirred suspicion in the Iranian leftist circles, especially in the Tudeh-inspired press and subsequently the Persian commentaries of Radio Moscow. In 1951 after his friend and host General Haj 'Ali Razmara, the pro-American prime minister, was murdered by radical Islamic terrorists of the Fada'ian-i Islam organization, Douglas noted:

> Both the 1949 and the 1950 trips brought the Moscow radio to a high pitch of excitement. I was charged with being the Big Devil [presumably his translation of *shaytan-i buzurg*], my son (who accompanied me in 1949) with being the Little Devil. . . . I was charged with being a spy for the American Army, with landing guns in the Persian Gulf, with laying plans for guerrilla warfare in the Middle East, with living in the tradition of the famous Lawrence of Arabia and the fabulous Major Robert T. Lincoln of more recent years.[18]

What makes this seemingly trivial quotation rather remarkable is the context Douglas provides. In his books he convincingly argues the breadth and the efficacy of Soviet propaganda broadcasting:

> Soviet propaganda beamed to the Middle East exploits the news of the day. It emphasizes and exaggerates the weaknesses and frailties in existing regimes. It constantly reminds the natives of their grievances. It whispers suspicions about those in power. It charges America and England with having designs on every nation in the region, with planning to make each one a subservient colony in the large imperial system. It represents the Soviets as the forces of Good in the world, America and England and all non-Communist governments as the forces of Evil. It identifies the Soviets with every minority cause, with every nationalist ambition.[19]

He goes on to say that Soviet propaganda does not neglect "religious prejudices," reminding the Muslim populations of religious rivalries and conflicts which in earlier days caused much bloodshed. "It was a Pope who in the twelfth century summoned the Christian world to war against the infidels. Soviet propaganda today resurrects the specter of that bloody conflict and links the Vatican with Wall Street and Anglo-American 'imperialists' in a conspiracy against the Middle East."[20]

Furthermore, he noted the way the Marxist message can be made to appear compatible with the message of Islam:

> When Marx and Engels wrote the Communist Manifesto in 1848, they dipped their pens in the New Testament and in the Jeffersonian philosophy to make their document popular among Europeans. Today in the Middle East the Communists use the same technique in preaching Soviet communism to those of the Islamic faith. They built elaborate syllogisms to show that their creed has support in the Koran.[21]

Despite his geopolitical insight and global scope, Douglas was influenced by fears of communism that engrossed his country especially during the McCarthy years. Yet, as a liberal observer and commentator sympathetic to the plight of the peoples of the Middle East, he did not fail to note that the reason Soviet propaganda appealed to the Iranians (as well as to the Arabs, Turks, Indians, and Greeks) was because in their view "America stood behind the British and apparently supported" their deeply resented and "unfair oil concession," which they insisted that the Persian government should honor. Time and again in his assessment of U.S. policy in the Middle East, Douglas was critical of U.S. reliance on military force, on empty advocacy of democracy while supporting dictatorships whose only redeeming quality was to be anti-communist, and for wrongly assuming that monetary assistance to the nations of the Middle East could transform ancient and complex societies such as Iran into the image of the United States.[22]

As if it were written today, a full half-century later, Douglas's critique of U.S. foreign policy is even more acute because he observed the growth of the media and especially the availability of radios all over Iran. Grudgingly admiring Soviet broadcasting for its "popular programs geared to the prejudices and interests of the people of the area," he noted:

> Radio propaganda is effective in the Middle East as it is here or in Europe. Arabs and Persians alike have radios. In the town of Khoy in northwestern Persia (not far from the Soviet boarder) there are forty thousand people and close to ten thousand radios (American made run by batteries). There are in fact some radios in every village I visited; I saw them even when I was in the mountains with the tribes.[23]

If villages and mountainous tribes in Iran were listening to Radio Moscow's Persian broadcasts, it is safe to assume that the mullas in Qom were listening, too. They must have been impressed by Soviet emphasis on the compatibility of Islam and communist social ideals. Indeed, at the time a group of Iranian exiles were mostly running the Moscow Persian broadcasting. They fled to the Soviet Union after the 1948 assassination attempt against Muhammad Reza Shah and the ensuing clampdown on the Tudeh Party. Among them was Ehsan Tabari, the well-known Marxist theoretician, intellectual, and historian who was assigned to read soviet-dictated political commentaries.[24] In his historical works, Tabari had accentuated the egalitarian features of Islamic religion and drawn parallels between Islamic principles and socialist ideals. Other Tudeh intellectuals also contributed. It is tantalizing to speculate that the term "Great Satan" thus was knowingly adopted by Persian commentators in describing the mischief of the "agents of the imperialist enemy" given the keen interest people like Ehsan Tabari showed in employing Islamic vocabulary in order to put their message across. They may even have found Marxist equivalents for the Great Satan in the works of Lenin and Stalin.

Tabari also recalled that in 1949 the directives handed down by the Soviet propaganda machine to the Persian broadcasting program emphasized attacks on the "global imperialist powers" and specifically the United States rather than criticizing the government of Iran and the shah. At the height of the Cold War, the United States signed treaties of cooperation with Iran offering military and financial aid and dispatched a military advisory mission to reorganize the Iranian army and gendarmerie. This, and efforts to nurture ties with the Iranian military under Razmara, alarmed the Soviet Union and further motivated anti-American propaganda.

Moreover, as Tabari noted, 1949 marked the beginning of an anti-Semitic campaign in Stalin's Soviet Union and a purging of the Jews at all levels in government and party posts. By the end of the first Arab-Israeli war in 1948, the Soviet position had shifted away from support for Israel and the socialist traits within the Zionist movement to one of criticism of world Zionism and worldwide Jewish support for Israel. Zionism was increasingly associated in Soviet propaganda, including in the Persian and Arabic broadcasts, with the United States and Great Britain. They were identified as supporters of Israel and the conspirers behind Israel's aggression against the Arab peoples.

It is, of course, naive to assume that Soviet Persian broadcasts were directly responsible for conceiving the notion of the Great Satan three decades later. Yet it is equally unrealistic to dismiss the impact of the Tudeh discourse and Soviet propaganda on the Shi'i clerical community and the course of its politicization in Qom and elsewhere. These were by all accounts the formative years of Khomeini's political thinking and marked his shift to radical politics, a process that bore fruit in his statements in the late 1950s and early 1960s. His perspective in these latter works in many respects resembled anti-American positions articulated in the propaganda of the Iranian Left. In contrast to his earlier work, *Kashf al-Asrar* (Unraveling the Secrets), a 1944 Persian polemic in defense of Shi'ism against Wahhabi-inspired attacks as well as against Ahmad Kasravi's critique, in later years Khomeini shifted toward more pointed anti-imperialist and anti-Zionist positions.

Such a shift of emphasis was in line with the greater politicization of the Qom milieu among the younger students and their radicalized teachers. As has often been noted, they were motivated by a range of international issues in the postcolonial world. First there was the Arab-Israeli conflict. As early as 1948, the creation of the State of Israel and the ensuing Arab-Israeli war incited strong pro-Palestinian and anti-Zionist sentiments within Iranian clerical circles. They were mostly led by the ambitious Ayatollah Abul-Qasim Kashani and his Fada'ian-i Islam organization modeled on the Muslim Brotherhood of Egypt. Both the 1956 Suez Crisis and the 1967 Six-Day War added to the intensity of the anti-Zionist feelings in clerical circles. The Algerian Revolution in the late 1950s also aroused strong feelings; but nothing perhaps like the Vietnam War in the 1960s and 1970s, which added to anti-American sentiment.

Yet Khomeini's resentment of the United States as an intrusive superpower was primarily tied to developments at home: the U.S. military role and military aid since 1946, the 1953 coup that the CIA inspired and executed (even though most clergy including Khomeini favored Kashani and ultimately the shah over Mohammad Musaddiq) and the strengthening of political, economic, commercial, and strategic ties between the government of the shah and the United States in the 1960s and 1970s. The United States thus invoked in the memory of these isolated clerical radicals the latest phase of an imperial intrusion. Khomeini belonged to a generation that remembered the Allied occupations of Iran during both world wars. As much as he hated Reza Shah and welcomed his abdication, he also resented the humiliation that came with the collapse of national resistance in the First World War against the Russians and the British and the surrender of the Iranian army to the Allied Forces in the Second World War.

Yet engaging in radical politics in clerical circles came at the high cost of disregarding legal and theological modernity. As discussed elsewhere,[25] the mullas' social isolation in Qom and other teaching circles after the Constitutional Revolution and later during the implementation of Pahlavi secular policies made them intellectually regressive and culturally obdurate. They seldom, if ever, engaged in transforming archaic legal concepts, language, classification, and methods of teaching in the hope of making Shi'i law more pertinent and adapted to the needs of their time. They paid even less attention to the principal issues of Islamic theology that were at the root of Shi'i (and Islamic) legal retardation. Instead, they compensated for their failure to modernize by resorting to ideological Islam and extremist politics. In part this was because state modernizing under the Pahlavids almost drove them out of the new legal and educational space and made their legal and theological expertise obsolete.

Cultural ossification among the clergy was particularly evident in the way Shi'i religious taboos persisted especially on issues of bodily pollutants and intricate rules for ritual purification. Chapters on ritual cleansing of the male urinary track *(istibra{p})*, correct ways of defecating and cleaning *(istinja')*, and minute details of the recommended *(mustahab)* and reprehensible *(makruh)* methods of vaginal and anal intercourse were prominent in the works of jurists. So was the obsession with women's menstrual periods and cleansing after intercourse. In another area of potential pollutants, even in the twentieth century the Shi'i mujtahids routinely ruled against using foreign leather products lest they were pigskin or treated with substances derived from pork fat.

Satanic temptations such as music, painting, and motion pictures and the threat of unveiled women and their intrusion into male spaces were beyond question. Likewise, there was a lack of toleration toward all kinds of outsiders, xenophobic avoidance of infidels, non-Muslims, and non-Shi'is, and active hostility toward secular intellectuals, Sufis, Baha'is, and nonbelievers (except for Tudeh party members or former Tudeh intellectuals who kept up the pretence of religiosity or became born-again Muslims). These alien influences were believed to corrupt the *nomos* of the Shi'i community and threaten the seed *(bayza)* of Islam. Ayatollah Husain Borujerdi (d. 1961), the first universally recognized Shi'i *marja'* since Mirza Hasan Shirazi in the late nineteenth century, built a career as an adamant anti-Baha'i. He was chiefly responsible for the 1956 anti-Baha'i campaign and persecution. Among other rulings he boycotted any dealing with members of the "despicable" *(dalla)* Baha'i community, even in small towns and villages, and he encouraged Muslims to confiscate their properties and forcibly drive them out of their ancestral hometowns. He also boycotted drinking Pepsi Cola, the first large-scale bottled soft drink in Iran, because the operation was owned by a Baha'i industrialist.

To preserve their last vestiges of social power in a fast-changing society, the religious establishment had to bridge the widening gap by some means other than intellectual modernity, openness, and legal reforms. To make this huge leap and make themselves socially relevant, they resorted to radical Islamic ideology. Bypassing the intellectual and legal ramifications of modern discourse, they instead adhered to radical anti-Westernism. In effect they tried to preserve the same pollutant taboos that maintained their communal purity albeit in a politicized guise. This was the price Iranians society had to pay for its clerical establishment clinging to Shi'i exclusionism and perceptions of Islamic superior morality. The remarkable asymmetry between resistance to secular modernity and acceptance of ideological radicalism is astounding and yet ironic: burning movie theaters in Qom but creating revolutionary posters inspired by Hollywood and later relying on cassette recordings to put across revolutionary messages while refusing to communicate by telephone.

This new fundamentalist discourse required the satanic enemy of old Shi'ism to be updated. Satan had to be brought out of the works of jurisprudence and ethics and be given more substantive powers than the mundane mischief assigned to him in popular beliefs. That task was accomplished with the recasting of the image of the United States as the ultimate threat to the purity and solidarity of the Islamic community worldwide. And, of course, the actions of today's "sole superpower," as American neoconservatives would like to refer to the United States, only helped to make Khomeini's Great Satan a self-fulfilling prophecy. Irrational and unbound support for the aggressive policies of the State of Israel toward Palestinians in the occupied territories, U.S. hypocritical double standards in dealing with democracy and territorial sovereignty in the Middle East, the two full-scale military invasions of the region since 1990, the disastrous consequences of the invasion of Iraq in 2003, and various manifestations of American counterculture exported to the non-West – all these have made Khomeini's label justifiable in the eyes of many Muslims and non-Muslims today.

## CHAPTER 10

# *Messianic Aspirations in Contemporary Iran*

Nearly three decades after the Islamic Revolution, the Iran of today is still rife with messianic aspirations; even more, arguably, than at anytime in recent Shi'i history. One would have expected that the Revolution would have put such yearnings to rest, at least for a while, if not forever. A Mahdi-like leader in the person of Ayatollah Khomeini, who adopted the honorific *na'ib al-Imam* (the Deputy of the Imam of the Age) and who was lavished with the title of *imam* for the first time in Shi'i history, had led a revolution that in many ways resembled the millenarian Shi'i movements of the past, only broader in its popular appeal and in its range.

And if an uncompromising *imam* was not a sufficient substitute for the apocalyptic Mahdi, there were revolutionary struggles in the offing that resembled the cosmic battles of the Mahdi with his enemies. Revolutionary Iran had found its nemesis in a superpower that it labeled the "Great Satan" while fighting a long and bloody war with the Ba'thist regime in neighboring Iraq; circumstances that helped Iranian revolutionaries see themselves as the besieged victim in the paradigm of Shi'i martyrs of early Islam who were to ultimately prevail in the cosmic battle of the forces of good against evil. Much of the revolutionary propaganda in the media, the sermons from mosque pulpits, the revolutionary posters, murals, slogans and battle songs aimed to carry the message of a utopian salvation to come. Revolutionary ferment as much as the overt narrative of the Karbala and tragedy of Husayn and his companions inspired resistance and sacrifice, as did the covert narrative of the Mahdi and his apocalyptic triumph over the forces of Dajjal and his collaborating oppressors.

Yet after a decade of devastating war with Iraq and the final admission of virtual defeat in 1988, the militant zeal of the Iranian revolutionaries was markedly fading, and they were ready to bury it in 1989 together with the man who first invoked such a messianic spirit at the turn of the fifteenth Islamic century. Once Khomeini declared that by accepting ceasefire he would be drinking the Socratic "chalice of poison," it was as if this former teacher of Greek philosophy was succumbing to the prevalence of temporal realities over utopian ideals.[1]

## *Revival of the Mahdi Cult*

Yet even before giving up the idea of exporting the revolution via Karbala to Quds – a popular wartime slogan of the Revolutionary Guards and their youthful vigilante "Recruitment Forces" (Quwa-yi Basij) – Khomeini was anxious to harness and eventually disband rival Shi'i messianic trends that promised to reshape his leadership and the direction of his revolution. Most significantly, in 1983 he had ordered the dismantling of the Hujjatiyya Society (Anjuman-i Hujjatiyya) by his former colleague, Shaykh Mahmoud Halabi, especially active in the 1960s and 1970s and still flourishing after the Revolution.

Founded in 1954 – a year after the coup that brought down the liberal nationalist government of Dr. Muhammad Musaddiq – the Hujjatiyya Society (i.e. devotees of *Hujjat al-Allah*: the Mahdi) for long advocated, as the title implied, vigilance for the impending advent of the Mahdi and for combating what they considered to be deniers of the Mahdi's return – above all, the Baha'is of Iran. The "Anti-Baha'i Society" (Anjuman-i zidd-i Baha'iyat) as the Hujjatiyya was initially known (or, alternatively, the Society of the Lord of the Age [Anjuman-i Sahib al-Zaman]) operated on a distinctly apolitical basis and chiefly (but not exclusively) recruited from the youth of the urban lower middle classes with a religious upbringing.[2] Some of the teachers, students, and graduates of the schools run by the Society for Islamic Teachings (Anjuman-i Ta'limat-i Islami) joined the Hujjatiyya ranks. The two major religious schools, the Haqqani and the 'Alawi schools in Tehran – which later provided the largest contingent of cadres for the Islamic Republic at highest level – also had a fair number of activists in the Society. Serving as an alternative conduit to any political association during the repressive decades of the 1960s and 1970s, Hujjatiyya was a sort of non-government organization with a distinct anti-revolutionary approach to Shi'i messianism. Such an approach, though condemned by pro-

Khomeini activists and other religious radicals, proved useful to the Pahlavi state and its security apparatus since it served as an effective tool in fending off the frustration of the religiously conscious youth and helped counter-balance the Shi'i revolutionary trend and also what at the time appeared to be the regime's favorable stance toward the Baha'is.[3]

Engaging in polemical debate with the Baha'is left a deep mark on the Society's ethos and the mentality of its members. In the long term, Baha'i modernity came to reshape Shi'i messianic thinking in several important ways both within the Society and beyond, in the general discourse of Shi'i messianism. In response to the Baha'i analogical approach to prophecies and their fulfillment, the Hujjatiyya, and soon after members of the clergy, began to introduce a certain coherence into the otherwise confused and contradictory corpus of Shi'i apocalyptic literature compiled over many centuries and with different subtexts. Among the earliest efforts to conjure up an updated version accessible to the general reader – though not necessarily a more coherent narrative – was a new Persian translation of volume thirteen of *Bihar al-Anwar;* a massive compendium of Shi'i hadith, of which this volume was exclusively devoted to the Occultation and Advent of the Mahdi.

The work was commissioned by Ayatollah Husain Burujerdi, the Shi'i *marja'* in direct response to Baha'i critique of Majlisi and its inconsistencies. Shaykh Ali Davani, a clerical scholar and historian, provided a new translation of the text just before Burujirdi's death in 1961. Over the years Davani added copious notes and revisions to his translation and in the process incorporated prophecies from other religious traditions. As with contemporaries among the Hujjatiyya, Davani thus implicitly heeded the notion of the comparative features of apocalypticism in various religions and societies.[4] In later years, other clerical advocates of Mahdism adopted with greater vigor the universalized notion of the Mahdi as fulfillment of all messianic prophecies (and not merely Shi'i Islam). Arguably, this was an adaptation of the Baha'i ecumenical view of presenting Baha'ullah as the messianic fulfillment of all ages. In the new Shi'i version the universal Mahdi was partially freed from the implausible shackles of Shi'i prophecies and was given a new mission to ultimately establish a "universal governance" *(hukumat-i jahani).*

Polemical encounters, moreover, sharpened rhetorical skills and theological casuistry and modernized in a peculiar way the method if not the substance of the Shi'i messianic discourse. Muslim writes and debaters began to emulate their nemesis by contemporizing the "signs" *(a'laim)* of the Mahdi's advent and applying them to various political crises and to the world's moral "decrepitude." They replicated the courteous Baha'i debating style and the ecumenical tone of their apologies, fashioned a hierarchy akin to the Baha'i administration, and even meetings such as the Baha'is' "investigation of the truth" *(taharri-yi haqiqat)*, in their aim to reconvert those who had strayed back to the true path of Islam.[5]

On the eve of the Islamic Revolution, despite a history of friendly relations with the Pahlavi state, a number of veterans of the Hujjatiyya quit ranks and were soon absorbed into the burgeoning Islamic movement. In the Revolution's spontaneity they found a unique chance to advance and consolidate their positions. Capitalizing on their Islamic experience – for they had long wrestled with the finer points of messianic theology with the Baha'i preachers *(muballiq)* and the Baha'i youth – they were well qualified to serve the newly established regime as "committed" *(muta'ahhid)* manpower. A few of the ex-Hujjatiyya activists continued to cherish their former affinities, albeit semi-clandestinely, while rising to prominence in the nascent Islamic Republic.

Shaykh Mahmoud Halabi, then an aging cleric who knew Khomeini from his madrasa years, was keen to preserve the Society's autonomy, yet was prudent enough never to deny Khomeini's leadership and the significance of the Revolution in initiating a committed Islamic discourse, and remained adamant in treating it as an overture to greater things to come. Revolution from this perspective was not a rationalized alternative to the eventual advent *(zuhur)* of the Mahdi; rather, Khomeini was seen mostly as a precursory messianic figure, and his revolution as a pre-millennial development in the move toward fulfillment of greater aspirations. Khomeini's call in 1984 for disbanding the Hujjatiyya came after veiled ideological challenges by its members to the doctrine of the Guardianship of the Jurists *(wilayat-i faqih)*, the founding principle of Islamic government. In effect the Hujjatiyya position aimed to diminish, if not overtly deny, the authority of the Guardian

Jurist as the best human alternative to the utopian reign of the Mahdi. This appeared as an implicit challenge to the prevailing, though latent, characterization of the Islamic Revolution as a post-millennial era.[6]

The official dismantling of the Society, however, did not entirely wipe out inherent loyalties among the old-timers. Semi-clandestine affiliations continued to allow a dormant existence. More importantly, the theological legacy of the Hujjatiyya continued to inspire newer messianic trends. In the mid-1990s, some years after the death of Khomeini, the pre-millennial tendency once again began to rise, perhaps as the direct outcome of the June 1997 shock that came with the presidential election and the landslide victory of the reformist Muhammad Khatami. The new messianic drive began to reorganize and recruit not primarily in pursuit of anti-Baha'i objectives but to consolidate a network of influence within the regime.

Halabi's death in 1998 seemed only to end the old loyalties and in turn helped diffuse to larger audiences the message of the Hujjatiyya, championed by a new class of younger clerics. Though not entirely wed to the clerical conservatives in Qom, the new messianic trend enjoyed warmer patronage of powerful figures such as Ayatollah Muhammad-Taqi MisbahYazdi, one of the founders of the Haqqani school and an influential figure in the conservative clerical clique of the post-Khomeini era. As a commentator on Shi'i theology, and particularly on the doctrine of the *wilayat-i faqih* and its theological and judicial ramifications, and an influential commissar to those who opposed Muhammad Khatami's "revisionist" doctrine, he soon rose to prominence in a new collision of clerics and laity that shared a messianic outlook.

The new drive was not overtly messianic in so much as diminishing the status of Khomeini as the Guardian Jurist or the office of the "supreme leader" as his successor came to be identified. Rather, it was to promote the Mahdi as an absolute sacred source of authority, primarily to counter the notion of the republic and the institution of an elected parliament. The Mahdist cult, then in gestation for some time and evidently independent of the old Hujjatiyya, seemed the appropriate avenue. The last years of Khatami's second presidency (2001–5) witnessed an even greater Mahdistic yearning advocated through selective mosque networks and Islamic associations. More than in his first term, Khatami's half-backed and halfhearted reformist initiative in the second term ran aground in the face of conservative challenges. As his government was riddled with inefficiency and indecision and his rhetoric of civil society, the rule of law, and the "dialogue of civilizations" weakened , the new spirit of messianic expectations and popular religiosity came to capture the public imagination and reflect its overall disillusionment with the unfulfilled promises of the Islamic Revolution.

This messianic enthusiasm was not an overt rejection of the early revolutionary rhetoric of the 1970s and 1980s. Rather, popular practices of Muharram and similar mourning rituals came into vogue (some like the "ten days of Fatimiya" in honor of the sufferings and death of Fatima long forgotten or never commemorated at all). Also of interest, even for the younger generations, were the miracle cults and supernatural feats of the Imams and the blessing of their offspring, the praise for piety and other-worldliness, beliefs in the healing qualities of sacred shrines, and eulogizing in praise of the Hidden Imam by reciters *(maddahs)* – aspects of Shi'ism that remained in hibernation during the Pahlavi era but flourished under the Islamic Republic. Within the environment of the "mourning associations" *(hay'at-i 'azadaran)*, recitation of stories of Karbala *(rawza)* and eulogies *(madh)* for the Mahdi – who was often referred to with the title of His Majesty the Imam of the Age *(a'la-hazrat imam-i zaman)* – and pietistic congregational prayers hastening the return of the Hidden Imam, a new spirit of camaraderie emerged, especially among the new Basij recruits and members of the Revolutionary Guards. Some clerical circles in Qom and their supporters in Tehran and elsewhere also contributed to this familiar brand of religiosity now touched by a sense of messianic awareness.

Devastating upheaval in the neighboring countries also contributed to the proto-messianic mood. The U.S. invasion of Iraq and its dire consequences, in particular, influenced the Iranian religious mood. The fall of the Ba'thist regime facilitated the pilgrimage of hundreds of thousands of Iranians to the holy shrines of Karbala and Najaf. Pilgrims sometimes traveled without proper visas and in the face of many hazards. The fall of Saddam Hussein was also viewed as the implicit triumph of the Islamic Republic and a just end to many crimes of the Iraqi president. The stubborn Iraqi Shi'i resistance movement working against the occupying U.S. forces convinced some in Iran that the course of events was a messianic precondition. Closer contacts with leaders of the Mahdi Army, who themselves entertained (and still entertain) messianic aspirations, and reportedly Muqtada al-Sadr's residence in Qom, further alerted Iranian radicals to the messianic dimension in Shi'i holy resistance. Scenes of confrontations with U.S. forces in historic venues of immense messianic significance, among them the mosque of Kufa, the headquarter of Muqtada al-Sadr and site of a deadly battle between the Mahdi Army and American troops in 2005, did not remain unnoticed. Being the site of 'Ali ibn Abi-Talib's assassination in 661, the Kufa mosque is of enormous importance in apocalyptic Shi'i literature, since it is the place where the Mahdi once made his Advent and will launch his cosmic struggle against the forces of evil and the enemies of his House.

## *Jamkaran and Appropriation of Popular Messianism*

Growing enthusiasm for the Hidden Imam is the central feature in the burgeoning cult associated with the mosque of Jamkaran. Since

**Figure 3.** The mosque of Jamkaran near Qom, on the night of 15th Sha'ban 1426/19 September 2005, in celebration of the anniversary of the birth of the Twelfth Imam, Muhammad ibn Hasan al-'Askari, the Mahdi.

the mid-1990s Jamkaran mosque has emerged as a site of great popular interest, epitomizing the revival of Mahdistic aspirations and the desire for personal and direct experience of the sacred. Yet it also revealed the Shi'i clerical establishment's clever exploitation of such sentiments for their own end. Primarily what makes Jamkaran popular with the Shi'i public is a proto-messianic hope for miraculous blessings and assistance from the world of invisible to resolve everyday pains and troubles, though an implicit aspiration for the Imam's physical advent is not entirely missing either. The Shi'i clergy, relying on the rich body of Mahdistic prophecies and veneration of the House of the Prophet, seeks to take advantage of popular enthusiasm and enhance its own standing as moral leaders of the community.

A minor shrine in the vicinity of Qom, nearly six miles to the west of the city, Jamkaran was for long known merely as a minor site with dubious associations with the cult of the Mahdi (fig. 3). It is named after a certain Shaykh Hasan ibn Muthla Jamkarani, a tenth-century local landowner whose holy vision in AH 373/974 of the Hidden Imam accompanied by the prophet Khidr (the Elijah of the apocryphal Islamic tradition) provided the shaykh with a timely excuse to declare the site as holy, build a humble shrine, and presumably appropriate the neighboring land. The mosque that was built on the site by the instruction of the holy figure of his vision was apparently in the vicinity of an earlier mosque, presumably the first to be built in Qom in the seventh century.

Known for many decades as a subsidiary pilgrimage site to the major shrine of Ma'suma in Qom, Jamkaran was distinguished from other popular Shi'i shrines for two unique characteristics. First, it was recognized as a "walking ground" *(ghadamgah)* of the Hidden Imam; a location now adorned with a modest structure known as the *Mahdiya*. Second, the dried hole adjacent to the back of the mosque, known as the "well of the Lord of the Age" *(chah-i sahib al-zaman)*, is believed to serve as a channel of communication with the Hidden Imam. With its slight connections to the shrine of Samarra in Iraq – where it was believed that the Hidden Imam was residing in an underground cellar – prior to the 1990s Jamkaran attracted a modest number of Shi'i local pilgrims, who submitted petitions to the Hidden Imam through the miraculous well or made pledges by tying strings of nuts to the well's metal grid in the hope that their wishes would soon to be granted (fig. 4). The whole Jamkaran

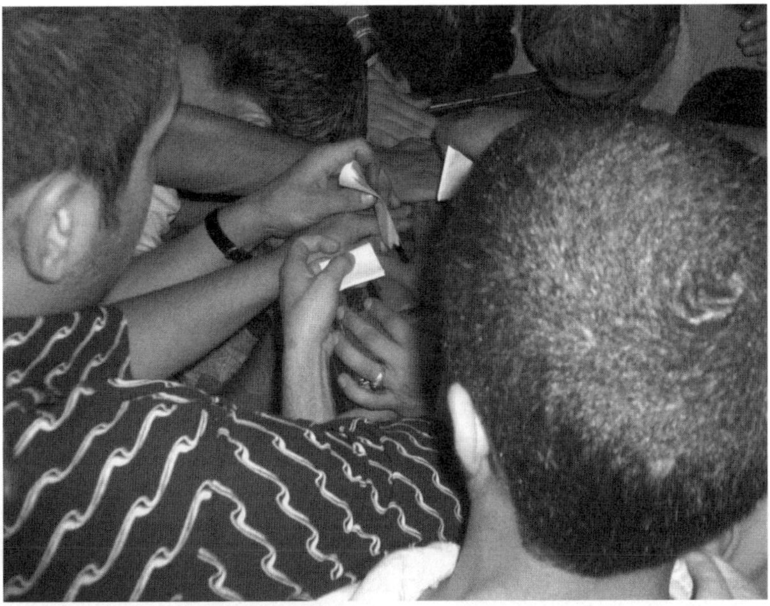

**Figure 4.** Dropping petitions unto the sacred well, mosque of Jamkaran, July 2005.

legend was based on an unreliable Shi'i report *(khabar)* that presumably originated in some version of a local history of Qom, itself a work of dubious authorship. Few Shi'i scholars before the twentieth century accepted its authenticity; yet like similar holy shrines in other religious traditions – Our Lady Fatima in Portugal and shrine of Santiago de Compostela in Spain are but two examples in Catholic Christianity – the question of authenticity did not affect Jamkaran's growing popularity.

The unassuming structure was restored a number of times both in the later Safavid period and in the late Qajar era. The celebrated Qajar statesman Mirza 'Ali Asghar Khan Amin al-Sultan carried out some renovations while residing in Qom (after his dismissal from the office of premiership in 1896–8). Seven decades later, in 1968, when the mosque's modest endowments were deemed insufficient, a grant was provided by the Pahlavi state (presumably from the office of the premier Amir Abbas Hoveyda) for basic renovation. Yet the site was barely known to the public save for local mullas in Qom who occasionally took devotional retirement there, and the poor of Qom who gathered there for modest food handouts during the holy days of the Shi'i calendar.[7]

Only in the mid-1990s, more than a decade into the Islamic Revolution, did the shrine rise to prominence at a time when the anti-Khatami campaign orchestrated by conservative clerics in Qom sought a focal point to counter the rising star of the reformists' trend. Resuscitating Shi'i folk culture offered Qom a convenient diversion. The transformation of Jamkaran into a major pilgrimage site is indeed a telling story of the conservative appropriation of diffuse popular messianic beliefs in order to consecrate the status of the ruling clerical elite by manipulating the public imagination and its disillusionment with the country's state of affairs. In 2000 Ayatollah 'Ali Khamanei, the Supreme Leader, presumably in agreement with the Qom clerics, appointed a certain Shaykh Abulqasim Wafi as Jamkaran's first official trustee. Simultaneously, a study undertaken for the reconstruction and development of the Jamkaran site forecasted a budget of 1,200 billion Rials (roughly $1.4 billion), which is to be expended on a site as large as 250 square hectares. Some two years later, at the cost of more than $400 million, the first phase of this massive expansion turned the modest mosque into an enormous shrine of five enclosures *(shabistan)*, twelve minarets (in the style of the new extension of the Holy Mosque of Mecca; a style entirely alien to the Iranian tradition of mosque architecture) and vast interior courtyards and facilities over 250,000 square meters of land designed to host hundreds of thousands of visitors.[8]

Revamping the Jamkaran image in the midst of the Qom desert under the aegis of the clerical leadership and selling it to public cost more than half a billion dollars of public funds. The Jamkaran institution soon produced its bureaucracy, which competed in size and budget with that of the Ma'suma shrine in Qom and was probably only second to the shrine of the Eighth Imam 'Ali al-Rida in Mashhad. Consisting of twelve departments and numerous units, the Jamkaran shrine has its own publications, exhibition, bookstore (including CD production), a research center specializing in all things messianic including assessment of reports of the Occultation of the Hidden Imam and his visual citations and instances of "miraculous" cures and other feats that took place in Jamkaran, a public relations bureau, a highly active Internet department (true to Qom's preoccupation with cyberspace), two "cultural" departments guiding Islamic brothers and sisters with their religious inquiries and questions concerning the Mahdi (the women's guidance department consists of seven units), guards, volunteers and security, an audiovisual department servicing several big screens throughout the site. Jamkaran also has its own farms, a sheep farm that produces meat, its own slaughterhouse, and a massive soup kitchen for free weekly meals open to all.

The vast number of visitors to Jamkaran demonstrates the resurgence of interest in the Mahdi among Iranians of all classes – including the affluent middle classes in the capital – and the triumph of the Islamic Republic in capitalizing on symbols of public piety. Every Wednesday evening (and to a lesser extent on Friday evenings) tens of thousands of pilgrims, some from destinations as far as Lahore and Bahrain but mostly from Iranian cities and especially from Tehran and Qom, gather in Jamkaran for the midnight congregational *faraj* (deliverance) prayer. A curious mix of solemnity and merriment characterizes Jamkaran: families picnicking, young men and women discreetly mixing, glancing at one another and even courting, thousands setting their nightly prayers under the dome of the mosque or under an open sky, women in black *chador* in pitch dark preparing the "charity soup" *(ash-i nazri)* on outdoor stoves, young people squatting in the courtyard filling the blanks on the printed "petition" *('ariza)* to the Imam of the Age while others huddle around the two segregated sections of the sacred well designated for "brothers" and "sisters," waiting for their turn to drop off their petitions onto the mailbox-like opening over the well. By the approach of midnight thousands stand in rows closer to the Mahdiya – the modest building erected on the presumed site of the "sacred steps of the Lord of the Age" *(Qadamgah-i Sahib al-Zaman)* – raising their hands and repeating after the *maddah* who recites on the loud audio system and visible on the big screens. Evidently moved by the surroundings, the youth and the elderly weep in an outpouring of religious emotions.

The congeniality of Jamkaran ritual may in part be attributed to the myth of miracle-making built around it, which helps to relieve the pains of everyday anxieties and aspirations, illnesses and disabilities, failures, financial troubles, and overall frustration with life. Serious illnesses are especially prominent in the list of meticulously documented "miracles" on the mosque's website: cancer, strokes, infertility, arthritis, nervous disorders, and even herniated discs. Testimonials of the cured are offered as proofs of how sincere faith in the Mahdi, good intent and moral purification prepares one for coming into contact with a "luminous sayyid" *(sayyid-i nurani)*, as the Imam of the Age is often euphemistically referred to. The chief reason the Mahdi is absent from the view of ordinary people, the Jamkaran website declares, is because they lack the moral rectitude to witness his presence: "If reports of the deeds of the Shi'is that every week are presented at his sacred threshold were not laden with such grave sins that are displeasing to His Excellency [the Mahdi] and far from what he expects from his supporters, his distance and separation would not have been prolonged to such an extent."[9] The nature of these "grave sins" is not revealed.

Miracles are but one aspect of Jamkaran's culture of piety. The need for moral reconstruction, often cast in melodramatic language peculiar to post-revolutionary Qom literature, is a precondition widely cited for the Advent of the Mahdi. The list of Jamkaran's publications (exceeding fifty titles) includes a guide for "Writing Petitions" *('ariza nivisi)* to the Mahdi, the "Discourse of Mahdism" *(guftman-i Mahdawiyat)*, "Anticipation and the Contemporary Man" *(intizar va insan-i ma'asir)*, and "Connecting with the Lord of the Age" *(irtibat ba imam-i zaman)*. The online library also offers a range of books and treatises primarily about the authenticity of the Jamkaran vision and other sacred sightings of the Mahdi. A curious mix of medieval Shi'i theological parlance and a melodramatic undertone – almost amorous – reveals a subtext reflective of the authors' state of mind. Anxious to rescue the Mahdi's image from the jumble of confused Shi'i apocalyptic texts and update it for the housewives, working men, and school children of the Islamic Republic, the custodians of Jamkaran even employ avant-garde Persian poetry and prose, modern computer graphics (Islamized to Qom's taste) as well as organizing painting and poetry contests, photographic exhibitions, text messaging, and downloadable wallpaper for cell phones and computer screensavers adorned with images of Jamkaran and calligraphy with Mahdistic images – all in the hope of sustaining their cult, maximizing donations and marketing a Qom version of hope for a pious future.[10]

## *The Mahdi of Cyberspace*

As a site of pilgrimage and piety Jamkaran presents a relatively familiar side of a multidimensional messianic project that currently engulfs the Islamic Republic. The appropriation of Mahdism by powerful circles within the Islamic Republic for their own ideological ends, moreover, covers a range of mass propaganda that borders on hate campaigns and reveals symptoms of paranoia. Beside press reports and publications about the Mahdi – his supranatural existence, his longevity, and the preconditions of his Advent – there is intense Internet coverage as well as conferences, seminars (another preoccupation of Qom), youth camps, night vigils and mourning ceremonies, recitations in praise of the Mahdi by *maddahs*, study groups, and lavish festivities celebrating the birthday of the Mahdi on the fifteenth of Sha'ban of the lunar Islamic calendar. To date there are at least sixty-five so called Mahdistic websites *(paygahha-yi ittila'-rasani Mahdawi)*, mostly in Persian but also in English, Arabic, Urdu, French and a host of other languages, engaged in revamping, promoting, modernizing, and politicizing the Mahdi's image for popular consumption. Some are more active than others, but these websites share a similar message and a similar ethos as if they all come from a common source and target a specific audience. Despite their technological advances and their sleek graphics (in tune with most religious-advocacy websites worldwide), their meager readership (judging by the limited number of "hits") betrays the intellectually impoverished sphere within which they operate and also their creators' acquired empowerment through the Internet. If one can judge by their readership, the effort to incite a public messianic alertness via the Internet seems largely to have been unsuccessful.

Among the most active is the website of the "Permanent Secretariat of the Biannual Symposium of Examining the Existential Dimensions of His Holiness the Mahdi" *(Dabirkhana-yi da'imi-yi ijlas-i dusalane-yi barrasi-yi ab'ad-i vujudi-yi hazrat-i Mahdi)*. First established in 1995, the Secretariat has since organized five biannual conventions *(hamayish)* on Mahdistic themes worthy of its impressive name: "The (spiritual) effects of His Holiness Mahdi's sacred existence" in 1996, "The existential persona of His Holiness and the philosophy of Islamic government during his Occultation" in 1998, "Examining theories of deliverance and the foundations of Mahdism" in 2000, "The rule of the reformer *(muslih)*: the great Ideal of humanity" in 2002 and the fifth convention without a specific theme in 2005.[11] The Secretariat appears to be one of the earliest examples of the recent messianic revival in the mid-1990s, possibly initiated by the former members of the Hujjatiyya. Not a mere coincidence, it is possible that the Secretariat was initiated when anticipation for the Christian millennium in the year 2000 invoked similar excitements especially in Christian Evangelical circles awaiting Christ's Second Coming. Congruent with these millennial excitements, Shi'i messianic circles could have contributed to the globalizing discourse of millennialism *(jahani-shudan)*. With Christ acting as the lieutenant of the Mahdi in the Shi'i apocalyptic narrative, such enthusiasm was not entirely out of place.

With more than one hundred affiliate clerics and lay figures, the Secretariat operates under the mentorship of Ayatollah Lutfullah Safi Gulpaygani, a recognized conservative and advocate of greater popularization of the Mahdi. Some former Hujjatiyya activists such as 'Ali Akbar Vilayati, longtime minister of foreign affairs in the 1980s and 1990s, also contributed to the Secretariat's conference and publication. The Secretariat's extensive publications (in print and online, to date numbering forty titles in Persian and six in English) cover a wide range of Mahdistic topics with a conscious updated approach: sixteen titles are on universalistic themes and primarily try to locate the Mahdi as the messianic fulfillment of all religious traditions.[12]

The undeniable resemblance between Islamic (more Shi'i) messianic prophecies and the Jewish and Christian traditions (and other non-Abrahamic religions) – defined in this literature as the "convergence theory" *(nazariya-yi hamgara'i)* – seemingly posed a theological challenge to these apocalyptic writers; a problem that is tackled in this burgeoning messianic output by empowering the Mahdi beyond the Islamic space and as the savior *(munji)* whose Advent is anticipated in all religions and who will erect upon his return the "universal government" *(hukumat-i jahani)* for all humanity. Seven women authors contributed in particular to the ecumenical discourse of Mahdism – indicative, perhaps, of their proclivity toward a more modernized image of the Mahdi beyond the traditional patriarchal bounds of Shi'i theology.[13]

By contrast, some twenty-two titles by male authors, mostly clerical, are devoted to familiar Shi'i and Islamic debates surrounding the Occultation and the preconditions of the Advent of the Mahdi, an attempt, no doubt, to systematize and streamline the bewildering corpus of Shi'i apocalyptics. Yet conservative clerical obstacles are evident in accomplishing such an objective. Seven polemical titles, again by male authors, were devoted to counter the "doubts" *(shubahat)* posed by Baha'i post-messianic discourse (four titles), by Ibn Khaldun's skeptical treatment of Mahdism in his monumental *Muqaddima*, by Ibn al-'Arabi's Sufi interpretation of Mahdism, and by contemporary Sunni authors. Throughout, the pamphlets are engaged with contemporary themes and even dabble in the predictable rhetoric of Occidentousis *(Gharbzadegi)*. Contrasting the greatness of Islamic millennial utopia under the Mahdi with Western, and especially American, "decadent" and "doomed" secular culture, they pay lip service to the regime's mainstay of anti-Americanism.[14]

Despite a facade of respectability and scholarship and despite the inclusion of Abrahamic and Zoroastrian prophecies in the Mahdi discourse, these and similar messianic publications remain decidedly ahistorical in perspective and uncritical in approach. True, several authors introduce civilizational and civil rights dimensions while others try to sort out the prophecies' varying degrees of probability and differentiate between the necessary preconditions for the Mahdi's coming from the unnecessary. Yet there is a distinct reluctance – as in most theological debates in today's Islamic Republic – to treat Shi'i apocalyptics and the phenomenon of Mahdism and its evolving nature by any measure of critical analysis.

For these authors the Mahdi is a living and historic figure rather than an expression of collective societal, moral, and religious aspirations. It is a personalized reality rather than a powerful myth symbolic of frustrations and yearnings of any historical juncture. He is still revered in this literature as an exceptional sacred being, in Occultation since 878, whose presumed return will miraculously transform the world, establish justice and annihilate his enemies (though perhaps not with such incredibly violent means as he does in traditional Shi'i apocalyptics). Rather than treating the Mahdi as part of the salvation paradigm shared by many traditions since ancient times that evolved over time and incorporated elements from earlier apocalyptic texts, the mainstream interpretation in today's Islamic Republic tends to treat the striking similarities between Shi'i apocalyptics and Judeo-Christian and Zoroastrian parallels as yet another miraculous sign of the Mahdi's foreknowledge.

Closer analysis of the plethora of messianic websites may reveal much about the powerful trends sponsored by the Islamic Republic and the ethos of their mentors. It may also reveal the behind-the-scene politics and inner dynamics. One thing, however, is clear: the visible proliferation of messianic expectations that first served as a counterforce to the reformism of the Khatami era increasingly became politicized and ideologically sharpened in its approach while universalizing the Mahdi as the global messiah.

## *A Journal for the Imam of the Age*

The most egregious example of politicizing the Mahdi cult perhaps appears in the monthly journal *Mouood* (*Ma'ud:* the promised one). Published regularly since 1996, *Mouood* is the first journal, as it claims on the cover, "about the Imam of the Age and for the Imam of the Age." With impressive graphics, diverse coverage, and an upbeat style, it embarks on the task of modernizing the radical apocalyptic aspirations and rationalizing conspiratorial obsessions associated with it. Merging anti-Western (and especially anti-American) xenophobia with arcane Shi'i literature on Occultation and Advent, the authors and editors of the journal employ every means to make viable the myth of the Mahdi and the scenario of the End. The bizarre perspective of its creators employs with dexterity fantastic Shi'i hadith narratives in Majlisi's *Bihar al-Anwar* about the Advent of the Mahdi and the End of the Time and mixes them with the outlandish pseudo-science and science-fiction theories concerning the physical possibility of the Mahdi's millennial longevity and the inevitable arrival of the End of the Time.

All kinds of material from diluted, Islamized, and domesticated versions of the philosophies of Nietzsche and Heidegger (via born-again devotees of Ahmad Fardid), Hollywood apocalyptic films, Nostradamus' prophecies, eclectic prophecies of various religious traditions, UFOs, and apocalyptic readings of natural disasters of different kinds find their way into the journal along with a heavy dose of anti-Semitism (often disguised as anti-Zionism) and ugly anti-Baha'i propaganda. A fair share of pronouncements from conservative ayatollahs and, since 2005, the remarks of President Ahmadinejad with messianic implications are also included. In *Mauood*'s worldview, history is a battlefield, a scene for an inevitable "clash of civi-

**Figure 5.** *Mouood* 8:25 (1383/2004). This cover depicts the biblical Four Horsemen of the Apocalypse. The lead is entitled "Now is the End of the Time" and articles include: "Key to understanding US policy," "the Jewish Messiah and the destiny of the world," "the awaited Mahdi and the end of history," and "End of the Time and the Universal Government of the Mahdi."

**Figure 6.** *Mouood* 6:36 (1381/2003). Here Mount Rushmore represents the twentieth century, the "American century," now an expired page on the calendar. The turn of the twenty-first century is illustrated as an exploding citadel embossed with the American coat-of-arms crowned by the Star of David. The Hammer and Sickle, symbol of the collapsing communism, is fading. The twenty-first century, too, is about to be folded away to be replaced by the blossoming twenty-second century. Blossoms are a familiar cliché depicting the spring of the Islamic Revolution. Articles include "The last government," "Qur'an and the end of history," "Destiny of history and the Last Man," "Iran the soul of the soulless world."

lizations" in which the cataclysmic forces of Islam will defeat the heathen forces of the secular West leading to the triumph of the Mahdi and his forces (figs. 5 and 6). American imperialism, Zionism, and the corrupt capitalism of the West are thus presented as allies that for a long time aimed to destroy Islam and dominate the world. Such radical readings of Samuel Huntington's *The Clash of Civilizations* is – and probably is meant to be – in diametric contrast to the "dialogue of civilizations" advocated by Muhammad Khatami.

*Mouood,* well funded by likeminded backers in high places, found a new lease of life, greater buoyancy and confidence with the election to office of Ahmadinejad. Following the "party line," it incessantly tries to introduce into Iran's hardline discourse an apocalyptic dimension, one that resonates with the Mahdi's absolute power, the "end of history" (or as its authors alternatively call "beginning of new history"), and prevalence of the moral forces of good over secular evil. In brazen tones such universal values as human rights, religious toleration, political moderation, democratic institutions, scientific objectivity, and even material prosperity is discredited as signs of Western decay. In contrast, adulation for the ultimate power of the Lord of the Age is highlighted and his vengeful campaign against his worldwide enemies of the "imperialist" and "world-devouring" camp is anticipated.[15]

The radical message is highlighted by a melodramatic tone and dated images of red tulips, blood-dripping martyrs, and the sunrays of the messianic coming. Also present are pictures of long-bearded clerics in reverential poses with "mystical" *('irfani)* undertones in the accompanying commentaries implying their personal experiences of the Imam of the Age and as if they received his joyful blessings. Homage to the high-ranking clergy and the supportive ayatollahs is also prevalent. Conspicuously underplayed, however, are references to Ayatollah Khomeini and the Islamic Revolution, and when they do appear they are primarily in the context of the future revolution of the Mahdi. The Islamic Revolution, the tone of the journal implies, was a preparatory stage for greater things to come. Nor is there any discussion of the current "evils" that envelop the Islamic Republic and that can be read as preconditions for the coming of the Mahdi: the corruption and racketeering of the Islamic Republic's elite, the failure of economic polices and industrial projects, massive institutional and individual kleptocracy, the striking level of drug addiction, prostitution and other ills, political suppression, and the widespread superstition that steadily creeps into the hearts and minds of the Iranian people – circumstances that according to the Shi'i apocalyptic may very well hasten the Advent of the Lord of the Age.

## *The Presidential Halo and Its Global Effects*

The Mahdistic message emanating from Qom and the propaganda machine associated with it was already in full swing when in 2005 Mahmoud Ahmadinejad was elected as President of the Islamic Republic. His much-discussed messianic convictions are indeed part and parcel of the chiliastic enthusiasm that has engulfed religious circles in Iran since the mid-1990s.

Born into an émigré working-class family, as a youth Ahmadinejad earned his revolutionary credentials through a few years of service in the front during the Iraq–Iran war as an intelligence officer. He represents a sector of war veterans – mostly former members of the Revolutionary Guards and the Basij volunteer recruits – who saw harrowing experiences in the trenches, when young men were sent forth in waves during failed offensives and battalions of their comrades were decimated by Iraqi chemical and biological weapons. The whole experience was charged with a sense of Islamic camaraderie and later by romanticized and sanctified memories of blood, sacrifice, and martyrdom. War could have been the devastating experience of a lifetime and yet Ahmadinejad – and seemingly many like him – successfully managed to integrate it, even capitalize on it, and to rise up in the emerging order of the post-war era.

The experience of the battlefront also seems to have been seminal in shaping Ahmadinejad's firm belief in the Mahdi and his seeking the Mahdi's support to overcome the odds. In effect he internalized the messianic culture nurtured at the front – the war cries calling for the Mahdi's support when young warriors fearlessly crossed enemy lines; silvered plastic keys given to volunteers as the symbolic keys to paradise; and vague sightings of the Mahdi as a white-clad warrior galloping on the horizon. Ahmadinejad seems to have been particularly enamored by such images through his ideological mentor, a behind-the-scene figure called Mujtaba Hashimi Samarih, who remained close to him during the war and in later years.[16]

Affiliated with the amorphous "hardliner" tendency in the post-war period, Ahmadinejad was assimilated into the Islamic Republic's second tier of political operators, serving in a number of provincial posts including governorship of Ardabil provinces from 1993 to 1997. He resigned from his post in the aftermath of Muhammad Khatami's landslide victory in the presidential election. He returned to his teaching post at the Amir Kabir technical university teaching civil engineering with a sub-specialty in urban traffic.

In 2003 Ahmadinejad returned to the political stage as the candidate of the conservative opposition in Tehran's mayoral election. His election to the office was seen as the outcome of popular displeasure with the pro-Khatami coalition and its dismal performance on the domestic front and against his conservative critics. His appointment benefited from the support of influential clerics both inside and outside of the government. Ahmadinejad came to represent a populist face of piety and commitment to revolutionary ideals among war veterans and radicals frustrated with post-revolutionary developments and with Khatami's relatively liberal message of civil society.

It was the same image of a war veteran devoted to the downtrodden and pious masses that brought Ahmadinejad to the presidential office in August 2005 with a message of social justice and return to true Islamic values. He came to power on the back of a constituency of Revolutionary Guards, Basij volunteers, and supporters of such conservative clerics as Ayatollah Muhammad Taqi Misbah and other vocal opponents of Khatami. If Ahmadinejad needed affirmative signs of the Mahdi's support they were provided by his meteoric rise to power from relative obscurity to the presidential office in less than two years. He started as the least-favored candidate in the presidential campaign and ended up winning the second round. Almost immediately afterwards, his international reputation as a radical leader – which in reality was due to his outrageous statements concerning Israel and the Holocaust – may have confirmed his conviction. In Ahmadinejad's worldview, he could not have achieved these results, as he repeatedly suggested, without the blessing of the Lord of the Age, or as he put it, his service under the Hidden Imam's "management" *(mudiriyat)*.[17] Shortly after assuming office, speculation on the time of the Hidden Imam's Advent was reported in pro-Ahmadinejad circles. One of the first acts of Ahmadinejad's government, it has been reported, was to donate a sizable budget (reportedly about $20 million) to the Jamkaran mosque's development project, in the belief that within two years the Hidden Imam would make himself manifest.[18]

Prognostications such as this coincided with the President's first address to the U.N. General Assembly in October 2005. Concluding his speech he noted that

> from the beginning of time, humanity has longed for the day when justice, peace, equality and compassion envelop the world. All of us can contribute to the establishment of such a world. When that day comes, the ultimate promise of all Divine religions will be fulfilled with the emergence of a perfect human being who is heir to all prophets and pious men. He will lead the world to justice and absolute peace. O mighty Lord, I pray to you to hasten the emergence of your last repository, the promised one, that perfect and pure human being, the one who will fill this world with justice and peace.[19]

A year later the messianic theme was more explicit. In his much publicized address to the 2006 United Nations' General Assembly Ahmadinejad began by pleading to God to "hasten the reappearance of the Imam of the times and grant to us victory and prosperity. Include us among his followers and martyrs." He ended by declaring that "today's world, more than ever before, longs for just and righteous people with love for all humanity; and above all longs for the perfect righteous human being and the real savior who has been promised to all peoples and who will establish justice, peace and brotherhood on the planet." He then uttered what appeared to be a modified passage from the "prayer of deliverance" *(du'a-yi faraj)* "O, Almighty God, all men and women are your creatures and you have ordained their guidance and salvation. Bestow upon humanity that thirsts for justice, the perfect human being promised to all by you, and make us among his followers and among those who strive for his return and his cause."[20]

Obviously impressed with his own performance, upon his return to Iran the President further revealed that at the time of his speech at the General Assembly he was enveloped by a halo of light – an allusion to the protective blessings of the Imam of the Age. "I felt that the atmosphere had suddenly changed, and for those twenty-seven or twenty-eight minutes, none of the leaders of the world blinked – and I say this without exaggeration. They were looking as if a hand was holding them there, and had just opened their eyes."[21] In other public speeches and interviews reaffirming the Hidden Imam's blessing, Ahmadinejad has unambiguously confirmed his mandate as one of paving "the path for the glorious reappearance of Imam Mahdi." He sees the hand of the Imam of the Age guiding him in affairs of the state, in his encounter with "the enemy," and in his advocacy of Muslim causes worldwide.

Whatever the personal dimensions of Ahmadinejad's convictions and his compliance with the "convergence theory" that looks for the Mahdi's universal governance, his enthusiasm and financial backing has given an unprecedented boost to the staff and funding of "research" institutes and indoctrinating "information" centers. Advocacy groups with the task of raising apocalyptic aspirations are to be seen at all levels, working within youth organizations and in public broadcasting and television programs, reviewing school text books, and promoting the Jamkaran cult.

Moreover, the resonance of Ahmadinejad's messianic persuasions among world opinion, especially in the West, when interspersed with questioning the accuracy of narratives of Jewish Holocaust – itself a reflection of deeper biases— and his predictions of the collapse of the Israeli state and the end of Zionism proved to be highly contentious. His insistence – especially in his addresses to international audiences – on the Advent of the Savior as a prelude to peace, social justice, prosperity, and happiness for all humanity is significant no doubt for its obvious contrast with the bloody image of the traditional Mahdi of some Shi'i traditions whose violent Uprising *(khuruj)* initiates a global apocalyptic confrontation between his "supporters" and the forces of "evil." One could be persuaded to view this as a major shift; perhaps a paradigmatic one. Yet Ahmadinejad's deep commitment to Iran's nuclear program is often presented by his critics in the West as a dangerous symptom of his apocalyptic aspirations, despite his repeated assertions that Iran's nuclear program is solely for peaceful purposes. It goes without saying that Ahmadinejad capitalizes on the Iranian people's sense of victimization and their desire for empowerment against a long history of deprivation and defeat especially in the face of Western hegemony. As has been observed elsewhere,

> It is easy to label Iran's quest for nuclear energy a dangerous adventure with grave regional and international repercussions. It is also comforting to heap scorn on President Mahmoud Ahmadinejad for his earlier denial of the Holocaust and his odious call for the obliteration of the state of Israel . . . Yet there is something deeper in Iran's story than the extremist utterances of a messianic president and the calculated maneuvering of the hard-line clerical leadership that stands behind him.[22]

Yet despite perceptions of Iran's nuclear program as a marker of nationalistic aspirations, and despite Ahmadinejad's utopian yearning for the peaceful advent of an ecumenical Mahdi, an unhealthy anxiety hovers over the Iranian President's continued preoccupation with the Hidden Imam and a final end to his prolonged Occultation.

As late as March 21, 2008, Ahmadinejad prefaced his Nouruz address to the Iranian people on the occasion of the Persian New Year by reciting the prayer pleading for the Hidden Imam's Deliverance.[23] Slightly earlier the Ahmadinejad Government's Chief of Cabinet also drew a curious parallel between the Hidden Imam and the present government. "Ahmadinejad's era is the period of his Lesser Advent *(zuhur-i sughra)*," he said, playing no doubt on the parallel with the Lesser Occultation *(ghaybat-i sughra)* of the Twelfth Imam and in effect implying some precursory function for the Iranian President in his first term which will soon lead to greater things to come presumably in his second term.[24]

The parallel, made by a confidant of Ahmadinejad, apparently was a reference to the President's pledge in the Cabinet meeting – he made the pledge three times – that during the second term of his presidency (if elected to the office) "he would not further a step but to fulfill his duty *(taklif)*, whether I stay for four years (in office) or not;" presumably his duty to act as the precursor to the Hidden Imam. With its fateful ring, the remark was quickly removed from the Iranian Students News Agency (ISNA) site.[25] Yet Ahmadinejad's aiming toward higher pre-messianic goals was not unusual. The Iranian network recently aired a previously unscreened speech of the President to the religious seminarians in Mashhad in which he posed as a victim from the attacks of his domestic opponents. He denounced the claim that he is in contact with the Imam of the Age but claimed in the meantime that his government acts "under the management of the Imam of the Age." He then concluded: "The endgame has started *(harakat-i akhir aghaz shudeh ast)*. We should quickly wrap up Iran's domestic problems so that we can commence the global responsibilities of the Revolution."[26]

## *Shifting the Mahdi Paradigm*

It may be observed that the encouragement and institutional support offered by Ahmadinejad's government and the senior ayatollahs to the cause of the Mahdi is a rare phenomenon in the history of Twelver Shi'i messianism. Throughout its history, urgent yearnings for the Advent of the Hidden Imam has been an expression of dissent by individual claimants or within movements of protest at odds with the clerical authorities of the time and with the political powers that support the 'ulama establishment. True, messianic "traditions" and apocalyptic literature were incorporated into the Shi'i belief system as a doctrine of faith primarily by Shi'i theologians of ninth and tenth centuries. And it is also true that over time this literature was further embellished by the Shi'i 'ulama, especially in the seventeenth to nineteenth centuries.

Yet the prime objective of this textual exercise and accumulation of a large and confused corpus of "traditions" was to authenticate and enhance clerical authority as the legitimate agent of the Mahdi. Though the Mahdi's very existence was naturally confirmed by Shi'i theology and made an item of faith, his Advent was invariably relegated to a distant and unspecified future (perhaps with the exception of the fourteenth-century Sarbadari state of Khurasan). Speculations on the return of the Hidden Imam were thus discouraged and any attempt to hasten the Mahdi's return was condemned. The thrust of the messianic literature was decidedly on the side of Occultation *(ghayba)* rather than Advent *(zuhur)*, hence providing the jurist theologians of the earlier centuries with a suitable climate for developing a stable judicial theory in the absence of the Imam and in due course consecrating their own authority as vicegerents of the Hidden Imam.

The shift of the Mahdi paradigm from the expression of popular anti-establishment yearnings to an ideological tool sponsored and advocated by the state and powerful circles within the Islamic Republic thus deserves explanation. At one level this seemingly curious phenomenon may be attributed to the religious convictions of Ahmadinejad and his cohorts who, being in control of the state, promoted their own messianic faith. At a deeper level however, the systematic advocacy of the Mahdi cult may be seen as a conscious policy to play on the people's frustration with the slogans of revolutionary Islam. By resorting to the Mahdistic faith the state, and more specifically conservative ayatollahs within the regime, hope to preserve their support base at a time when old revolutionary rhetoric alone no longer spawned grassroots loyalty.

It appears that a number of senior clerics and their younger cliques in Qom opposed to the second of Khurdad reformist movement that brought Khatami to power gave their blessing to the state-sponsored messianic drive. They were backed in this venture by "committed" veterans of the Iraq–Iran war especially among former Revolutionary Guards and the Basij recruits who lend their support to the cause of messianism in the hope of gaining what could not have been accomplished on the battlefields. It is in their yearnings for the Mahdi that we see aspirations of a generation of Islamic hardliners whose worldview was shaped by the experience of the war and for whom Ahmadinejad represents the prelude to a power monopoly.

This apocalyptic trend promoted by Ahmadinejad and likeminded advocates could have been dismissed as benign eccentricity or a demagogic charade if it had not been obliquely connected to disturbing anti-semitic and anti-Baha'i expressions. An implicit connection also between the coming of the Mahdi and the end of worldly "injustices" and political "arrogance" invariably implicates the United States and Israel. Furthermore, Israel's prolonged occupation of the Palestinian territories and oppressive treatment of its population provide ample ammunition to the likes of Ahmadinejad and widespread support for his anti-Zionist stance. Likewise, the United States' disastrous invasion of Iraq – an illegal and unjustifiable act of aggression – in turn vindicated the Islamic Republic's anti-American stance and made its rhetoric popular throughout the non-West. And, needless to say, Ahmadinejad intends to take full advantage of anti-American and anti-Israeli sentiment.

Conservative clerics such as Ayatollah Safi Gulpaygani, on the other hand, promote the Mahdi cause for their own ends despite their recent claim to the contrary. It may be argued that the doctrine of Occultation and its corollary, the Advent of the Imam at an unknown point in time, undermine the near total authority of the Guardian Jurist (especially after the demise of Khomeini). Conversely, the Mahdi doctrine put at the disposal of the grand ayatollahs, who consider their own positions as *marja'-i taqlid* (the sources of emulation), a far greater judicial autonomy, greater public recognition, more jockeying for political influence and greater financial resources. There is, one may conclude therefore, a return in the late 1990s to the Hujjatiyya thesis of partial compliance with the doctrine of the *wilayat-i faqih* and treatment of the Islamic Revolution as a mere prelude to an eventual Advent of the Imam of the Age.

All doctrinal implications aside, one may see in the Qom clerics' advocacy of the Mahdi and overzealous effort to market it for public consumption not only demagogy and cynicism but an irrational and politically dangerous motivation. It is comforting to note that neither the entire clerical body in Qom and elsewhere nor the Iranian public at large, as much as it has been willing to buy into the superstitious and miracle-making aspects of the state's messianic travesty, has so far remained unexcited by the politicization of the Mahdi's myth. Jamkaran is no doubt popular with ordinary Shi'is because it reflects disillusionment with the revolutionary utopia and offers a remedy for the personal troubles of everyday life. In private at least, Ahmadinejad's statements about the support of the Hidden Imam are mocked or viewed as an eccentric trait. Likewise, the Iranian public and the progressive clergy appear to see through the pious pronouncements of the conservative clergy whose call for the Mahdi seems to be one more act in the popularity contest.

Promoting messianism and giving it a certain sense of urgency has nonetheless been accompanied by unabashed vitriolic attacks on Baha'i post-millennial beliefs and on the Baha'i community. The unmistakable tone of religious intolerance associated with the most recent phase of Mahdistic pandemonium, seems to mime the Hujjatiyya rhetoric of earlier decades. Yet the recent propaganda campaign in the press, on the Internet and from the pulpit comes in the wake of three decades of discrimination and persecution that considerably weakened Iran's Baha'i community. Anti-Baha'i politicized propaganda paints this community not merely as heretics but as disloyal to the Islamic Republic, accusing them of serving the cause of Zionism and British and American imperialism. The number of Iranian Baha'is is dwindling and their economic status far less prominent than at any time over the past century, thanks to the discriminatory treatment under the Islamic Republic.

The radical clerics and their allies responsible for disseminating hate do not seem to be able even to tolerate reduced numbers of Baha'is, even though they are still the largest religious minority in Iran, as if the Baha'i post-millennial counter-narrative to the Shi'i expectations has been particularly troubling. Ironically, a vast majority of disseminators of anti-Baha'i propaganda have never met, let alone engaged in debate, with a Baha'i. Baha'is are for the most part just imagined enemies, ones that were exorcized from the deep recesses of a collective memory shared almost unanimously by the Shi'i clergy, by the conspiratorial theorists of the Pahlavi era who first politicized anti-Baha'i polemics and tried to present them as despised agents of foreign powers or domestic allies of the Pahlavi dictatorship at home. Anti-Baha'ism may thus be compared, as noted by Fred Halliday, with the entrenched anti-Semitism in European culture espoused by the church, conservative, right-wing radicals, and by conspiratorial theorists.[27]

By breathing urgency into the Mahdi myth, influential circles within the Iranian regime seem to be playing with a double-edged sword. The activities of one such messianic circle, the Cultural Center of Pavers of the Path of Deliverance *(Kanun-i Farhangi-i Rahpuyan-i Visal)* in Shiraz provides one example. Under the aegis of a hard-liner cleric, a rabble-rouser with a messianic slant named Muhammad Anjawinijad, the Center attracted a large following, mostly among Shiraz's émigré community in a newly developed neighborhood. The massive bomb explosion on April 13, 2008, in the Husayniya Sayyid al-Shuhada, the Center's congregational venue, resulted in fourteen deaths and close to one hundred injured. After some hesitation, the government agencies declared the incident as a Zionist and American imperialist conspiracy and subsequently a number of Baha'is of Shiraz were arrested as perpetrators of the terrorist act, without slightest shred of evidence. Though some were later released, others remained in detention. The thrust of Anjawinijad's sermons on moral reconstruction, and apparently the key to his popularity, was his routine attacks on the Baha'is and the Wahhabis; he declared them enemies of the House of the Prophet and devotees of the House, by which he meant the Shi'is. Messianic insinuations in Anjawinijad's sermons, exaggerated claims on behalf of the Mahdi and the House of the Prophet, and sordid melodramatic mystico-moral teachings to prepare devotees for the moment of deliverance, seem to have created inner tensions and enmities within Shiraz and infringed presumably on the vested interests of other Islamic influential groups leading in turn to retaliations for which the Baha'is are to be the scapegoats.

## *An Heir to Husayn's Legacy*

The popularity of messianic themes in today's Iran naturally motivated others outside the regime to lay claims to moral authority. One remarkable example is the emergence of the crypto-messianic movement of the self-assumed "ayatollah" Sayyid Muhammad Kazameini Boroujerdi, a charismatic middle-class preacher and prophet of the sort whose large following and critical views brought him into confrontation with the regime's security forces in October 2006 and resulted in his arrest and imprisonment. Evidently active since 1997 as an independent preacher – presumably with rudimentary theological training under a mentor of similar leanings – in his public statements Boroujerdi criticized the Iranian regime for politicizing Islam and turning it into a tool of hegemony and aggression.

In his sermons Boroujerdi remained loyal to the traditional forms of *rawza* recitation and invoking the Shi'i vocabulary of bereavement, victimization *(mazlumiyat)*, and final salvation. Making repeated references to the sufferings of his sacred ancestry – Muhammad the Prophet, 'Ali ibn Abi-Talib, Husayn ibn 'Ali, and Zayn al-'Abidin (the Sajjad) – he often drew parallels with his own mission to counter religious oppression, combat poverty and corruption as well as inevitable arrest and imprisonment. The crowds of thousands who gathered in his Husayniya in Tehran, a makeshift structure with a corrugated roof, represented a cross-section of Iranian urban society with a noticeable female constituency from the poorer section of the city alongside more affluent women of the middle classes. Giving blessings, distributing alms, attending to people's plight seemingly widened his appeal as what he indulgingly referred to as being the "refuge for the troubled" *(marja'-i giriftaran)*. Referring with pride to his sacred lineage, he first assumed such titles as "heir to Husayni legacy" *(warith al-Husayniyya)*, "paragon of Haydari (i.e. 'Alid) ancestry" *(bashir al-Haydariyya)*, the "Fatimid emissary" *(mandub al-Fatamiyya)* and claimed to be of the twenty-seventh son from the progeny of Sajjad. These titles presumably referred to his vague assumption of the Mahdihood, a claim which remained unarticulated, at least in public.

His audacity in criticizing the Islamic regime in public and on the Internet (and lately on You Tube) brought Boroujerdi into a showdown with agents of the Ministry of Information and the Revolutionary Guards who were dispatched to his home in a middle-class neighborhood of central Tehran in late October 2006. Clashes with the security forces, barrages of machine-gun fire, and injuries to his devotees eventually resulted in his arrest and imprisonment. What seemed to have triggered the regime into action (rather than putting up with him as a minor thorn in its side) was Boroujerdi's open criticism of the senior clergy, whom he repeatedly referred to with the demeaning label of *akhund* (ironically he himself appeared in clerical garb and he proudly assumed the title of *ayatollah*), calling them oppressors, criminals, thieves, and liars. The jurists *(fuqaha)*, he declared, were opponents of the Imam of the Age who rely on spurious juristic treatises *(risala)* rather than moral honesty to authenticate their leadership.

More threatening, perhaps, was his objection to the Islamic Republic's antagonistic foreign policy and dissemination of hate, which he argued has darkened the name of Islam and distorted Iran's image. Calling for peaceful coexistence with all nations, and a non-political Islam, his stance was in sharp contrast to Ahmadinejad's rhetoric, and the regime's routine propaganda. In Boroujerdi's letter to the pope, for example, he underscored the non-political nature of his mission and his divine calling.

The Islamic regime's concern with Boroujerdi's appeal and his pacifist Mahdistic claim had to be deflected with a propaganda counter-offensive. Under arrest and possibly by means of medical and other interrogation techniques, he was persuaded, or more likely forced under the threat of torture, to make a familiar TV "confession." Snippets of this confession were shown on Iranian TV, even though his face was blurred and his statements doctored, presumably from fear of inciting further protest by his followers. Retracting his presumption of divine agency and lowering his critical tone against the regime, however, has failed so far to facilitate his release from prison. His following has seemingly subsided, or at least for the time being is in hibernation.[28]

## *Limited Shelf Life*

Propaganda, scapegoating, and volatile rhetoric are the fruits of a state-sponsored messianic venture in today's Iran. The whole operation, it can be argued, betrays signs of the regime's moral and political vulnerability. It is as if the idea of the Mahdi is a weapon in the arsenal of the conservative mullas to mobilize and bring into line an army of preachers, reciting *maddahs*, Basij recruiters, and ideological commissars of the Revolutionary Guards. With free access to the press, media and Internet and with the financial backing of the state, they seem to have momentarily captured the public imagination, played to their unfulfilled aspirations, and steered their deep-seated religious beliefs. If the revolutionary Guardianship of the Jurist *(wilayat-i faqih)* of *Imam* Khomeini, the declared vicegerent of the Imam of the Age *(na'ib Imam)*, no longer seems to motivate Iranians and persuade them to submit to the senior clerics, perhaps a call for the Advent of the Hidden Imam himself can incite enthusiasm.

Yet the Shi'i clergy, despite centuries-old experience of eluding messianic expressions, does not seem to realize that there is a limit to the marketing of Mahdism. The "shelf life" for any intense messianic anticipation is alarmingly short, as the history of millenarian movements abundantly demonstrates. Sooner rather than later there will be an unpredictable turn from merely expecting the Mahdi to the actual manifestation of the Mahdi that does not necessarily bend to their authority. Messianism, as has often been observed, has its own complex dynamics, transforming pre-messianic speculations and proto-messianic anticipations – no matter how artificially induced by the clerical authorities – into a fully-fledged apocalyptic movement of incalculable proportions. If contained and controlled by the conservative clergy and their cohorts, developments such as those in Shiraz may have the potential of breeding an ideology even more absolutist than that acceptable in today's

Islamic Republic. If, on the other hand, the messianic euphoria no longer remains under the regime's control, it may evolve into a powerful movement of popular protest capable of challenging the Islamic Republic and its leaders. Such a possibility is not unrealistic given Shi'ism's past examples of such revolutionary mutations.

On a more positive concluding note, we may view the revival of millennial aspirations, and the shift of the messianic paradigm even among the clergy, as an indigenous accommodation to modernity. This is in effect the encounter of modern Shi'ism with one of its deepest and most enduring beliefs, an encounter which is taking place against the backdrop of social realities and social expectations for a better future in contemporary Iran and beyond in the Muslim world. Whether it is the popular desire for communicating with the Mahdi, Lilliputian speculation on the circumstances of his appearance and the grand utopian order that he will establish, Mahdism is an issue that can no longer be interpreted or be bound by arcane images of the suffering and frustration of early Shi'ism. We may even venture to speculate that current engagement with the myth of the Mahdi is a prelude to a new fashioning of the old Iranian quest for salvation, one that may aspire this time for a collective, perhaps a more democratic, savior.

# Notes

## Preface

1 For the ceramic bowl in question see *The Legacy of Genghis Khan, Courtly Art and Culture in Western Asia, 1256–1353,* ed. L. Komaroff and S. Carboni (New Haven, 2002), 58. For the mosque of Jamkaran and the popular cult associated with it see below Chapter 10.
2 See below Chapter 4 for Kashifi and the shaping of the *rawza* narrative.
3 See below Chapter 3 on the Nuqtavis and their fate.
4 For the arrival of the Bab, Hajji Mirza Jani and his family and the early Babis of Kashan see A. Amanat, *Resurrection and Renewal: The Making of the Babi Movement in Iran, 1844–1850* (Ithaca, 1989), 344–7.
5 The Jewish community of Kashan, one the oldest in the world and important in the intellectual life of Iranian Jewry, completely disappeared in the 1970s. So did the smaller but equally ancient Zoroastrian community of Kashan, along with the few Armenians.

## Chapter 1

1 See for example B. Batto, *Slaying the Dragon: Myth Making in the Biblical Tradition* (Louisville, KT, 1992); N. Cohn, *Cosmos, Chaos and the World to Come: The Ancient Roots of Apocalyptic Faith* (New Haven, 1993) esp. chs. 4 and 5.
2 For Zoroastrian millennial cycles see P. G. Kreyenbroek, "Millennialism and Eschatology in the Zoroastrian Tradition," *Imagining the End: Visions of Apocalypse from the Ancient Middle East to Modern America,* ed. A. Amanat and M. T. Bernhardsson (London and New York, 2002), 33–55, and A. Hultgard, "Persian Apocalypticism," *The Encyclopedia of Apocalypticism,* vol. 1, ed. J.J. Collins (New York, 1998), 39–83, reprinted in *Continuum History of Apocalypticism,* ed. J. J. Collins *et al.* (New York, 2003), 30–63.
3 See for example J.J. Collins, "From Prophecy to Apocalypticism: The Expectation of the End," *Encyclopedia of Apocalypticism,* vol. 1, 141–5.
4 For Ann Lee see S. J. Stein, *The Shaker Experience in America: A History of the United Society of Believers* (New Haven, CT, 1992); for Hildegard see B. Newman, ed., *Voices of the Living Light: Hildegard of Bingen and Her World* (New York, 1998); for Qurrat al-'Ayn see A. Amanat, *Resurrection and Renewal: The Making of the Babi Movement in Iran, 1844–1850* (Ithaca, 1989), 295–331. For a postmodern but still useful reading of feminine apocalypticism see C. Keller, *Apocalypse Now and Then* (Boston, 1996), esp. 224–44.
5 For a relatively recent bibliographical survey of the field see T. Daniel, *Millennialism: An International Bibliography* (New York, 1992). For a general appraisal of the field C. B. Strozier and M. Flynn, *The Year 2000: Essays on the End* (New York, 1997) and especially B. McGinn, 'Apocalyptic Spirituality: Approaching the Third Millennium', 73–80, and more recently R.

K. Emmerson, "The Secret," *American Historical Review*, 104/5 (Dec. 1999): 1603–14 and cited sources. See also B. McGinn, "Apocalypticism in the Middle Ages: An Historiographical Sketch," *Medieval Studies*, 37 (1975): 252–86, and H. Schwartz, "The End of the Beginning: Millenarian Studies, 1969-1975," *Religious Studies Review*, 2 (1976): 1–15.

6 Among the most substantive studies on comparative basis are *Apocalypticism in the Mediterranean World and the Near East* (Tubingen, 1983) which concentrates on ancient period but excludes Islam, and the more comprehensive and accessible *The Encyclopedia of Apocalypticism*, ed. J. J. Collins, B. McGinn, and S. S. Stein, 3 vols. (New York, 1998). For a popular survey of the largely Western apocalypticism see D. Thompson, *The End of Time: Faith and Fear in the Shadow of the Millennium* (Hanover and London, 1996). More recently Eugen Weber's *Apocalypses: Prophecies, Cults, and Millennial Beliefs through the Ages* (Cambridge, MA, 1999) offers a succinct (though at times hurried) overview of Western and largely early modern and modern European apocalypticism.

7 For further discussion of Zoroastrian influence on Jewish apocalyptic see Cohn, *Cosmos, Chaos,* esp. ch. 13 (220–6) and sources cited in n. 1 (263–4); G. Widengren, A. Hultgard, and M. Philonenko, *Apocalytique iranienne et dualisme qoumranien* (Paris, 1995); and most recently A. Hultgard, "Persian Apocalypticism," *Encyclopedia of Apocalypticism,* vol. 1, 39–83, and esp. 79–81. See also J. J. Collins, *Apocalypticism in the Dead Sea Scrolls* (London and New York, 1997) 41–51, 99–106. For Judeo-Christian origins of Islamic apocalypticism see S. A. Arjomand, "Islamic Apocalypticism in the Classical Period," *Encyclopedia of Apocalypticism,* vol. 2, ed. B. McGinn (New York, 1998), 238–86 and *idem*, "Messianism, Millennialism and Revolution in Early Islamic History," *Imagining the End,* 106–28.

8 R. I. Moore, "Medieval Europe: Religious Enthusiasm and Social Change in 'Millennial Generation'," *Imagining the End*, 129–47 offers in-depth text analysis of the historical setting around the year 1000 CE in Europe. In addition to the literature discussed by Moore, see also Richard Landes, "The Apocalyptic Year 1000: Millennial Fervor and the Origins of the Modern West," in Strozier and Flynn (eds.), *The Year 2000: Essays on the End* (New York, 1997), 13–29 and Emmerson, "The Secret," 1604. For a recent survey of European medieval apocalypticism see C. W. Bynum and P. Freedman, eds., *Last Things: Death and the Apocalypse in the Middle Ages* (Philadelphia, 2000), 1–20. Articles in this volume address a range of new questions and concerns.

9 See for instance S. Bashir, "Deciphering the Cosmos from Creation to Apocalypse: The Hurufiyya Movement and Medieval Islamic Esotericism," *Imagining the End,* 168–86.

10 See for instance J. Cole, "Millennialism in Modern Iranian History," *Imagining the End,* 282–311.

11 For a general appraisal of methodological issues see for example S. D. O'Leary, *Arguing the Apocalypse*: *A Theory of Millennial Rhetoric* (New York and Oxford, 1994), 3–92. For an apocalyptic rereading for early Islam see for example J. Wansbrough, *The Sectarian Milieu: Content and Composition of Islamic Salvation History* (Oxford and New York, 1978) and M. Cook and P. Crone, *Hagarism: The Making of the Islamic World;* and *Early Mahdism: Politics and Religion in the Formative Period of Islam* (Leiden, 1985).

12 For an early exposition of this theory see D. Aberle, "A Note on Relative Deprivation Theory as Applied to Millenarian and Other Cult Movements," *Millennial Dreams in Action*. See also R. R. Wilson, 'The Biblical Roots of Apocalyptic,' *Imagining the End*, 56–66.

13 For articulation of the effect of natural disasters and sudden social change in triggering apocalyptic processes see for example M. Barkun, *Disaster and the Millennium* (New Haven, 1974) and his more recent *Crucible of the Millennium* (Syracuse, NY, 1986).

14 S. O'Leary, *Arguing the Apocalypse: A Theory of Millennial Rhetoric* (New York, 1994).

15 For dynamics of Shi'i apocalypticism see for example Amanat, *Resurrection and Renewal* 1–29 and *Encyclopaedia Iranica*, 'Islam in Iran' section 2.v. (A. Amanat); vi. (S. Arjomand); vii. (M. Amir-Moezzi); ix. (V. Klemm). For an early treatment of Latin American millenarianism see V. Lanternari, *The Religions of the Oppressed: A Study of Modern Messianic Cults*, tr. L. Sergio (London, 1963), 158–95. See also P. Pessar, 'Masking the Politics of Religion: The Case of Brazilian Millenarianism', *Journal of the Latin American Lore*, 7 (Winter 1981): 255–77. See also the case study by P. Vanderwood, *The Power of God against the Guns of Government: Religious Upheaval in Mexico at the Turn of the Nineteenth Century* (Stanford, 1998) and A. C. Metcalf, "Millenarian Slaves? The Santidade de Jaguaripe and Slave Resistance in the Americas," *American Historical Review*, 104/5 (Dec. 1999): 1531–59 which also surveys Latin American millennial studies.

## *Chapter 2*

1 For Islamic messianism, see J. Blichfeldt, *Early Mahdism: Politics and Religion in the Formative Period of Islam* (Leiden, 1985); J. Darmesteter, *Le Mahdi depuis les origines de L'islam jusqu'a nos jours* (Paris, 1885); A. A. Sachedina, *Islamic Messianism: The Idea of the Mahdi in Twelver Shi'sm* (Albany, 1981). See also W. Madelung, "al-Mahdi," in *The Encyclopedia of Islam*, 2nd edn. (Leiden, I960–). For a selection of primary sources on Mahdism, see J. A. Williams, ed., *Themes of Islamic Civilization* (Berkeley, 1971), 189–251. See also J. Macdonald's series of seven articles in the *Journal of Islamic Studies* on aspects of Islamic eschatology. "The Creation of Man and Angels in Eschatological Literature," 3 (1964): 285–308; "The Angel of Death in Late Islamic Tradition," 3 (1964): 485–519; "The Twilight of the Dead," 4 (1965): 55–102; "The Preliminaries to the Resurrection and Judgment," 4 (1965): 137–79; "The Day of Resurrection," 5 (1966): 129–97; and "Paradise," 5 (1966): 331–83.

2 See W. L. Cleaveland, *A History of the Modern Middle East* (Boulder, CO, 1994); A. H. Hourani, *A History of the Arab Peoples* (Cambridge, MA, 1991), 265–458; M. G. S. Hodgson, *The Venture of Islam.* 3 vols. (Chicago, 1974); B. Lewis, *The Shaping of the Modern Middle East* (New York, 1994). For reform and renewal in Islam, see A. Merad, H. Algar, N. Berkes, and A. Ahmad, "Islah," in *Encyclopedia of Islam*, vol. 2. J. O. Voll, *Islam: Continuity and Change in the Modern World* (Boulder, CO, 1982).

3 For North African Islam, see A. Faure, "Islam in North-West Africa *(Maghrib),*" in *Religion in the Middle East*, ed. A. J. Arberry (London, 1969), 171–86. For the Muhammadan Way, see R. S. O'Fahey, *Enigmatic Saint: Ahmad Ibn Idris and the Idrisi Tradition* (Evanston, IL, 1990) 1–24.

See also A. Dallal, "The Origins and Objectives of Islamic Revivalist Thought, 1750–1850," *Journal of the American Oriental Society*, 113 (1993): 341–59.

4 For North Africa in the eighteenth and the early nineteenth centuries, see A. Raymond, "North Africa in the Pre-Colonial period," in *The Cambridge History of Islam,* ed. P. M. Holt, A. K. S. Lambton, and B. Lewis, 2 vols. (Cambridge, 1970), 2: 266–98; *Eighteenth-Century Renewal and Reform in Islam,* ed. N. Levtzion and J. Voll (Syracuse, NY, 1987), 3–38.

5 J. Abun-Nasr, *The Tijaniyya: A Sufi Order in the Modern World* (London, 1965), 14–50; J. S. Trimingham, *The Sufi Orders in Islam* (Oxford, 1971), 107–10.

6 O'Fahey, *Enigmatic Saint*, 46–9, 73,105–10.

7 Dallal, "Origins," 355–8; K. S. Vikor, *Sufi and Scholar on the Desert Edge* (Evanston, IL, 1995), 218–40; N. Ziadeh, *Sanusiyah* (Leiden, 1958), 35–51, 73–98.

8 P. M. Holt, *The Mahdist State in the Sudan, 1881–1898* (Oxford, 1970) 329–38.

9 Ibid. 37, 116. H. Shaked in *The Life of the Sudanese Mahdi: A Historical Study of Kitab sa'adat al-mustadhi bi-sirat al-Imam al-Mahdi* (New Brunswick, NJ, 1978), 50–200 provides an annotated translation of an apologia and chronicle of the Mahdi of the Sudan by Isma'il b. 'Abd al-Qadir accompanied with a useful introduction and notes. See also J. O. Voll, "The Sudanese Mahdi: Frontier Fundamentalism," *International Journal of Middle East Studies* 10 (1979): 145–66.

10 N. Daniel, *Islam, Europe, and Empire* (Edinburgh, 1966), 416–58.

11 M. Gilbert, *Churchill: A Life* (New York, 1991), 90–100. British strategic concerns were primarily with French advances in central Africa, which in the same year as the battle of Omdurman led to the famous Fashoda incident in south Sudan.

12 Holt, *Mahdist State,* 202–4.

13 On Shi'i Mahdism and the Occultation, see M. A. Amir-Moezzi, *Divine Guide in Early Shi'ism* (Albany, 1994); S. A. Arjomand, "The Crisis of Imamate and the Institution of Occultation in Twelver Shi'ism: A Sociohistorical Perspective," *International Journal of Middle East Studies* 28 (1996): 491–515; H. Modarresi, *Crisis and Consolidation in the Formative Period of Shi'i Islam* (Princeton, 1993), 53–105; Sachedina, *Islamic Messianism*, 78–183.

14 For Shi'i messianism in the early modern period, see S. A. Arjomand, *The Shadow of God and the Hidden Imam: Religion, Political Order and Societal Change in Shi'i Iran from the Beginning to 1890* (Chicago, 1984), 66–104; H. Halm, *Shiism* (Edinburgh, 1991), 71–91. See also below Chapter 4.

15 See below Chapters 3 and 4.

16 J. W. Morris, *The Wisdom of the Throne: An Introduction to the Philosophy of Mulla Sadra* (Princeton, 1981) 119–29.

17 For further details see below Chapter 3.

18 A. Amanat, *Resurrection and Renewal: The Making of the Babi Movement in Iran, 1844–1850* (Ithaca, 1989), 109–211.

19 *Bayan* (Tehran, n.d.), 2:7 (pp. 30–3) and 3:13 (93–7); cf. *Le Beyan Persan,* tr. A. L. M. Nicolas (Paris, 1911), 68–73, 50–8. For other pertinent references, see E. G. Browne's "Index of chief contents of the Persian Bayan," in his edition of Hajji Mirza Jani of Kashan, *Kitab-i Nuq tatul'-Kaf*

(Leiden and London, 1910) under "Resurrection" (p. lxxxvii), "Revelation" (p. lxxxvii), and *"Zuhur"* (p. xciv).

20 For a summary of the Babi doctrine, see E. G. Browne, "The Babis of Persia: II, Their Literature and Doctrines," *Journal of the Royal Asiatic Society*, 21 (1889): 881–933, reprinted in *Selections from the Writings of E.G. Browne on the Babi and the Baha'i Religions,* ed. M. Momeri (Oxford: 1987), 187–239.

21 Amanat, *Resurrection and Renewal,* 260–94, 332–71.

22 Ibid. 295–331, and sources cited there.

23 Ibid. 372–416. See also *Encyclopaedia Iranica*, ed. Ehsan Yarshater (New York, 1985–), "Baha'allah" (J. Cole).

24 For Babi-Baha'i fulfillment of past prophecies, see Baha'ullah, *Kitab-i Iqan* (Cairo, n.d.), trans. Shoghi Effendi as *Kitab-i Iqan, the Book of Certitude* (Wilmette, IL, 1931). See also C. Buck, *Symbol and Secret* (Los Angeles, 1995). On the intellectual formation of the Baha'i faith, see J. R. I. Cole, *Modernity and the Millennium: The Genesis of the Baha'i Faith in the Nineteenth Century Middle East* (New York, 1998) and P. Smith, *The Babi-Baha'i Religions: From Messianic Shi'ism to a World Religion* (Cambridge, 1987). S. Lavan, The Ahmadiyah Movement: A History and Perspective (Delhi, 1974), 22–63.

25 S. Lavan, *The Ahmadiyah Movement: A History and Perspective* (Delhi, 1974), 22–63.

26 Ibid. 92–121.

27 M. Bazargan, *Zarrih-i bi intiha* (Tehran, 1966).

28 'A. Shari'ati, *Intizar mazhab-i i'tiraz,* 3rd edn. (n.p., 1396 Q./1976).

29 Ibid. 25–53.

30 M. Mutahhari, *Qiyam va inqilab-i mahdi az didgah-i falsafah-yi tarikh* (The uprising and the revolution of the Mahdi from the perspective of philosophy of history) (Tehran, 1354 Sh./1975), 5–10.

31 Ibid. 57–60.

32 See also M. Mutahhari's discussion on Resurrection *(ma'ad)* and his debates with the Mahdi Bazargan during late 1960s in his *Majmu'a-i asar* (Tehran, 1374 Sh./1995), 4:621–840.

33 R. Khomeini, *Wilayat-i Faqih* (Tehran, 1971; new edn. 1357 Sh./1978). Translated and annotated by H. Algar as *Islam and Revolution: Writings and Declarations of Imam Khomeini* (Berkeley, 1981), 27–149. First delivered as a series of lectures in Arabic in the early 1970s, this work was then translated into Persian for publication.

34 For further discussion see below Chapter 8.

35 Khomeini, *Wilayat-i Faqih*, 6–24; English trans. Algar, *Islam and Revolution*, 27–54. For the development of the Great Satan in Khomeni's revolutionary rhetoric see below Chapter 9.

36 For Khomeini and the ideology of the Islamic Revolution, see S. A. Arjomand, *The Turban for the Crown: Islamic Revolution in Iran* (New York, 1988), 91–102, 147–88; S. Bakhash, *The Reign of the Ayatollahs* (New York, 1984) and H. Munson, *Islamic Revolution in the Middle East* (New Haven, 1988).

37 A. Baqi, *Dar shinakht-i hizb-i qa'idin-i Zaman* (Tehran, 1363 Sh./1984). For upsurge of messianic aspirations in contemporary Iran and remnant of the Hujjatiyya see below Chapter 10.

## Chapter 3

1 Iskandar Beg Munshi, *Ta'rikh-i 'alam-ara-yi 'Abbasi*, ed. I. Afshar (Tehran, 1334–5/1955–6), vol. 2, 475–6. Iskandar Beg eulogizes Darwish Kuchak's death with a sarcastic hemistich: "He has gone and gone and gone and gone and is still going."

2 Beyond Sadiq Kiya's pioneering work, *Nuqtaviyan ya Pasikhaniyan* (Tehran, 1320/1941), there is no critical treatment of the history and doctrines of Nuqtavism. Kiya's collection of primary material is superseded neither by A. Bausani's entry in *Encyclopedia of Islam*, 2nd edn. (Leiden, 1954–2005) (henceforth *EI2*) nor by the ideologically coloured rehash of 'A. Mirfitrus, *Junbish-i Hurufiyya va Nahzat-i Pasikhaniyan 'Nuqtaviyan* (Tehran, 1356/1976). Paucity of primary sources and lack of access to the surviving Nuqtavi manuscripts have obliged most scholars to rely on Kiya's gleanings from historical sources, biographical dictionaries, and selections of Nuqtavi writings, the only fragments so far published.

3 Mirfitrus, *Junbish*, 60.

4 For the Hurufi movement, see H. Ritter, "Studien zur Geschichte der islamischen Frömmigkeit, II: Die Anfänge der Hurufisekte," *Oriens*, 7 (1954): 1–54; Persian trans. by H. Mu'ayyad as "Aghaz-i firqa-yi Hurufiyya," in *Farhang-i Iranzamin*, 10 (1341/1962): 319–3; E. G. Browne, "Some Notes on the Literature and Doctrines of the Hurufi Sect," *Journal of the Royal Asiatic Society* (1898): 61–94, and his "Further Notes on the Literature of the Hurufis and their Connection with the Bektashi Order of Dervishes," *Journal of the Royal Asiatic Society* (1907): 533–81; *Textes Persans relatifs à la secte des Houroufis*, ed. C. Huart (London, 1909); S. Kiya, *Vazhih-nama-yi Gurgani* (Tehran, 1330/1951), and A. Bausani "Hurufiyya", *EI2*, vol. 3, 600–1.

5 Kiya, *Vazhih-nama*, 26, and Ritter (Persian trans.), 328, 367, 375.

6 Taqi al-Din Awhadi Baliyani, *'Arafat-i 'ashiqin*, MS. Malik Library, cited in Kiya, *Nuqtaviyan*, 58.

7 Reference to Mahmud's life appears primarily in the anonymous *Dabistan-i madhabib*, ed. R. Ridazada Malik (Tehran, 1362/1983), 273–8; English trans., *The Dabistan, or School of Manners*, tr. D. Shea and A. Troyer (London, 1901), 337–44. The *Dabistan* is the only source that refers to the Nuqtavis as *Wahidiyya* (Unitarians). In addition to the nomenclature *Nuqtaviyya*, most hostile Safavid and Mughal accounts identify them with the generic term *mulhid* (heretic), and occasionally as followers of Pasikhani (Pasikhaniyan). Nuqtavism is occasionally identified as "Mahmud's religion" *(din-i Mahmud)*. See Kiya, *Nuqtaviyan*, 5, for further sources on Mahmud's life.

8 *Rasid nawbat-i rindan-i 'aqibat mahmud/guzasht ankih 'Arab ta'na bar'Ajam mizad (Dabistan*, p. 276). Both *rind* and *mahmud* are intentional puns with obvious Nuqtavi connotations.

9 *Dabistan*, 275

10 Nuqtavi catechism, cited in Kiya, *Nuqtaviyan*, 84. Identified by Kiya as "a Nuqtavi work" *(niwishtih-yi Nuqtavi)*, this catechism is apparently authored by a certain Abu'l-Maryam in 820/1417–18 and at the time of Kiya's writing was in private hands. The original manuscript consist of 188 folios but Kiya only cites excerpts in the appendix.

11 Catechism, Kiya, *Nuqtaviyan*, 76.

12 Ibid., 102.

13 Ibid. 120-1.
14 Ibid. 84–6.
15 Ahmad b. Nasr Allah Qadizada Tatawi, MS. Malik Library, cited in Kiya, *Nuqtaviyan,* no. 13, p. 36. The same Isma'ili revolt is cited in Qadi Mir Ahmad Munshi Qummi's *Khulasat al-tawarikh*, ed. I. Ishraqi (Tehran, 1359/1980), vol. 1, 582–4, under the year 981/1573–4 but with no explicit reference to the Nuqtavis.
16 Iskandar Beg, *Alam-ara*, vol. 2, 476.
17 Awhadi Baliyani, *'Arafat-i 'ashiqin*, in Kiya, *Nuqtaviyan*, 59–60.
18 Iskandar Beg, *Alam-ara*, vol. 2, 476.
19 Ibid. Darwish Yusuf's story was a source of inspiration for another antinomian of later times. Mirza Fath 'Ali Akhundzada's Persian play *Sitarihgan-i farib khurdih ya hikayat-i Yusuf Shah Sarraj* (Betrayed Stars or the Story of Yusuf Shah, the Saddler), first published in Tiflis (Tbilisi) in 1857, is a sympathetic dramatization of Yusuf's ephemeral reign and the Nuqtavi massacre of 1593. Nuqtavi *qalandars* were also a source of inspiration for J. Al Ahmad's novel *Nun w'l-Qalam* (Tehran, 1390/1961).
20 'Abd al-Qadir Bada'uni, *Muntakhab al-tawarikh* (Calcutta, 1865–9), vol. 2, 286–8.
21 For Sarmad, see Jalali Na'inis introduction to Dara Shukoh's Persian translation of the *Upanishads* entitled *Sir-i akbar*, ed. H. Jalali Na'ini (Tehran, 1340/1961), 129–30, 246.
22 The points of affinity between the Nuqtavi and the Babi doctrines are alluded to (beyond Kiya's brief reference in his *Nuqtaviyan*, p. I5n) in A. Amanat, *Resurrection and Renewal: The Making of the Babi Movement in Iran, 1844-1850* (Ithaca, 1989), 13–14, I44–5, 333.
23 *Dabistan*, 277.

## *Chapter 4*

1 *Rawdat al-Shuhada* enjoyed a wide readership throughout the Persian-speaking world. A. Munzavi (*Fihrist Nuskhaha-yi Khatti Farsi*, vol. 6: 4473–76 [Tehran, 1353/1974]) identifies sixty-nine manuscript copies dating back to 939/1532 of which twenty-five are in Iranian libraries. K. Mushar (*Fihrist-i Kitabha-yi Chappi Farsi*, vol. 2: 1790 [Tehran, 1352/1973]) identifies twelve nineteenth-century lithographic editions, mostly published in India, with the earliest dating Bombay, 1285Q./1868. All references in this article are to Husayn Wa'iz Kashifi, *Rawdat al-Shuhada*, Abul-Hasan Sha'rani edn. (Tehran, n.d. [1358/1979 ?]). The term *rawda* has often been rendered as garden. Its original meaning however is "meadow" or "field," hence here implying the plane of Karbala irrigated with the blood of martyrs. Kashifi also uses *rawda* for graveyard.
2 *Rawdat al-Jannat,* 2nd edn. (Tehran, 1367/1947), 255–56. Today *rawda-khwani* is a general term for all recitations of the sufferings of Karbala regardless of the text or texts used by the professional narrators. None of the approximates in English corresponds fully to *rawda-khwani: dirge* is not performed by a professional nor is it limited to a particular commemoration narrative. Similarly, *oraison funèbre* in French relates to a funerary rite. Kashifi's *Rawad al-Shuhada* has been superseded by a number of later eulogies *(marathi)* including, in the the seventeenth century, Muhammad Baqir Majlisi's *Jala' al-'Uyun* (purifier of the eyes) and, in the nineteenth century, Ahmad Naraqi's *Muhriq al-Qulub* (incinerator of the hearts) and

Muhammad Baqir Hiravi Qazvini, *Tufan al-Buka'* (deluge of tears).

3 For *Rawdat al-Shuhadas* influence on the *ta'ziya* narrative and style see for example P.J. Chelkowski, ed., *Ta'ziyeh: Ritual Drama in Iran* (New York, 1979); J. Malikpur, *Adabiyat-i Nimayishi dar Iran*, 2 vols. (Tehran, 1363/1984), vol. 2, 211–42.

4 For the Muharram ceremony in the kingdom of Awadh see J. R. I. Cole, *Roots of North Indian Shi'ism in Iran and Iraq* (Berkeley, 1988), 101–16 and in Hyderabad see D. Pinault, *The Shiites: Ritual and Popular Piety in a Muslim Community* (New York, 1992), 125–36. For revolutionary Iran see above Chapter 2. For the political significance of martyrdom in modern Shi'ism see H. Enayat, *Modern Islamic Political Thought* (London, 1982), 181–94.

5 For Shi'i *maqatil* literature see J. Calmard, "Le chiisme umamite en Iran à l'époque seldjoukide d'après le *Kitab al-Naqd,*" *Le Mond iranien et l'Islam* IV (1971): 64–70; and A. Bausani, *Religion in Iran from Zoroaster to Baha'ullah,* tr. J. M. Marchesi (New York, 2000), 355–9; and H. S. Jafri, *Origins and Early Development of Shi'i Islam* (London, 1979). See also Shaykh al-Mufid, *Kitab al-Irshad*, tr. I. K. A. Howard (London, 1981).

6 For a recent summary of debates about Kashifi's religious affiliation see J. 'Abbasi's introduction to his edition of Kashifi's *Jawahir al-Tafsir* (Tehran, 1379/2000), 83–93.

7 For later Sarbadaris see for example I. P. Pertrushevsky, "Dizhenie Serbedarow v Khurasane," *Uchennye Zapiski Instituta Vostokovedeniya AN SSSR* 14 (1956): 91–162 tr. K. Kishavarz, *Nahzat-i Sarbadaran-i Khurasan,* 3rd edn. (Tehran, 1351 Sh./1972), 94–7 and the cited passage by Ahmad Fasihi Khwafi, *Mujmal*, ed. M. Farrukh (Mashhad, 1339 Sh./1950), 115–19. For 'Ali Muayyad's promotion of orthodox Shi'ism see also S. Arjomand, *The Shadow of God and the Hidden Imam* (Chicago, 1984), 70–1.

8 One example is Abu Sa'id Hasan ibn Husayn Shi'i Sabzivari (alive in 753/1352) *Rahat al-Arwah wa Munis al-Ashbah* (comfort of the souls and companion of the spirits) on the life of the Prophet, Fatima, and the Twelve Imams. For manuscript copies see A. Munzavi, *Fihrist*, 6: 4465–66. For a similar work by the same author see ibid. 6: 4420–21.

9 In his scholarly introduction to *Futuwwat-nama-yi Sultani* (Tehran, 1350 Sh./1971) M. J. Mahjub overlooked the importance of the Sarbadari connection in the creation of this work (see intro. 73–104 and 98–104).

10 Ibid. 4.

11 For Kashifi's chain of hadith see the facsimile of his 872/1467 license *(ijaza)* for a student of his cited in a manuscript copy of *Sahifa al-Razawiya* now in the library of the Masjid A'zam in Qom. It appears in an appendix to *Rawda,* 420.

12 Fakhr al-Din 'Ali Safi, *Rashahat 'Ayn al-Hayat* (Laknaw, 1308/1890), 144–5 cited in J. 'Abbasi's introduction to *Jawahir,* 44–5.

13 Nizam al-Din 'Abd al-Wasi' Nizami, *Makhzan al-Insha'* collected by Ahmad Khwafi (Munshi), ed. R. Humayn-Farrukh (Tehran, 1357/1978), vol. 1, 116. This source cites a decree *(farman)* by Sultan Husayn ibn Bayqura appointing Kashifi to the Sabzevar chief judgeship for the second time (therefore after 1470). A second *farman* (ibid. 158) acknowledges his resignation but exempts Kashifi from some taxes in the region and other privileges.

14 Nurullah Shushtari, *Majalis al-Ma'wminin* (Tehran, 1335/1956), vol. 1, 548.

15 Throughout his many works in *Shawahid al-Nubuwwa*, Jami expresses

pro-'Ali sympathies. See below for Kashifi's extensive use of this work in his *Rawda*. Jami's biographers, including modern writers, tend to overlook these sentiments. See for example A. Afsahzad, *Naqd wa Barrasi-yi Athar wa Shar-i Ahwal-i Jammi* (Tehran, 1378/1999), 105–40.

16 His title was *Murshid al-Dawla* (Kashifi, *Rawda*, 13). See below for further details.

17 For Qasim Anwar and his mission see R. Savory, "A 15th-Century Safavid Propagandist at Herat," *American Oriental Society, Middle West Branch*, ed. D. Sinor (London, 1969), 189–97; and *Kulliyat-i Qasim Anwar*, ed. S. Nafisi (Tehran, 1337/1958), Introd., 59–107.

18 *Makarim al-Akhlaq*, ed. Muhammad Akbar 'Ashiq (Tehran, 1378/1999), 112–13. Khawnd Mir names Kashifi in a group of seven scholars which includes Ahmad Taftazani, the Shaykh al-Islam of Herat, and son of the famous theologian. He was later executed by the Safavids for his refusal to curse the Sunni caliphs. Earlier (103–8) Khwand Mir cites a letter by Sultan Husayn Bayqura in which the reluctant ruler eventually grants Nav'i permission to embark on a Hajj pilgrimage.

19 For Shaibanid conquest of the Timurid empire see Ghiath al-Din Khwand Mir, *Habib al-Siyar fi Akhbar al-Afrad al-Bashar*, ed. J. Huma'i , 4 vols., 3rd edn. (Tehran, 1362/1983), vol. 4, 273–319. A vivid contrast to the leisurely culture of Herat appears in *Majalis al-'Ushshaq*, arguably written by Husayn Bayqura himself (ed. G. Tabataba'i Majd [Tehran, 1376/1997]).

20 Kashifi himself gives the date of composing his work as 847 years after Husayn's martyrdom (in AH 61/680) which corresponds to July 1508 to June 1509 (*Rawda*, 354).

21 For the Safavid conquest of Herat see Khwand Mir, *Habib al-Siyar*, vol. 4, 514–20.

22 The above-mentioned reference to turmoil in "Iraq and Sham" in July 1500 may be taken as an allusion to the earliest Qizilbash clashes with the Aq Qoyunlu and other political contenders in northern Mesopotamia and eastern Syria. For a summery of Isma'il's early campaigns during the year 905/1500 in eastern Anatolia and northern Mesopotamia before the capture of Tabriz in 1501 see H. R. Romer, "The Safavid period," in the *Cambridge History of Iran* (Cambridge, 1986), vol. 6, 203–15.

23 Kashifi, *Rawda*, 405 cf. 419–20.

24 Khwand Mir, *Habib al-Siyar*, vol. 4, 248–9, 318, 321, 376, 387. See also idem, *Makarim al-Akhlaq*, 108. We know that several of Sayyid Mirza's allies among the Timurid princes took refuge with Shah Isma'il and remained in his service. Badi' al-Zaman himself first took refuge with Shah Isma'il and then with the Mughal ruler Babur before defecting again to Isma'il. After the battle of Chalduran (1514) Badi' al-Zaman took refuge with Sultan Salim and was sent off from Tabriz to Istanbul, where he died shortly after.

25 *Habib al-Siyar*, vol. 4, 345. Khawnd Mir's mentions that the royal Dar al-Siyada was located on the main junction *(chahar suq)* of the city of Herat. In another of his works, *Khatamat al-Akhbar fi Ahwal-i al-Akhyar* (final reports about the lives of friends) Khwand Mir describes Dar al-Siyada as one of grand monuments of Amir 'Ali Shir Nawa'i: "Everyday in that noble edifice the poor and the dervishes (or the needy) are fed." A certain Mawlana 'Abd al-Jalil was the teacher there who received an appropriate royal pension (*Ma'athir al-Muluk bi zamima-yi Khatama-yi Khulasat al-Akhbar wa Qanun-i Humayuni*, ed. Mir Hashim Muhaddis [Tehran, 1372/1993], 192). If we apply the more technical meaning of *dar al-*

*siyyada* in the Iranian context it is possible to assume that this institution was devoted to charity and study of the *sayyids* of Herat, probably supervised by Shi'i dignitaries.

26 Ibid.

27 For a list of his works see *Encyclopedia of Islam,* vol. 2: "Kashifi" (Gh. Yusufi) and A. Sha'rani's intro. to his edition of *Rawda*, 3–4.

28 Also variably known as Wa'iz-i Harati, Muhaddith Shirazi, and by his penname, Asili.

29 For his biography see Khwand Mir, *Habib*, vol. 4: 332–3 and 'Ashiq's, notes to *Makarim al-Akhlaq,* 175–6 (and the cited sources). 'Ashiq refers to Jamal al-Din's Shi'i proclivity based on his recommendation from the pulpit to the people of Herat to accept Shi'ism after the capture of the city by the Safavids. Yet according to his friend and protégé Khwand Mir, he remained a Sunni to the end despite Safavid pressure on him to conform.

30 Munzavi, *Fihrist,* 6: 4467–72. Mnuzawi identifies ninety-five manuscripts, most of them from the early sixteenth century. This may indicate the instant popularity of this work. The earliest copy (in the Chester Beatty Library, Dublin) dates to 888/1484 and only has the first part on the life of the Prophet, hence suggesting the addition of the latter parts in 903/1497. In the earlier chapters of his work Kashifi makes occasional use of Jamal Husayn's *Rawdat al-Ahbab* (e.g. *Rawda,* 71).

31 Kashifi, *Rawda*, 12.

32 *Tazkira-i Majalis al-Nafa'is,* Persian tr. Sultan Muhammad Harati and Hakim Shah Muhammad Qazvini, ed. A. A. Hikmat (Tehran, 1363/1984), 268.

33 Ibid.

34 *Wa'izan kin jilwih bar mihrab u minbar mikunand/ chun bi khalwat miravand an kar-i digar mikunand.* "That other act" in Hafiz may have been an allusion to drinking. In this context, it probably means the "best of the acts" (*khayr al-'amal*), as in the Shi'i *adhan*, which the Sunnis mocked as being a reference to Shi'i temporary marriage *(mut'a)*.

35 Safi , *Rashahat*, vol. 2: 491.

36 After a sermon in the Sabzevar Jami' mosque, in which Kashifi stated that the Archangel Gabriel appeared to the Prophet twelve thousand times, a hostile old man in the audience put him on the spot. He asked if Gabriel also appeared to 'Ali. Facing a zealous pro-'Ali audience, the artful Kashifi claimed that Gabriel appeared to 'Ali twenty-four thousand times. He backed this claim by quoting the famous Prophetic hadith: "I am the city of knowledge and 'Ali is my gate;" hence each time Gabriel visited the Prophet, he must have passed through 'Ali's gate twice (Shushtari, *Majalis,* vol. 1: 548).

37 *Anwar Suhayli,* is an ornate, and rather longwinded, Persian rendering of Bidpa'i's famous *Kilila wa Dimina*. It is based on the masterful Persian translation by Abul-Ma'ali Nasrullah Munshi. A Turkish translation of *Anwar Suhayli* was translated into French by the order of the Louis XIV, and was to be a source for La Fontaine's *Les Fables.*

38 For Turkish accounts of Karbala' see I. Melikoff, "Le drame de Kerbela dans la littérature épique turque," *Revue des études islamiques*, 34 (1966): 133–48.

39 Kashifi, *Rawda*, 276.

40 For a brief description of this work see Afsahzad, *Naqd*, 188. For manuscript copies and table of content see Munzavi, *Fihrist*, 2(1): 1264–5 and 6: 4499–501.

41 Also his *Durj al-Durrar fi Milad Sayyid al-Bashar* (a treasure chest on the birth of the Lord of the Humanity [Muhammad]).

42 Of the sixty-seven works that Kashifi mentioned by title, the largest number of citation, twenty-six, belongs to Jami's *Shawahid*. With the exception of the Qur'an, the second most frequently cited is *Nur al-A'ima* by the well-known twelfth-century Abul-Mu'ayyad Muhammad al-Khwarazmi, a hadith scholar with evidently pro-Shi'i tendencies, which is mentioned twenty times. *Kanz al-Ghara'ib*, an account of Shi'i sufferings by an anonymous author, is mentioned twelve times. Neither of the latter two works can be found in Shi'i bibliographies. See for example Agha Buzug Tihrani's *al-Dharia ila Tasanif and Shi'a* and Munzavi's *Fihrist*. See also Abul-Hasan Sha'rani's introductory note (*Rawda*, 6) which considers them as lost.
43 Kashifi, *Rawda*, 341
44 Ibid. 254.
45 Ibid. 15.
46 This constitutes chapter one of *Rawda* (15–67). The enigma of Jesus' absence from the narrative of Karbala may be explained by the Islamic denial of the Christian doctrine of the crucifixion. Kashifi's sources for biblical prophets apparently are the Qur'an and the apocryphal stories of the *qisas al-anbiya'*.
47 Ibid. 67–117. These are subjects of chapters two and three, corresponding to the second and the third day of Muharram mourning.
48 Ibid. 192–3, cf. 242–3 where the author provides a fuller and more passionate account as a prelude to Husayn's entry to the plain of Karbala.
49 Ibid. 63–4.
50 Bausani, *Religion*, 352–3; H. Halm, *Shi'ism* (Edinburgh, 1991) 139–41. For a full study of the subject see M. Ayoub, *Redemptive Suffering in Islam: A Study of the Devotional Aspects of 'Ashura' in Twelver Shi'ism* (The Hague, 1978).
51 Ibid. 136–7. The four other great weepers consist of three prophets of the Old Testament: Adam, Jacob, and Joseph, and Zayn al-'Abidin 'Ali, the Forth Shi'i Imam. The latter is credited for weeping forty years for the massacre of his family in Karbala.
52 Ibid. 62.
53 Ibid. 248–9. And again (p. 250): "I am entangled in a noose (*kamand*) that has been thrown from the Heavens." Indeed, the whole section prior to his entry into the Karbala plane revolves around the theme of destiny.
54 See Bausani, *Religion,* 353–4 and Halm, *Shi'ism,* 141–2 and cited sources. All accounts trace the rite of Siyavush to Narshakhi's *Tarikh-i Bukhara.*
55 Ibid. 418. On the other hand, *maghrib* may be understood in its classical sense as the geographical west of the Islamic world and hence Kashifi's remark is to be taken as a relic of the Fatimid messianic legacy in North Africa.
56 The study of *Rawdat al-Shuhada*'s impact on later works of the same genre deserves a separate study, as does the tracing of mourning literature on the shaping of a Shi'i-Iranian psyche and its historical manifestation.

## *Chapter 5*

1 See above Chapter 3.
2 From the Arabic root *b-y-n* (to be or become plain, to explain, to come out) thus *bayan* denotes clearness, manifestation, elucidation, and explanation. The Qur'anic verse (3:138) reads; "This is a clear explanation/evidence for people and is a guide and counsel for those who fear God." The other occurrence (55:4) implies teaching mankind the

sacred word: "God the merciful; taught the Qur'an; He created man; taught him to speak/ the explanation *('allama-hu al-bayan).*"

3 At the time of writing the *Bayan,* the Bab was familiar with the new Persian translation of the New Testament and may have read John's Book of Revelation. Yet it is doubtful that he was inspired by it in his composition of the *Bayan* or in the choice of the title. Henry Martyn translated St. John's Book of Apocalypse (or Book of Revelation) as *Mukashifiat-i Yuhana.* Nowhere in the *Bayan* does this term occur in any form. For the Bab's familiarity with the NT see A. Amanat, *Resurrection and Renewal: the Making of the Babi Movement in Iran, 1844-1850* (Ithaca, 1989), 197–8. For the new translation of the NT see below Chapter 6.

4 This also corresponds to the NT notion of *logos* as in John's Gospel.

5 Altogether the *Bayan* has received little scholarly attention. Exceptions are the French translation by A. L. M. Nicolas and E. G. Browne's classification of its contents (*Nuqtatul'-Kaf being the Earliest History of the Babis compiled by Hajji Mirza Jani of Kashan* (London, 1910), liv-xcv). See also D. MacEoin, *Rituals in Babism and Baha'ism,* Pembroke Persian Papers, vol. 2 (London, 1994) and his entry, "Bayan," in *Encyclopaedia Iranica*, ed. Ehsan Yarshater (New York, 1985–). Baha'i apathy toward the study of Babi texts is disheartening given the place that the *Bayan* holds in the evolution of Baha'i law and outlook. As late as the 1860s in Edirne, Baha'ullah in the Muslim tradition of addressing the Qur'an referred to the *Bayan* as "the mother book" *(umm al-kitab).* The impact of the *Bayan* on the Babi-Azali view is also worthy of attention. It is possible to argue that the teachings of the *Bayan* influenced Babi activists during the Constitutional Revolution. See A. Amanat, "Memory and Amnesia in the Historiography of the Constitutional Revolution," *Iran in the 20th Century: Historiography and Political Culture,* ed. T. Atabaki (London and New York, 2009 [forthcoming]). The early Azali treatment of the *Bayan* was largely in line with the Islamic notion of scripture as a source of the shari'a, as for instance in the writings of Mirza Yahya Subh Azal.

6 See for example Qur'an 21:34. See also Amanat, *Resurrection*, 191–3.

7 *Bayan* (Tehran, n.d.) appendix p. 340. The Arabic *Bayan*, written at the same time as the Persian version, and with an identical structure, was completed up to the end of unit 11. Based on the Arabic version, Subh Azal added twenty-eight units to the Persian *Bayan*, which brought it to the end of unit 11. He left the rest incomplete for the time of glory *('izza)*, as the Bab had requested. Baha'ullah's *Iqan* and later *Aqdas* are both viewed by the early Baha'is as addenda of the *Bayan*.

8 The most widely used work of Shi'i law available to the general public for instance was still Shaykh Baha' al-Din 'Amili's *Jami'-i 'Abbasi,* a *fiqh* compendium commissioned by Shah 'Abbas I in the early seventeenth century.

9 *Bayan* 8:7 (188).

10 Ibid. 7:10 (252). See also MacEoin, *Rituals,* 14–21.

11 *Bayan* 7:6 (245). The *Bayan* even goes so far as to prohibit believers from carrying weapons of any sort, an aversion no doubt reflecting the level of violence the Bab witnessed in his urban surroundings and at a national scale.

12 It is questionable however whether the Bab condoned Tahira's emergence after 1848 as the prime leader of the radical wing of the movement during the Badasht gathering.

13 Ibid. 6:6 (198–200).

14 Not surprisingly, after the execution of the Bab the same spirit of democratic epiphany came to haunt the distressed Babi community for decades.

## Chapter 6

1 D. Bently-Tylor, *My Love Must Wait, the Story of Henry Martyn* (London, 1975), 73, 53, 97 citing Martyn's *Journal*.
2 N. Daniel, *Islam, Europe and Empire* (Edinburgh, 1966), 255–6, 263, 501.
3 S. Wilberforce, *Journal and Letters of Reverent Henry Martyn*, 2 vols. (London, 1837), vol. 1, 310.
4 Bently-Tylor, *My Love Must Wait*, 118.
5 Wilberforce, *Journal*, vol. 2, 347.
6 Ibid. 717.
7 Ibid. 357, 371.
8 Ibid. 724.
9 Ibid. 724–5.
10 Earlier he had read anti-Islamic polemics by a certain Lord Valentia while writing his own Arabic tracts in Bombay (J. Sargent, *A Memoir of the Reverent Henry Martyn,* 5th edn. [London, 1844], 309, 314).
11 For Mirza Ibrahim Fasa'i (1173–1255/1759–1839) see for example Hasan Fasa'i, *Fars-namah-i Nasiri*, 2nd edn. M. Rastigar-Fasa'i, ed. (Tehran, 1367/1989), vol. 2, 927–9 which offers some details about his juristic career and his altercations with the government of Fars. None of the Persian biographical dictionaries, so far as I know, makes any reference to Fasa'i's exchanges with Martyn.
12 Mirza Ibrahim Fasa'i, *Risala,* Bodleian Library, Oxford, Persian MS. no. 1826 [Bodl. Or. 765], folios 1–2, trans. in S. Lee, *Controversial Tracks on Christianity and Mohammedanism* (Cambridge, 1824), 1–2.
13 For a bibliography of mostly medieval Islamic polemics see M. Steinschneider, *Polemische und Apolgetische Literatur in Arabischer Sprache, Zwischen Muslimen, Christian and Juden* (Leipzig, 1877) which does not make any reference to the literature resulting from the Martyn controversy.
14 'Alawi was commissioned by 'Abbas I to respond to refutations by Heionuymo Xavier just before the Safavid expulsion of the Portuguese from the Island of Hormuz in 1622. 'Alawi's rejoinder, needless to say, was an excellent piece of propaganda needed by the canny Shah 'Abbas to fortify his military action with a religious justification. For this work and its author and the exchanges with Jesuits see Lee, *Controversial Tracks,* v–cxiii; E. G. Browne, *A Handlist of the Persian Manuscripts in the Library of the University of Cambridge* (Cambridge, 1896), 12. Only one manuscript copy of this work appears in the Iranian collections (M. 'A. Rawzati, *Fihrist-i Nuskhahay-i Khatti-i Kitabkhanaha-yi Isfahan*, vol. 1 (Isfahan, 169).
15 See *Jahadiyya* (Tehran, 1234/1819); 2nd edn., J. Qa'im-Maqami ed. (Tehran, 1353/1974). For the circumstances leading to its production and publication see A. Amanat, "'Russian Intrusion into the Guarded Domain: Reflections of a Qajar Statesman on European Expansion," *Journal of the American Oriental Society,* 113/1 (1993): 35–56.
16 Fasa'i, *Risala, folio,* 38/23; trans. in Lee, *Controversial Tracks*, 38.
17 Martyn, *Risala* (I), Bodleian Library, Oxford, Persian Ms. 1826, folios 24–47, trans. in Lee, *Controversial Tracts,* 80–101.
18 Martyn, *Risala* (II), Bodleian Library, Oxford, Persian Ms. 1826, folio, 48–59a., trans. in Lee, *Controversial Tracts*, 102–23.
19 Cambridge Central Library, MS. Add. 3231 (see E. G. Browne, *Handlist of*

*Persian Manuscripts*, 415). Excerpts of the original and partial translation in Lee, *Controversial Tracts*, Appendix A, 40–69.

20 Earlier, in 1215/1800, Aqa Muhammad 'Ali Bihbahani (son of Aqa Muhammad Baqir Wahid) also addressed Christian attacks, though without reference to any European missionary, in his general anti-Jewish and anti-Christian polemic *Radd Shubahat al-Kuffar* (Refuting the Infidels' Illusions), infamously titled *Sufi-kush* (killer of the Sufis), which was produced at the request of Fath 'Ali Shah.

21 Shortly after his other compilation, *jihadiyya*, which was a composite statement based on several fatwas by contemporary Mujtahids, was published in Tabriz in 1819.

22 Entitled *Padri-nama* it consisted of about 250 verses. Rustam al-Hukama lists it in the inventory of his own works that appears as an appendix to a manuscript copy of his *Pand-nama*. In the same inventory he also lists a digest he prepared of treaties about the veracity of Judaism, Christianity, and Islam and of the Shi'i Imams that he compiled for Muhammad Shah and Hajji Mirza Aqasi. These treatises were originally written by Mirza Muhammad 'Ali Darbandi, Rustam al-Hukama's teacher, and were presented to the Russian emperor Nicholas I and the Russian royal princes.

23 Mirza Abul-Qasim Qumi, *Risala dar Radd Padri*, MS. Mar'ashi Library, Qum; for excerpts see H. Modarrisi Tabataba'i ed. *"Risala dar radd-i Henry Mrtyn," Vahid,* 10 (1351/1972): 1223–37. I am truly indebted to Dr. Hossein Modarrisi also for many years of sharing notes with me on the subject of Shi'i responses to Martyn and for his valuable references to lesser-known accounts which he assiduously gleaned from various collections and generously made available to me. In a more extensive version of this study I am hoping to make a wider use of some of the material which he first brought to my attention.

24 Ahmad ibn Mahdi Naraqi, *Sayf al-Umma wa Burhan al-Milla dar Radd-i Padri-yi Nasrani (*n.p. [Tabriz?], 1267 Q.), 41–68.

25 Ibid. 85–120. See also Muhammad Tunikabuni, *Qisas al-'Ulama* (Tehran, n.d., 129–30) on Naraqi's invitation to ten Jewish rabbis and his use of the library of a certain rabbi, Mulla Musha (Moses), in compiling his work.

26 Lee's edition of the *Controversial Tracts* included a long preface including remarks on earlier controversies of the Safavid period, translation of tracts by Ibrahim Fasa'i's, Martyn, Aqa 'Ali Akbar Shirazi, a full translation of Hamadani's work and Lee's own rejoinder to Hamadani. He dedicated his book to the Earl of Liverpool "as a public acknowledgement of one hundred pound per annum made from his Majesty's Treasury for the purpose of enabling the Arabic professor of this University [i.e. Cambridge] to deliver a public course of Arabic and Hebrew lectures."

27 It is not a coincidence perhaps that at the time the Shi'i philosopher and founder of the Shaykhi school, Shaykh Ahmad Ahsa'i, was advocating his doctrine of the Perfect Shi'i *(Shi'a al-kamil).*

28 Hamadani, *Irshad al-Muddillin,* manuscript, Minasian Collection, Wadham Library, Oxford (no ms. available), 1254 Q [?], Introduction and first *misbah*, pp. 1–20, abridged [and inaccurate] trans. in Lee, *Controversial Tracts*, 161–91.

29 Martyn, *Journal,* 374–5 cf. *Memoir,* 332. For Mir Sayyid 'Ali Fasa'i's biography see *Fars-namih,* vol. 2, 1104–8 which praises him as a master calligrapher and a physician and cites specimens of his poetry. It acknowledges his two-year stay in India around 1815 but does not refer to the translation of the New Testament. He died in 1263/1847 in Shiraz.

30 Martyn, *Journal*, 358–87. Ahsa'i resided in Yazd between 1808 and 1813. According to his son during this period "the cause of his reverence was disseminated in towns and publicized in provinces." Shaykh 'Abd-Allah Ahsa'i, *Sharh-i Ahwal-i . . . Shaykh Ahmad ibn Zayn al-Din Ahsa'i*, tr. Muhammad Tahir Kirmani (2nd edn., Kirman, 1387 Q.), 28–9. See also A. Amanat, *Resurrection and Renewal: The Making of the Babi Movement in Iran, 1844–1850* (Ithaca, 1989), 275.

31 The Latin title page reads: Novum Testamentum Dominiet Solvatoris Nostri Jesu Christi E Craeca in Persicam Linguam a viro reverendo Henrico Martyno (Petropoli, 1815). The Persian title page reads: Payman-i tazih-i khudavand va rahanandih-i ma 'Isa Masih ki afzal al-fuzala' Henry Martyn-i Ingilisi az zaban-i Yunani bi Farsi dar dar al-'ilm-i Shiraz tarjama nimudih ast. Taba' fi sana (Masihiya, 1815). The Bodleian copy (N.T. Pers. d.1) presumably belonged to Gore Ouseley.

32 An inquiry into the literary style and translation techniques of this work and its impact on the Persian of the Qajar period requires a separate study.

33 Ibid. 1st edn., 759–60.

34 The English translation of Fath 'Ali Shah's *farman* appears in G. Fowler, *Three Years in Persia* (London, 1841), 126–7.

35 Abul-Qasim Qa'im Maqam, *Munsha'at* (Tehran, 1280 Q.), 134–8.

36 Ibid. 281–90. For further details see Amanat, "Russian Intrusion."

37 Naraqi, *Sayf al-Umma*, 321.

## *Chapter 7*

1 Cited in N. Amir Sadiqi Tihrani, *Ruhaniyat dar Shi'a* (Tehran (?), 1349/1970), 91. The author, a critic of the clerical establishment, attributes this saying to "one of the Shi'i scholars of the past."

2 On the evolution of the doctrine of *ijtihad* in pre-eighteenth-century Shi'ism, see N. Calder, "The Structure of Authority in Imami Shi'i Jurisprudence," Ph.D. thesis (University of London, School of Oriental and African Studies, 1980); S. A. Arjomand, *The Shadow of God and the Hidden Imam* (Chicago, 1984), 51–6, 137–44; J. Eliash, "The Ithna 'Ashari-Shi'i Juristic Theory of Political and Legal Authority," *Studia Islamica*, 29 (1969): 17–30; E. Kohlberg, "From Imamiyya to Ithna-'Ashariyya," *Bulletin of the School of Oriental and African Studies*, 39 (1976): 521–34. For the survey of the Shi'i literature on *ijtihad*, see H. Modarressi Tabataba'i, *An Introduction to Shi'i Law; a Bibliographical Study* (London, 1984), 1–11, 39–50.

3 More recent Shi'i works of *usul al-fiqh* under the heading of *ijtihad* specify certain conditions for the jurist to be eligible as "absolute" *(mutlaq)* or "fully qualified" *(jami' al-sharayit) mujtahid*. To be able to possess the "power" *(quwwa)* of *ijtihad*, the jurist must have command of Arabic grammar and syntax, the jurisprudence *(fiqh)*, and the precedence for opinions *(fatawi)* and consensus *(ijma')* on legal and doctrinal issues, as well as a fair knowledge of Qur'anic exegesis, *hadith* and its narrators *(rijal)*, logic, and theology *(kalam)*.The "partial" *(mutajazzi) mujtahid* would only be qualified to express authoritative opinions on specific areas of his expertise. For a summary of the conditions of *ijtihad*, see Ghulam-Rida 'Irfaniyan, *al-Ra'y al-Sadid fi al-Ijtihad wa al-Taqlid* (based on lectures by Sayyid Abu'l-Qasim Khu'i) (Najaf, 1386/1967), 9–22; M. Rashad, *Usul al-Fiqh* (Tehran, 1355/1976), 585–9.

4 The final recognition of superiority in learnedness *(a'lamiyai)* as the chief requisite for *sole marja'iyat* may have emerged as late as the time of Aqa Husayn Burujirdi in the late 1950s. An example of retrospective classification of past Shi'i scholars as *maraji'* (plural of marja'*)* may be found in 'Ali Davani *Zindigani-yi Za'im-i Buzurg... Ayatallah Burujirdi* (Qumm, 1340/1961, 18–35), which takes the chain of *maraji'* as far back as the time of Muhammad Kulayni (d. 940). However, as Aqa Buzurg Tihrani takes care to point out, unified authority emerged under Burujirdi when the "majority of people" turned towards him "until he came to be recognized as the source of the emulation for all" *(Tabaqat A'lam al-Shi'a,* vol. 1: *Nuqaba' al-Bashar fi Qarn al-Rabi' 'Ashar* [Najaf, 1373/1954], 606–7). After Burujirdi (d. 1960), the doctrine of the sole marja' was questioned by a number of the 'ulama and the laity, including contributors to *Marja'iyat va Ruhaniyat* (Tehran (?), 1341/1962). For a critical study of this work, see A. K. S. Lambton, "A Reconsideration of the Position of the *Marja' al-Taqlid and* the Religious Institution," *Studia Islamica*, 20 (1964): 116–35.

5 First published in 1291/1874–5 in Tehran, this Persian catechism on *taqlid* and other related issues was compiled by Hajji Mulla Muhammad 'Ali Yazdi on the basis of his teacher's legal rulings. It is annotated and endorsed by Mirza Hasan Shirazi and carries the subtitle *Risalat al-Taj al-Hujjaj*. (The above-mentioned statement appears on page 2.) The significance of this *risala* may be gauged by its wide circulation. Between the date of the first publication and 1327/1909–10), at least ten editions of this work were produced (see K. Mushar, *Fihrist-i Kitabha-yi Chappi-yi Farsi* [Tehran, 1352/1973], vol. 2, 2219–21). The 1323/1906 edition entitled *Majma' al-Rasa'il* contains additional annotations in the margin by six leading mujtahids of the Constitutional period (see below). The section dealing with *taqlid* (but not the marginal commentaries) has been studied by J. R. Cole in his "Imami Jurisprudence and the Role of the 'Ulama: Murtaza Ansari on Emulating the Supreme Exemplar," in *Religion and Politics in Iran; Shi'ism from Quietism to Revolution,* ed. N. R. Keddie (New Haven and London, 1983), 33–46. Cole comes close to suggesting that the learnedness was indeed the determining factor in the emergence of the sole *marja'iyat*. I am thankful to J. Cole and to S. Arjomand for providing me with two different editions of this *risala*.

6 *Majma' al-Rasa'il,* 9.

7 Ibid.

8 Ibid.

9 Ibid.

10 *Sirat,* 2; *Majma',* 10.

11 Ibid.

12 A number of contributors to *Marja'iyat va Ruhaniyat* – particularly, the editor (introduction pp. jim-dal), M. Mutahhari (pp. 105–30), and M. Jazayiri (pp. 136–47) – have pointed out the relativity of *a'lamiyat* and have implicitly acknowledged the inadequacy of such criteria in determining the marja'.

13 Muhammad Baqir Khawansari, 2nd edn. (Tehran, 1367/1947), 28 (under the biography of Mulla Ahmad Naraqi). It is interesting to note that the author did not allocate an independent entry for Ansari. See also pp. 132 and 637. [It is worth noting that the entry on Ansari in *Qisas al-'Ulama* is very brief, but refers to him as *a'lam* to all the 'ulama and describes his position as *riyasat* (ed.)]

14 These are Shaykh Muhammad Hasan Najafi Isfahani the author of *Jawahir*

*al-Kalam* (ibid. 182), Shaykh Hasan Najafi son of Shaykh Ja'far Kashif al-Ghita' (ibid. 182) and Sayyid Ibrahim Qazvini (ibid. 12).

15 See, for instance, Muhammad 'All Mudarris Khayabani, *Rayhanat al-Adab,* 3 vols. (Tehran, 1324/1945), 116, who identifies the "absolute scholarly leadership" *(riyast-i mutlaqa-yi 'ilmiya)* with the position of *"marja'-i taqlid* of all the Shi'a."

16 The term *hubb-i riyasat* (drive for leadership) is often applied pejoratively by critics – mostly lay writers, mystics, and nonconformists – to denote the exceedingly worldly ambitions entertained by some religious leaders.

17 On the Usulis' gradual rise to prominence under Bihbahani and his disciples, see 'Ali Davani, *Vahid-i Bihbahani,* 2d edn. (Tehran, 1362/1983), particularly 122–28 and 169–252; H. Algar, *Religion and State in Iran, 1785-1906* (Berkeley and Los Angeles, 1969), 32–6.

18 For these and other titles, see Davani, *Vahid,* 109–10, 131–6; Muhammad 'Ali Mu'allim Habibabadi, *Makarim al-Athar* (Isfahan, 1337/1958), vol. 1, 222.

19 See 'A. al-'Azzawi, *Tarikh al-'Iraq Bayn Ihtilalayn,* 8 vols. (Baghdad, [1375/1955]), vol. 7, 10–60; 'A. Wardi, *Lamahat Ijtima'iyya min Tarikh al-'Iraq al-Hadith,* 3 vols. (Baghdad, [1971]), vol. 2, 15–111; S. T. Longrigg, *Four Centuries of Modern Iraq* (Oxford, 1925), 216–49. For economic conditions in the first half of the nineteenth century, see J. G. Lorimer, *Gazetteer of the Persian Gulf, Omamn and Central Arabia,* 2 vols. (Calcutta, 1915), vol. 1, parts I and II; C. Issawi, *The Economic History of the Middle East, 1800-1814* (Chicago, 1966), 131–6.

20 Aqa Buzurg Tihrani, *al-Dhari'a ila Tasanif al-Shi'a,* 25 vols. (Najaf and Tehran, 1387–1898/1968–78), vol. 18, 45; cf. Modarressi, *Shi'i Law;* 91.

21 See Muhammad Tunikabuni, *Qisas al-Ulama* (Tehran, 1378/1967), 183–98, for an interesting account of Najafi's life and personality. See also Tihrani, *Tabaqat,* vol. 2: *al-Karam al-Barrara* (Najaf, 1374/1954), 248–52; Khawansari, *Rawdat,* pp. 154–6.

22 Arjomand, *The Shadow of God,* 224–45 and 230–2, and cited sources.

23 For his biography, see Tihrani, *Tabaqat,* vol. 2, 52–4, and cited sources. Passing through Qom in 1812, Mirza Salih Shirazi notes the dilapidated state of madrasas in the town, but also new religious buildings under construction with Fath 'Ali Shah's patronage. He also notes that the students in the madrasas of Qom are solely engaged in the study of *fiqh* and *usul,* since Mirza Abu'l-Qasim Qumi does not permit the teaching or study of any other subject *(Ruznama-yi Mirza Salih Shirazi,* MS. Ouseley Collection, no. 159, Bodleian Library, Oxford, fol. 25b).

24 Fath 'Ali Shah to Mirza Abu'l-Qasim Qumi, "Panj Nama az Fath 'Ali Shah bi Mirza-yi Qumi," letter no. 5, H. Modarressi Tabataba'i, ed., supplement to *Barrasiha-yi Tarikhi,* vol. 10, no. 4, 274.

25 Ibid. 270 (letter no. 3).

26 Ibid. 1–18.

27 Beside Muhammad Baqir Shafti who has often been singled out as the most prosperous *mujtahid* of the nineteenth century, other Usuli mujtahids also amassed large fortunes. Among the better known, though by no means the only examples, are: in Isfahan, Mir Muhammad Husayn *imam jum'a* and his family, and later the Najafi family (Shaykh Muhammad Baqir and Shaykh Muhammad Taqi, known as Aqa Najafi); in Tabriz, Mulla Murtaza 'Alam al-Huda, Shaykh 'Ali-Asghar, Shaykh al-Islam and his family, and the *imam jum'a* Mulla Ahmad and his family; in Qazvin, Mulla Muhammad Taqi Baraqani and his brothers; in Mashhad, the *imam jum'a* Mirza-yi 'Askari; in Shiraz, Hajji Muhammad Hasan Mujta-hid; in

Kashan, Mulla Mahdi Naraqi and his family; and in Tehran, Mulla 'Ali Kani. Because of government backing, some holders of official and semi-official positions such as *imam jum'as,* and *shaykh al-Islams* were the beneficiaries of this favorable economic climate; however, the independent mujtahids were no less eager to have a share of the material wealth.

28 On Shafti and his economic ventures in Isfahan, see *Qisas al-'Ulama,* 135–67. Together with *Rawdat* (125–6), they are the chief sources for later accounts. See also 'A. Jazzi, *Rijal-i Isfahan ya Tadhkirat al-Qubur*, 2d edn., M. Mahdavi, ed. (Isfahan, 1328/1949), 146–53; Habibabadi, *Makarim*, vol. 3,, 1614–20; Tihrani, *Tabaqat*, vol. 2, 192–6. For a summary, see Algar, *Religion and State,* 59–63; 'A. Iqbal, "Hujjat al-Islam ... Shafti," *Yadgar* V, 10: 28–43.

29 Habibabadi, *Makarim*, vol. 5, 1614. It is not clear whether this title was adopted by Shafti or had been conferred upon him.

30 On Sayyid Muhammad and the Khatunabadis, see Habibabadi, *Makarim*, vol. 2, 314–20; Asadallah Fadil Mazandarani, *Zuhur al-Haqq* (Tehran, n.d.), vol. 3, 94–6.

31 Sayyid Muhammad Baqir Shafti, *Kitab-i Su'al va Javab,* 2 vols., rev. edn. (Tabriz, 1247/1832), vol. 1, 6.

32 On the sociopolitical aspects of the Babi movement see A. Amanat, *Resurrection and Renewal; The Emergence of the Babi Movement in Iran, 1844-1850* (Ithaca and London, 1989); M. Momen, "The Social Basis of the Babi Upheavals in Iran (1848–53)," *IJMES* (1983): 157–83; D. M. MacEion, "From Shaykhism to Babism: A study in Charismatic Renewal in Shi'i Islam," (Cambridge University, Ph.D. thesis, 1979); M. S. Ivanov, *The Babi Uprising in Iran (1848–1852)* (Moscow, 1939 [in Russian]).

33 His leadership is attested by most contemporary sources. See Khawansari, *Rawdat,* 181–2; Muhammad Hasan Khan I'timad al-Saltana, *al-Ma'athir wa al-Athar* (Tehran, 1306/1888–89), 135–6.

34 A collection of anecdotes and praiseful statements about Ansari's scholarship and moral accomplishments appears in Murtada al-Ansari, *Zindagani va Shakhsiyat-i Shaykh-i Ansari* (Tehran (?), 1339/1960), 75–105.

35 Ansari, *Zindigani*, 85–6.

36 In this respect he was reportedly following his teacher Shaykh Hasan Al-i Kashif al-Ghita'. See Ibid. 89–90, citing N. Turab Dizfull, a confidant of Shaykh Murtaza.

37 Ibid. 79–80.

38 I'timad al-Saltana, *Ma'athir,* 137; cf. Ansari, *Zindagani* which gives the figure of 100,000 *tumans.*

39 Ansari, *Zindagani*, 169. This source gives the short biography of 277 of his students (168–322).

40 Ibid., p. 169; cf. *Ma'athir*, 137.

41 Ansari, *Zindagani* (354–87) lists 144 scholars who wrote commentaries on Ansari's works.

42 Tihrani, *al-Dhari'a*, vol. 16, 132.

43 Ibid., vol. 22, 151.

44 Ansari briefly visited Shaykh Asadallah Burujirdi, a scholar with esoteric inclinations (possibly a student of Shaykh Ja'far Kashfi, a renowned scholar-mystic with Akhbari tendencies) who had claims to be the *a'lam* and a "gate of knowledge" *(bab-i 'ilm)* to the Imam. This encounter may not have been without influence in Shaykh Murtaza's pietistic tendencies (see *Ma'athir*, 140; *Zindagani*, 66–7).

45 Ansari, *Zindagani*, 77; cf. 110–11 (citing *Luma'at* of Dizfuli). This report

asserts that Ansari was endorsed by his teacher Muhammad Hasan Najafi, when, in his deathbed, the latter addressed a gathering of the learned, saying, "This is your *marja'* after me" (ibid. 73).

46 Ansari, *Zindagani*, 74.

47 For his biography, see *Rayhanat al-Adab,* vol. 1, 201–2; Tihrani, *Jabaqat*, vol. 2, 599. For his anti-Babi campaign, see Muhammad Nabil Zarandi, *The Dawn Breakers,* S. Effendi, trans. (Wilmette, IL, 1932), 430–3; Mazandarani, *Zuhur al-Haqq*, vol. 3, 430–3; Muhammad Taqi Sipihr, Lisan al-Mulk, *Nasikh al-Tawarikh (Qajariya)* (Tehran, 1385/1965), vol. 3, 240ff.

48 Ansari, *Zindagani*, 84.

49 E. G. Browne, ed., *A Traveller's Narrative* (Cambridge, 1891), 86; cf. Mirza Husayn 'Ali Baha'ullah, *Lawh-i Sulfan-i Iran* (Tehran, 1976); E. G. Browne, ed., *The New History* (Cambridge, 1893), 187–8.

50 Ansari, *Zindagani*, 120.

51 'Ali Va'iz Khayabani Tabrizi, *Kitab-i al-'Ulama al-Mu'asirin* (Tabriz, 1366/1848), 3–6; Tihrani, *Tabaqat*, vol. 2, 420–3. The latter source recognizes him as a successor to Ansari who achieved "authority in teaching" *(al-marja'iyat-i fi al-tadris)*.

52 Tihrani, *Tabaqat*, vol. 2, p. 421.

53 Ibid., vol. 1, p. 438. In this biography of Shirazi, Aqa Buzurg summarized his own work *Hadayyat al-Razi ila Mujadid al-Shirazi* (Najaf, 1388/1968) and that of Muhammad 'Ali Urdubadi, *Hayat al-Imam al-Mujadid al-Shirazi*. See also his *al-Dhari'a,* vol. 7, 116 and vol. 25, 207–8.

54 *Tabaqat*, vol. 1, 484.

55 Muhammad Mahdi al-Musavi al-Kazimi, *Ahsan al-Wadi'a, 2* vols. (Baghdad, n.d.), vol. 1, 160.

56 *Tabaqat*, vol. 1, 439.

57 *Hadayyat al-Razi* lists the biographies of close to 360 of Shirazi's students. See also Va'iz Khayabani, *'Ulama*, 48; Habibabadi, *Makarim*, vol. 3, 888.

58 Khayabani, *'Ulama,* 80–2; Tihrani, *Tabaqat,* vol. 1, 409–11.

59 Kazimi, *Ahsan*, I, 162–3; Khayabani, *'Ulama*, 50–2.

60 Ansari, *Zindagani*, 85.

61 Shirazi's works mostly consist of commentaries on the works of his teacher, Ansari. He also wrote a general work of jurisprudence on earnings *(makasib)* and contracts *(mu'amalai)*, (*Tabaqat,* vol. 1, 441; Habibabadi, *Makarim*, vol. 3, 887).

62 For his family background, see Hasan Fasa'i, *Farsnama-yi Nasiri* (Tehran, 1313/1896-97), vol. 2, 54; Amanat, *Resurrection and the Renewal*, ch. 2 and the cited sources.

63 Tihrani, *Tabaqat*, vol. 1, 274; Yahya Kirmani, *Farmandihan-i Kirman,* Bastani Parizi, ed. (Tehran, 1344/1965), 26, 50.

64 Tihrani, *Tabaqat*, vol. 1, 440; Habibabadi, *Makarim*, vol. 3, 886.

65 *Takmalat al-Amal al-Amil,* MS cited in Tihrani, *Tabaqat*, vol. 1, 440.

66 For the correspondence between the 'ulama during the Regie episode, see Shaykh Hasan Karbala'i, *Tarikh-i Dukhaniya ya Tarikh Inhisar-i Dukhaniyat,* I. Dihgan, ed. (Arak, 1333/1954); also cited in I. Taymuri, *Tahrim-i Tanbaku* (Tehran, 1328/1949). N. R. Kiddie, *Religion and Rebellion, the Iranian Tobacco Protest of 1891-1892* (London, 1966), and F. Adamiyat, *Shurish bar Imtiyaznam-yi Regie* (Tehran, 1360/1981), all of whom discuss the role of the merchants in persuading the 'ulama to support their cause. See also F. Kazimzadeh *Russia and Britain in Persia, 1864-1914* (New Haven and London, 1968), 241–301 for the Russian anti-Regie provocations.

67 Karbala'i, *Tarikh-i Dukhaniya;* also cited in Taymuri, *Tahrim,* 120. It asserts that "all the *mujtahids* of the time were unanimous that this [i.e., Shirazi's declaration] was a ruling and not an opinion. The distinction between the two is that compliance with a ruling of a fully qualified mujtahid is an obligation for all, whereas the opinion is only obligatory for the deliverer of the opinion *(mufti)* and his emulators.

68 On the merchants' initiative in Shiraz, which was taken in spite of the 'ulama's early reluctance, see M. H. I'timad al-Saltana, *Khalsa ya Khwabnama,* M. Katira'i, ed. (Tehran, 1348/1969), 122–5; 'Abbas Mirza Mulkara, *Sharh-i Hal,* 'A. Iqbal, ed. 2nd edn. (Tehran, 1355/1976), 183–4. For Falasiri, see *Farsnama,* vol. 2, 23.

69 Rajab 4, 1309/February 4, 1892. Cited in Muhammad Nazim al-Islam Kirmani, *Tarikh-i Bidari-yi Iranian,* 2nd edn., A. A. Sa'idi Sirjani, ed., 3 vols. (Tehran, 1346/1967), vol. 1, 34–5.

70 The original Arabic text of this letter appears in Kirmani, *Bidari,* vol. 1, 88–92. The Persian translation then in circulation is cited in Taymuri, *Tahrim.* For the English translation, see E. G. Browne, *The Persian Revolution of 1905-1909* (Cambridge, 1910), 15–21.

71 Browne, *Revolution*, 16. The Arabic original reads: *"hibr al-umma, bariqat al-anwar al-a'amma, da'amat al-'arsh al-din wa lisan al-natiq 'an al-shar' al-mubin"* (*Bidari*, vol. 1, 88).

72 Ibid.

73 Ibid. 17.

74 See *Bidari,* vol. 1, 12; cf. Browne, *Revolution*, 22; Keddie, *Rebellion*, 96, n. 1. For Ashtiyani, see Tihrani, *Tabaqat,* vol. 1, 389–90.

75 Keddie, *Religion and Rebellion,* 114–19; V. A. Kosogovski, *Khatirat,* 'A. Jali, tr., 2nd edn. (Tehran, 1355/1976), 177.

76 M. Mahmud, *Tarikh-i Rawabit-i Siyasi-yi Iran va Inglis dar Qarn-i Nuzdahum-i Miladi,* 8 vols. (Tehran, 1333–40/1954–61), vol. 6, 1343–4; the memoirs of Muhammad Baqir Ulfat written in 1343/1964 (copy in possession of S. A. Arjomand).

77 Ulfat, *Memoirs*; A. Kasravi, *Tarikh-i Mashruta-yi Iran,* 13th edn. (Tehran, 1356/1977), 294, 381–5, 496–8; A. H. Hairi, *Shi'ism and Constitutionalism in Iran* (Lieden, 1977).

78 See, for instance, the joint *fatwa* (perhaps an *ijma')* on "the prohibition of travelling via the mountain route to Mecca" *(risala bar hurmat-i istitraq az tariq-i jabal bi Macca-yi Mu'azzama* (Sha'ban, 1320/1902). Initiated by Shaykh Fadlallah Nuri, this fatwa is endorsed by twenty leading *mujtahids* of the time. Appearing presumably in the order of seniority, the first in the list, Muhammad Fadil Sharabiyani, is addressed as "the head of *faqihs* and *mujtahids" (ra'is al-fuqaha'wa al-mujtahidin);* the second, Fadlallah Nuri, and the third, Mirza Husayn Tihrani, are addressed as "the head of the nation and the faith" *(ra'is al-millat wa al-din);* the fourth and fifth, Muhammad Kazim Khurasani and Muhammad Hasan Mamaqani, were addressed as "the pride *(iftikhar)* of *faqihs* and *mujtahids";* while the rest were referred to as the refuge *(maladh),* the supporter *(zhir),* and the pillar *('imad)* of Islam and Muslims. This *risala,* though on a relatively minor issue, demonstrates the tendency to preserve a united clerical front on the eve of the Constitutional movement. It may also be taken, however, as an indication of the ongoing struggle for clerical supremacy in the decade following the death of Shirazi. See also Khayabani, *'Ulama*, 77–8.

79 Ulfat's memoirs (extract 6–9). See also Aqa Najafi Quchani, *Siyabat-i Sharq,* 2nd edn. (Tehran, 1362/1983), 455–82, who gives an amusing

account of the students' dependence on Khurasani and Yazdi for their subsistence.

80 Muhammad Baqir Ulfat marks the death of Mulla Muhammad Kazim Khurasani as the end of an era of intervention by the 'ulama in the political affairs of Iran; an era which he believes had started some twenty years earlier with the tobacco protest of 1891–2 (memoirs, extract p. 12).

## *Chapter 8*

1 Aghajari's speech was delivered at Mu'allem lecture hall in Hamadan on 29th Khurdad 1381/19 June 2002. It was first published in *Binish-i Sabz* monthly (Tehran, 9th Amurdad 1381/31 July 2002) and in *Umid-e Javan* weekly (Tehran, no. 306, Daymah 1381/January 2003) and widely cited in papers and on the Internet. The full text appears in P. Hajizada, ed. *Aqajari: Matn-I Kamil-i Sukhanrani-yi Hamadan* (Tehran, 1382/2003), 36–7. Although refreshing and courageous for the Islamic Republic, Aghajari's speech draws a rather pedestrian, and largely ahistorical, comparison between Christianity and Islam. He portrays Shari'ati as a prophet of Protestant Islam while seeking in his thoughts and his lifestory a "humanist" message.

2 For the institutional and historical obstacles to the development of the *marja'iyya* in the ninteenth and twentieth centuries see above Chapter 7. See also L. Walbridge ed., *The Most Learned of the Shi'a: The Institution of the Marja' Taqlid* (New York, 2001); A. K. S. Lambton, "A "Reconsideration of the Position of the *Marja' al-Taqlid* and the Religious Institution," *Studia Islamica*, 20 (1964): 115–35.

3 For the doctrine of Occultation (*ghayba*) in Shi'ism see for example S. A. Arjomand, "Crisis of the Imamate and the Institution of Occultation in Twelver Shi'ism: A Sociohistorical Perspective," *International Journal of Middle East Studies*, 28/4 (1996): 491–515; idem, "The Consolation of Theology: The Shi'i Doctrine of Occultation and the Transition from Chiliasm to Law," *Journal of Religion*, 76/4 (1996): 548–71; E. Kohlberg, "From Imamiya to Ithna-'ashariya," *Bulletin of the School of Oriental and African Studies*, 39 (1976): 521–34. See also A. Amanat, *Resurrection and Renewal: The Making of the Babi Movement in Iran, 1844-1850* (Ithaca, 1989), 1–9 and cited sources.

4 For the historical evidence in the Safavid and Qajar period see for example Amanat, *Resurrection and Renewal,* 33–69; S. A. Arjomand, *The Shadow of God and the Hidden Imam: Religion, Political Order and Societal Change in Shi'i Iran from the Beginning to 1890* (Chicago, 1984), 171–201, 238–59.

5 The development of *ijtihad* in Shi'ism still awaits a full-length modern treatment. See M. Arkoun, "The Concept of Authority in Islamic Thought," in Klaus Ferdinand and M. Mozaffari, eds., *Islam: State and Society* (London, 1988); R. Brunschvig, "Les usul al-fiqh imamites à leur stade ancien (X et XI siècles)," in T. Fahd, ed., *Le Shi'isme imamate* (Paris, 1970), 201–13; N. Calder, "Doubt and Prerogative: The Emergence of an Imami Shi'i Theory of Ijtihad," *Studia Islamica,* 70 (1989): 57–77; W. Madelung, "Authority in Twelver Shiism in the Absence of the Imam," in *Religious Schools and Sects in Medieval Islam* (London, 1985), 163–73 and A. Zysow, "Ejtehad (in Shi'ism)", in *Encyclopaedia Iranica*, ed. Ehsan Yarshater (New York, 1985–). For theological debates in early Shi'ism see

H. Modarressi, *Crisis and Consolidation in the Formative Period of Shi'i Islam* (Princeton, 1993) and A. J. Newman, *The Formative Period of Shi'i Law: Hadith as Discourse between Qum and Baghdad* (Richmond, Surrey, 2000).

6 For Safavid conversion to Twelver Shi'ism see Arjomand, *The Shadow of God*, 105–214; R. Jurdi Abisaab, *Converting Persia: Religion and Power in the Safavid Empire* (London and New York, 2004) and R. Ja'farian, *Din va Siyasat dar 'Asr-i Safaviya* (Qom, 1370/1991). Abisaab demonstrates the emergence of the *Akhbari* school as the outcome of a complex interplay between the Arabic-speaking 'ulama and their descendants and the Persian 'ulama of the Safavid period.

7 For the Akhbari-Usuli controversy see R. Gleave, *Inevitable Doubt: Two Theories of Shi'i Jurisprudence* (Leiden and Boston, 2000); A. J. Newman, "The Nature of the Akhbari-Usuli Dispute in Late Safawid Iran," *Bulletin of the School of Oriental and African Studies*, 55/1 (1992): 22–51; 55/2 (1992): 250–61; "Anti-Akhbari Sentiments among the Qajar 'ulama: The Case of Muhammad Baqir al-Khwansari, 1313/1895", in R. Gleave, ed., *Religion and Society in Qajar Iran* (London: 2005), 155–73.

8 The extensive patronage networks in Shi'i Iraq in the nineteenth century are discussed in M. Litvak, *Shi'i Schools of Nineteenth-Century Iraq: The* 'ulama' *of Najaf and Karbala'* (Cambridge, 1998). See also above Chapter 7.

9 The conventional treatment of clerical–state relations in the nineteenth century is H. Algar, *Religion and State in Iran, 1785-1906: The Role of the* 'ulama *in the Qajar Period* (Berkeley, 1969). Algar, like most scholars in the 1960s, was inclined to portray the 'ulama as a unanimous voice of opposition against the Qajar state who questioned its legitimacy and enjoyed the support of their constituency. Yet, even the selective evidence in Algar's study points to a pattern of collaboration rather than confrontation between the 'ulama and the state. To preserve their vested interests, to prevail in inter-clerical rivalries, and to preserve power and prestige the 'ulama frequently sought collaboration with the state. From the theoretical perspective, during the Qajar and most of the Pahlavi periods the 'ulama did not produce any substantive account of theory of government – nor even an oral pronouncement of any substance – that denies the legitimacy of the Shi'i state.

10 Aspects of clerical transformation under the Pahalvids are studied in S. Akhavi, *Religion and Politics in Contemporary Iran: Clergy-State Relations in the Pahlavi Period* (Albany, 1980) and M. Fischer, *Iran: From Dispute to Revolution* (Cambridge, MA, 1980). See also two recent accounts with new details but with a pro-clerical bias: H. Basirat-mansih, *'Ulama va Rizhim-i Riza Shah* (Tehran, 1376/1997) and R. Ja'farian, *Jarayanha va Sazemanha-ye Mazhabi-Siyasi Iran az Ru-yi-kar Amadan-I Riza Shah ta Piruzi-yi Inqilab-I Islami, 1320-1357,* 6th edn. (Qum, 1385).

11 Among the few exceptions was Muhammad Baqir Sadr's trilogy on politics, society, and economics from the perspective of Shi'i jurisprudence, though here too Sadr's attempt takes a more rhetorical turn toward apologia than a serious reconstruction of the legal theory. See C. Mallat, *The Renewal of the Shi'i Law: Muhammad Baqir Sadr, Najaf and the Shi'i International* 2nd edn. (Cambridge, 1993). For a translation and extensive commentary on Sadr's work on *usul al-fiqh* see R. P. Mottahedeh, tr., *Lessons in Islamic Jurisprudence: Muhammad Baqir as-Sadr* (Oxford, 2003).

12 A collection of papers of this conference appeared in M. Tabataba'i *et al.*,

eds., *Bahsi dar Bara-yi Marja'iyat va Ruhaniyat* (Tehran, 1342/1963). A. K. S. Lambton was among the few outside Iran to discuss the new debate in her "Reconsideration of the Position of the *Marja' al-Taqlid.*"

13 See for example *Khatirat-iI Ayatullah Muntaziri* (n.p. [Germany], 2001), 42–102.

14 See Ja'farian, *Jarayanha*, 703–54. Khomeini's *Kashf al-Asrar* (Tehran, 1323/1944) was in response to Shi'i revisionist trends. Hakami-zadih's anti-clerical tract, *Asrar-i Hazar-sala* (Tehran, n.d. [1323/1924]), was refuted by Khomeini's first published work, *Kashf al-Asrar (*Tehran, 1323/1924).

15 Most of Mutahhari's work in the late 1960s and through the 1970s was devoted to popularizing Islamic (and to a lesser extent Shi'i) theology, fundamentals of religion *(usul-i 'aqa'i*d), Islamic philosophy (hikma), and exegesis *(tafsir)* rather than jurisprudence and *usul al-fiqh*. His lectures in Husayniya Irsah and other places and bulk of his writings, even when implicitly refuting 'Ali Shari'ati's revolutionary reading of Shi'ism, are shaped by an Islamic modernist discourse that was safely distant from the traditional teachings of the *hawza*. To a lesser extent other radical clerics of Qom and other centers, many of them Khomeini's students, moved away from *fiqh*. Mutahhari's collected works, *Majmu'a-yi Asar-i Ustad-i Shahid Mutahhari,* 7 vols. (Tehran, 1368-1374/1989–95), clearly reflect such modernist tendencies.

16 Khomeini's thirteen lectures in Najaf on the "authority of the jurist" *(wilayat-i faqih)* in early 1970 was apparently delivered at the request of Jalal al-Din Farsi, an Islamic activist and author of a number of works on political Islam, and was first published by Farsi in Persian (Beirut, 1349/1970) and later in Qom, Najaf, and Tehran. The idea of *wilayat-i faqih* was not entirely unknown to Shi'i dissident circles from the early 1950s, though it was Khomeini who first developed it as a political doctrine. See, for example, Ja'farian, *Jarayanha,* 237–49. For the English translation see H. Algar tr. and ann., *Islam and Revolution: Writings and Declarations of Imam Khomeini* (Berkeley, 1981). See also M. Fischer's critical review of Algar's edition in *Iranian Studies,* 14 (1981): 263.

17 Algar, *Islam and Revolution*, 29.

18 Such an assertion comes despite the fact the Khomeini himself had produced one such "practical treatise of jurisprudence" with all the familiar conventionalities and customary preoccupations with ritual acts, cleanliness *[taharat]*, and similar debates. See R. Khumayni, *Risala-yi Tawdih al-Masa'il* (Qom, 1381 Q./1961) which is a commentary on Husain Burujirdi's voluminous work on the subject. It is translated as *A Clarification of Questions: An Unabridged Translation of Resaleh Towzih al-Masael,* tr. J. Borujerdi (pseudonym) with a foreword by Michael M. J. Fischer and Mehdi Abedi (Boulder, CO, 1984). Moreover, Khomeini produced at least twenty-seven titles on *fiqh* and *usul al-fiqh* in Arabic and Persian on all aspects of *furu'*. For an annotated list see *Paygah-i Ittila'rasani-yi Imam Khumayni* (http://www.imam-khomeini.com) under "*asar wa asha'r-i Imam.*" Also, H. Ruhani (Ziyarati), *Barrasi va Tahlili az Nahzat-I Imam Khumayni,* 2 vols., 11th edn. (Tehran, 1360/1981), vol. 1, 55–62. For a discussion of Khomeini's early interests in jurisproduce see H. Algar, "Imam Khomeini: Pre-Revolutionary Years, 1902-1962," in E. Burke and I. Lapidous eds., *Islam, Politics and Social Movements* (Berkeley, 1989), 263–88.

19 The early reference to Khomeini as *imam* appears in the tracts of the Najaf-based clandestine publisher Panzdah-i Khurdad (better known as

Davazdah-i Muharram), operated by Khomeini's students Mahmud Du'ai, 'Ali Akbar Muhtashimipur, and others. Among its publications were the Arabic *Mawqaf al-Imam al-Khumayni Tujah Isra'il* (Najaf, 1971?) and a two-volume Persian hagiography of Khomeini, *Biugrafi-i Pishva* 2 vols. (n.p. [Najaf ?], 1394 Q./1974) where the aforementioned *qasida* appears at the outset of the first volume (7–11). The biographer(s) repeatedly refer to Khomeini with the title *pishva*, a term ominously used in Persian from the 1930s for the German *Führer.* The Persian editions of Khomeini's *Hukumat-i Islami* published in the early 1970s appear under the pseudonym "Imam Kashif al-Ghita'," a camouflage under the cover of the well-known anti-British Iraqi Shi'i leader of the 1920s. Another example of Shi'i adoption of the term *imam* in the 1970s is in the case of the Iranian-Lebanese Shi'i leader, Imam Musa Sadr.

20 M. Kadivar, *Hukumat-i Wila'i,* 3rd edn. (Tehran, 1378/1999).

21 *Nazariyaha-yi Dawlat dar Fiqh-i Shi'a*, 4th edn. (Tehran, 1378/1999).

22 For the indictment of Aghajari and his defense see P. Hajizada, ed., *Aghajari*, 47–170.

## *Chapter 9*

1 Remarks at a meeting in Qom with the staff of the Central Insurance Company, Nov. 5, 1979, excerpts from news bulletin, Tehran home radio broadcast service, BBC Summary of the World Broadcasts, Nov. 7, 1979 (ME/6264/A/5).

2 For a summary of events, see S. Bakhash, *The Reign of the Ayatollahs* (New York, 1985). See also M. Milani, "Hostage Crisis," in *Encyclopaedia Iranica*, ed. Ehsan Yarshater (New York, 1985–).

3 For early references to Great Satan in the U.S. media, see "Doing Satan's Work in Iran," *New York Times,* Nov. 6, 1979. The editorial begins: "In the zealous eyes of Ayatollah Khomeini, America is the 'great satan' and Great Britain is its 'evil' ally." See also W. O. Beeman, *The "Great Satan" vs. "the Mad Mulla": How the United States and Iran Demonize Each Other* (Westport, CT, 2005), 49–68, which offers a socio-psychological interpretation of Iranian political culture and its demonizing of the United States. Beeman's treatment, however, is not concerned with the concept's religious ramifications nor with its historical origins.

4 The seizure of the American Embassy by the militant Students Following the Imam's Path was preceded by a similar attempt by Marxist students. On Feb. 14, 1979, the Fedai'an-e Khalq attacked the embassy in Tehran and took some of the staff hostage, including Ambassador William Sullivan. The episode ended quickly after the provisional government of Mahdi Bazargan intervened. See *EIr:* "Hostage Crisis" (M. Milani).

5 For a study of how the verses were debated in premodern Islam, see S. Ahmed, "Ibn Taymiyyah and the Satanic Verses," *Studia Islamica*, 87 (1998): 67–125.

6 See R. Khomeini, *Wilayat-i Faqih (Hukumat-i Islami)* (Tehran, 1357/1978), 13–21.

7 See A. Rippin, "Shaytan," and A. J. Wensinck [L. Gardet], "Iblis" in *Encyclopedia of Islam*, 2nd edn., vol. I2.

8 The thirteenth-century mystic Hamadani is preoccupied with Lucifer (Iblis). This is evident in his works and collection of letters. See, e.g., *Namihha-yi*

*'Ayn al-Qudat Hamadani,* ed. 'A. Monzavi and 'A. 'Usayran, 3 vols. (Tehran, 1377/1998), 1:313–15, 2:95–96 (where he is recognized as the "lord of the forsaken"), 409–19, 449–50. See also Monzavi's introduction to vol. 3, 237–47.

9 For susceptibility to Satan see, e.g., Muhammad Baqir Majlisi, *Hilyat al-Muttaqin* (Tehran, 1367/1988), 10 (naked bodies); 12 (unmatched shoes); 61 (during intercourse); 83 (clipping nails); 96 (washing hair), 103 (sleeping with greasy fingers and unwashed children); 104 (sleeping on one's stomach); 107 (nightmares); 115 (in toilet); 197 (yawning); 202 (forgetting to remember the Prophet). See also idem, *Bihar al-Anwar* (Beirut, 1983) 2:1319. For references to satanic temptation in *Bihar,* see 'A. Qumi, *Safinat al-Bihar* (Najaf, 1355 q./1936), 2:654–55.

10 Muhsin al-Tabataba'i al-Hakim, *Mustamsak al-'Urwat al-Wuthqa*, 4 vols., 4th edn. (Najaf, 1391 q./1971), 1:273–554. For defiling the nature of the infidels, see 1:367–98.

11 For a brief survey of the vast literature on the subject, see P. G. Kreyenbroek, "Millennialism and Eschatology in the Zoroastrian Tradition," in *Imagining the End: Visions of Apocalypse form the Ancient Middle East to Modern America,* ed. A. Amanat and M. T. Bernhardsson (London and New York, 2002), 33–55.

12 See for instance the dialogue between Zarathustra and Ahriman in M. Moazami, "The Confrontation of Zarathustra with the Evil Sprit: Chapter 19 of the *Pahlavi Videvdad,*" *East and West*, vol. 52 (Rome, December 2002), 151–71 (161–71).

13 For a study of Self versus Other in the *Shahnama* see A. Amanat, "Divided Patrimony, Tree of Royal Power and Fruit of Vengeance: Political Paradigms and Iranian Self-Image in the Story of Faridun in the *Shahnama,*" *Shahnama Studies,* ed. C. Melville (Cambridge, 2006), 71–96.

14 Khomeini, *Wilayat-i Faqih (Hukumat-i Islami*), 193–5.

15 R. Khumayni, *Risala Tawdith al-Masa'il* (Tehran, 1378/1999). At least one-fifth of this work concerns laws of purification, pollutants, and ritual cleansing (parts 2–10, pp. 14–126). For an online edition, see Paygah-i Ittela'-rasani-yi Imam Khomayni (http://www.imam-khomeini.com/Resaleh/index.htm). See also above Chapter 8.

16 For Qur'anic reference to the *taghut*, see T. Fahd and F. H. Stewart, "Taghut," in *Encylopedia of Islam,* 2nd edn. Typical of the archaic approach of the second edition of the *Encylopedia of Islam*, this entry is devoid of even a minor reference to the modern usage of the term especially during the Islamic Revolution of 1979.

17 For the messianic dimensions of the Islamic Revolution see above Chapter 2 and below Chapter 10.

18 W. O. Douglas, *Strange Lands and Friendly People* (New York, 1951), xiii. In his *West of the Indus* (Garden City, NY, 1958), Douglas again mentions (i–ix) Radio Moscow's commentary on the occasion of his visit in 1957 and the Iranian newspapers who cast doubt on the altruistic nature of his visit then. In this citation there is no mention of the Big Devil, however. Douglas claims on both of his accounts that he was more offended by the charge that he was a decrepit mountaineer. According to his recent biographer, Douglas was not disabled and had never contracted polio, as he apparently claimed later. See B. A. Murphy, *Wild Bill: The Legend and Life of William O. Douglas* (New York, 2003).

19 Douglas, *Strange Lands*, 1.

20 Ibid.

21 Ibid. 1–2.
22 Ibid. 3–4, 318–24.
23 Ibid. 4.
24 Ehsan Tabari, *Kazh-rahe: Khaterati az Tarikh-e Hezb-e Tudeh* (Tehran, 1373/1994), 103–6. Although Tabari wrote this "confessional" autobiography while in the prison in the Islamic Republic, awaiting trial, his account is in many ways revealing. It contains numerous details of the life and culture of Iranian Communist exiles.
25 See above Chapter 8.

## *Chapter 10*

1 For a summary of messianic traits in the early years of the Islamic Revolution see above, Chapter 2.
2 There is some confusion about the Society's nomenclature and the history of its establishment. Although Hujjatiyya seems to have been the original name, the Islamic activists with counter-Baha'i zeal in the 1960s and 1970s were generally known as members of the Society of Islamic Teaching (*Anjuman-i Ta'limat-i Islami*). The Anti-Baha'i objective of the Society, if indeed there was an organized objective, was concealed. The title "*Hujjatiyya*" came into vogue after the Islamic Revolution. A. Baghi in his book and M. Sadri in his *EIr* entry (see below) identify it as a charitable society *(Anjuman-i Khayriya-i Mahdawiya-yi Hujjatiyya)* presumably the name adopted under pressure from SAVAK to provide a more acceptable guise. Abedi (see below) also recalls the Society being identified as *Anjuman-i Imam-i Zaman.*
3 For the history of Hujjatiyya see A. Baghi, *Dar Shenakht-i Hezb-i Qa'edin-i Zaman* (Tehran, 1984). See also *EIr:* "Hojjatiya" (M. Sadri) and *EIr:* "Halabi" (M. Sadri). Mehdi Abedi "Autobiographical Stories of Mehdi Abedi: the Anti-Baha'i Society" in M. Abedi and M. J. Fischer, *Debating Muslims: Cultural Dialogues in Postmodernity and Tradition* (Madison, 1990) offers a valuable vignette of the Society's activities in the late 1960s. See also above Chapter 2.
4 Davani, 'A. *Mahdi-yi Maw'ud*, 1st. edn. (Tehran, 1962 [?]). By 2006 this translation had reportedly reached its 30th edition. For this translation see below in this chapter.
5 The history of the Baha'i-Muslim interaction remains to be written. Among pioneering attempts are essays by H. Chehabi, M. Tavakoli-Targhi, R. Afshari and A. Amanat in *The Baha'is of Iran: Socio-Historical Studies* ed. D. Brookshow and S. Fazel (London and New York, 2008). See also the abovementioned entries by M. Sadri in *EIr*. Some of the assertions in the passage above concerning Islamic activists and their dealings with the Baha'is is based on personal observation.
6 See above Chapter 2 for further details.
7 For the early history of Jamkaran see for example *Tarikhchih-yi Masjid-i Muqaddas-i Jamkaran* published by Masjid Jamkaran (Qom, n.d.) and H. Karim Qumi, *A'inih-yi Asrar,* chap. 1 (online publication: http://jamkaran.info/fa/library/asrar.htm).
8 Details of the Jamkaran development project appear under "Master Plan" (*tarh-i jami'*) section of Jamkaran website referred to as Paygah-i Ittela'-rasani-yi Masjid-i Muqaddas-i Jamkaran (http://www.jamkaran.info).
9 Ibid. cited in the "miraculous feats" (*karamat*) section.

10 Based on the author's observations in 2005 and on information gleaned from various sources.

11 The Secretariat operates under the "Office of the Vice Chairman for Research" of the Islamic Propagation Organization (Saziman-i Tablighat-i Islami); a governmental-funded organ of the Islamic Republic. See http://www.ejlasmahdi.com.

12 Ibid. See "Manshurat-i Jadid" (new publications). Persian pamphlets (they are hardly books) all have a print run of 5,000 and are in universal format denoting a considerable budget allocated for their production, presumably from public funds.

13 For the "convergence theory" see M. Akhundi, *Hamgara'i-yi Adyan va Mazahib dar I'tiqad-i bi Maw'ud* (Tehran, 1385/2006) and *Convergance* [*sic.*] *of Religions in Their Belief in Savior,* ed. Hawza-yi Ijtihadiya-yi Muhsiniya (Tehran, 1385/2006).

14 See for example 'A. A. Vilayati, *Imam Mahdi va Shokufa'i-yi Farhang va Tamaddun Islami dar Jahan* (Tehran, 1385/1996), English trans. *Imam Mahdi and Manifestation of Islamic Culture and Civilization* (Tehran, 1996); B. Akhavan Kazimi, *Hukumat-i Jahani-yi Imam-i 'Asr va Nazariyi-yi Jahani-shudan dar 'Asr-i Ma* (Tehran, 1385/2006), English trans. *The Universal Government of Imam Mahdi and Globalization* (Tehran, 2006). For more pamphlets on various topics see the above website. A similar website of the Entizar-i Nur (Awaiting the Light) research center, presumably established in 1998, also promotes study of the Mahdi and his Occultation through conferences and publications at all levels.

15 True to the cybernetic spirit of messianic propaganda, the complete archive and current issue of *Mouood* is available online (http://mouood.org). Detailed content analysis of the journal requires a separate study.

16 For a revealing report on Samarih's personality, his "psychology of infidels" (*ravanshinasi-i kufr*), and his influence on Ahmadinejad see Arash Mahdavi (pseudo.?) "Mardi kih Ra'is-jumhur Pusht-i U Namaz Mikhanad," *Rooz* Online, 11 Aban 1384/ Oct 2005. He seems to have been Ahmadinejad's vital connection with Ayatollah Mesbah Yazdi.

17 Young Ahmadinejad's acute yearning for the Imam of the Age is reported by some of his early associates. On a trip to the shrine of Imam Riza in Mashhad in the early 1980s Ahmadinejad's reportedly profound urge to come into contact with the Hidden Imam was eventually answered (after an initial disappointment). When walking through the city's bazaar, he was approached by an elderly person – presumably the Hidden Imam – who foretold some details about Ahmadinejad's cohorts. See A. Ebrahimi in his weblog *Goftaniha,* May 2008 (?)

18 A. La Guardia, "Divine Mission' Driving Iran's New Leader," *Daily Telegraph,* Jan. 15, 2006. Keeping up with the President's anticipation, a prayer leader in the Mosque of Adineh in Tehran, Muhammad Razi Hujjati, published a brochure (curiously, in response to Hujjatiyya's "deviating" and "corrupt" propaganda) asserting that upon collective and simultaneous prayer in all mosques throughout Iran (and especially in Jamkaran), the Hidden Imam will duly make himself manifest. As a proof of his veracity, he further pledged that if the Advent does not occur, he and his supporters are ready to be executed. A. Mu'tamad (psoudo.?), "Zuhur-i Imam ta do sal-i digar," *Rooz* Online 26 Mehr 1384/ Oct.18, 2005 citing M. Armin, an MP of the Islamic Republic. See also *Baztab* Online (27 Shahrivar 1384/Oct. 3, 2005).

19 For the full the text of President Ahmadinejad's speech at the General Assembly, IRNA, Oct. 17, 2005, see English trans. at http.//www.globalsecurity.org/wmd/library/news/iran/2005.
20 For the full text of President Ahmadinejad's speech at the General Assembly, IRNA, Sept. 20 2006, see English trans. at http://www.globalsecurity.org/wmd/library/news/iran/2006.
21 Transcript of a videotaped meeting with Ayatollah Javadi-Amuli in Tehran, October 2006.
22 This expression of Iranian nationalism by means of acquiring nuclear technology is discussed in A. Amanat, "Persian Complex," OpEd (the title is the editor's), *New York Times,* May 25, 2006. For an online version see http://www.nytimes.com/2006/05/25/opinion/25Amanat.html.
23 Reported by M. Farahmand, BBC Persian, 2nd Farvardin 1387/March 21, 2008.
24 A. Musazadih (pseudo.?) "Dawran-i Ahmadinejad, dwran-i zuhur-*i* sughra'", *Rooz* Online, 22 Isfand 1386/March 12, 2008.
25 Ibid.
26 Amin Ra'ufinijad (psoud.?) "Bayad dakhil-i Iran ra sari' jam' va jur kunim," *Rooz* Online, 18 Urdibihisht 1387/May 7, 2008.
27 Anti-Jewish hatred was shared by most Christian millenarian trends in Europe of medieval and modern times as amply demonstrated by Norman Cohn in his classic *The Pursuit of the Millennium* (London, 1970) and by others. See for example *Antisemitism through the Ages*, ed. S. Almog and tr. N. H. Reisner (Oxford, 1988) and A. C. Gow, *The Red Jews: Antisemitism in an Apocalyptic Age, 1200-1600* (Leiden, 1995). For the Shi'i 'ulama attitude toward Jews see for example D. Tsadik, *Between Foreigners and Shi'is: Nineteenth-Century Iran and the Jewish Minority* (Stanford, 2007).
28 Most information about Kazameini Boroujerdi is gleaned from the Internet (including You Tube) and newspaper articles. See for example N. Fathi, "Iran Arrests Outspoken Cleric Who Opposes Religious Rule," *New York Times*, Oct. 9, 2006 and S. Saba, "Iran arrests controversial cleric," BBC News, Oct. 8, 2006 (http://news.bbc.co.uk/2/hi/middle_east/6032217.stm). According to this latter report, Boroujerdi denied any claim to be the Hidden Imam.

# Index